Ichnographia Rustica

One of the most significant occurrences in the history of design was the creation of the English Landscape Garden. Accounts of its genesis – the surprising structural change from the formal to the seemingly informal – are numerous. But none has ever been quite convincing, and none satisfactorily placed the contributions of Stephen Switzer.

Unlike his contemporaries, Switzer – an 18th century author of books on gardening and agricultural improvement – grasped a quite new principle: that the fashionable pursuit of great gardens should be "rural and extensive", rather than merely the ornamentation of a particular part of an estate. Switzer saw that a whole estate could be enjoyed as an aesthetic experience, and that the process of improving its value could increase wealth. By encouraging improvers to see the garden in his enlarged sense, he opened up the adjoining countryside, the landscape, and made the whole a subject of unified design. Some few followed his advice immediately, such as Bathurst at Cirencester. But it took some time for his ideas to become generally accepted.

Could this vision, and its working out in practice between 1710 and 1740, be the very reason for such changes? Three hundred years after the first volume of Switzer's writings began to be published, this book offers a timely critical examination of the lessons learned and Switzer's roles. In major influential early works at Castle Howard and Blenheim, and later in the more "minor" works such as Spye Park, Leeswood and Rhual, the relationships between these designs and his writings is demonstrated. In doing so, this book makes possible a major re-assessment of the developments, and thus our attitudes to well-known works. It provides an explanation of how Switzer, and his colleagues and contemporaries, first made what he had called Ichnographia Rustica, or more familiarly Modern Gardening, from the mid-1740s, and later landscape gardens.

It reveals an exceptional innovator who, by transforming the philosophical way in which nature was viewed, integrated good design with good farming and horticultural practice for the first time. It raises the issue of the cleavage in thought of the later 18th century, essentially whether the *ferme ornée* as the mixture of *utile* and *dulci* was the perfect designed landscape, or whether this was the enlarged garden with features of "unadorned nature"? The book discusses these considerable and continuing contrary influences on later work, and suggests that Switzer has many lessons for how contemporary landscape and garden design ought to be perceived and practised.

William Alvis Brogden is an architectural historian, critic and consultant based in Aberdeen. He has served on the councils of the National Trust for Scotland, the Garden History Society and the Architectural Heritage Society of Scotland. His interests in architecture are wide and include landscape, old buildings and towns. He has fought to enhance the city of Aberdeen and to protect its very strong architectural heritage from foolish depredation, and occasionally is called on to advise on historic interiors, the reclamation of old gardens and the expansion of designed townscapes. He taught student architects in these subjects until his retirement. His recent book *A City's Architecture: Aberdeen as Designed City* (Ashgate) was published in 2012. The same year saw the fourth edition of his *Aberdeen: An Illustrated Architectural Guide* (Rutland).

Ichnographia Rustica
Stephen Switzer and the designed landscape

William Alvis Brogden

LONDON AND NEW YORK

First published 2017
by Routledge
2 Park Square, Milton Park, Abingdon, Oxon OX14 4RN

and by Routledge
711 Third Avenue, New York, NY 10017

Routledge is an imprint of the Taylor & Francis Group, an informa business

© 2017 William Alvis Brogden

The right of William Alvis Brogden to be identified as author of this work has been asserted by him in accordance with sections 77 and 78 of the Copyright, Designs and Patents Act 1988.

All rights reserved. No part of this book may be reprinted or reproduced or utilised in any form or by any electronic, mechanical, or other means, now known or hereafter invented, including photocopying and recording, or in any information storage or retrieval system, without permission in writing from the publishers.

Trademark notice: Product or corporate names may be trademarks or registered trademarks, and are used only for identification and explanation without intent to infringe.

British Library Cataloguing-in-Publication Data
A catalogue record for this book is available from the British Library

Library of Congress Cataloging-in-Publication Data
Names: Brogden, William A.
Title: Ichnographia rustica : Stephen Switzer and the designed landscape / by William Alvis Brogden.
Description: Burlington, VT : Ashgate, 2015. | Includes bibliographical references and index.
Identifiers: LCCN 2015025291 | ISBN 9781472434401 (hardback : alk. paper) | ISBN 9781472434418 (ebook) | ISBN 9781472434425 (epub)
Subjects: LCSH: Switzer, Stephen, 1682?–1745. | Landscape gardening—Great Britain—History—18th century. | Gardens—Great Britain—Design—History—18th century. | Agriculture—Great Britain—History—18th century.
Classification: LCC SB470.55.G7 B76 2015 | DDC 712.0941—dc23
LC record available at http://lccn.loc.gov/2015025291

ISBN: 978-1-4724-3440-1 (hbk)
ISBN: 978-1-315-58771-4 (ebk)

Typeset in Sabon
by Apex CoVantage, LLC

To Zian Chi Lamb

Contents

List of figures   ix
Abbreviations of sources   xiii

Introduction   1

1 **A fine genius for gardening**   8

Garden history; Brompton Park, Cassiobury, Hertfordshire; Longleat, Wiltshire and Bretby, Derbyshire; London and Wise, Castle Howard, Yorkshire and the new gardens at Kensington, London; Blenheim, Oxfordshire; Heythrop, Oxfordshire; Hampton Court, Bushy Park Middlesex; Magdalen College, Oxford; Chargate, Surrey

2 **Towards a rural and farm-like way of gardening**   44

Grimsthorpe, Lincolnshire; Riskins, Buckinghamshire; How to make a rural and extensive garden; Dyrham, Gloucestershire; Hopetoun, West Lothian; Whetham, Wiltshire

3 **Early landscapes**   79

Cirencester Park, Gloucestershire; Marston, Somerset; Hampton Court, Herefordshire; Stourhead, Wiltshire; Leeswood, Flintshire; Cliveden-Taplow Court, Buckinghamshire

4 **"Nature to advantage dress'd"**   119

Caversham, Berkshire; Holme Lacy, Herefordshire; Ebberston, Yorkshire; Shotover, Oxfordshire; Lumley Castle, County Durham; Studley Royal, Yorkshire; Belvoir, Rutland/Lincolnshire; Wilton, Wiltshire; Marlborough House, Wiltshire; Spye Park, Wiltshire; Lacock Abbey, Wiltshire

5 **A public figure**   158

Seedshop in Westminster Hall; Societies of Improvers, Lord Cathcart, Cannons, Middlesex; Lord Burlington, William Kent and Chiswick House,

Middlesex; Kent and Carlton House, London; Rokeby and the North; Switzer's improvers; Rhual, Flintshire

6 **Essays in the landscape style** 192

Cirencester Lodge Park, Gloucestershire; Sherborne Lodge Park, Gloucestershire; Tottenham Park, Wiltshire; Stowe, Buckinghamshire and Castle Howard, Yorkshire; Nostell Priory, Yorkshire and Mereworth Castle, Kent; Exton, Rutland; Garendon, Leicestershire; Beaumanor, Leicestershire; Wilton, Wiltshire

7 *Furor hortensis* 231

Lord Petre, Thorndon, Essex; Gisbourne, Lancashire/Yorkshire; Formark House, Derbyshire; Stowe, Buckinghamshire, Home Park; Elysian Fields and Hawkwell Field; The Leasowes, Worcestershire; Hagley, Worcestershire and Enville, Worcestershire; Castle Kennedy, Dumfries-shire; Blenheim, Oxfordshire, The Lake (Queen Pool); Wroxton, Oxfordshire; Kiddlington, Oxfordshire; Lowther, Westmorland; Badminton, Gloucestershire; Wimpole, Cambridgeshire; Stowe, the Grecian Valley; Brown and the English Landscape Garden: Croome Court, Worcestershire

8 **Legacy** 259

Alternative genesis of the Modern Taste; Whately and the English Landscape Garden; neo-classical landscape and beginnings of urban design; taste into philosophy, Association of Ideas, arts and science estranged; the Modern Movement; *Envoi*

Switzer's publications 273
Works consulted 276
Acknowledgements 289
Index 292

Figures

0.1	Stephen Switzer (?), presumed self-portrait	xiv
1.1	Kensington Palace, London: gravel-pit amphitheatre	8
1.2	Wilton, Wiltshire: aerial view of garden	15
1.3	Cassiobury, Hertfordshire	17
1.4	Bretby, Derbyshire	18
1.5	Castle Howard, Yorkshire: design for the grounds, ca 1699, by George London	21
1.6	Castle Howard, Yorkshire: working plan, early 18th century	24
1.7	Castle Howard, Yorkshire: prospect from the south in 1732	26
1.8	Blenheim, Oxfordshire: anonymous plan of the early Bridge-Canals, ca 1708	28
1.9	Blenheim, Oxfordshire: 1719 part of the estate plan	29
1.10	Heythrop, Oxfordshire: plan of the grounds, ca 1707	31
1.11	Upper Lodge, Bushy Park, Hampton Court, Middlesex	33
1.12	Upper Lodge, Bushy Park, Hampton Court, Middlesex	35
1.13	Chargate/Claremont, Surrey: view from the north-west, by William Stukeley, 1722	37
1.14	Chargate, Surrey: plan of the fruit garden where the walls are bevel	40
1.15	Chargate/Claremont, Surrey: partial plan	42
2.1	Grimsthorpe, Lincolnshire: prospect of the estate	45
2.2	Grimsthorpe, Lincolnshire: view of Duchess' Bastion, by William Stukeley, 1736	47
2.3	Grimsthorpe, Lincolnshire: view of the parterre from the east, by William Stukeley, 1736	48
2.4	Grimsthorpe, Lincolnshire: view of Grime's Walk, by William Stukeley, 1736	49
2.5	Grimsthorpe, Lincolnshire: estate plan from the 1752 plan book	50
2.6	Riskins, Berkshire: plan	52
2.7	Riskins, Berkshire: Stephen Switzer's "regulated Epitomy"	54
2.8	Houghton Hall, Norfolk: plan of the grounds	57
2.9	The Manor of Paston plan as divided into rural gardens	60
2.10	"The Mannour of Paston" as found	65
2.11	Whetham, Wiltshire: anonymous 1846 view from the south-east	66
2.12	Whetham, Wiltshire: cascade-house analogy	68
2.13	Dyrham, Gloucestershire	70
2.14	Whetham, Wiltshire: plan of the estate in the early 18th century	73

Figures

3.1	Stephen Switzer's "Plan of a Forest or Rural Garden"	80
3.2	Cirencester, Gloucestershire: garden front of the house	81
3.3	Cirencester, Gloucestershire: diagram of the layout of the grounds	83
3.4	Cirencester, Gloucestershire: grounds, eastern section	85
3.5	Cirencester, Gloucestershire: details of north woodland walks, the "Riskins" terrace walks	88
3.6	Cirencester, Gloucestershire: plan of Seven Rides	90
3.7	Marston, Somerset: plan of the estate in the mid-18th century	92
3.8	Marston, Somerset	93
3.9	Marston, Somerset: plan of part of Marston Pond and wood	95
3.10	Hampton Court, Herefordshire: plan of the gardens	97
3.11	Hampton Court, Herefordshire: plan of the estate in the early 18th century	99
3.12	Leeswood, Flintshire: plan of the grounds	100
3.13	Leeswood, Flintshire: plan of the estate in the early 18th century	103
3.14	Cliveden/Taplow Court, Buckinghamshire: painting at Cliveden House of prospect from the south, undated (ca 1760)	105
3.15	Cliveden/Taplow Court, Buckinghamshire: plan of the estates in 1752	109
3.16	Stourhead, Wiltshire: plan of the estate in the early 1740s	116
4.1	Caversham, Berkshire: plan of the estate	119
4.2	Caversham, Berkshire: plan of the gardens	121
4.3	Holme Lacy, Herefordshire: view of the house from the south, ca 1780	125
4.4	Holme Lacy, Herefordshire: plan of a kitchen garden, related to the layout of Holme Lacy, ca 1716	126
4.5	Ebberston Lodge, Yorkshire: prospect of the gardens from the house	127
4.6	Shotover, Oxfordshire: view of the gardens and landscape, by George Bickham, 1752	130
4.7	Lumley Castle, County Durham: anonymous plan, ca 1720	133
4.8	Belvoir Castle, Rutland: prospect from the south, by Thomas Badeslade	136
4.9	Belvoir Castle, Rutland: prospect from the north, by Thomas Badeslade	136
4.10	Wilton, Wiltshire: prospect from the north, by William Stukeley, 1723	138
4.11	Wilton, Wiltshire: prospect from the south, by William Stukeley, undated (early 1720s)	138
4.12	Castle House, Marlborough, Wiltshire: prospect, by William Stukeley, 1723	140
4.13	Spye Park, Wiltshire: house and grounds in the 17th century	142
4.14	Spye Park, Wiltshire: plan of the terrace, grotto pavilion, west cascade	144
4.15	Spye Park, Wiltshire: prospect of the east cascades	146
4.16	Spye Park, Wiltshire: plan of the house, west cascade, basin etc from "The Plan of a Kitchen or Fruit Garden"	147
4.17	Lacock Abbey, Wiltshire: *Beeches at Lacock*, photograph of trees in the gardens by Henry Fox Talbot, 1844	150

4.18	Lacock Abbey, Wiltshire: "Exact Plan of the Demean and Manor of Lacock 1764"	153
5.1	Cannons, Middlesex: plan of the estate in 1754	161
5.2	Richmond Palace, Surrey: John Rocque's plan of the grounds between Richmond and Kew, now site of Kew Gardens	162
5.3	Chiswick House, Middlesex: south view from the river in 1750	164
5.4	Chiswick House, Middlesex: partial plan of the gardens, by John Rocque	166
5.5	William Kent, watercolour design drawing for an unidentified landscape scheme with deer house, ca 1735	171
5.6	Carlton House, St James', London: plan of the gardens, by John Rocque, undated (early 1740s)	172
5.7	Rokeby Park, Yorkshire: plan of the grounds, 1741	174
5.8	Corby Castle, Cumberland: Samuel Buck's prospect of Wetheral Priory showing the grounds of Corby Castle with reference to Rokeby, 1739	177
5.9	Aqualate, Staffordshire: the Menagerie, from a survey of 1767	187
5.10	Rhual, Flintshire: plan of the grounds as in the 1740s	188
6.1	Cirencester, Gloucestershire: Ivy Lodge Park and Seven Rides sections, from joined plans of the whole estate	192
6.2	Cirencester, Gloucestershire: views of the garden at Alfred's Hall	194
6.3	Cirencester, Gloucestershire: plan of the garden at Alfred's Hall, Oakley Great Park	195
6.4	Lodge Park, Sherborne, Gloucestershire: Charles Bridgeman's design for the park landscape, 1729	197
6.5	Nostell Priory, Yorkshire: design	199
6.6	Nostell Priory, Yorkshire: plan of house siting	202
6.7	Nostell Priory, Yorkshire: plan of central section	204
6.8	Mereworth Castle, Kent: plan of the grounds in the 18th century	206
6.9	Exton, Rutland: detail of view of the church and house, undated (mid-18th century)	209
6.10	Exton Park, Rutland: south prospect of the house and grounds	210
6.11	Exton Park, Rutland: cascade, south view	212
6.12	Exton Park, Rutland: plan by Stephen Switzer for the water-works, undated (1730s)	213
6.13	St Giles House, Dorset: engraved south prospect of the house and grounds by François Vivares, 1772	215
6.14	Garendon Park, Leicestershire: anonymous drawing of the Triumphal Arch, 1826	216
6.15	Garendon Park, Leicestershire: survey plan from the late 18th century	218
6.16a	Beaumanor, Leicestershire: Stephen Switzer's design for the grounds, 1737	220
6.16b	Beaumanor, Leicestershire: detail of Stephen Switzer's design for the grounds 1737	221
6.17	Wilton House, Wiltshire: part of the engraved view by Luke Sullivan 1759	223
6.18	Wilton House, Wiltshire: engraved plan of the grounds by John Rocque, 1746 (ed 1752)	225

6.19	Wilton House, Wiltshire: Bridge of Communication from the west with the Nadder as a lake	228
6.20	Wilton House, Wiltshire: engraved later 18th century, west prospect from the Bridge of Communication or dam based on Richard Wilson's painting at Wilton	230
7.1	Gisbourne, Yorkshire/Lancashire: Peter Bourguignon's design for the grounds, ca 1735	233
7.2	Formark, Derbyshire: plan of the grounds based on an anonymous design for the grounds, ca 1737	234
7.3	Formark, Derbyshire: detail from an anonymous design for the grounds	235
7.4	Formark, Derbyshire: detail from an anonymous design for the grounds, showing escarpment above the River Trent	236
7.5	Formark, Derbyshire: the Anchor Church, engraved view by Thomas Smith of Derby and François Vivares, from a painting of 1745	237
7.6	Stowe House, Buckinghamshire: plan of the gardens with Elysian Fields, based on Sarah Bridgeman's plan of 1739	238
7.7	The Leasowes, Shropshire: plan of the grounds in 1745 by H F Clark, 1943	242
7.8	The Leasowes, Shropshire: *The Grove*, by William Shenstone, ca 1753	244
7.9	Blenheim, Oxfordshire: detail of John Spyers' estate plan, 1763	250
7.10	Stowe House, Buckinghamshire: plan of the eastern additions, part of Hawkwell Field and Grecian Valley	253
7.11	Stowe House, Buckinghamshire: J B C Chatelain's 1753 engraved view from the north of the Grecian Valley as designed by Lancelot Brown	256
8.1	Belton House, Lincolnshire: the new Waterwork from the south	266

Abbreviations of sources

DNB   *Oxford Dictionary of National Biography*
FG   *The Practical Fruit Gardener*
Hydro   *An Introduction To a general System of Hydrostaticks and Hydraulicks, Philosophical and Practical*
IR   *Ichnographia Rustica*
KG   *The Practical Kitchen Gardener*
PH&P   *The Practical Husbandman and Planter*
Vit Brit   *Vitruvius Britannicus*

Figure 0.1 Stephen Switzer (?), presumed self-portrait. From Stephen Switzer, *Ichnographia Rustica*, 1718, II plate 11. Private collection.

Introduction

Stephen Switzer (1682–1745) is an author known for his writings on gardening and agricultural improvement. He is remembered now for his early advocacy of the 18th century landscape style of gardening, a reputation clouded somewhat by perceptions that his conception was not sufficiently full-blown. Perhaps for that reason alone, there has not been a book devoted to his contributions. Yet even a cursory glance at his major works is enough to excite interest, and the subject of garden history has matured in the last half century enough to show that such a study is now needed, indeed wanted. Work here and abroad on the developments of the 18th century, notably of the picturesque and its very considerable and continuing influence, has indicated anomalies in the standard accounts that require us to look at the subject afresh. And doing so from Switzer's point of view will provide a refreshing and stimulating corrective. (And the far from least outcome will be to appreciate these various essays in designed landscapes for their own qualities as works of creative art, rather than as harbingers of a new and superior taste, or more likely as the mildly regrettable examples of *retarditare*.)

For a long time our basic ideas about how a landscape can and should be planned have rested on the clear and generally pleasing notion of the primacy of either formal or informal modes. These are best exemplified in the works of Andre Le Notre, working for Louis XIV at Versailles and elsewhere, and its alternative can be seen a century later in the works of Lancelot Brown in the service of a variety of aristocratic improvers in England. Many other matters in exercising power, from the political through the economic to the personal, have become involved. Since its creation, or perhaps better since its recognition, the informal has been stronger, and even for a time was fashionable. In the 19th century matters were often mixed. Whatever the local issues and perceptions, this dichotomy has served as the robust limits for subsequent thought and practice in the appreciation of designed landscapes.

Stephen Switzer received his training and education and his early practice at the formal pole. Then in the early 18th century he published his *Ichnographia Rustica*, which effectively posited the second pole, the informal. In following his career in the first half of the 18th century, as author and designer, an alternative story to that which has prevailed for so long presents itself. In demonstrating just how the designs for grounds, from garden to countryside, changed over 50 years this calls into question the truth of our proposed fundamental oppositions. Switzer did not perceive them as opposites. Rather, he appreciated both modes and early on discovered that they might be mixed together, to the advantage of both. Thus, *Ichnographia Rustica* and its clear understanding of Switzer's *both-and* pattern invites a new reading of the period and perhaps a renewed regard for his methods and a consequent emulation.

The idea of making gardens, and then large gardens and estates, into works of art can only occur in times of stability, power and will. Naturally following the best examples of Continental practice, men and women in these islands (from the early 18th century a securely united Britain, with Ireland) as commissioners of designs, as designers, as contractors and suppliers, and also as interested friends and neighbours, collectively the *improvers*, began to do just that. Given that the land then *was* wealth, its ownership gave power, and its improvement in terms of advances in agriculture and forestry, especially with the perceived necessity to replenish and expand the navy from a much depleted resource, became both a personal and national good. Political legitimacy, and power, also was then based only on landowning. Recent constitutional reforms had ensured security for those landowners and thus encouraged improvements. In the Continental wars British success provided even more confidence, and with the returning generals and senior officers the body of determined early 18th century improvers was increased.

This was the culture into which Switzer was born, and from the beginning of the new century he became a student-improver, then a full player and leader. But, as he lacked an estate and thus wealth and power, his role had to be professional, at a time when there was hardly such a thing. His masters, George London and Henry Wise, were senior servants as head gardeners who had been encouraged by their powerful patrons to establish the very successful enterprise of Brompton Park Nurseries, as Switzer put it, "from which the Nation was stock'd". As designers, contractors and then (to a degree) managers of these new works or art they thrived, and Wise as surviving partner sold his shares at the firm's peak of esteem and was able to move into power as a landowner. Switzer had to find a role, and this forms the subject of this book.

The rural neighbourhood of Winchester where Switzer's family had long been established still retained its dangers in the late 17th century, as the trial for treason of their landlord, Lord William Russell, clearly showed. Switzer's own path in life might have been a trifle more genteel otherwise, but his apprenticeship at the Brompton Park Nurseries nonetheless was most fortunate: in a time when very large gardens were numerous, and desired by many, London and his partners were the most esteemed, and the busiest, and they were patronized by both royal families and revolutionaries, by Whigs and also by Tories. Switzer, who worked and studied under London and Wise, was closely involved in all aspects of this period of extraordinary re-designing of landscapes.

Although big gardens and estates aspired to being works of art they never became fabricated objects of value, as, for example, statuary or paintings were. Like buildings, but much more so, they were a social rather than an individual work. Although London and Wise were courted for advice, and they may have made a design on paper, they never could (nor would) charge enough from that to make a living. Rather, their living and wealth came from the contracts to carry out designs, and these naturally became protracted, as changes were desired, and as plantations succeeded or failed, and this occurred over time. These smaller, although very significant, charges were easily and contentedly paid by their clients, with whatever moiety went to running and sustaining the business unnoticed by them. Of course, as making the designs into gardens and estates lasted years, often many years, opportunities for changes occurred. Usually these were seemingly inconsiderable, but sometimes not. But natural growth and maturing sensibility or altered tastes were thus accommodated. Thus, it is never an easy matter, and most often a matter approaching impossibility, to determine what decisions were made about design, or who made them. The surviving evidence has to be examined in each case, and a judgement reached. Sadly, but perhaps predictably, such evidence is often entirely missing. The Orrerys' improvements at Marston, Somerset, were made from about 1715 and were continuing at Switzer's death: he was involved with the place, and his advice sought, for 30 years or so. Yet the only indication of what they did rests on one engraved view, a partial view of another part, and meagre references to difficulties in carrying out his designs. Neither Orrery thought to commission artists to record their efforts, although their cousin Burlington patronized many artists to record his place at Chiswick, although not his other, and bigger, estate. Where evidence exists it is often scant: for example Switzer's late design for Rhual, Flintshire, is known only from one references in one surviving letter.

Much of our evidence comes from Switzer's own published works. In 1715 he records the meritorious decision making, then on behalf of Queen Anne, taken by his employer Henry Wise in the formation of part of the new gardens at Kensington, making no further claim, although he is later confirmed as the author of the design. Rarely is he so effusive as he was in 1718 in his praise of Lord Carlisle for the decision to adopt Wray Wood in its existing state and make it, effectively, the *garden* for Castle Howard. And even there he sensibly calls attention to the appropriate decision and does not claim any role for himself. However, the suspicion arises that that may hardly have pleased its owner. His other scattered references to places and people are disguised and discreet. However, these usually are reinforced by some other evidence. There are only two surviving design drawings for a scheme of improvement, and these are both signed. Of the large collection of drawings made by the early topographer Richard Gough, most of which are anonymous, only a very few appear to be by Switzer: his surviving drawings are too few to identify characteristics of style of draughtsmanship. His published illustrations, which confirm his skill as an artist, are confined by their size, as folded plates normally in octavo format, and are thus conventional rather than perfectly accurate formal records. There are occasions when later surveys of Switzer's designs survive, such as that for Leeswood from the 1780s, that indicate his intentions. Some of the earliest drawings made for the nascent Ordnance Survey maps, for example in the late 1780s for Mereworth in Kent, or for Abb's Court, Surrey, can be used, with appropriate caution.

One of the greatest of these 18th century schemes, and the most influential, was Castle Howard, near York, a brand new house (still unfinished in the 1740s) for Lord Carlisle. It was undertaken as if its owner were a prince, and by men who were as experimental in the design of buildings and landscapes as their colleagues of the Royal Society were in matters of natural philosophy. Novelty was not sought, but when it arose through following hard headed experiment it certainly was not despised. By these means Castle Howard set a standard for judgement for the next two generations of improvers. Blenheim, an even more princely and palatial house, celebrated national pride in the military leadership of Marlborough, and the stormy struggles of the Queen and her sometime favourite servant, his wife. It also presented unprecedented design problems with which Switzer struggled along with John Vanbrugh and Nicholas Hawksmoor, as well as Wise, and even Sir Christopher Wren.

In the second decade of the 18th century he moved into independent practice. Access to the funds needed to undertake great gardening schemes was available only to few, often to those who could tap into public revenues, managed from the Crown by a system of patronage. Two of Marlborough's lieutenants, Lord Coningsby and Lord Cadogan, were such clients. He worked also for the Monarch's Ministers of State or their close relations: grandly at Hampton Court for Lord Halifax, closely with London for William Blathwayt at Dyrham, and more enigmatically at nearby Whetham for John Kyrle Ernle, where Switzer seems to have produced the earliest of his Rural and Extensive, Farm-like or, as they would soon be called, Landscape gardens. With the Earl of Pembroke and his family, masters of one of the greatest of the great European gardens of the previous century at Wilton, Switzer began a lifelong relationship, as he did also with the Boyle family, initially Charles, Earl of Orrery, whose library soon became the jewel of Christ Church, Oxford. There were also rural grandee clients such as the Duke of Ancaster at Grimsthorpe, and at least one Tory, the famous Lord Bathurst at Cirencester and at Riskins.

Based on his experience, and doubtless also spurred by the publication of the translation of A J Dezalier D'Argenville's *Theory and Practice of Gardening*, which presented the style of Louis XIV to British improvers, Switzer pulled together his own thoughts on the design of great gardens. A trial volume was published in 1715 as *The Nobleman Gentleman and Gardener's Recreation*, and enlarged to three volumes with numerous illustrations in 1718 as *Ichnographia Rustica*. This was effectively the manifesto for a designed landscape; agrarian in nature, taking the seat of the landowner as the grand core certainly, but also demonstrating improved agriculture, and forests as elements combining garden and farm, and including parks, and tenanted farmlands . . . the whole business of country life designed to unite utility and delight in the manner that Virgil had written about. It brought together aspirations to ancient culture with the decent attempt to re-establish something of the deservedly lost but longed for Paradise.

There was a lot of material for Switzer's readers to understand, and to be convinced of. The advantages of pursuing his advice were clearly stated, and there were flattering references to its congeniality to their habits and aspirations, and to the superiority of British materials and climate. And he cited recent support by Alexander Pope and Joseph Addison. But it was all new, not only different from what the French were doing, but different too from what his British neighbours had already achieved, and not all potential patrons were so keen as Lord Molesworth, who wished to lure Switzer away from England to Ireland to work with him near Dublin. Others may have thought the notions of both men rather peculiar, as John Laurence, one of his rival authors, did.

What was clear as absolutely right in the late 1750s, and what had been sensed as early as the 1730s as the coming fashion, was much less than obvious in 1718. Like Colen Campbell's contemporary *Vitruvius Britannicus*, which sought to reform the design of buildings, Switzer's manifesto needed time to find supporters and wide acceptance. Besides that, the first flush of excitement in making great gardens had passed, and of the few who could aspire to such works many had already committed themselves. Of the wealthy adventurers in the South Sea speculation only John Aislaby's Studley Royal near York was completed; many other schemes were abandoned when the bubble burst. In the 1720s and 1730s noticeably fewer very great schemes were undertaken. However, the smaller schemes then begun not only were what Switzer advocated but were relatively more easily achieved: during that period, however slow the acceptance of his ideas might have seemed at the time, within a little more than a decade a new manner began to emerge.

With the publication of this books, the pattern of Switzer's life changed somewhat. He had become a public person. And as he had very fully instructed potential improvers on what they needed to do, and what qualities they needed to develop, and precisely how to make a pretty *landskip* of their possessions (offering, apart from the works of his colleague Charles Bridgeman, the only advances in this period), thus he will have enlarged his own reputation. This only increased from 1724 with the first of his supplementary books, *The Practical Fruit Gardener*, followed by *The Practical Kitchen Gardener*, plus a series of pamphlets on grasses. These more fully covered his ideas on the horticultural side of his concerns, while the more magisterial *An Introduction to a General System of Hydrostaticks and Hydraulicks* followed in 1729. This drew on his own experience in making complex, elaborate or simply large water-works of various kinds. This last had required significant access to the specialist libraries of his patrons, Orrery's no doubt, but also, and specifically, the young Lord Brooke's at Breamore, as well as lore about current practice gleaned from friends such as William Stukeley.

After beginnings in Berkshire and Wiltshire in smaller versions of Brompton Park, Switzer settled in London in the lucrative and jealously guarded trade in seeds from a shop in Westminster Hall. There he could meet even more of his fellow improvers, and be consulted by them, as well as supplying seeds for the burgeoning experiments in improving soils. While the shop remained his headquarters, manned by assistants overseen by his wife, Elizabeth, he travelled extensively giving advice, staying in various parts of the country for a few days, or rather longer, as required. His practice in these mature years was an extensive one, and although the evidence which has come down to us remains more fragmentary and unsatisfying than we could wish it is clear that he gave advice about making extensive gardens and also smaller aspects of his *Farm-like Way of Gardening*. These include the full, although relatively small, design for Henry Hoare at Stourhead, the grand but short-lived water-works for Anne Baynton at Spye, an apparently abortive scheme for Thomas Broadley at Ferriby, the provision of specialist features such as menageries (for example at Lacock Abbey), and at least one scheme whose expense, if not aspiration, rivalled those of Queen Anne's time, Leeswood in north Wales.

A great garden scheme might be a discrete effort designed and then executed timeously; more often it was much longer term, in the case of Castle Howard and Cirencester an effort of decades. So even exemplars of Switzer's way of designing gardens were not instantly persuasive. The old Wray Wood dominated Castle Howard from the beginning, and directed its character. At Cirencester, as elsewhere, the major elements, Switzer's *Boldest Strokes* of a new scheme, had to carry the design from the beginning, but as it and the other areas – blocks of plantation, or parterres, or walks – asserted their own characters as they grew to maturity, so then new ideas or appreciations occurred, and these in turn suggested improvements or even new departures.

In the deliberations that accompanied these developments at Cirencester, from about 1718 the poet Alexander Pope was involved, and had he had his way, would have been more thoroughly involved. And he also becomes during that period a major apologist for *Rural and Extensive Gardening*. His moral essays especially, those long poems about the uses of power and riches, which included the theory of design and were dedicated to Lord Bathurst, and to Lord Burlington, bring the strength of his poetic voice and make memorable and timeless observations on how best to design things, especially landscapes. Other writers had also contributed to the dissemination of these new ideas about garden design, not least Thomas Tickell, Joseph Addison's protégée, in the curious *Kensington Gardens*, but also Robert Castell's *Villas of the Ancients Illustrated* (1728), which sought to show just how the great gardens of Virgil's time were made. At a more popular and professional level Batty Langley contributed his *New Principles of Gardening* (1728), while new editions of John James' *Theory and Practice of Gardening* appeared.

These iterations in others' words promulgated many of Switzer's ideas and indicate that after ten years they were about to establish a new fashion. Although Switzer wished to be listened to, and to have his ideas accepted, *Ichnographia Rustica* could never have been fashionable . . . there are just too many nuances, ifs, ands and buts. But, perhaps sensing the drift of taste, in 1728 he wrote material for a new edition in which he attempted to restate his ideas in simpler fashion, and in doing that he introduces the term *ferme ornée*. Despite all this, when Philip Miller's *Dictionary of Gardening* appeared, the short section on design reiterated the notions of James. That attests the continuing power of gardens in the French manner. This was continued in the many following editions. Switzer's message was not yet fully accepted until well past mid-century, in the 1760s.

Yet towards the middle of the 1730s a breakthrough begins to be recognized, and although *nature* is cited and curving forms of various kinds are employed, neither is the actual cause, nor, in all probability, is political stance. The *edges* of gardens begin to be a major concern, often because they are literally the next obvious issue, and the attention of improvers shifts. That indicates another aspect which is even more important. What becomes pronounced in the 1730s is a much greater preponderance of space . . . whether it is called parade, lawn or park. Open, that is to say, effectively "empty", space becomes progressively more noticeable. With Switzer at Nostell Priory or later in 1737 at Beaumanor the amount of open space relative to conventionally planted space is striking, as it is similarly at Exton Park. At Lord Petre's contemporary design for himself at Thorndon, or with Bridgeman's last work at Amesbury, spaciousness is also characteristic. Larger spaces, mostly parkland, were historically enlivened by groups of trees, and characteristically by great singletons: when they (or park-like adjuncts) become the subjects of design they have clumps at trees, in the 1730s almost always roughly in a figure. Parades and avenues, while wider, are ornamented by buildings, almost invariably the house, and still defined by forest trees still predominantly en masse.

Lawns are the new design element which allows the easier acceptance of Switzer's proposal to mix pleasure with profit: the pleasure element is the smart parterre (now increasingly empty), which has the contiguous field as the contrasting profitable part. This can be seen, for example, in the works at Rousham. If a field is also ornamented by a building, then the placement of the building tends to nestle into the edge, usually the far edge. And as Switzer had indicated, a walk between, or along, these two hitherto contrary parts of country life, is not only very pleasing but easily becomes the *raison d'être* of the whole scheme. Hagley, where old sheep walks (or lauds, an early form of lawns) were added in the later 1730s, illustrates this well. Soon it and its neighbour Enville and also Painshill in Surrey become mostly a matter of decorated lawns connected by walks.

As contiguous fields are the obvious next place for improvers to expand into, it is hardly surprising when fields become the defining part even of Wilton. In its next and most profound iteration, begun in the early 1730s, clearly the intention was to enlarge the gardens. Removing the old walls had the immediate effect of shifting the centre of the composition also, so the point where the River Nadder ran out of Isaac De Caus's design unnoticed has from a century later been marked by the marvellous "Palladian" bridge of 1737. This mostly transparent building becomes the garden's new centre. Around it are a new series of garden-fields differentiated only by their kinds of grass, some close cropped, others less so. The house lies to one side of the enlarged scheme (but is now seen obliquely), rising ground and a formal entry to Sydney's Walk occupy the other, and to the east the Nadder is dammed at a new edge and forms a fair sized lake-like piece of water ornamented by re-sited old De Caus elements and the distant spire of Salisbury cathedral. Thus, the "new" Wilton declared to be in the *Modern Taste* is surprising in appearance. Although it is the result of skilful revision, these developments also have the revolutionary effect of making it into a landscape garden.

In Switzer's late years he continued in business and publication (the second edition of *Ichnographia Rustica* appeared in 1742), and he continued to advise on garden design. His principal concerns revolved around ways of more fully incorporating horticulture and agriculture into one scheme. So attention to the perfection and uses of grasses, for enrichment of ground, as feed for animals, and as ornament, is evident, such as his quarrel with Jethro Tull about seed-drilling, numerous pamphlets and the developing predominance of fields in designs. As always, his work continues to have its surprises and defies easy assessment. For those who would follow art historical division there remain curiously baroque elements, especially in water-works. For example there is the Waterwork, a scheme of river and cascade, added to Belton for Lord Tyrconnel in 1742. Whereas the River is up-to-date, the Cascade remains as amazingly grotesque as his imitation at Spye of the Aldobrandini a decade before, confirming Switzer's long expressed admiration for such, derived as he said from Homer: yet the design is still similar to 16th and 17th century Roman work. Conversely, the placement of these extraordinary elements in contrast with their large empty and smooth contexts makes them equally comparable to a surreal landscape as painted by of Salvador Dalí, still two centuries into the future. Clearly for Switzer, as for his clients, gardens are never finished; his latest recorded effort was in the ongoing improvements to Marston, where he was then working with the young Orrery. By his death in the summer of 1745 taste had almost caught up with Switzer's advice from 1715. H F Clark long ago (Clark 1943) identified William Shenstone's The Leasowes, by 1745 largely in place, as the earliest example of the new and still not named manner, and also as its most perfect pattern: its amateur designer-owner even used the term *ferme ornée* to describe it. But Shenstone never acknowledged Switzer, and as Stukeley observed in his diary others were also ignorant of Switzer's role.

Conventions

There are conventions employed for this book in the interests of clarity and ease. The thorn, often rendered as "y" in 18th century usage, has normally been replaced by "th"; the value of sterling has been given as found, and also rendered in current values (£1 = £300) for guidance. Obvious misspellings in Switzer's publications have been corrected.

1 A fine genius for gardening

Figure 1.1 Kensington Palace, London: gravel-pit amphitheatre (north to top). Plan reproduced from Thomas Tickell, *Kensington Gardens*, 1722. Private collection.

As his is the first history of gardening Switzer begins it with a little trepidation and an apology for presuming to venture into a subject where readers might rather expect "valiant Atchievements, Heroick Examples and Lives of Great Soldiers, and the solemn Debates and Councils of Learned Statesmen and Senators . . ." (*IR* I 1). He goes on to argue that gardening, unlike high deeds, is the concern of many, if not all, and in any case the great men were also deeply interested in this subject and contributed to it. He naturally starts with Creation and notes, quoting Scripture with some modesty, that it was only on the third day that "[t]he Lord God planted a Garden eastward in Eden, and there he the Man whom he had form'd". Of its "Mathematical Distribution" Switzer ventures no guess, but asserts that after the Flood, probably somewhere near Armenia, Noah "began to be a Husbandman, and he Planted a Vineyard" (*IR* I 5). Thus, Scripture attests the founding of humankind's history of gardening, and, by Switzer's adoption of Zoroaster actually being one of the sons of Noah, this is confirmed in one of Switzer's most trusted non-Biblical ancient sources, Pliny the Elder's *Natural History*.

Thus, Switzer's ideas are founded in Scripture and the classics, and he uses them freely to trace the early part of his narrative. For the second part he relies rather more on the poetry of the 17th century, that of Browne, Cowley, Milton and Temple. These are selected to further his own attitudes and give strength and colour to his opinions. Then the substantial last part of his history traces his own knowledge of the period following the Glorious Revolution and paints a rather Whiggish and progressive account of the making of the great gardens of Longleat, Chatsworth and Badminton up to the death of the Duchess of Beaufort there in the spring of 1715.

For Switzer the Biblical ancients, having been driven out of Paradise, worked slowly and with much toil, "living a Pastoral Life in open Fields and moveable Tents . . . Gard'ning was doubtless little known or practis'd by them . . ." before David's or Solomon's time. But then Solomon "made me Gardens and Orchards, and planted Trees in them of all kinds of Fruit; I made me Pools of Water, to water therewith the Wood that bringeth forth Trees" (*IR* I 6). The earliest description of a garden in classical sources is roughly contemporary, found in Homer's long passage about Alcinous, and there he gives a trifle more detail but shows the same kind of garden. A well-watered enclosed ground of some four acres adjacent to the house is planted with lofty fruit trees . . . apple, pear, pomegranate, fig and olive with grapes from "order'd Vines in equal Ranks appear," while "Beds of all various Herbs for ever Green, in beauteous Order terminate the Scene." As a perfect idea few can surpass this, and doubtless this has remained the ideal well into modern times. The Villa d'Este at Tivoli from the 1540s and the Botanic Garden at Oxford, about a century later, are of similar size and composition.

For the more extensive plantations Switzer looks to the elder Pliny's account of Epicurus (341–270 BC), who was "the first that brought into Athens the custom of having, under the name of *Hortus*, a Garden, the Delights of Fields and country mansions . . . and hence we may conjecture . . . that this was the Place which Pausanias reports to have been called, even in his Time, the *Garden of Philosophy*; adding that there was in it a Statue made by Alcemenes . . . and that the Temple of Venus did join to it" (*IR* I 12–13). Unusually, perhaps uniquely, for Switzer, the tillage and dressing of land, and agriculture in its developed forms, are allied to gardening and his History. The Romans' "great Veneration for Gard'ning, Agriculture, &c . . ." is almost sufficient in itself. And as gardens had provided a home for philosophy, so Switzer believes that early Romans dwelt communally in gardens (*IR* I 19), but unlike the more arid wilderness of their Biblical neighbours, the Latin countryside was "the nearest Resemblance to Heaven that could possibly be found on Earth . . .", as Vitruvius also asserted. Switzer cites Aeneas' visit to Elysium with the Sybil, when on enquiring of his father where the Blissful lived he was told, ". . . In no fix'd Place the happy Souls abide; In Groves we live, and lie on mossie Beds, By Chrystal Streams that murmur'd thro' the Meads" (Dryden, quoted in *IR* I 20). Not only did he draw from Virgil notions of the countryside as Paradise, but he could populate its imagined scenes with characters and stories, especially of the shepherds and ploughmen familiar to his own country experience, and could even find "as to the Designing Part" the arrangement of trees in "Quadratic and Quincuncial Form" in the *Georgics*. Virgil's works and life seem to provide the very pattern for his *Ichnographia Rustica*, and thus he cited these higher realms of poetry, greatly esteemed as they were in the late 17th century, as his foundation.

Few treatises specifically on country life and farming had survived from classical times. But this handful of sources indicated to Switzer the very high standard of knowledge, practice and even philosophical attitude of the ancient Romans. These tracts had the same literary aspirations and qualities set by the poetry. The oldest of these is Marcus Porcius Cato's *De Agricultura*. Cato (234–149 BC) was a venerated Roman of the old school, that is, the Republican period. He was a soldier, and a most resolute one; he disliked luxury and had little time for the idea of nobility. His surname meant "the shrewd", and his interest in farming was lifelong and included what is now sometimes called agribusiness, and on a very large scale. An old farmer from the Sabine country, he embodied the most esteemed Roman virtues. He took his oratory seriously and worked on his speeches and wrote them out for improvement. His literary output was great and ranged to witty aphorisms but consisted mostly of history, ethnology and antiquities. All of that is lost; only the *De Agricultura*, incidentally the earliest composition of Latin prose, survives, and it is looser and less polished than he would have approved of.

Switzer found in Cato two qualities very congenial to his argument: the character of the farmer, and the pattern of the farm. For these really form the basis of *Ichnographia Rustica*. According to Cato, who relays it as information well known rather than his particular opinion, ". . . it is from the tillers of the soil that spring the best citizens, the staunchest soldiers; and theirs are the enduring rewards which are most grateful and least envied. Such as devote themselves to that pursuit are least of all given to evil counsels." He is drawn to commerce, but that career is full of risks and pitfalls. For Cato banking too has its great rewards, if honestly pursued, but he observes that is most unlikely to happen. The farmer's life is best, for himself and for Rome.

His ideal farm will face south, be backed by hills, be in a flourishing country near a good sized town and be at the sea-side, or on a navigable river. Frugality is all. "Know that with a farm, as with a man, however productive it may be, if it has the spending habit, not much will be left over." The best disposition of a farm for Cato has a vineyard (if it promises good yields), an irrigated garden, an osier bed, an olive orchard, a meadow, a cornfield, a wood, a cultivated orchard and a mast grove. This estate will consist of about 66 acres and may be all there is. It will always act as home-place, home-farm or mains. Planting should come first, and if it succeeds then, in his middle age, a farmer can begin to build, according to his means and always furnished for a country life. Such a place will be attractive; the owner will visit often and find fewer mistakes and better crops. "The face of master is good for the land." The roadways and field divisions should be planted with elms, and near the house is the place for the cultivated orchard, as also a "garden with garland flowers and vegetables of all kinds, and set about with myrtle hedges . . ." This is also the pattern of a Switzer garden.

A farm in Latin is *villa* and of course refers to the whole. In Switzer's time *villa* was used to describe a small house only but one of some distinction because of its design, contents or setting. This is also after ancient usage, and by the time of Marcus Terentius Varro (116–27 BC) *villa* was being used in this sense too. Varro was another polymath and public figure. He backed Pompey in the civil wars that ended the Republic. Julius Caesar restored his property to him, but then Mark Antony had him proscribed: so he spent his last years in forced retirement, in study and writing. His literary works were numerous and distinguished. His *Nine Books of Disciplines* about the liberal arts established that very significant grouping, and also the notion of encyclopaedic knowledge later taken up by Pliny. They covered a very wide range, from *belles lettres*, essentially poetry, to works about history and antiquities, and various technical works about how to do things, which includes his only work that has survived in full, *Rerum Rusticarum Libri Tres*, which he wrote in old age.

Varro's text is strikingly modern when compared to Cato's declarative statements of what one ought to know about farming. Varro uses the form of dialogue, sometimes several voices, and enjoys all sorts of discursive, and also enlightening, departures. He has enough of the old Romans' contempt for the foolish excesses of fashion. Naturally he recognizes, and to a degree deprecates, the modern form of the villa with its expensive furnishings and decorations, and often complete lack of the agricultural aspect. Rather than build "according to the thrift of the ancients than the luxury of the moderns . . . the effort is to have as large and handsome a dwelling-house as possible; and they vie with the 'farm-houses' of Metelus and Lucullus, which they have built to the great damage of the state" (Varro, book 1, chap 13). But it is an almost formal condemnation and without real sting. This becomes clear when he gets to the heart of his matter, which is that a farm, and by extension any kind of villa, ought to make money. So he extols those near Rome which cater to the luxury trade. The subject of book 3, *Of Poultry, Fish and Dormice*, indicates just how lucrative preparing these delicacies for the Romans could be, and in his description of his own *Ornithon* (book 3, chap 5, p 447 et seq) Varro gives hints that Switzer very likely followed in his forays into the design of menageries, and perhaps more widely (see below). And although Varro, probably to discredit Cato's authority, misreads his intentions in the description of the standard farm, Varro also tells of the kinds of divisions of fields used by the Romans, which Switzer finds very helpful. One suspects Switzer also found Varro's style of writing congenial, and followed it rather more than that of Cato.

With Lucius J M Columella (AD 4–70) comes the definitive treatise on Roman husbandry. It provides the pattern for all subsequent work before modern times, and itself appeared in a scholarly and substantial quarto edition in London in 1745. Sadly, its translator remains anonymous. Switzer recognized the value of Columella's *De Re Rustica*, and found references there for his history as well as justification for his arguments for Rural and Extensive Gardening. Columella lived and wrote in the post-Augustan age, when the old Roman virtues had been supplanted by some of its greatest vices: still he upholds the former while acknowledging the luxury of his time. In his section on the disposition of a villa, the *Manor House* of the 1745 translation, we find the first modern understanding of how a villa, or any Roman house, was designed – or, it should be said, early evidence of the great misunderstanding which had bedevilled architects and designers from the 16th century, which was the confusion that a great number of *rooms* signified *palatial* standards. As the translator puts it in his note: ". . . as their riches and luxury increased, they became much more magnificent; and a sumptuous and magnificent villa seems to have been the darling even of the wisest and most moderate among them . . . and when those of private persons were so stately, what must those of the more eminent station have been, as that of Maecenas, Lucullus, Cicero &c. As for those of the Caesars . . ." (Columella 31, see also 338). That these many rooms were really no more than closets never occurred to them, but the core problem of the appropriate manner in which to live for those with wealth and power, as well as the aspirations of those with neither, remained Switzer's concern and also the concern of his time.

Columella accepts the principal divisions of the villa grounds, as presumably also their size of roughly 60 acres each, and structures his text accordingly. For Switzer, apart from his various assertions that vineyards in parts of England produce very good wine, the very significant portion of Columella about Trees, which is always an aspect of the production of wine, is rather passed over, whereas the treatment of the tillage part, the *Meadow* and to a slightly lesser extent the livestock parts, the *Park* or *Coney-ground*, becomes central to his idea of a garden and to his work in improvement more generally. Once the idea is established that a Meadow or Park is integral to the design of Rural and Extensive Gardens, then to read these chapters (Columella 95 et seq) is to encounter the same concerns as those of the improvers of the 1730s.

Columella's treatment of the *Garden* assumes enclosed grounds as described in Homer and Cato, but with the vineyard and productive groves for olives (which he calls the *Palladian berry*) removed, and he concentrates on the finer vegetation. He carries on where Virgil, sadly for lack of time, had declined to continue and casts his remarks in verse in imitation. This tenth book (Columella 417 et seq) the translator renders in blank verse. This is followed, in book 11, chapter 3 "as the culture of gardens and of garden-herbs, in prose" for the benefit of the unpoetical bailiff. With significant exceptions Switzer's treatment of the Kitchen garden, and also occasionally the Fruit garden, as an enclosed place with its own nature and rules, but within easy reach and in correspondence with the rest of what he came to call a *Rural and Extensive* scheme, follows his understanding of Roman practice as well as the best modern (late 17th to early 18th century) good sense.

Like any historian Switzer has to follow his sources, but some are more congenial and richer than others. Some greats are, surprisingly, given short shrift. Vitruvius Polio, despite his "excellent Directions relating to Situations", warrants only a paragraph, not because he is obscure, but because "[t]hese are quoted by most Authors that treat of *Gard'ning*, at the Beginning of their Books; for which Reason I shall content myself, after I have paid this short, but willing, Tribute to the Memory of this great Architect and Gard'ner, and proceed to [new paragraph] *Horace* the next in my List of Garden Heroes . . ." (*IR* I 28). Unlike the ideal historian Switzer is not so much wishing to present a clear and true account of past events as he is seeking to find justification among the acknowledged greats for his particular vision of how best to make big gardens in early 18th century Britain, of landscape scale, but as yet without a settled name. In Horace he finds justification for a preference for the country instead of the capital in his long quotation from Thomas Creech's translation of the Epistles. As evidence it brings allusion, and some colour perhaps, but little "information". Thus, it is sufficient to Switzer to enumerate evidence of the fondness the great men of Rome had for their farms and gardens, and for the countryside generally, and the disdain for the business, intrigues and follies of cities, to which they resorted only because of duty.

His treatment of modern great men is also brief, although his choices are most apt. The Cardinal of Ferrara at the Villa d'Este at Tivoli, and the Pope at the Villa Belvidere (Aldobrandini) at Frascati are noted as creators of great works, "[b]ut the more useful Part of my Subject, I mean Agriculture, Planting &c have not appear'd with that Lustre as it had formerly done in those Countries and the Reasons of it are drawn from the Despotick Power and Pride of the *Roman* Church" (*IR* I 38).

Switzer's readers may therefore conclude that while they are being encouraged to admire the Villa d'Este, and perhaps to emulate some of its beauties, they are being addressed by a good Englishman of suitably Anglican persuasions. When he comes to praise Louis XIV he is equally clear. As one of the greatest characters yet produced he made a masterpiece at Versailles, but "whether by an innate Love or virtuous Disposition to the Glory and pleasures of *Gard'ning* or that by the Encouragement of Arts and Sciences (and amongst them of *Gard'ning*) he might allure and dazle [sic] the Eyes of Europe, and thereby the easier carry on the Scheme of Universal Monarchy he had been aiming at, is not my Business, neither do I pretend to determine" (*IR* I 39–40). If this were not sufficiently clear to later historians, it must have been perfectly plain to his readers: the gardens at Versailles and Marly are great and worthy of admiration, so take note; the polices of the King of France are very dangerous to the interests of Britain, so beware.

Switzer feigns ignorance of who the actual author of these French works might have been. Although he must have known of Andre Le Notre, either from George London or from the most idle investigation, he chooses rather to praise Louis' gardener Jean De La Quintinye for his produce, and the poet-dramatists Nicholas Boileau and Rene Rapin for their spiritual content. The gardener De La Quintinye (whose book was notably translated by John Evelyn, and then abridged by London and Wise) civilizes Louis by appealing to him through the wondrous fruits and vegetables to forget, or at least to mollify, his war-like natural instincts. Switzer praises Rapin's *Of Gardens* for its elegant raising of a treatise on horticulture to literature. "In this Poem is contain'd the whole Body of *Gard'ning*, and, by the additional Help of Notes, would be of excellent use to the World" (*IR* I 44). And to Boileau Switzer leaves the rapturous injunction,

> Give me the Shades, the Forests, and the Fields,
> And the soft Sweets Rural Quiet yields;
> Oh, leave me to the fresh, the fragrant Breeze,
> And let me here awhile enjoy my Ease:
> Let me *Pomona's* plentious Blessings crop,
> And see rich Autumn's ripen'd Burthen drop;
> 'Til Bacchus with full Clusters crowns the Year,
> And gladdens with his load the Vinatger.

Switzer will have felt the power to influence the compilation of Le Notre's ideas in A J Dezalier D'Argenville's already well-regarded *Theory and Practice of Gardening*, recently translated into English by John James. In introducing his very clear alternative Switzer will have realized that to further the reputation of a great French designer might be to weaken his own message. He therefore praises practical execution on the one hand, allied to ideals seemingly far distant from the business of making landscapes. He is clearly playing a long game, and subtly. For Switzer gardens are not to be splendid things which might be copied by rich men in emulation of each other. Rather, they were to be useful and delightful employments in planting and agricultural improvement which incidentally would have many of the characteristics that were to be admired at Marly or the Villa d'Este.

Thus, the mighty French, and no less the great Renaissance Italians, join the ancients in introducing the story of the role of Great Britain, where successive governments "encouraged the Planting and Preserving of Wood, Husbandry, and the like, the Laws made by them is a sufficient Demonstration" (*IR* I 47). To the evidence of laws Switzer adds Sir Henry Wotton's *Elements of Architecture* for providing the first "Thoughts of that Rule, Proportion, and Design which has since took place in *Gardening*". Physical remains of earlier gardens Switzer traces back no further than a century: ". . . we may suppose some of the Old Avenues and Walks adjoining to Noblemens Houses, were planted, and of that Date [late 16th century] seems to be the Old Walks at *Hatfield* (and at several other Places,) planted no doubt, by that great Minister of State the Lord Treasurer *Burliegh*".

Of Wilton Switzer was then still apparently ignorant. His history, until he comes to men he knew, remained literary. His choices for this "information" are even more surprising than his choices abroad. From *Paradise Lost* he quotes at length Milton's imagination of Eden as if it were a real garden, and Switzer invites his readers to accept it as such, and as worthy of imitation. "Thus sweetly did this great Poet paint the Innocence and Beauty of a Country Life, in the happy Possession of *Paradise* by our First Parents. Happy, thrice happy Man, had his Pen been employ'd upon no other Subject" (*IR* I 52). From the reign of Charles II on, Switzer seems more assured of his facts and their context; he knew all the characters by reputation, and others he will have met, and he will have studied their works thoroughly. He notes the garden virtuosi as the Lords Essex and Capel, John Evelyn and Sir William Temple, Abraham Cowley and John Rose. Lord Capel's was one of the smallish Thames-side estates on the Surrey side opposite Brentford. Lord Rochester's New Park and, of course, Temple's Moor Park were others. Capel's place became Kew in the early 18th century and was used by the children of George I, becoming part of an extended Richmond estate in the later 1720s (see below). His claim to Switzer's notice was his importation and improvement of fruit stocks, and his friendship with De La Quintinye. According to Switzer, Lord Essex at Cassiobury in Hertfordshire was the first to plant a Forest Garden.

It was John Evelyn to whom "it is owing that *Gard'ning* can speak proper *English*" (*IR* I 59), and from Evelyn Switzer likely drew his very inspiration for *Ichnographia Rustica* and his love of forest trees and woodlands as the soul of gardens and then landscapes. Evelyn (1620–1706) had written his *Sylva* in 1664 and in addition to many other works was still adding to his great and unpublished *Elysium Britannicum* when he died. If Switzer met Evelyn he did not mention it. To assess Evelyn's importance is difficult: his contributions to information and thought about gardens and garden design were immense. He freely gave advice about the design of gardens, and was sufficiently skilled to be counted as what later was called a *Professor*; so the temptation is to look to him as the fount of all things. But the later 17th century abounded in such prodigies. One of these was Sir William Temple (1628–1699), who figures in Switzer's History as the author of *Upon the Gardens of Epicurus*, "one

A fine genius for gardening 15

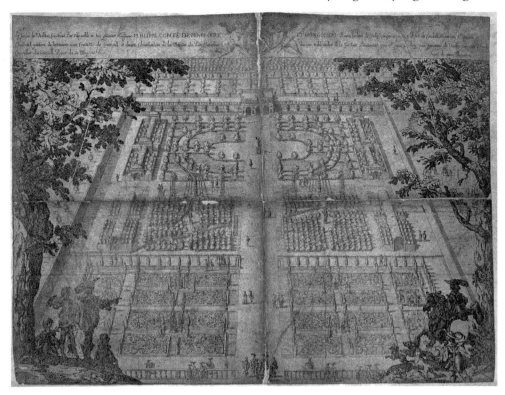

Figure 1.2 Wilton, Wiltshire: aerial view of garden. From *Hortus Pembrocianus*, mid-17th century. Bodleian Library.

of the politest Essays . . . that has yet appeared". Temple's essay is in the manner of Montaigne, reflective, humane and self-deprecating. In it he mused on the delights of making gardens and the joys they can bring, and, as a kind of essayist's afterthought observed, in essence, that of course the Chinese have a quite different taste in these matters. This was how Temple rather slyly introduced the idea of the Chinese manner of esteeming gardens: he called it *Sharawaggi*. His gardens were in no way extraordinary for their day, although in part of his gardens at Sheen he used serpentine paths in his wilderness as early as the 1690s, likely the first such to be seen in these islands.

Abraham Cowley composed four books in Latin verse "upon Herbs Plants Trees &c", initially as a ruse to spy out the state of England under Cromwell for the Royalists; as Switzer puts it, "That which he had made use of as a Vizor, grew afterwards familiar, and so broke through the cloudly Shades of a domestick Exile. His Delight in *Gard'ning*, and the other Diversions of a Country Life, afterwards encreasing with his Liberty, he surpass'd (if possible) the Divine Virgil himself" (*IR* I 68). John Rose (1619–1677) was Switzer's professional grandfather and had been gardener to Lord Essex at Essex House in the Strand, and then became gardener to Charles II at St James'. He wrote about vines as well as a treatise on fruit trees, and is famously, if not universally, accepted as giving the first native grown pineapple to King Charles in the celebrated double portrait set in the Royal Gardens. More certainly he was later master to George London (c1640–1714), one of the founders of the Brompton Park Nurseries.

Switzer recognized the contributions of the members of the Royal Society as examples of the "Virtuoso's of this Age" by commending their works on *Vegetative Philosophy*, and instances the cellular structure of plants, "which means there is a constant Passage for the Lymphatic Tuboes as well as Air, which is as necessary in the Vegetable as Animal Life", and that as water abounds in particles this is the means of nourishment. He also applauds other *Rustic Authors*, Mortimer, Hartlib, Blythe, Plat, Sharrock, Nourse, Laurence and Ray. These writers not only had "the sublimest taste of Gard'ning that ever any had" but were not content with matters as commonly received but made it their business to learn by experiment. "And when they came to make those Inferences, which are, or ought to be the Result of every virtuous Man's Labour and Practice, as they studied it on purpose to demonstrate the Being of a God infinitely Wise, Powerful and Good; so they always concluded their Speculations in this or the like Phrase, *O Lord, how manifold are thy Works! in wisdom hast thou made them all: the earth is full of thy riches*" (*IR* I 63–64).

For the 1690s Switzer was fully contemporary with the events and issues he discussed in the History, and from 1697, the year he became an apprentice at Brompton Park, he was very close indeed, and often personally involved. Indeed, his inclusion of the events surrounding the trial and execution of Lord William Russell in the summer of 1683, the same year as Switzer's birth (can he have been an intended godson?), derives from close family knowledge, and his own early life was thus influenced by the affair. The Russells, close relations to the Bedfords of Woburn Abbey, lived at Stratton Park, Hampshire, and Switzer's father held the family farm nearby at Micheldever on copy-hold from them. Thus, the Switzers and the Russells were close. When Switzer came to his maturity he also held the Russells in personal regard, and, from the tenor of his relation of the affair, he clearly also shared their politics. But what were their politics? Russell was *whig* before the party actually formed. He was opposed to a Roman Catholic being king in England. He was accused of treasonable involvement in the Rye House Plot to murder King Charles, and after trial was beheaded for it. He maintained his innocence throughout, and was soon formally cleared of the charges. His views and the Whig Party very soon prevailed, and William and Mary succeeded as joint monarchs. From the tenor of Switzer's opinions expressed in his works it appears that he too was Whiggish by nature, personal attachment and background. But as Switzer never stood for election, nor assumed a public office, we cannot know for certain what his politics were.

Through Switzer's History we know of the foundation and scope of the Brompton Park Nurseries, near Kensington at the west end of Hyde Park, and much of its work. In 1681 George London, with the encouragement of Henry Compton, Bishop of London, and doubtless also with Royal Gardener John Rose's backing, seems to have been the senior partner. He was joined by Moses Cook (d 1715), Lord Essex's gardener and designer of Cassiobury, and also "Mr. *Lucre*, Gardener to the Queen-Dowager at *Somerset House*, and Mr *Field*, Gardener to the Earl of *Bedford-House* in the *Strand*" (*IR* I 78). Lucre and Field died, and in 1687 Cook sold his share to Henry Wise (1653–1738), so that the great period of Brompton Park is more often known as simply London and Wise. Cassiobury was the prototype for the firm's work and set a high standard, which was soon refined by London's exposure to French designs on his expeditions, arranged by Rose. Switzer wrote of Cassiobury, more forest than garden, "I never see that truly-delightful Place, without being more than ordinarily ravish'd with its Natural Beauty" (*IR* I 62). Its design was a conventional one, in the sense that it was composed about two major axes which crossed in the centre of the house, newly built by Hugh May. It was the "quarters" which were all different, in character and in design: these were predominantly made of plantations of very large blocks of forest trees. There had been much design development since its beginning, most likely in the parterres on the main fronts, which do seem later, and perhaps also elaborations within the forest cover planted by Cook. It was composed of a series of avenues and walks; in 1707 when Johannes Kip and Leonard Knyff's view of it was published the forest still dominated its character as "garden", or more properly as landscape.

The first joint enterprise of the four partners, in which each took a turn directing the works, was at Longleat in Wiltshire from 1683. In 1725 its plan was published in the third volume of Campbell's *Vitruvius Britannicus* long after its heyday, but with its sophistication much in evidence. It is one of the most subtle of large garden designs, whose seemingly "standard" elements at first sight are soon shown to be no such things. The principal axis is nominal only, partly because the plan of the old house (from the 1580s), though regular, is not hierarchical as a contemporary one would have been: also disconcerting (in an almost Mannerist-playful sense) is that the real main axis runs parallel to the principal front, and the transition between the expected and real is skilfully handled by means of the horizontal framing of a terrace walk.

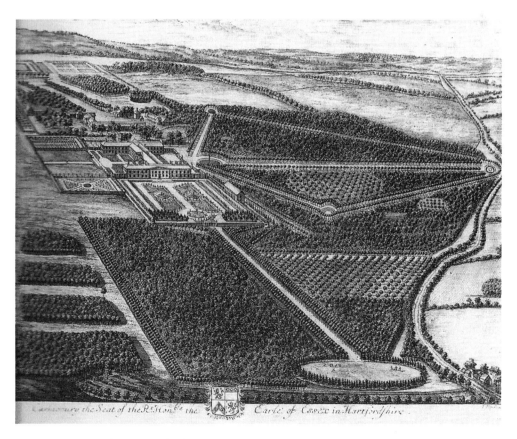

Figure 1.3 Cassiobury, Hertfordshire (north to top). Reproduced from Johannes Kip and Leonard Knyff, *Les Delices de la Grand' Bretagne*, 1707. Private collection.

18 *A fine genius for gardening*

All remains geometrically straight-forward, yet in use the surprises abound. It shows Brompton Park designing at the level of Le Notre. If London is the leader of the team, his partners are never far behind.

Lord Chesterfield's country house in Derbyshire, Bretby, is thought to be London's best work (Harris *DNB*), and it also dates from the 1680s. It shows a similar mastery in playing with axes, and semi-enclosed spaces, where they are on a more condensed scale, in a more changeful topography so the vertical sense of movement is more keenly appreciated. It is less extensive in aim than Longleat and is content to be more a series of exterior spaces, which though very large remain room-like. That quality is noted in Celia Fiennes' unusually detailed account of her visit there in 1695 (Fiennes 1888 140–143). Her meticulous descriptions add the richness of the furnishings . . . the textures of the surfaces, the potted fine plants, the more decorative plantings and ornaments of the parterres, the identification of the young Cedar of Lebanon given pride of place at the centre of one parterre, the sculpture and the water-works (one of which struck the time of day, another of which played Lillebollero) are evoked by her, even more than in the large format rendering by Kip and Knyff. The duodecimo version of the same view stresses the more architectural aspects of the design.

There are references in Switzer's works to incidents and places with London and Wise, and two of these were quite important to his development as a thinker about

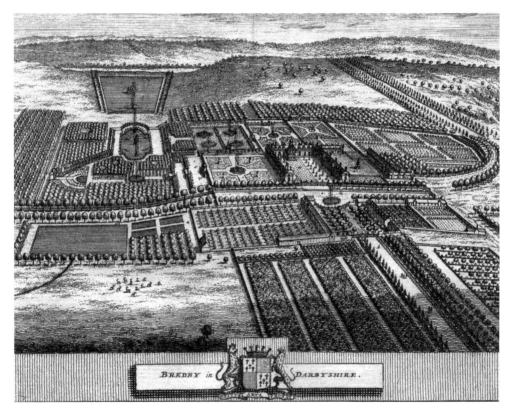

Figure 1.4 Bretby, Derbyshire (north to bottom). Reproduced from Johannes Kip and Leonard Knyff, *Les Delices de la Grand' Bretagne*, 1707. Private collection.

design, and to the designs he subsequently produced. The earliest of these was at Castle Howard, where he was assisting London, and the second, a few years later, was at Kensington with Wise. These two were genuine apprentice pieces where his youth and semi-detachment allowed him to "see" issues, possibilities and designs which others had not seen. These not only were taken up but then received great approbation, in the case of Kensington to an extraordinary degree. These newer revelations he added to the pattern learned from Brompton Park, of the Moses Cook-George London tendency, which he had imbibed over his whole time there. This for him was not only the accumulated wisdom and practice of the greatest gardeners but also that knowledge directed through "the Noble and Correct Judgement and Taste of Things" encapsulated in the "Rustick Verse, *Utile qui dulci miscens, ingentia Rura, / Simplex Munditiis ornat, punctum hic tulit omne*" (*IR* I xvi et seq). This good Augustan example, the triad of Horace's seeming oppositions about which "every one makes what Judgement he pleases, and thereby leaves *Design* in Confusion," Switzer adopts as his "three Motto's". By *utile et dulci* he means the mixture of the "Pleasures of the Country with the Profits" and, specifically, "that all my Designs tend that Way: And by mixing the useful and profitable Parts of Gardening with the pleasurable in the Interior Parts of my *Designs*, and Paddocks, obscure Enclosures, &c in the Outward: My Designs are thereby vastly enlarged, and both Profit and Pleasure may be said to be agreeably mix'd together . . .". Thus, he widens the scope of "gardens" now to include contiguous agriculture, and at least to begin to become "landscape".

With *ingentia Rura* Switzer introduces his notion of style or manner, "that Extensive Way of Gard'ning that I have already hinted at, and shall more fully handle; that the *French* call *La Grand Manier*, and is oppos'd to those crimping, diminutive, and wretched Performances we everywhere meet with . . . the Top of these Designs being in Clipt Plants, Flowers, and other trifling Decorations . . . fit only for little Town-Gardens, and not for the expansive Tracts of Country" (*IR* I xviii). Also related to style is his third motto, *Simplex Munditiis*. "In Gardening, and all the whole Cycle of Arts, it signifies noble Elegance and Decency, a due Proportion and clear Majestick Mien in the several corresponding Parts thereof; and without straining it too hard, may very well demonstrate the beautiful and harmonious Rules of Symmetry and Variety. However, 'tis a well-govern'd pursuit of Nature, whose Rules, tho' often fortuitous, are not the less beauteous, but rather more admirable. And if this was more followed, if the Beauties of Nature were not corrupted by Art, Gardens would be much more valuable" (*IR* I xix).

The Brompton Park enterprise brought together the best design skills, vast quantities of healthy plants and expertise in the making of a great garden or landscape. These included land architecture, site preparation, provision of water and water-works, laying out, planting and site supervision, plus the after-care attention gardens must have, especially great ones. All this was supervised by London and Wise, and the longer term care was provided after 1689 by London, largely in the country, or by Wise nearer London. Each of these many stages will have carried a moiety from the bills, thus sustaining and then enriching the business. To master these skills and attain the character of London or Wise required talent and receptive intelligence over a long period. Wise added a contract from the Crown for the care of the Royal Gardens, which he retained until the mid-1720s. On his retirement Brompton Park still supplied plants and skills, and continued to do so into the 1740s. But its heyday was from the 1690s until London's death, a period delivered to us in great detail by engravings by Kip and Knyff published as individual prints, or as collections in *Les Delices de la Grand' Bretagne* or *Britannia Illustrata* from 1707 on. It also provided an education for young potential gardeners, notably Switzer from 1697 on and Charles Bridgeman by 1709. Details of their indenture as apprentices do not survive, but the term was normally seven years as an apprentice followed by a further seven years of journeyman status. Switzer's first independent work dates from 1711, and Bridgeman's was a little later, in 1716. Bridgeman's first known work is the great drawing of the estate of Blenheim of 1709, from which date we might infer his beginnings as journeyman: Bridgeman was noted for his fine draughtsmanship, and he "shadowed" Wise in the following years, succeeding him as Royal Gardener to George II. Switzer clearly admired London, and his journeyman efforts are more on the engineering side of Brompton Park's affairs, for example, scouting Oxfordshire for suitable stone to quarry, and then planting out the great parterre at Blenheim, and then "[t]he Business of the Bridge". But the most influencing events in his work with London and Wise were the issue of the gravel-pit at Kensington Gardens and the matter of Wray Wood at Castle Howard.

Charles Howard (1669–1738), Earl of Carlisle, decided to rebuild his place, then called Henderskelfe, north-east of York, which had an ample park but whose grounds were empty and unimproved. The old house with its straggling village had one asset in the big mature woodland called Wray Wood. As for the rest of the estate, it was as if it were a new world waiting to be made. And Carlisle was minded to build and to plant to match this opportunity. He engaged William Talman as architect, and Talman brought in his great friend and favourite collaborator, London. By 1700 they had proposed two schemes for what was now to be Castle Howard. Both included a grand new house, a new and regularly planned village (the first of its kind) and naturally enough a landscape plan to accommodate both of these and the improved estate. For reasons we do not know, Talman and Carlisle quarrelled and parted company. They were both men of decided opinion, but who would be so foolish as to employ a non-entity as his architect? But Talman had also fallen out with others of his grand clients, and his own lordliness might have been the issue. Carlisle, himself exceptionally bold, maybe a little mercurial, and ever the lord, then appointed his friend John Vanbrugh, a sometime soldier, then playwright and sort of impresario, and drinking buddy, as his architect . . . prompting Jonathan Swift to tease, "Van's genius without Thought or Lecture / Is hugely turn'd to Architecture". London remained.

A sign of Talman's and Carlisle's disaffection was that Talman lost his post as Comptroller of His Majesty's Works through the authority of Carlisle, then in office as First Lord of the Treasury. In 1703 Vanbrugh was appointed in his place. One of Vanbrugh's first official engagements was the Orangery at Kensington, on which Nicholas Hawksmoor (1661–1736) was already at work. Kensington Palace had been home to William and Mary, who preferred it to Whitehall for their town residence. It had been made comfortable for them by the Board of Works, under Sir Christopher Wren's surveyorship . The gardens made then, in the 1690s, were in what Switzer called the "*Dutch* Taste", by which he meant over-furnished with plants and ornaments, stuffed, as he put it, and these furnishings were expensive (because tender or rare) and costly to keep. Their design and installation had been overseen by the Duke of Portland, an old friend and confidant of William's, who held the post of Royal Gardener as a sinecure, with London as his working deputy. On Queen Anne's accession she moved to Kensington. Officially because of the expense of keeping the old gardens, the contract was reviewed, and, prudently, the new bid from Brompton Park

Figure 1.5 Castle Howard, Yorkshire: design for the grounds, ca 1699, by George London (north to bottom). Bute Collection, © Victoria and Albert Museum.

was led by Wise, who proposed keeping the gardens for significantly less, so long as they were also much simplified. That suited the new Queen, and her ministers, and also Brompton Park, but it meant that as Wise became the contractor he got the post of Royal Gardener.

The new Orangery to the north-east towards Hyde Park was carried on, but the rest of the gardens were greatly simplified and extended northwards into what was called the New (or Upper) Garden. Kensington had never had a master-plan, as neither English, nor Dutch, practice saw much value in such, and all were content to add or subtract features as thought desirable. The New Garden is such an addition, a filling of the next contiguous space with more rectangular gardens. As Switzer puts it, Queen Anne's first works ". . . were the Rooting up of the Box, and giving an *English* Model to the Old-made Gardens at *Kensington*; and in 1704 made that New Garden amongst the most valuable Pieces of Work that has been done any-where. The Place where that beautiful Hollow now is, was a large irregular Gravel-pit, which, according to several Designs given in, was to have been fill'd; but that Mr. *Wise* prevail'd, and has given it that surprizing Model it now appears in. As great a Piece of Work as that whole Ground is, 'twas near all completed in one Season, viz. between *Michaelmas* and *Lady-Day*; which demonstrates to what a pitch Gard'ning is arriv'd within these twenty or thirty Years" (*IR* I 83).

Wise's biographer, David Green, was somewhat bemused at the fame this design had in its time, and one suspects many others will share his attitude (Green 1956 76). However, famous it was. Queen Anne is said to have believed it to be healthy for her son and heir, the Duke of Gloucester. And its fame caused Thomas Tickell to compose his *Kensington Gardens* in 1722, a long didactic poem about these gardens and their denizens, led by *Albion*, the king of fairies, with the Gravel-Pit Amphitheatre as the putative city and home of these fairies. Kensington Gardens were thus famous long before J M Barrie wrote about them. (Tickell's other claim to fame was as Joseph Addison's assistant, biographer and literary executor.) The Hollow was "balanced" by a new "Mount". One of King William's "*Dutch* Style" designs rooted up by his sister-in-law's fit of economy was an elaborate Fortress and Battle, all in box, to which the Hollow and Mount succeeded in public esteem, and seemingly affection too. The Mount was no such thing but simply appeared as if it were one: its plants were kept clipped very low at the edges, then regularly taller towards the centre. It looked like a Mount, and as if conjured there, like the Amphitheatre as a miniature city-palace had apparently also been conjured . . . by the *fairies*.

Contemporary with these works, the two designs by London were being debated at Castle Howard. Both have the outreaching axes of forest trees providing a sense of structure in the otherwise open estate. The more elaborate design owes much to Talman and London in partnership, for the spaces defined by the great blocks of trees have what seem like a tendency to become designed landscape almost as a super sized sort of "building". This plan (neither is dated, but they are believed to be on the cusp of the new century) shows just how fused the landscape and building parts have become. The composition is close to the union flag with the up-and-down axes of the St George part taking the lines of entrance and movement with the diagonals of St Andrew leading to and from huge circular spaces, one of which contains the new model Henderskelfe village. Both plans have large water-works of canals and ponds in the low ground to the north. Rather than having the house at its customary place in the centre Talman and London have a huge courtyard space instead, whose edges are complex and made of the subsidiary stables, kitchens and other necessary service buildings, and on its east side, stopping the east-west entry axis, is the big house. The other and grander of the orthogonal axes runs across this courtyard north to the lake and canals, and south through the gardens into parkland. The large "emptiness" beyond and between London's plantations is undefined.

The second plan has the same elements, but in a rather simpler design, also with the noticeable spaciousness. It also has a great house in standard form and place, which is to become the kernel of Castle Howard under Vanbrugh's direction, a block with wings, and small quadrants connecting to the service flankers. The landscape features show the lakes developed but no smaller, the model village is still in its big roundel to the south-west, but the whole east side of the scheme is made into a much enlarged single woodland "star". From these plans we can follow Switzer's own design development, as they clearly lie at the heart of his ideas about design. His "officious Boldness" began benignly enough. Although before the 20th century designers' plans do not indicate slopes or declivities unless they are significant, even extreme, an awareness of the shape of the ground was necessary then as much as it was later. At Castle Howard Switzer took his appreciation of the site more to heart than his master did. This will become a core preoccupation which derives from a desire to humour the site. As Alexander Pope phrased it so tellingly in 1732, "Consult the *Genius of the Place* in all / That tells the waters where to rise or fall" (*To Burlington*). For Switzer that modern sensibility begins with these plans and this site. Was it Switzer who suggested to Carlisle that an alternative to the designed new plantation of Wray Wood in star formation was to seize the opportunity of the ancient woodland, accept it for what it was and transform it into a new sort of garden? Undoubtedly.

The topography of Castle Howard presented a series of big undulating land forms. The old house and village lay on one of the flattish areas, a sort of plateau, and overlooked a much broader and lower stretch of shallow valley to the north. Wray Wood, a plantation of at least a hundred years' growth, occupied the highest ground on the estate and lay to the east side of the house site. London had already recognized the opportunities of the valley, and his schemes for canals and ponds mixed with large blocks of forest plantations were suitable solutions, as were his avenues and other major lines of his design. If there had not been a wood already in place then the site of Wray Wood would have called out for one. For London, who doubtless was as open to the charms of the old wood as Switzer, or indeed anyone else, took a much longer view. He knew that as the new plantations matured, with the building of the house, together with the finer plantings of the gardens (still not planned beyond designation of places), the whole ensemble would be all of a piece, and likely thought to be perfect. To Switzer the qualities to be found in the existing wood could not be compensated for in the newly planted one, even at its maturity, never mind in the lifetime until then. It was not only the plan form of the design but also its fit onto the far from "faultless" site.

"Some there are that esteem nothing well in a Design, but long, large, wide, regular ridings and walks; and this, in truth, is right in an open Park or Forest . . . but that a garden Design for walking in only . . . it would be too great a Fault to set too great a Value upon them in a Garden; and for the sake of long level Walks, to level all those little Eminences and pleasing Labyrinths of Nature . . . It is an unpardonable Fault . . .

24 *A fine genius for gardening*

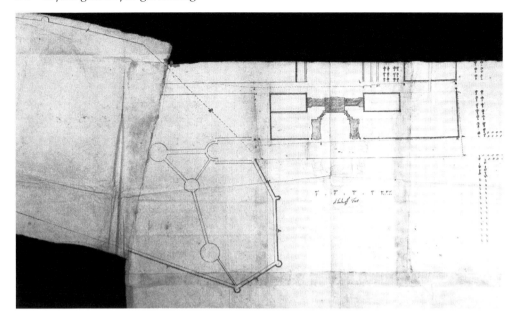

Figure 1.6 Castle Howard, Yorkshire: working plan, early 18th century (north to bottom). © Victoria and Albert Museum.

to have scarce any Thing in a whole Design, but carries open Walks; so that be the Garden 40, 50, or 60 Acres, one shall scarce find any private or natural Turn in the Whole . . . And this seems to be the greatest Difference in the Opinion of Persons as to Design". This point he illustrates by reference to Wray Wood, "where Mr *London* design'd a Star, which would have spoil'd the Wood; but that his Lordship's superlative Genius prevented it, and to the great advancement of the Design, has given it that Labyrinth diverting Model we now see it; and it is, at this Time, a Proverb of that Place, *York against London* in Allusion to the Design of a *Londoner*, and Mr *London* the Designer" (*IR* II 197–198).

The grounds at Castle Howard, in similar manner to the house, occupied Carlisle for nearly 40 years. He never seemed to be in a hurry to finish either: rather, he appears to have relished the doing much more than the completion. We can be more certain about the development of the buildings, and we may infer from them, and other scant sources, the making of the landscape. Roughly speaking, apart from the abandonment of the model village (as the old one likely remained in use for some time), the elements of London's scheme were retained, and Carlisle may well have thought himself following it as the master-plan, even if London would hardly have recognized the result. Although he continued to be involved at Castle Howard, the realization of the landscape there proceeded as slowly as the rest of the works. The array of ponds, canals and woods in the northern lowland was finally realized as an early naturalistic looking lake in the later 1730s, having first been essayed as a tightly serpentine "River" a few years earlier. The Parterre, only sketchily indicated by London, was carried out to the developed design Campbell published in 1725: this was based on a drawing of Vanbrugh and Hawksmoor's whole intended ensemble, as yet without the famous obelisks which followed immediately. Similarly, the walled gardens had proceeded, and the north-south axis had been laid out as the Great Avenue. But on the very earliest surviving plans, and as early as 1705, Switzer's story about Wray Wood shows itself already accepted.

But really the Parterre, and perhaps the other works too, had been taken over by the wood: Wray Wood *became* the garden. Switzer was rhapsodic about it, members of the family also exercised their poetic skills in praising it, and early travellers like Tracy Atkyns in 1732 described some of its features, but no one ever made a plan of it, nor did anyone draw it. Although Carlisle's son-in-law Sir Thomas Robinson asked for permission to have its landscape portrayed no such picture is known to exist. The earliest plan shows three straight walks in irregular composition, and the 1727 estate survey shows the outline and the trees, but no paths, cabinets, water-works, amphitheatre or sites of statuary. They existed in the Wood, but as to how and where they were arranged, there is no evidence. Even the system of paths is only attested to in a plan of the later 18th century, and as it shows none of the known features in place, we must conclude that they had disappeared. We know it was extended in the early 1730s, and that on its extreme north-east edge Hawksmoor added the Temple of Venus, then, joining Vanbrugh's last work, the Temple of the Four Winds sited at the south-east corner. We also know that on its highest point, and on the major east-west axis there was a large circular reservoir. For the rest we have to use our imaginations... following Switzer's indication of the mood, where

> ... that truly Ingenious lover of Architecture and Gard'ning, the Right Honourable the Earl of *Carlisle*, in his Wood at *Castle-howard*, [has reached] the highest Pitch that Natural and Polite Gard'ning can possibly arrive to: 'Tis There that Nature is truly imitated, if not excell'd, and from which the Ingenious may draw the best of their Schemes in Natural and Rural Gardening: 'Tis There that she is by a kind of fortuitous Conduct pursued through all her most intricate Mazes, and taught even to exceed her own self in the *Natura-Linear*, and much more Natural and Promiscuous Disposition of all her Beauties.
>
> (*IR* I 87)

The Wood, of course, existed before any of the works, and it therefore had the power to "colour" the way the designs in development and construction were perceived. As really the only significant feature in the open and unimproved but agricultural estate it could not be ignored. It would not take much, given its high timber and lofty site, to begin to suggest the kind of nobility of ancient groves, which gave it an added value. By the time London's design was being perused Wray Wood had become, at least to Switzer and Carlisle, a stand-in for the gardens of their imaginations, and then perhaps a kind of garden itself. As such it necessarily gave a bias to any views of the ongoing work on the house and its ancillaries.

By the middle to later years of the first decade of the new century the designers (assuming that *Carlisle's superlative Genius* was a poetical expression) had hit on the idea of enclosing Wray Wood with a terrace walk, for that appears on the earliest plan. Switzer, at several places, gives Vanbrugh the credit for suggesting the revival of this old Roman means of enclosing gardens, specifically of course at Blenheim, roughly contemporary with its use at Wray Wood. It had been discussed by both Cato

26 *A fine genius for gardening*

and Columella in their works on gardening and agriculture: both put it at the expensive end of the possible means of enclosure and make no comment about any other qualities. The idea could have been seen at York in the remains of the city's walls. But whatever the source of its use at Castle Howard, since the raised terrace is fully visible from *outside*, that is, from the house and its approaches, it turned Wray Wood into a seemingly fortified wood, increasing its nobility by association. The walk along the top of the wall, which followed the irregular edge of the old Wood, provided a new and structured way to see the ongoing building works, almost forcing a quasi-picturesque appreciation of them. It also gave a pleasing, sociable and comfortable means to view the buildings rising and the landscape being improved, and in a serial, that is, constantly varying, manner. Of course it gave similarly new perspectives into Wray Wood at the same time. As Switzer points out elsewhere, one of the prime virtues of a woodland garden is the changing mixture of prospects through the woods, in close views and in more distant ones.

In 1705 Switzer's time as an apprentice will have finished; no longer was he "Servant to Mr *London* and Mr *Wise*", and he will have had to make his way as a journeyman. Such mediaeval structures around pupillage and its aftermath were no longer strictly in force, but like recent graduates from professional courses today his professors will have not only wished him well but taken pains to see that he was suitably engaged, and will have given him short term employment from time to time as needed. He left Brompton Park with a developing aesthetic sense, honed if not actually acquired in his time with them, and with new ideas from his limited observations in practice.

There is a glimmer of his interest in architecture at the end of his time as an apprentice. He was one of the subscribers to the translation into English of Claude Perrault's *Ordinance for the Five Kinds of Columns after the Method of the Ancients* (Perrault 1993), a curious thing for a young man coming out of the first half of his education to do, considering the expense and the marginal nature of the work for an intending

Figure 1.7 Castle Howard, Yorkshire: prospect from the south in 1732. Reproduced from Thomas Gent, *The Antient and Modern History of the Loyal Town of Rippon*, 1733.

professional gardener. Perrault was the most intellectual of the architects of his time, a translator of Vitruvius certainly, but more a thoughtful and remarkably modern seeming man. The East Front of the Louvre is his main (almost his only) built work, and it is a milestone in the history of architecture, which, of course, sums up his extraordinary nature. Throughout his History, as elsewhere in his writings, Switzer always showed an inclination to the structural side of garden design, and thus an interest in architecture as much as in horticulture, poetry or philosophical musings is characteristic.

In 1705 London had begun his most lavish project at Wanstead to the east of London in Essex. This was for the banker Sir Richard Child, and its ambition, and nearly its scale as well, matched that of the King of France. A few years later he began another great palatial project at Cannons, north-west of London at Edgeware, for James Brydges, Duke of Chandos, almost as rich as a banker but much more powerful. He was, as he called himself, "paymaster of the foreign forces" (Jenkins 2007 88 quoting Chandos to Marlborough June 1710). These were the projects of the age (Defoe 1725). They were the grandest, most noticed and most admired. But Switzer was involved in neither of these projects, and it may have been to his chagrin, but London had other apprentices to look after, and a nephew to train up, Thomas Acres. Acres was involved with London at Wrest Park for the Duke of Kent, and also at Wanstead. And despite Switzer's glowing words about Chandos' project he was not one of the gardeners chosen to be employed there. Vanbrugh had the same ill luck in securing a commission at Cannons, and never forgave Chandos: however, Switzer and Chandos worked together much later, in the 1730s.

The palace Queen Anne chose to bestow on the Duke of Marlborough to honour his great victories in the Continental wars was to employ both Switzer and Vanbrugh in these years. The estate of Woodstock a few miles north-west of Oxford had been a royal holding for centuries, and it was chosen as the site for the Marlboroughs' new house and gardens. On that project it was Wise in his capacity as warrant holder to the Queen who was responsible for the gardens and grounds, and he employed Switzer in a variety of roles from 1705. As a royal gift Blenheim was a public project, and managed by interests from the Treasury and the Board of Works, on which Vanbrugh and Hawksmoor as well as Wise held posts. Vanbrugh and the Duke of Marlborough were also friends. The Duchess of Marlborough was a great personal friend and confidante of the Queen, from whom she held various posts, including Keeper of the Privy Purse. The project's future bode very well indeed.

Marlborough and Vanbrugh visited Woodstock and determined the placement of the house in the winter of 1704, and in the following spring the project had begun. It ran smoothly until 1710 when the weaknesses in its inception emerged, the changed personal relationships of the Queen and the duchess effectively cut off funds, and political developments and a change of ministers questioned the whole basis of the project: all these occurred at the height of discussions about an interesting but most difficult series of site planning matters and brought the project to a halt. Fortunately, by then the house was built (but not complete internally), and the gardens and the grounds planted.

Switzer's roles there were managerial and included overseeing the planting of the great parterre, and the forest trees adjacent, and also scouting the neighbouring estates of Oxfordshire to find suitable stone quarries to furnish materials for the vast projects at Woodstock. These were to supply good stone not only for a very large house and

28   *A fine genius for gardening*

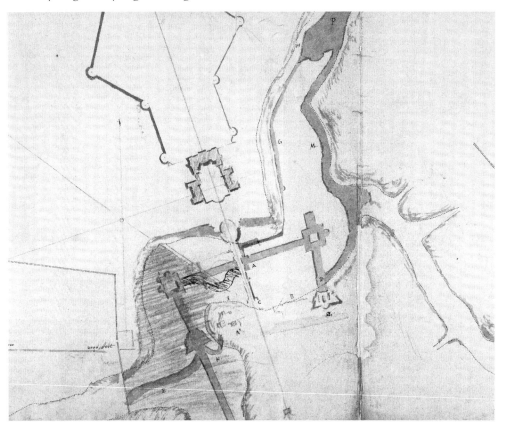

Figure 1.8 Blenheim, Oxfordshire: anonymous plan of the early Bridge-Canals, ca 1708 (north to left). Oxford Bodleian Library, MS Top. a.37.

dependencies (a deal bigger than Castle Howard) but also for the park walls, very extensive garden walls and other buildings, not the least among these the Bridge . . . soon seen to be the essential solution to join the two halves of the awkward site at Woodstock. The Glyme had made a large valley which meandered through the heart of Woodstock: sadly, the Glyme as a river was tiny compared to its valley, and to the works planned for this site. Switzer's engineering skills were thus developed in the related site works at the Bridge. Specifically, these called for forming "The Carriage that plays the Water-works", that is, the lade or canal system that powered the waterworks at an Engine House (soon to be incorporated into the Bridge, which supplied the big house through tanks in its attics) near the old palace of Woodstock, called the Mansion House on contemporary plans. As part of these works the very course of the River Glyme, its banks in the park and the modifications needed to make the Bridge and the entries to the house from Woodstock and the park fell to Switzer.

"The Carriage that Plays the Water-works" is how Switzer terms this man-made river, his first. It started its course as close to the edge of the Woodstock estate as possible, immediately west of the town of Woodstock, and from there it was led in a series of irregularly composed sections of canal-like water-way to deliver the greatest possible weight of water to its end just south of the old Mansion House. To accomplish that, Switzer kept its course as close as he could to the highest ground, hugging the slope between the high park and the Glyme valley floor. It is a design whose form comes from its required performance. A canal-like course is chosen as far as the big collecting basin just north of the Mansion House, and from there it follows a broadly shallow curve around the fortifications added at the time of the Civil Wars, and thence through two more irregular bends takes its canal form to the Engine House. Thus, it follows a natural course, but it is a course that does not yet mimic that of a *natural* river. (Such *arti-natural* shapes for water courses do not appear for another two decades, and then enjoy a rather brief life of fashion, as in the seemingly unexecuted example of the design for Castle Howard of the early 1730s noted above.) Switzer's Carriage remained in place until the later 1720s, when it was used to form the south and west edges of the first lake at Blenheim, called the Queen's Lake (see below).

The central problem at Blenheim was how the new work and the remaining ancient works could be reconciled by design while also making a handsome feature of the Glyme and its valley. The very thought of it enraged the Duchess, who had begun to fear that she and the Duke would have to pay for it. And every alternative offered seemed to increase the debt. The problem arose from Vanbrugh's and the Duke's decision on siting the new house, as they aligned its generating axis to run between the two poles of antiquity on the opposite side of the Glyme, the Old Palace or Mansion House and its companion site, Fair Rosamund's Well. Vanbrugh made the point, fairly and professionally, that the problem would not go away by being ignored; indeed, it

Figure 1.9 Blenheim, Oxfordshire: 1719 part of the estate plan (north to right). Blenheim Estate Archives.

could only grow greater. He was appalled when the Duchess made it clear she wanted the "offending" site cleared, with not a penny more to be spent on it.

The real pity is that a solution was so easily to be had, and that several workable alternatives had been offered. As early as 1705 or 1706, a design shows the problem, and a fair shot at its solution. The valley was to be made into a series of broad-ish canals in an irregular pattern; on the west side, opposite the main front of Blenheim Palace are the old Mansion with its outworks on the right hand side, and Rosamund's Well (or Bower) opposite it (and largely in imagination) on the left hand side, while between was to be an earthwork, a great scoop or amphitheatrical semi-circle joining the two, while beyond it were to be the great figures laid out in forest trees. This would have made a suitable, strong and quite new "picture" as a prospect from the front of the palace. The actual crossing was to be by a low causeway, also on axis, but visible only when one was close to it. That solution had the advantage of working both from the axial prospect from Blenheim but also when seen from the Woodstock town gate (thus far not recognized as part of the problem, but shortly to be central to it). Vanbrugh, of course, would never be able to "see" it and always had in mind his monumental Bridge; the Duchess was vexed by any scheme.

The discussions about how the Glyme, the old Mansion House and the two sides of the estate were to be dealt with raged in the period 1709 and 1710, and many were consulted. Sir Christopher Wren was asked by the Duchess of Marlborough to offer an alternative design, and Hawksmoor had designs as well. Vanbrugh's scheme for a grand Bridge with a handsome superstructure was pressed, and its housing of the engines to raise the water occupied much of the park side's accommodation, but the supplementary rooms to be provided on the palace side, and in the lower floors, seemed only to enrage those against the scheme even further. Although it was resisted, the Bridge in Vanbrugh's design was accepted, but the planned buildings above the roadway level were never finished. The fuller story can be seen in my thesis (Brogden 1973 154–160). No one came away satisfied, and the unresolved issues remained when Colonel John Armstrong took over the finishing work, since Vanbrugh had been dismissed, Switzer employed elsewhere and the other workmen turned out unpaid.

There were many lessons for Switzer to take from his time at Blenheim, many purely cautionary, but one of the most profound is the attitude he soon shows in treating ancient remains. He was able to transfer his already keen appreciation for the grotesque . . . misshapen lumps of rocks, in cave form or as adjuncts to waterfalls or cascades. This taste he was to justify both Biblically and by reference to other ancient texts, specifically to Homer. Within five years he introduced in his essay "Of Statues" the idea of making ruin-like buildings useful adjuncts in a designed landscape. He recommends ". . . the Erection of all Lodges, Granges, and other Buildings that Gentlemen are obliged to build for Conveniency, in the Form of some Antiquated Place, which will be more beautiful than the most curious Architecture: There seems to be a much more inexpressible Entertainment to a Virtuous and Thoughtful Mind, in Desolate Prospects, Cool murmuring Streams, and Grots, and in several other Cheap and Natural Embellishments, than in what many of our modern Designers have recommended, in themselves very Expensive" (*IR* I 317).

There is a further lesson Switzer learned in these years, a lesson he credits as the beginnings, or perhaps the clarification, of his thoughts about garden design. That is the connection between the enjoyment of gardens and the pleasures of country life

A fine genius for gardening 31

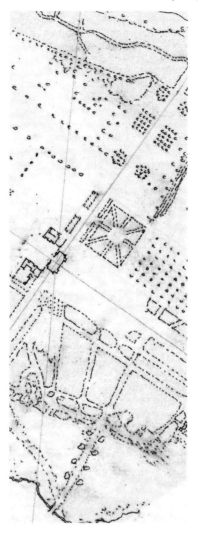

Figure 1.10 Heythrop, Oxfordshire: plan of the grounds, ca 1707 (north to top). Image by the author, based on Helen Lawrence, "New Light on Thomas Archer as Garden-Maker", *Garden History 38:1* (2010).

outside the garden . . . the fields, the woods, the estates or the countryside in general. His epiphany (at least his strongest example) was at Heythrop in about 1708. Heythrop was the Oxfordshire estate of Charles Talbot, Duke of Shrewsbury, and his great house was being built at the same time as Blenheim Palace, 1705–1708, under the direction of Thomas Archer. The author of the design for its contemporary grounds is unknown but is likely to have been Archer himself (Lawrence 2010 50 et seq). A much later survey shows the early 18th century design unchanged. It is structured in pleasing abstraction as a series of many parallel avenues, made up of rows of forest trees in both line and platoon formation. The central axis carries the house and its customary dependencies. One of the effects of this structure, and the one Switzer notices, is the close relationships these lines of garden planting make with the more agricultural parts of the estate. On the south side of the scheme, opposite the wooded Wilderness, are Meadows, while even more tellingly on the northern side an extended linear plantation of woods (with laid out walks) borders the avenues on the "inside", and on the "outside" runs along a made but incipient "natural" stream with arable fields beyond. This "first attempt" leads Switzer to observe:

> It is very happy for such Gentlemen, as find little Hedge-Rows, Coppices, and Lawns, mix'd one amongst another by Nature; for there they may easily cut a Walk of about six, or eight Foot wide, just through the middle of it; and, as there is always a Terrace ready made on one side of them, so 'tis easy having their materials at their Fingers Ends, to make another; and so to fence themselves in on both sides; as not only to keep the Cattle, that feed on the Lawns and Enclosures, that lie between them, within their own Bounds; but also, from coming into, and cropping the Hedge-Rows, and spoiling the Wood, and Walk; and these Hedge-Rows being mix'd with Primroses, Violets, and such natural sweet, and pleasant Flowers; the Walks that lead through afford as much Pleasure as (nay I may venture to say more than) the most elaborate, fine Gardens.
>
> (*IR* III 87–88)

This simple measure becomes the thread of his theory – he later calls it *enfilade* – which connects all elements into a designed landscape.

Switzer had left Woodstock before the works were so summarily concluded, and in 1711 was working in Lincolnshire. At the same time Charles Montagu, 1st Earl of Halifax (1661–1715), sometime Chancellor of the Exchequer for King William, had the Upper Lodge at Bushy Park, part of Hampton Court Palace grounds. Switzer knew the project well, spoke of it in glowing terms and compared it to Castle Howard and London's New Park, Richmond (*IR* I xxxiii, *IR* II 166) and illustrated one of its cascades (*Hydro* II plate 34 403). He comes close to claiming it as his, and it is likely one of his works of this period, from about 1710 onward. The project at Bushy Park is very similar to his work at Blenheim, but at Hampton Court its purpose was decorative. Essentially, Upper Lodge was already well supplied with a designed landscape, since a subsidiary avenue ran eastward from it to connect to the greater works of the park, and there was a small garden attached on its west side. The addition of the Water Garden, which has remained in place, introduced a new axis, close to and parallel with the Lodge's south front, where an oval basin marked its crossing with the avenue and lay at the centre of a lateral parterre-like garden. To either side canals led to a further five basins, and the whole was, as it were, dropped into the existing park. This was done on purpose, and Switzer credits it to "the Judgement of the noble Lord [Halifax] and which is his not endeavouring to crowd much Wood, about this Cascade, as the *Italians* and *French* do" (*Hydro* II 403). Towards the Engine House the canal form even becomes serpentine. A number of related water gardens follow, and most of these have a connection to Switzer himself. John Aislaby's famous Studley Royal has been nurtured and is the most intact and gives a character to the type: however, on present evidence it appears this water garden cannot confidently be ascribed to Switzer. The Upper Lodge water gardens have been restored to a state close to that painted by Marco Ricci in about 1715.

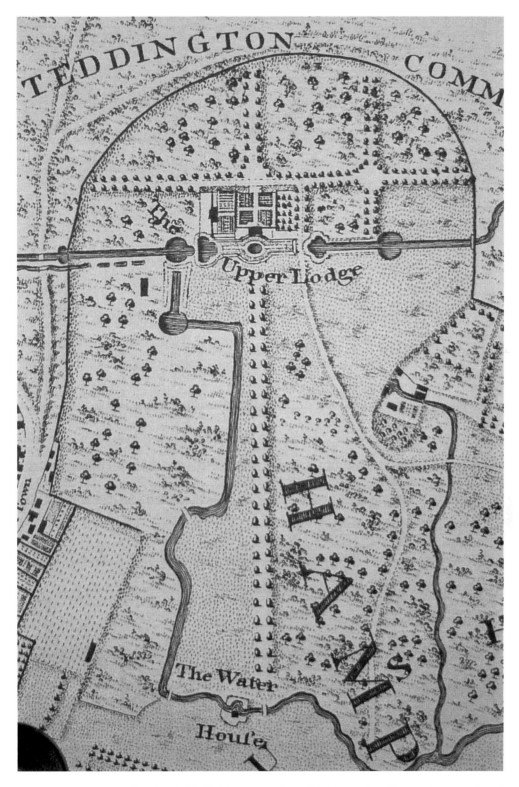

Figure 1.11 Upper Lodge, Bushy Park, Hampton Court, Middlesex (north to top). Reproduced from John Rocque, *An Exact Survey of the City's of London Westminster the Borough of Southwark and the Country near 10 Miles Round*, 1746. Private collection.

Halifax was an important politician and had acted as a patron to many, including Joseph Addison (1672–1719) a few years earlier. When Addison took his degree at Oxford he was awarded a fellowship by Magdalene College. That was not a position to be demeaned, but he was ambitious and believed himself capable of public work. For public work he required connections, and with little in prospect through his family, he had to rely on strong political friends, and there needed to be a suitable position for him. In 1698 Halifax secured a post for Addison to travel to the Continent in preparation for work as a diplomat. After a spell near Paris and a longer sojourn in Italy Addison, on King William's death and his Whig patrons' dismissal from office, had to return to England. In 1704, without public employment, he addressed himself to turning his Italian journey to account. Fortunately, a public post was proposed for him, but to secure it he was asked to write a panegyric to Marlborough and the recently won Battle of Blenheim. He rose, and rose splendidly, to that occasion and thus also became an esteemed public figure. Shortly afterwards, his *Remarks on Several Parts of Italy* came, and as his political patrons gained power again, his prospects in public life brightened and his public career began.

He claims our attention for several reasons, and all have to do with his aptitude to appreciate landscape and his interests in it. This came early. When his college laid out a walk across a meadow to the Isis, as the Thames is called in Oxford, thus making a circuit, he was involved in this. It is through his writings about it that it became famous, and it has long been known as Addison's Walk. One of his early patrons was John Dryden, then at work on his translation of Virgil's *Georgics*, which may have spurred Addison's appreciation of the Italian countryside and its potential to raise an association of ideas. These informed his *Remarks on Several Parts of Italy*. Then in the following decade come his essays on the "Pleasures of Imagination." These appeared in *The Spectator*, one of his ventures in journalism, conducted of course with Richard Steele, and on which his fame has rested since. It has been to Addison's words that critics, commentators and then historians have always turned as the scriptural source for developments in the appreciation and design of landscape in the 18th century. The first of these was Switzer, and it appears that his approbation was reciprocated.

Although London possessed an excellent library of his own, kept at Brompton Park House and at his Thames Ditton villa, neither he nor his partner, Wise, had the leisure to write their thoughts on making gardens. However, in 1699 they were selected by Evelyn to edit and abridge his translation of Jean De La Quintinye's famous book on gardening. It appeared as *The Compleat Gardener* and ran to several editions. In those days gardeners, even royal ones, did not figure in the newspapers. But when the new style of papers, affable, friendly and conversational, began to appear, gardening matters were occasionally covered. Addison was the first journalist to write about gardening seriously as an art, that is, writing as a critic. This he essayed in *The Spectator*. His series on the "Pleasures of Imagination," and his more tangential thoughts on the "Reading Habits of Women," for example, refer to gardens and the appreciation of value in them. (Myers 2013). Later, in one of his more ruminative papers he casts himself in the role of a simple man possessed of a few acres only, to poke gentle fun at the makers of more pretentious gardens. Keeping to his assumed amiable simplicity he resorts to familiarity by analogy, comparing gardening to poetry. Thus, he introduces the forms as well-understood types with associated tropes his readers could follow easily and with an amused interest. He describes Switzer's manner of making gardens as his "Confusion of Kitchen and Parterre, Orchard and Flower Garden, which lie so mixt and interwoven with one another, that if a Foreigner who had seen nothing

Figure 1.12 Upper Lodge, Bushy Park, Hampton Court, Middlesex (north to left). Painting by Marco Ricci, ca 1715. Royal Collection Trust / © Queen Elizabeth II 2014.

of our Country should he be conveyed into my Garden at his first landing, he would look upon it as a natural Wildness". Later he writes, "Your Makers of Parterres and flower Gardens, are Epigrammists and Sonneteers in this Art, Contrivers of Bowers and Grotto's, Treillage and Cascades are Romance Writers. *Wise* and *London* are our *Heroick* Poets . . . As for myself, you will find . . . that my compositions are altogether after the *Pindarick* Manner, and run into the beautiful Wildness of Nature without affecting the nicer Elegancies of Art" (*The Spectator* 477, quoted in Hunt and Willis 1975 146).

It is in this amiably instructive essay that Addison praises the *Heroick* Kensington Gardens Amphitheatre: "If as a Critick I may single out any passage of their Works to commend I shall take Notice of that Part in the Upper Garden at Kensington which was at first nothing but a Gravel-Pitt. It must have been a fine Genius for Gardening that could have thought of such an unsightly Hollow into so beautiful an Area and to have hit the Eye with so uncommon and agreeable a Scene as that which it is now wrought into . . ." (*The Spectator* 477, 6 September 1712). The Heroick Poets of Garden Making, London and Wise, will have known full well that it was Switzer who was the author of this scheme for Kensington Gardens, as would Vanbrugh and Hawksmoor also, and doubtless Addison too. No one could guess it from Addison's essay, and although Switzer alludes to the design, and Tickell wrote his long poem about it and published the plan of the amphitheatre as its frontispiece, none of them names Switzer as the author.

> . . . That Hollow space, where now in living rowes,
> Line above line the Yew's sad verdure grows,
> Was, ere the planter's hand its beauty gave
> A common Pit, a rude unfashion'd Cave.

> The landskip now so sweet we well may praise
> But far sweeter in its ancient days,
> With Fairy domes and dazling tow'rs was crown'd
> Where in the midst those verdant Pillars spring,
> Rose the Proud Palace of the Elfin King . . .
>   (Tickell *Kensington Gardens* 1722 lines 35–44)

In fairness, apprentices never do get such credit, nor usually do employees in a firm of architects or other kinds of designers. Convention decrees that any such approbation goes to the principals. We know that Switzer was indeed the designer only because of William Stukeley's private recollection in his diary nearly 40 years later.

The compliment will have been most encouraging to a man hard at work on his first book about his ideas about garden making, much of which he got, of course, from London and Wise, but the *Pindarick* parts do not derive from them, nor I believe from Addison either, but from Switzer himself. Addison had an ability to listen, to absorb and to distil matters and discussions which were of interest to his contemporaries: it would have been most exceptional to believe he also generated those ideas. That Addison was able to put them so clear and strong and still amiable, so persuasive and economical, was his gift as a writer, in his justly celebrated mode of journalism.

Oxford colleges possessed most of the constituents of a good sized country house, and its contiguous estate was easily imagined in the open spaces in and around the town. Many of its students, and tutors also, will have passed pleasant hours in re-arranging, imaginatively, these elements so as to reach their own Arcadias as the perfect idea of a place for good living. The college buildings each had elements of the country house: they were commodious; they had their halls, whose arrangement and forms were shared with the older country houses; they were arranged around courtyards, many of which were laid out as gardens. Their proximity to the river and open countryside, and the time for contemplation essential at universities, would have invited long walks there. If that were not enough there had been for more than half a century the Botanic Garden, a modern realization of Alcinous' garden, and, sited axially opposite Magdalen College, its monumental gateway, often attributed to the most esteemed of native architects, Inigo Jones. In the early 18th century there were experiments by Dean Aldrich and others also in how modern architecture might be best rendered to achieve parity with the ancients, and these were equally in advance of fashion and the most imaginative of private individuals like Carlisle. Addison's Walk, famous through his reflections on his habitual use of it (or several walks at Magdalen), is simply one of these elements. Given the constantly renewing population of the town these elements were rather more public and potentially influential to the student body here made up almost entirely of landowners, vicars and men of government (Batey 1981, Batey and Lambert 1990 141–146). Many of these, of course, figure in this study about Switzer.

Addison's Walk is the element of garden making to lead these students into the 18th century. Of course, it is not the first walk laid out to make a constitutional stroll into the countryside easy, and country folk have been going, and will continue to go, for walks through their own place, and more likely through their neighbours' places, and soon also into the wilder country of mountains and moors. In the *Spectator* papers the literate world shares many fruits of Addison's contemplative walks, so his promoting it as a good thing, and a thing to be imitated where possible, will have been eagerly accepted. While being manly, it does not exclude women and children, and having a made up and well-drained surface to walk on it positively encourages use by them. And this is reinforced by the potential for education: the observation and identification of plants in various season, similarly the oversight of livestock, or of crops. It takes little imagination to see such tree-lined walks becoming grander and thus turning into avenues, or being further enlarged to open up and civilize parks or fields. In small estates such walks encourage their seeming enlargement, and soon in cities they will appear as resort for the citizen, as in Edinburgh in the Meadows, or the Walks along the Ouse in York. In bigger estates walks can be the means to give them structure and allow an easy comprehension. And walks like Addison's Walk encourage the exercise not only of body but of imagination. Apart from the core garden element, that is, the plain rectangular enclosure, whether parterre or cabbage-patch, they make the simplest of elements with which to form gardens and designed landscapes. Switzer prefers the walk as his primary element of design, and he interprets it in so many and various ways.

Switzer had some hopes also to be given the supervision of the gardens at Blenheim after their planting, which suggests he was ambitious: the post went, not surprisingly, to Tilleman Bobart, son of the esteemed keeper of the Botanic Gardens at Oxford. Bobart was not only qualified but older too, and his famous father and their connections would have spoken very much in his favour. As fleeting as these pieces of evidence may be they do suggest that pursuing the life of a professional gardener was not quite what Switzer had in view. At twenty-two and only half way through his course of work and study under London and Wise his options were indeed pretty much open. Fortunately, assisting Wise in the Business of the Bridge kept him occupied there in the next years, and it was one of the most interesting, and instructive, episodes he ever encountered.

Chargate, Surrey

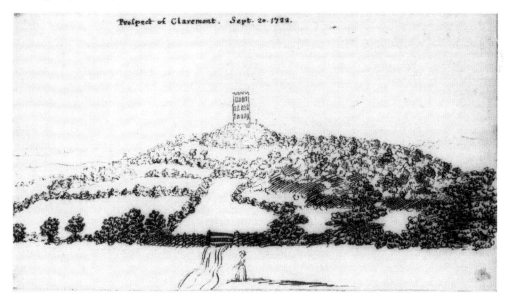

Figure 1.13 Chargate/Claremont, Surrey: view from the north-west, by William Stukeley, 1722. The Bodleian Libraries, University of Oxford, [shelf mark and folio TBD].

About this time Vanbrugh acquired his little country place, a home for him but also for his mother and sister. It was these simplest of elements, garden and walk, that he chose to employ in the design. In 1709 the site was a farm of 60 acres or so near Esher in Surrey and he had very little to spend on it. Vanbrugh was able, indeed more than able, to design his own garden-estate, certainly one as simple as Chargate, and he clearly designed his own house. But according to John Harris, Vanbrugh chose his colleague Switzer to design the grounds (Harris 1993). Harris, one of the earliest and most distinguished of garden historians of this present generation, rarely attributes, so when he does we all listen. Vanbrugh and Switzer knew each other from their time at Castle Howard, and of course at Blenheim. And Switzer acknowledged his debt in matters of design to Vanbrugh fully. It is about this time, before he started in earnest to work on the Bridge site, that Switzer's time at Blenheim seemed to be coming to an end and thus making him available to help Vanbrugh on this new project. Or, more likely, Vanbrugh would simply have valued the expertise and company of the younger man on the project: certainly he and Switzer would have been well matched, and with Vanbrugh, naturally as the owner, ultimately in charge. Given their history Switzer would have been most happy to work on it with him. Of course, and critically perhaps, they had Wray Wood in common.

The design that Harris based his attribution on is one of those drawings assembled by the 18th century antiquary Richard Gough and for long housed at the Bodleian Library in Oxford. Some of these have been identified as being from Charles Bridgeman's hand. I examined the Chargate drawing, along with the rest some time ago, and I recall it, but did not identify it as being by Switzer. Nor did Peter Willis recognize it as being by Bridgeman, and recorded it as unidentified (but see Willis 2002 427, 193b). It is exceptionally simple (certainly a deal simpler than the others in the collection, which are often so splendidly Bridgemannick, as Pope had it), and although the bowling green, for example, has more flourishes perhaps than I would have anticipated, sadly there are too few drawings surviving by Switzer to be certain. The design with which Vanbrugh began at Chargate was overtaken a few years later by its sale, a change of name to Claremont and the great expansion of the design of the grounds for the Duke of Newcastle, as it has been assumed first under Bridgeman's direction (Willis 2002), augmented by William Kent in the later 1730s and finally effectively overwhelmed by Lancelot Brown for the great Nabob, Lord Clive.

Like Castle Howard Chargate also had a large and mature woodland, and Vanbrugh's lease allowed him to cut this as he pleased. It already had a house, and he had permission to rebuild it, but seemingly only on the same site. This all presented problems for him. There is a prominent hill, also called the Mount in early references, which, presumably, was always the heart of Chargate Wood. This lies to the north-west of the house site, whose entrance was from the east. Therefore, if its entrance would probably have to remain to the east any parterre features could not be set aside on the south side for pleasure only as was the convention, with an entrance and service opposite to the north. We might assume that as the house was for Vanbrugh, and it most certainly is in a castle-style very much of his invention, that an unconventional arrangement would be cheerfully seized upon, and a rather Lodge-like character sought. But that is to wish a lack of convention too far. Vanbrugh's mother was a principal occupant, and she was a daughter of Sir Dudley

Carleton and thus related, however tangentially, to many of Vanbrugh's clients and his friends. She was also a widow returned to live near her relations in Surrey. Therefore, it would of needs be a proper country house, with no more flouting of convention like he could get past, for example, the Duke of Manchester at Kimbolton, where he pressed such matters, not too far but close enough. These site problems were issues, when properly managed, to give a surprising originality to the place, in which they clearly succeeded, as Colen Campbell dubbed it "singularly romantick" (*Vit Brit* II 11).

The wooded Mount fortunately did not block sunlight on the house, but did rather overshadow the park-like ground on the north-east side of the house. Finally, the wood and its Mount were very close on the house. In the absence of any survey of the state before the design drawing was made it appears that the woodland may have been extended eastward to cover that half of the farm. (For example there are more closely planted trees shown around a large roundel to the east, and similarly defining the edges of the drive and parade, which suggest new plantation.) Whether done purposely or accepted as a condition Chargate is very much a Forest Garden. Therefore, the open spaces will have had an even greater significance. Entrance is gained by drives from the south, and a rather longer one from the north-east: these curve but hardly in the manner of the *arti-natural* as John Harris has taught us to call the Sharawaggi curves, and which used to be offered as evidence of "forward thinking" in design matters. Apart from the walks snaking up the Mount here are no further hints of the serpentine to be seen.

The drives approach the south front by the sides of a quite large rectangular clearing, much too big to be called a courtyard, whose axis establishes the axis of the whole scheme, which extends laterally east-west. Its edges parallel to the axis are straight and defined by the close planted woodland. There is no hint of reinforcement here by hedging. The east side is shaped with stepped plantings and an oval apse, whereas the west "edge" beyond the big grass oval is shaped by quadrants stepping forward to define and support a large grass splay banked platform. This is the size of the house, and is left quite unfurnished. At the extreme edges are two straight ways up to two small support buildings to either side of the house standing in flanking "courtyards" (with no apparent walls to enclose them). The other has a further building, presumably a stable, within the woodland's edge.

Beyond the house is a broad parade which runs roughly east-west across the axis ending in the large roundel on the east end, and opposite to a gate at the edge of property. The parterre lies northward and is bigger than its companion, the platform on the other side of the house. It lies beyond the parade on the axis of house and estate, and is splayed in V fashion and lined with hedges and some eight pedestals presumably supporting statues, and the two great walks which lead into the woodland garden. These also lead into the open park-like ground. So Vanbrugh's house occupies the point of this great V, and the two arms make two very different kinds of *Addison's Walks*. The splayed parterre is a rather peculiar restatement of the conventional kind, and its placement underlines its peculiarity. Its form is close to one of Switzer's published designs for "A Fruit Garden where ye Walls are bevel" (*FG* 1724 299). At Chargate there is an ornamental building on axis opposite the house, whereas the Fruit Garden has a *jet d'eau* in a semi-circular basin occupying the same place. The parterre proper lies between the two great walks, and appears to be set off, perhaps lowered by a small

40 *A fine genius for gardening*

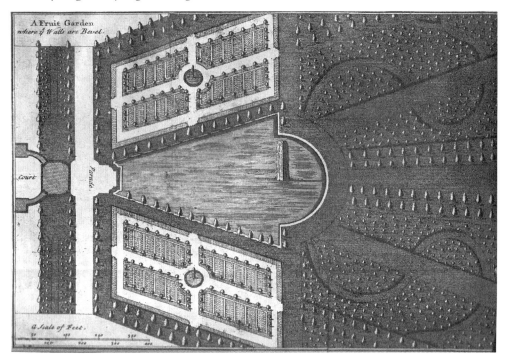

Figure 1.14 Chargate, Surrey: plan of the fruit garden where the walls are bevel (north to lower right corner). Reproduced from Stephen Switzer, *The Practical Fruit Gardener*, 1724. Private collection.

bank, or dwarf wall, and although it is shaped slightly at the north side, at the sharp end it is otherwise unfurnished.

The two walks at Chargate lead to very different experiences. The right-hand walk leads on the level simply between two pieces of dense woodland to an open park-like area which abuts the woodland of the rest of the farm. Its edges with the wood are defined by a narrow and somewhat meandering walk, and where the walk breaks out of the wood is shown bastion-like, but in a rather unfinished manner. To its northeast is what remained park-like ground, that is, un-gardened, whereas to the west and south the 1709 drawing indicates walks in a more formal disposition, but still unresolved. The walk defining the other side of the parterre leads upwards into the hill as a sloped ramp cut and embanked into the hillside. This way is augmented by pairs of shadier woodland walks to either side. All these lead to the top of the hill, to a flattened and circular glade which is known as the Mount. Its shape is elaborated by square wings to humour the opening made by the walk, whose westward extension also offers extensive views over Esher and the Thames valley. In the foreground to the north-west are two large gardens laid out along the axis as parterre, and beyond it a bowling green: both of these are almost landscape in scale and appear to belong more to that region than to the house or woodland.

The Chargate design experiments with Wray Wood themes, which at this date are still to be realized and remained largely imaginary or unresolved. The tiny castle-like house is in plan almost identical to what Vanbrugh tried to make of old Woodstock, where the close but "out-scale" axis of the Bridge and its earthen approaches suggest the same strong formal connection between the terrace or parade at Castle Howard on the north side. There it intersects Wray Wood in a decidedly vigorous manner, and similarly at Chargate is designed to connect house and Mount and not in a humouring serpentine entry. In the end a more serpentine way is in fact adopted to reach the Mount and the surprising view north-west. The contrast at the end of the alternative, and the easier walk with its views of park or pasture, will have brought its own and varied pleasure. The grounds adjacent to the bowling green and parterre north-west of the Mount remained at the heart of the unresolved series of walks mentioned above, and this part will become the centre of the design concerns of the next phases of Chargate, as Claremont.

This begins in 1715 when the Mount becomes the site of Vanbrugh's tower called Belvedere. Vanbrugh had Chargate for a scant five years. He was never a rich man and in that period was especially stretched, and he could not call on credit as his landed relations and friends could. But the house was finished and also the grounds and sold on for a good profit to Newcastle in 1714, who took over not only the house and small farm but also the design, and acted almost as Vanbrugh's surrogate in developing them. Immediately the Mount is transformed into an important building, and its ground forms there and elsewhere in the wood are further sculpted military fashion, provided with an easy and serpentine route from the house, and the edges fronting the park are made into terrace walks with bastions. This phase of expansion and re-design may have been the work of Bridgeman, and its first iteration is shown in *Vitruvius Britannicus*. Although Switzer remained an interested commentator on the project, its development, certainly from the later 1720s, seems to have been entrusted to other hands (*Vit Brit III* 1731).

Notwithstanding the unfinished parts of the Chargate design, when taken as a Forest Garden, its play and balance of open clearings and woodland managed in slightly awkward circumstances, it shows much merit. This is most notable in its mien of minimalist contrast of open and closed space, seen from the long curving drive, "unrelieved" through the dense trees, to the entrance spaces, much larger, and utterly plain until the banked platform where the house presents itself. Without lateral walls it is both incredibly small and articulated, plain (that is, with no architectural ornamentation) and yet changeful, and with movement. This quality, of course, is the only one later 18th century professional, and academic, critics felt due to Vanbrugh. Sometimes called castle-style when used as here entirely symmetrically it really ought to bear other names. Its articulation of parts is due to Vanbrugh's bent; as James Gibbs will, and Colen Campbell knows he should but sometimes forgets, or as John James or specially Francis Smith always achieves, Vanbrugh will never make that flat topped, tall, square house which is so characteristic of the early 18th century, whether in more baroque or Palladian mode. Much of this comes naturally from his penchant to make aedicular passages and ante-rooms, or bays or bows within major rooms, and this is much in evidence internally at Chargate. This we can be certain is Vanbrugh by himself.

These qualities are not exported to the garden design. There the elements are strong, largish and without elaboration: they are apt to be plain rectangles or squares, except as centres like the Mount itself (even there the "wings" are plain smaller rectangles)

42 *A fine genius for gardening*

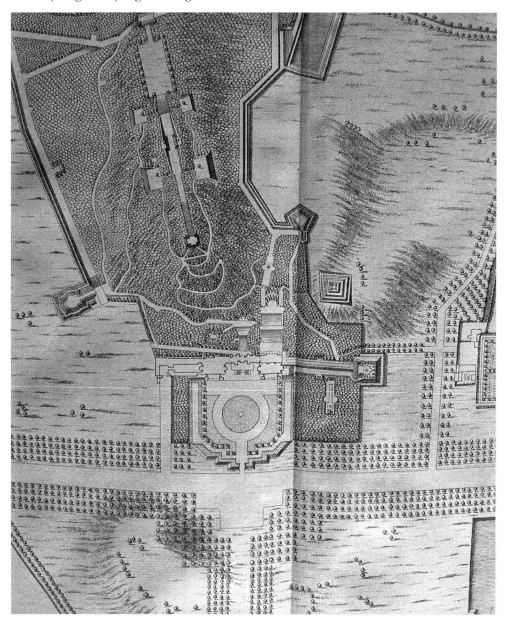

Figure 1.15 Chargate/Claremont, Surrey: partial plan (north to upper right corner). Reproduced from Colen Campbell, *Vitruvius Britannicus, or the British Architect*, 1725 (ed 1731), III plates 77 and 78. Private collection.

or at the roundel at the east end of the parade. There, where some elaboration is anticipated, it is kept relatively plain. The roundel has very short rectangular wings, and its centre is square with quadrant corners recollecting the big circular form. Bastions, insofar as they exist, are also plain. It is in the following developments that the earthworks and bastions take on added articulation when they become, as here suitably, elaborate in Bridgeman's manner but not so in the original. With its out-size entrance court (it is only full size, but the tiny house makes it appear grander) and the very ample parade beyond, set in old woodland, it does make a simple, even noble show. The easy access to the quirky parterre (which masterfully manages to be in scale with both house and parade) and the shorter walk towards the park manages to make it also sociable and convenient for an old lady's use.

2 Towards a rural and farm-like way of gardening

Grimsthorpe

Stephen Switzer was established with the Bertie family in Lincolnshire by 1711 and was engaged on the expansion of the gardens at Grimsthorpe, and very probably at Swinstead Belleau and Eresby as well. And it appears that it was there that he began writing *Ichnographia Rustica*. When I first wrote about Grimsthorpe (Brogden 1973) I suggested that Switzer might have been an agent in introducing John Vanbrugh to the family, which led to his work there from 1715. It is much more likely that the reverse is true and that it was Vanbrugh's kind offices which brought Switzer to work for the Berties. For of course Vanbrugh and Robert Bertie (1660–1723) had known each other from the earliest days, and had attended on the Stadtholder Willem in 1688 just before he assumed the throne as the husband of Queen Mary as William III. It was apparently the high spirits of his youth in praising Willem in Paris a bit later that landed Vanbrugh his stint in Vincennes, gaoled as a suspected spy. Vanbrugh was also distantly related to the Willoughbys, so his friendship with Robert, and his even closer relationship with Robert's brother Peregrine, was easy, intimate and long standing (Field 2008, Hart 2008).

The grounds at Grimsthorpe had been designed and laid out in the 1670s for Robert Bertie's mother, Lady Lindsey, who figured in Switzer's History. She was a great planter and was very personally involved. She was probably also instrumental in making the series of ponds, later to be combined as a great lake, in the park west of the house. The gardens consisted of parterres running the full width of the south side of Grimsthorpe, neatly flanked by regular beds for vegetables and fruit. These the family were happy to enjoy, alongside their unimproved and old-fashioned house built rather college-like around the four sides of a good sized courtyard. The Best Garden lay on the east front. It had a large, square bowling green with a pair of pavilions, a broad terrace and a double avenue if shade were wanted, all enclosed by walls bearing more fruits, there espaliered. The north side of the house had recently been made a regular nine bay composition with short advancing wings and a central pediment, but without a basement and with its roof in full view. Although perfectly and reticently classical it remained friendly, even homey.

This side was approached from a broad avenue, and its entrance court was separated only by a low wall and equally friendly gatehouses (there must have been a gate, but Kip's view shows none). So Grimsthorpe was an almost academic exercise in modern place making, which is to say it could have been held up for comparison with a composition from Andre Mollet, or A J Dezalier D'Argenville, and shows that

A rural and farm-like way of gardening 45

the Willoughbys were as modern and up-to-date as any Continental. The composition of the grounds, and the extended approaches, were designed symmetrically about the north-south axis and without discomfort. And there are slightly quirky touches which take it beyond any text-book designs. For a start the axis does not run through a walk; rather, it is carried across a relatively simple series of beds, flanked by fancier ones to east and west beyond broad walks which are of unequal widths. And directly opposite the garden front, and of course on axis, is an octagonal garden house (itself perfectly and classically formed) standing at the south side of the parterres, which paused the eye rather than stopped it, as a strong avenue lay behind it to be explored further southward. Here was Lady Lindsey's plantation of four square blocks of forest trees, and a further broad avenue extending into the far distance between a park and hayfield, each seen through a single row of forest trees. Not only was Grimsthorpe perfectly presentable to informed and international company, but it also exhibited evidence of talent in its design.

Although it did not need to be updated or further improved, further improvements continued well into the 18th century. As early as 1710 (Hart 2008) there is a hunting lodge design by Vanbrugh for a site near Grimsthorpe, and also on the estate is his Swinstead summer house of 1720 (very like his Chargate), which is all that remains

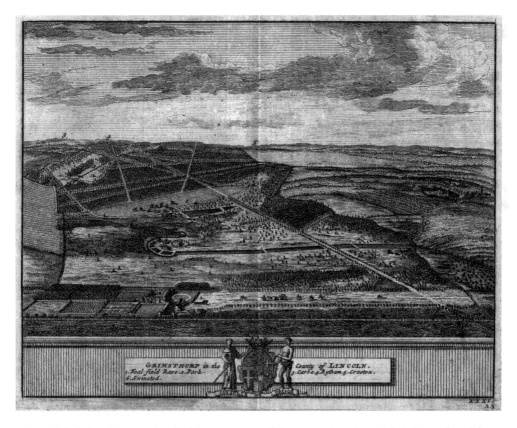

Figure 2.1 Grimsthorpe, Lincolnshire: prospect of the estate (north to right). Reproduced from Johannes Kip and Leonard Knyff, *Les Delices de la Grand' Bretagne*, 1707. Private collection.

of the project to build a new house there. And of course his last major project was to re-case the whole of Grimsthorpe. The north front is all that was realized. So, like at Blenheim, Castle Howard and Chargate Vanbrugh and Switzer are colleagues at Grimsthorpe. Switzer's role appears at first sight to have been simply to extend Lady Lindsey's woodland and to make the parterres less fussy. In the manner of carrying that work out, however, the results yielded much more than a simple extension. In a recent study of Vanbrugh Caroline Dalton (Dalton 2012) has presented Vanbrugh's role as a putative landscape designer, and has produced much new and interesting information and re-evaluation. The thrust of her message would reverse much of the judgement of writers about him, from Laurence Whistler onwards, as she would credit to him and to him alone almost all the landscape works with which he was connected. That aspect of her work does not convince, and seems at odds not only with Vanbrugh's amiable and generous character but also with the individual cases argued. There were more than sufficient works to have kept both Vanbrugh and Switzer employed as architects or as garden designers. Certainly for Switzer and for Vanbrugh, where they are known to be associated, this is so, nor do analogous arguments which would exclude the roles of other designers elsewhere convince. This notwithstanding, Grimsthorpe was the beneficiary of their working on it at the same time, as indeed was the legacy which Lady Lindsey had bequeathed, as well as that of William Stukeley, the antiquary whom Switzer introduced to the Berties, and with whom essential qualities from their joint imaginations/research gave depth and further enrichment to the designs as they developed. Doubtless also are the contributions, which had to have been profoundly important, from Robert Bertie, perhaps Uncle Peregrine also, certainly his nephew, the second duke and other members of the family as well. But, sadly, their contributions will simply have to be accepted as critical, but just how we cannot at present tell. And doubtless none of these contributors would wish to exclude Vanbrugh's influence for an instant.

The wood at Grimsthorpe was only a quarter as old as the venerable wood at Castle Howard. It was thus at the perfect stage to be both recognizably a mature wood but still amenable to alteration and improvement. Its maturity would make sure that those trees which were exceptionally strong and had a special appeal or beauty could be protected and perhaps celebrated, while those which had struggled could be sacrificed and either replaced or more likely removed to make room for some feature. It presented the four cardinal views or prospects, north to the garden front of Grimsthorpe, or to the countryside southward, across the park to the west, or to fields, and the grounds let to tenants, in the east. These are of course concentrated views, and if the most interesting objects lay in the way they were excellent, not only as views, but also from their ends as prospects. Already there was a terrace running along the west side of the garden, and that gave varied views into the park, albeit across kitchen garden beds. But being open as they were, these prospects might, and most likely would, be reckoned to lack the variety so admired in the early 18th century. And as much as they might be appreciated from the terrace, they are hardly celebrated. And of course from the wood there was only the single view to the park at a time, as the wood had apparently only the four walks, as from the Kip view no others are visible, and in a youngish woodland that would have been expected, and hardly regretted.

With marvellous prospects to enjoy already to hand, the designer's (or designers') project was to capture, enhance and celebrate these while opening the maturing woodland, expanding it where appropriate and making it into something like Wray

Figure 2.2 Grimsthorpe, Lincolnshire: view of Duchess' Bastion, by William Stukeley, 1736 (north to top). Oxford Bodleian Library, MS Top. gen d.14 fols. 44 38v.

Wood, and using the lessons from Chargate and elsewhere in the bargain. Switzer's solution was to multiply the number and directions of the walks, and to lead the terrace all around the wood. Thus, the wood is expanded into a polygon, and the number of views is greatly increased, and their variety as well, not only as set pieces of framed views where one stops and contemplates, but also as views multiplied and seen surprisingly in new contexts. In the revision these become garden views, woodland views, views across the park or views into hayfields.

Another, perhaps primary, purpose is to enhance Grimsthorpe as it is viewed from the park, and from any distance. Like at Blenheim and Castle Howard, and Chargate too, there is a plain desire to extend the house into the landscape because it makes the house seem bigger and more important, a part of and a flattering adjunct to that landscape. It also ensures that it makes that finer show so much admired. This was achieved in seemingly the same manner as at Blenheim, which Switzer will cheerfully acknowledge as Vanbrugh's design, where the big polygon of the bastioned parterre is mimicked in plan form. But instead of the stone fortress appropriate to Blenheim, a cheaper, more easily constructed manner is used at Grimsthorpe, and one familiar to any soldier . . . that of field fortification, with its ditches and scarps and counter-scarps and embanked bastions. From the great distances westward across the park and its ponds, the ridge with Grimsthorpe extended southward as a natural fortress, and thus made it all grander, in fact and in impact.

The parterres in Switzer's revision are drastically simplified, becoming grass plots marked by conical dwarf greens between the gravelled walks. And the emphasis of the gardens, as a whole, is now shifted, from the parterres seemingly into the wood.

48   *A rural and farm-like way of gardening*

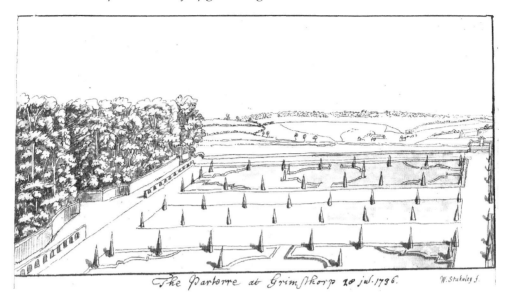

Figure 2.3 Grimsthorpe, Lincolnshire: view of the parterre from the east, by William Stukeley, 1736. Oxford Bodleian Library, MS Top. gen d.14 fols. 44 37v.

Although that is true, the wood really becomes more a means of appreciating an even wider garden than the primary destination in itself. Not only are the extra views and their varieties now in addition, but the adjacent grounds begin to take on garden aspects themselves. Whereas the parterres have lost their horticultural colour and variety the extensions of the wood have more than made up for it. Certainly by their maturing state at the time when Stukeley's drawings of them are dated, that is, in 1736, they exhibit a great variety of plant shape and size against the mature forest trees, indicating that the wood had been enriched with the flowering and fragrant shrubs Switzer employed elsewhere (such as Beaumanor, see below) and that they show the promiscuous plantation he prefers in such places.

The avenue Lady Lindsey had laid out south of the wood Switzer transforms into a different kind of avenue, where the rows of trees are replaced by platoons or square clumps. These allow the avenue to move into a different scale, and become larger, potentially much larger, without becoming also tiresomely repetitive. It also introduces in the spaces of the avenue between the platoons wider open views which can be had to either side into, as here, either field or park. Occasionally these gaps became the means to depart from the gardens proper and allow company to wander into the adjacent fields to enjoy them as if they were gardens. To make sure interest is maintained Switzer waits until the very end of the extended walk is reached, and then he offers a meandering side walk to assure its attraction and installs at the end of it, well out of sight of any other part of the scheme, a place set aside for contemplation, whose power is boosted by its association with the early local king Grime. At Grimsthorpe what could be better than a seat, sequestered on several sides, but with open views across the parkland, called Grime's Seat? Or, for visitors who know the grounds already, the subterfuge can work in reverse. As the straight Grime's Walk is

Figure 2.4 Grimsthorpe, Lincolnshire: view of Grime's Walk, by William Stukeley, 1736 (north to top). Oxford Bodleian Library, MS Top. gen d.14 fols. 44 37.

also presented earlier as a walk, as it were, in the park already and at an angle to the rest of the scheme, when its end is reached Grime's Seat can be enjoyed and fully contemplated, then the meandering way can be offered as an alternative for the return.

The topography of Grimsthorpe is ample and somewhat rolling, and the ridge where the house and extended gardens are sited has the character of a pronounced swell at sea. So although there are fairly extensive views to both west and east the sense of the landscape is planar. In that topography the appropriate gestures of a designer of landscape will be different from those in a hilly and quickly changing place, so big and formal elements will be at home and will suit the nature of the place. The platoons we have observed in the new south avenue have their counterparts in the extended grounds to the north, where Switzer planted blocks of woodland as great groves; there, not only are the trees laid out regularly, but the groves themselves have geometric shapes. *Platoons* is derived of course from military usage, if not field fortification, certainly as an orderly means of marshalling soldiers, and its seeming Dutch spelling suggests a recent introduction from the Low Countries. In the early 18th century the furnishing of a park, or any big open space, is often encountered, and the means used seem equally often similar to battle lines and formations explaining the important engagements, such as the recent Battle of Blenheim. And the similarity seems most appropriate especially in the very recently set out park west of the house at Blenheim Palace. But of course that is not a restatement of Marlborough's troop formations, nor anything close, but the seeming similarity at a distance was strong, and with some remains so. In fact, these great figures have what Switzer called (as Isaac Newton had observed, or would shortly observe, about the cosmos) an incomprehensible regularity. In other words, although they

50 *A rural and farm-like way of gardening*

exhibit no particular or recognizable form, insofar as they are known to have, and can be shown to have, form, this brings a necessary comfort. Although Switzer does not use such forms after the early 1730s, more generally they remain in use until well past 1750.

At Grimsthorpe the northern plantations share the same basic appeal but also have a different kind. Here the "confusion" comes both from the enlargement of scale of apparent and actual shapes and from the maze-like tricking of the eye that comes from being inside a complex, geometrically laid out grove, here of 30 acres, but which "might in any such like Case be two or three hundred" (*IR* II 206), where all the undergrowth is kept clear, and the ground is level and grazed with a canopy of trees above also kept at the same height so that the tree trunks only show the pattern of their layouts occasionally, and otherwise seem in a sort of constant confusion. Thus, variety is ensured, while openness is assured and sunshine not excluded, "besides the Beauty and Nobleness there is in seeing of the Deer feed in the open Lawns, and running backward and forward through our whole Design" (*IR* II 205).

Of nearby Eresby we can sadly tell little. John Harris, when researching Lincolnshire with Nikolaus Pevsner, combed over the site of the house and grounds more than 50 years ago, recorded the gate piers and sensed Switzer's ghostly presence, but was unable to transmit more. When Bill Spink and I attempted the same we puzzled over seemingly important lumps in a woodland, but even Switzer's ghost eluded us. Later still a single plan of the grounds was found in the Lincolnshire Archives, and that gives the outlines of the designed grounds, and shows that the house was a regular rectangle in plan and had two advanced and good sized square pavilions defining an entrance courtyard. Apart from that there is only the grand avenue, the width of

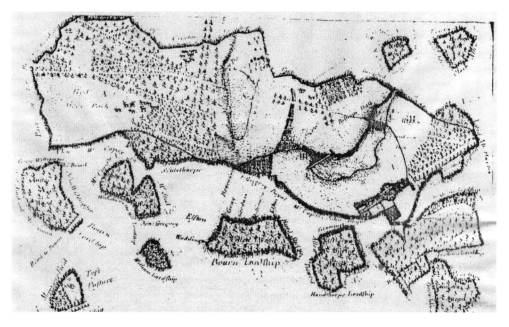

Figure 2.5 Grimsthorpe, Lincolnshire: estate plan from the 1752 plan book (north to right). Lincoln Castle, Ancaster MSS. With the permission of the Grimsthorpe and Drummond Castle Trust and Lincolnshire Archives.

the house frontage, which runs northwards to Spilsby. The house had disappeared by the time of early Ordnance Surveys although one of the pavilions survived until 1890 to carry the name Eresby House, which attests to how large they were. Also from then we can see a large rectangular basin on axis southward of the house site with its longer side parallel, and rather wider than the house. It is there marked Fish Pond, and is rather closer to the house than it might be expected to be. Could it indicate that there was some sort of water-parterre? This idea is reinforced by two large woodlands close by: that to the east is still designated Wilderness, and its larger neighbour across the axis is called Eresby Mount. And just to the west of the northern avenue, and hard by the house site, is Mont Holt, which contains a somewhat curvilinear fish pond called The Moat, and a further woodland with earthworks (perhaps my ghostly lumps?). For the rest of the estate there are the fields, roughly rectangular but in no sense seemingly designed.

Riskins, Berkshire

Among Switzer's patrons were Allen Bathurst, 1st Earl Bathurst (1684–1775), and Algernon Seymour (1684–1750), Earl of Hertford (and briefly 7th Duke of Somerset), and his wife, Frances Thynne (1699–1754), who was also a poet and generous correspondent. These three created and improved one of the most important, yet still too little known, gardens, the *extravagante bergerie*, as Lady Frances Hertford called it, of Riskins near Windsor. Bathurst had inherited it and gave it form and early fame. He was a Member of the Commons in Parliament and then raised to the Lords to insure the Treaty of Utrecht. As a Tory he soon left government, and devoted his life until the 1740s and Robert Walpole's departure to improving his estates, from 1714 at Cirencester on the very largest scale (see below), and at Riskins, where he began one of the first of what was later called *ferme ornée*, sometime after he inherited in 1704, and most probably in the very early 1710s. Both these estates are important ones from the point of view of landscape design, and they have been recognized as such practically from their beginnings. However, it is less easy, in fact positively difficult, to chart just how they were conceived, designed and carried on, and from whom the ideas which shaped them came, and in just what manner. I believe Switzer provided that guidance for both estates until the 1740s, when both were complete. But there are other contenders, such as Alexander Pope, who is the most distinguished, and, of course, Bathurst himself, whose old Roman virtue of turning political disappointment (if indeed it was such) into service to his country through improvement of his estates ensured his esteem. For it was Bathurst who remained central to their development. Indeed, he was one of James Lees-Milne's *Earls of Creation* where that aspect of patronage control and design was thoroughly presented and argued back in the 1960s.

Although they are generated from precisely the same principles Riskins is much the smaller and more garden-like, and it shares many features with Grimsthorpe and Whetham (see below). It is also, like Chargate, one of the several (soon to be many) nearby with which it can be compared. Riskins is one of those small estates within easy reach of Westminster and Windsor, and these had initially been esteemed by the powerful as almost royal places such as Fulham Palace, and so also became attractive to slightly less powerful men. During the long 18th century their qualities as power houses were thus changed. Lord Rochester's New Park at Richmond, which remained one of the most admired gardens of the day, may have carried a whiff of rakish power of a 17th century kind, whereas the retirement site of Sir William Temple's Moor Park nearby had power, but of a subtler kind. When this type of new small estate was developed in the early 18th century these estates began to wear their power quite lightly, and with some grace. And soon they became positively desirable in themselves. But that is to run ahead. It is also the case that for those who had these little estates, and often little else despite their distinction and duty to govern if of the right party, these farms, for that is really what they were, allowed a cheap, cheerful and decent alternative to trying to keep up an establishment in Westminster or London. At least they could grow their own food and supply much of their own needs, and keep their dependants in a healthy place, without too many of the temptations of the capital. The Thames made a good and easy way to move about, and in dangerous times the countryside, or abroad, was easier to reach.

Riskins lies north of the Thames on the Colnbrook in country that is decidedly flat. There is plenty of water, and the principal feature of the place has always been its brook, or is it canal? Was it straight, crooked or sort of meandering? It was too narrow to be made a pond, and besides a pond was not needed. It is an irony, and one hardly lost on

Figure 2.6 Riskins, Berkshire: plan (north to top). Reproduced from John Rocque, Berkshire, 1752. © National Library of Scotland.

Bathurst, who was not one of the stuffier Earls of Creation, that he possessed one of the earliest streams "to depart from the straight line" (quote ascribed to Lord Stafford by Barrington 1785) knowing that if he had bothered he might have easily mended it, but then discovering that he might be in fashion. His comments also suggest that the Riskins water pre-dated John Aislaby's abstraction of the river at Studley Royal (see below), which was towards the earlier end of the second decade. When in the late 1730s the Hertfords took Riskins over they made a circular basin where the canal turned its corner, and even later they extended the gardens and canal/stream and made the new water course straight. Of course on a flat site the genius of the place cannot be certain whether it wishes to be one or the other. (Pope and then many of the younger critics like Horace Walpole forgot this.) Generally it was decided that the stream wanted to be straight, and that is how Switzer illustrates it in what he called a regulated Epitomy, as does the topographically very correct John Rocque, who also shows it as such on the earliest plan we have which shows the place as surveyed. This is all not so silly as it may seem. For an early 18th century observer with knowledge, sensibility and education the positive nature of the serpentine line, which the painter William Hogarth would soon declare to be the Line of Beauty, had to be learned. And at places like Riskins it is a close run thing. During Bathurst's time, and as long as the Hertfords lived there, it remained in the form shown by Rocque in 1752. Sometime in the early 19th century the water was curved through its former 90 degree turn, and like the Serpentine in Kensington Gardens (see below) it only became natural looking much later.

The other thing they had to learn to accept, and then to celebrate, was that the water course gave the character to the place, and served the same validating function as the avenue or parterre or court in other schemes. That is Riskins' lesson, and that is perhaps why Switzer's presentation of it as a canal with a walk on either side, which is technically true, took so much soul-searching by him, and by Bathurst. They had always loved the place, as had Pope and the poets, even if grudgingly including Jonathan Swift. The layout of Riskins is arranged to either side of this dominant feature, and appeared to be essentially woodland. This made a clearly defined wooded and irregular form, approaching, if any regular feature, then a hexagon, and its sharpish edges recall some of the earlier design trials for the Great Parterre at Blenheim. On the east, south and west the wood lies adjacent to fields; to the west, with views to Windsor Castle, there is also a roadway, whereas the north is indicated by Rocque to be more like open grove work with walks, and that is also the site of the house. In shape, size and nature it is similar to Switzer's reworking of Lady Lindsey's wood at Grimsthorpe, or of Chargate.

Except for Switzer's, no view or plan is known for Riskins during the period of its design and layout. It is mentioned from time to time from 1713, and always in the manner and terms of approval, but never actually described. Switzer is the first to do so in 1727, and he is still rather allusive. It is thought his plan of it, his regulated Epitomy, was prepared then although it was not actually published until 1742, two or three years after the place had passed from Bathurst to the Hertfords and they had renamed it Percy Lodge. So from these, and Switzer's we can reconstruct its early nature. From Switzer and Lady Hertford we can also add details of some of the significant structural parts, and thus build up a fuller picture of the place, and put it into context with other designs of the period.

Both of Rocque's plans (the *Topographical Map of Middlesex* and *Berkshire*) show a compact and somewhat irregular wooded farm north-east of Colnbrook. If only

54 *A rural and farm-like way of gardening*

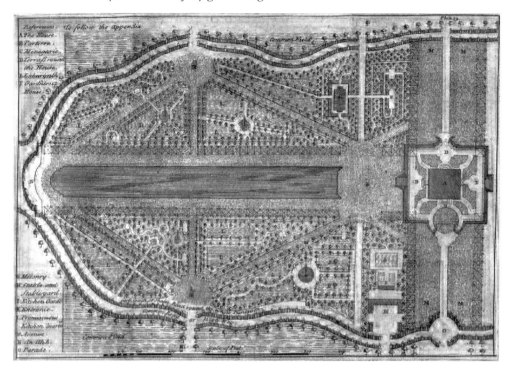

Figure 2.7 Riskins, Berkshire: Stephen Switzer's "regulated Epitomy" (north to right). Reproduced from Switzer, *Ichnographia Rustica*, 1742, III, plate 39. Private collection.

Rocque's plans existed it is most doubtful anyone would suspect a special place and look further, for there is little to tempt. There is a canal with a circular swelling at is centre which does bespeak designed gardens, and the rest appears to be woodlands only; Frances Hertford writing in 1740 characterized them as "laid out in the manner of a French park [by which she meant] interspersed with woods and lawn" (quoted in Brown 2006 77 et seq). These seeming wooded blocks between the walks were where the kitchen quarters were sited, and where fruit gardens were planted, making the wood the garden part surrounded by arable fields and "fenced" by an *enfilade*, the "cart, coach or shaise (sic) Road round the whole Plantation" (*IR* III 1742 plate 39). This character comes only from the references in the published "regulated Epitomy." The house was at the extreme north edge of the scheme, and it sat on a raised terrace embanked with grass slopes, and set back behind pairs of small grass plats differently shaped on each front. Lying to the west and east sides are grassed forecourts, as they were the full width of the house with a walk in the centre, replaced by a drive on the east which led by a perron of ramps to a circular drive hard by the front door. The north front of the house opened across its terrace directly into an avenue, a tree-lined alley between fields, more in the nature of a park than part of the garden. The opposite front was exactly the same, but commanded the garden.

There the grassed forecourt is replaced by the same thing, if rather smaller, and on this side designated "Parterre," axially aligned with the canal-stream. These formal spaces are really defined by the pleached walks which begin at each of the four corners of the terrace, where they "connect" with four quadrant walks to the house, and allow shaded walks alongside the canal with views and ways through to "Promiscuous kitchen quarters" on the west, past the principal cross axis, to the canal's end at the shaped "Ah Ah,h" (sic; Switzer's expression for what is more often called a Ha Ha, named from the expression of surprise when encountering the sunk fence where there was the expectation of a continuing and open walk), and open views to the south over hayfields, then back towards the house with differently shaped quarters of kitchen stuffs now on the east side of the canal. The kitchen garden proper lies just south-east of the house, with a melonry, the stable block and the gardener's house. The entrance green is also defined by pleached walks, as is its neighbour to the west, from which there is access to a small maze, and a menagerie tucked in next to the promiscuous kitchen quarters. These all amount to structural changes in how gardens were conceived and designed, and although there are interesting aspects about the forms used, it is really these more fundamental changes in how parts of gardens were perceived and put together which signal Riskins' importance. Hitherto discrete elements are here designed to be seen together and to benefit from the obvious mixing of what designers had taken great pains to keep separate. This wilful mixing of *dulci* and *utile* brought variety of form and surprised by unconventional juxtaposition. This included trim walks beside a civilized canal, shaded by regularly planted trees, hard by flourishing kitchen stuffs and fruit trees in plots of various shapes, across which, as it were through, one caught glimpses of hayfields and meadows and ploughed arable land.

These principal walks led into serpentine and meandering ones through and past the kitchen quarters and around the whole plantation if one wished. But the surrounding fields are clearly better appreciated from a chaise, or perhaps a Bath-chair, following the way which meanders around the edges of Riskins' heart, now contrasting kitchen quarters mixed with woodland, and the "common fields" on the other side. The "real" Riskins, then, was more extensive and sprawling than the octavo folding plate, about which Switzer had warned in his commentary of 1727 when it was meant to be published. The surrounding fields are merely identified in the printed version but are open to see in the county map version, and we can also deduce something of the crops they bore when surveyed by Rocque and his team. His convention of rendering ploughed fields, predictably enough, is broken horizontal lines representing the ridges and furrows. These fields will have borne crops, such as cabbages or turnips. These are rather further away from the heart of the scheme than the other field type planted broadcast fashion, such as hay. The controversy which Switzer had with Jethro Tull in the 1730s (see below) had as much to do with the manner of sowing and the consequent appearance of productive fields as any other factor. Broadcast planted fields next to tidier ones, even if promiscuously planted by type, would have given the more satisfying contrast and variety sought after. At Riskins the only seemingly ploughed ground lies to the west beyond a lane and one of the meandering streams with Windsor Castle in the distance. The greatest exposure of the inner garden to these outer gardens occurs along the south and east. The canal axis is aligned across the Ha Ha at its end to a large hayfield, and the wood quarters on its east side also look over hayfields, and seem to be separated from them by an extended terrace walk with Ha Ha. And one of the fields juts into the wooded garden quarters on the site of Switzer's east cardinal cross axis. The rest, that is, the north-east corner and the north flank of the grounds, is where the stables, carriage entrance and house are located, in both Switzer's epitome and Rocque's survey, and the boundary there appears more conventional. The canal in Rocque turns 90 degrees westward, and may swell again to make a basin by the house.

It is most helpful to be mindful of how Switzer's plates illustrating his texts are to be "taken". Although he has been very precise in pointing out differences in scale and idealizations or epitomes historians and critics have consistently continued to apply the visual conventions of their own times, and have thus missed the point, to usually a greater degree. But at Riskins we can compare his efforts alongside Lady Hertford's poetic and contemporary descriptions of essentially the same things. As the Hertfords were also Switzer's patrons they would have been well acquainted by the time they bought Riskins. The first volume of his *Introduction to a General System of Hydrostaticks and Hydraulicks* has been dedicated to the Earl of Hertford, and it is most probable that Switzer helped them with their improvements at Marlborough House. They had also taken Lord Brooke under their wings in his minority, and thus Switzer's use of his library at Breamore in preparing his *Hydrostaticks and Hydraulicks* would be a manifestation of their patronage. They made improvements and additions to Riskins, notably garden buildings including a grotto, and, finally taking Pope's advice (which Bathurst had avoided), they made a pavilion on a sort of mount, "on the highest spot that Bathurst had ordained" (quoted in Brown 2006 137; see Brown for more on the Hertfords' tenure). Crucially as Lady Hertford was also a published poet she was able to bring a personal music to her own great appreciation and enjoyment of the place, and she also gives us valuable information about how Riskins was thought of in the 1740s and 1750s. It is she who terms Riskins "a scene from Arcadia", and it is she who waxes quite lyrical about the cathedral-like nobility of the rows of old trees, that is, the pleached allies of Switzer's avenues. And it is she who adopts Pope's poetics of that *extravagante bergerie* which is much more memorably charming than the prose of Switzer's "upon the plan of La Ferme Ornée" (*IR* III Appendix 9).

Switzer wrote much in his 40 year career as an author; beginning without a pattern to follow he invented one of his own, and as he wrote about new and then undefined subjects he became something of a pioneer. His manner of writing is genial if didactic, and he is apt to attempt more than he can complete with polish. Happily for us he included anecdotes of those things in life that helped him make, or illustrate, his points. In later works these more personal asides diminished, but fortunately were not abandoned. He attempted to account for his own conception of making great gardens, and he sought to persuade improvers to adopt his ideas, and he methodically gave them the means to do so. But, instead of adopting the template John James had used in 1712, where an ideal was set, then the variations required to make it fit various circumstances and sites were illustrated, he was obliged to begin by offering the variations, likely to be confusing when first encountered. For him a great garden, one not unlike Louis XIV's works, was, despite everybody's perception, not a thing to imitate, a sort of commodity. Rather, for him a most firmly held notion was that designs for landscape had to come from their sites and circumstances: therefore, a deep knowledge of the place was necessary before a design could be contemplated, never mind commenced. And also perhaps an idealization of Switzer's was his belief that no one was in a better position to know this than the estate's owner.

At that time, however, "[t]he Method commonly taken in this Affair, is, Gentlemen have their Ground survey'd, and perhaps the Levels taken, and then 'tis brought to London, where there are a great many Drafts-men and Paper Engineers, so a regular fine Scheme is made . . ." (*IR* III xii). The appeal, and indeed the beauty, of that method

A rural and farm-like way of gardening 57

had been most ably illustrated in James' *Theory and Practice of Gardening*. This very fully illustrated book, a translation of A J D'Argenville's *Theorie et Practique du Jardinage*, showed how gardens in the French manner can be understood, and provided the means to achieve them. This was very clearly laid out. There secrets of composition were also revealed. An orderly progression from complex to simple should be followed from the house along the major axis. Lateral design follows the same principle, from elaborate to simple, either from the house, or in bigger schemes beginning from any point along the major axis. Thus an estate may be laid out. Designs showing how the parts are handled are given also, simpler and grander.

Switzer warns improvers to avoid this way of proceeding. Rather, they should first ensure close study of their situations . . . how best to improve them, to save expense, to mix pleasure and profit and to grasp the nature of the place so as to discover how to draw all into "an agreeable and easy Correspondence of one Part of an Estate with another . . .". He genuinely wants them to take the most active role, and so he sets out his ideas, describes the history and the philosophy and spirit guiding him, and commends this also to them. All this is covered in *The Nobleman Gentleman and Gardener's Recreation*. There he explained also why he was proposing such a curious, even extraordinary, manner of thinking about, and laying out, large gardens. These were a mixture of the attitudes he brought with him to Brompton Park, and the things he learned while there which he drew together in his Preface, History and, in

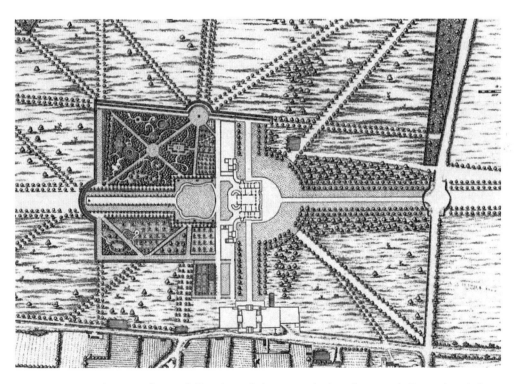

Figure 2.8 Houghton Hall, Norfolk: plan of the grounds (north to top). Reproduced from Colen Campbell, *Vitruvius Britannicus, or the British Architect*, 1725 (ed 1731), III plates 27 and 28. Private collection.

imitating classical elements, his first attempts at exposition . . . essentially his initial *essay*. Switzer's subsequent writings are all additions, of course, but are still revisions of these ideas introduced in 1715. He was then well aware that received taste was the continuation of current practice, best seen, for example, in Norfolk at Narford or Houghton, both large, well made and stylish, certainly in their constituent parts, but lacking any real grandeur, or "correspondence of Parts". Houghton was the creation of Sir Robert Walpole, the coming great man of British politics, and his new house was his bid to join the improvements recently undertaken by his senior Whigs, such as Carlisle and Halifax. At Houghton he was assisted by Kingsmill Eyre (Eburne 2003) to form grounds still with much of the "*Dutch* Taste" in evidence. (Walpole was as canny in matters of taste as in politics, and therefore would never be the first to take up new ideas.)

The alternative taste was based on revisions of the received manner to emulate the style perfected in France, the subject of James' translation, and realized magnificently by the new King George at his then almost finished Herenhausen in Hanover. Switzer knew this, and wished to encourage improvers of both attitudes to adopt his thinking. But anticipating an expected charge ". . . that I am setting up new Schemes in Gard'ning, which may, 'till the Prints come out, cause divers Reflections, as the Readers are disposed to think; but, on the contrary, I can affirm, that 'tis much the same as has been us'd already in some parts of the Kingdom . . . and for Antiquity . . . [I]t appears to be the same kind as the Gardens of *Epicurus* . . . was and is the manner of Gard'ning amongst the *Chinese* . . . And the *Designs* that tend the Way I am speaking . . . [are] such as that incomparable Wood of my Lord *Carlisle's* at *Castle-howard*, the Wood at *New-Park* . . . the Woods at *Cassiobury*, the *Design* of *Bushy Park*, &c" (*IR* I xxxvii–xxxviii).

Another disclaimer he felt obliged to make was his assertion that there were two sorts of gardens: those appropriate to ". . . City, and Country; the first for Flowers, &c and the last, Woods, Coppices, Groves, and the busie and laborious Employs of Agriculture, with which *Gardening* is unavoidably as well as pleasantly mix'd" (*IR* I xl). Switzer was not a *florist*: rarely does he treat of flowers. Apart from pointing out the fondness Roman women had for flowers in their religious rites in his History, or grudgingly acknowledging that since improvers are normally still engaged in London when flowers bloom they had better concentrate their attentions on agriculture or useful horticulture, he does not mention flowers. As exotics are useful – to eat, to enrich soils, to diversify a plantation or to shelter – Switzer is positive about them. He does not appear to value them otherwise. But his City type excludes gardens like Riskins or Chargate, those "Gardens . . . that are four, five, six, or seven Miles out of Town, whither the Fatigues of the Court and Senate often force the illustrious Patriots of their Country to retreat, and breathe the sweet and fragrant Air of Gardens; and these are generally too pent up" (*IR* I xl), and he promised a future work about these: no such work ever appeared; rather, the type became subsumed in his general advice. He allows grounds of the size of 25 acres or more to count as estate-size and thus qualify to be Rural and Natural, such as Riskins.

How to make a rural and extensive garden

He begins very positively and clearly by stating that gardens should appear as large as possible: ". . . if they were a hundred Acres or more, still the nobler; but how this should be done without the loss of too much Ground, or how many Gentlemen should be contented to be at so great an Expense, is not obvious . . . at first sight" (*IR* I 335). So first just what makes a "garden"? The immediate setting of a house, its parterre and the like he accepts as customary, if greatly simplified. However, Switzer observes that "our Modern Wildernesses", as the woody parts of great schemes were then known, are largely composed of expensive exotics, whereas native woods are cheaper to sow and manage, and nothing is nobler. Therefore, instead of using these wildernesses he proposes using large plantations of native woods as the major element to make big gardens with, but, "That in the Heart of all Quarters and Division [of these] there shall be a large Lawn or open Square, or other Polygonar or Natural Plot." These can also be the sites of fruit or kitchen gardens or orchards. Therefore, what has always been kept like with like, as it were, should rather mixed together, *utile* and *dulci*, but the particular placement of these elements will depend on the individual site to accommodate what may be there already, to exploit the more fertile or less promising grounds to their best advantages. That these "Extensive Plantations . . . adorn'd with Water and Statues, add as great a Grace to our Country Seats as the most elaborate Gardens of the *French*, will, I believe, not be denied, when 'tis consider'd that our Grass and Gravel is so much handsomer than theirs, in which Respect our Parks and common Ridings excel them by Nature; but if to that be added Rowling and Levelling the Mould [Mole] Hills, and a little Exactitude near the Bounds of the inner Parts of our Gardens; how much better may it not be than the best of their Turf and Carpet Walks and Gardens in *France* or *Holland*?" (*IR* I 336).

As had transpired at Castle Howard, where Wray Wood's 40 acres was becoming the *garden*, here Switzer generalizes that idea into a system for all. Of course, just how large (or small) each of the wooded quarters would be is a matter of judgement, taste and the particular site. Similarly their shapes could be as variable. As the enclosing woods could be densely planted, or more open, and made up of one sort of timber, or more likely several, and include Exoticks and flowering shrubs, so also it would not take too much imagination to understand that the various lawns (or whatever) contained in these divisions might be very large or very small. The walks leading to and from them might become objects of design as well, to be broader, or curved, or of whatever shape fancy or site might suggest. If these variations did not occur to an improver, then there were designers, such as Switzer, available to make suggestions. But it is clear that he is content, and indeed expects, that such decisions will arise more or less by themselves once his general idea of *Ichnographia Rustica* is accepted. Henceforth Switzer invites his readers to accept that *Garden* no longer means the legacy of up to four acres that Homer first described (for the early 18th century, the parterre and its adjacent walks and enclosures) but that for *Ichnographia Rustica* its contents and qualities need to be dispersed and scattered throughout an estate, and thus create a new kind of "garden" . . . a designed landscape.

Before concluding he remembers a few more practical observations about keeping his extensive gardens tidy. For these *Outer Lines* as he calls them, "The Cattle shall be the Mowers; and for Rowling, a Boy and Horse will do a great deal; and 'tis not incredible to affirm, 100 Acres will not cost above 50 *l. per annum* [£15,000 currently] the keeping, since there is no occasion of keeping those Outer Plantations very fine; a Paddle to cut up any staring Thistles and other things of that kind, and a Scythe fix'd into a long Handle, are the chief Instruments in this Rural way of Gard'ning" (*IR* I 336–337).

60   *A rural and farm-like way of gardening*

Reference to Abraham Cowley, and an early recognition of Pope in praising his "Windsor Forest" and a long quotation from *The Spectator*, concludes Switzer's *Nobleman Gentleman and Gardener's Recreation*. To reinforce Switzer's dislike for what he called the "*Dutch* Taste", that tendency to fussy, overcrowded and expensive designs of little nobility, Joseph Addison, like Queen Anne before, is called as a witness. In his *Spectator* 414, about the relationships of beauties of nature and art, he had written, "Our *British* Gardeners . . . instead of humouring Nature, love to deviate from it as much as possible. On this account our *English* Gardens are not so entertaining to the Fancy, as those in *France* and *Italy*, where we see a large Extent of Ground covered over with an agreeable Mixture of Garden and Forest, which represent everywhere an artificial Rudeness, is much more charming than the Neatness and Elegancy which we meet with those of our own Country" (quoted in *IR* I 342, 341).

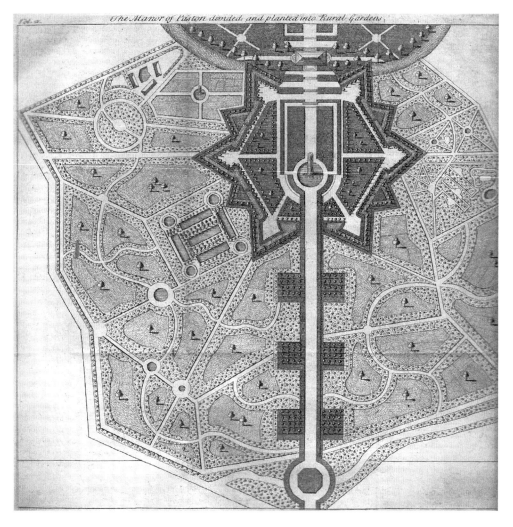

Figure 2.9 The Manor of Paston plan as divided into rural gardens. Reproduced from Stephen Switzer, *Ichnographia Rustica*, 1718, II 115. Private collection.

One has to wonder whether Switzer's ideas as expressed in 1715 will have been sufficient to convert his readers, or to what extent it could provide the guidance for others to make designs. Fearing that a somewhat negative response would be bound to come he had always planned to include explanatory plates, and these duly appeared in the 1718 edition, now expanded into three volumes under the general title *Ichnographia Rustica*. The contrast to volume 1 is strong; from rhapsodic praises of the countryside and the superiority of nature Switzer begins his next volume with the basics . . . of number, geometry and instruments. The move from the poetic to the mundane is characteristic of him; both seem to be ever present with him, and no exploration of the nature of landscape and its design can be had without this basic acceptance. However great an artist, or critic, may become all starts with the pencil and empty paper: thus he begins volume 2 with the consideration of the point, and then the line . . . He takes his intending improvers methodically through the constituents of design by setting simple exercises for them to work out. He then teaches how these very basic shapes may be transferred from drawing board abstraction into a sort of reality with simple surveying techniques; and, more potent for his message, how observed reality can be abstracted onto the drawing board to be considered, manipulated, shaded, embellished or changed to be a new design. These exercises working through simple propositions and proofs take up half of his volume 2, and result in the notional survey and commitment to paper of the Manor of Paston, an imaginary small estate of about 25 acres, as yet unimproved, which is typical of England (and based really on elements of the Bertie family's estates in southern Lincolnshire).

It is through such close study, then meticulous measurement, and finally drawing of its plan that an understanding of the nature of his place begins to form in the mind of an improver, and its abstracted image on paper becomes his means of beginning, by design. But Switzer puts off talking about the design which may come from all this; indeed, he puts it off until his student-improver has finished reading, and digesting, the matter in this volume and is half way through the final volume, before any Rural Design can be usefully addressed. In the meantime Switzer reverts to types, then the major constituents of a country seat. He begins with Courtyards, the entry and busy heart of the place where all must meet, have their business or needs attended to and then dispatched further: if company, then entry into the house proper (not to be seen again until they come out into the gardens beyond). But for the would be designer under Switzer's tuition there is still much to consider about the Courtyard, such as its pavement (whether with turf centre or more likely without) and the proper separation of paved areas to allow the house staff to come and go, and other staff to interact, and then move on to the stables or to other jobs. Switzer rather scolds his over-exuberant improvers who are apt to spend much too much on these architectural preliminaries in order to impress: his advice to them, given at length, is to be canny here and spend those funds in the extended grounds.

His first *garden* element is the Terrace Walk, with which he would prove his point. For Switzer the main terrace is the critical mediation between house and grounds: it should be magnificent to the same degree as the rooms within the house, the main reception rooms, and as it is the place where best to enjoy the magnificence of the best front of the house, it ought therefore to be quite broad, likely broader than common, significantly more than the height of the garden façade. Hampton Court Palace is singled out for its deficiency in this regard (*IR* II 154). It is the place for parade, for company to disport themselves in the same manner and dress as they might inside the house, and apart from their customary conversations and gossip to admire both the grounds and the main front of the house.

The importance Switzer places on the terrace is apt to be overlooked: for him it is the prime exterior space . . . the most elaborate and well finished, and the nearest to the best interior of a great house. It could bear furnishing, as in the example he gives. There the depth of the terrace, between the wall of the house and the first slope to the parterre, works out to be a staggering 105 feet, or 33 metres (which is as long as many parterres). Its breadth should be well beyond that of the garden front of the house, roughly three times at least. Of course it has to be meticulously constructed, seeming utterly flat and consistently so throughout its breadth and its depth. Thus, it is a very large element which has a standard equivalent to an interior room of reception. In his illustrated example there is first a series of strips of smooth gravel (or cockle shells) ten feet broad, then a six foot verge of grass, followed by a repeat of gravel and grass strips to a narrow verge of sand (at feet) to reach the centrepiece, the pavement, indicated as stone in checkerboard. But, "Whether the Verges of Grass before the House be best plain, or planted with Pyramid Yew and Vasa's between them, I leave to the Discretion of the Owner. I must confess there is a becoming Decency and Grandeur in plain Grass only; and of that Kind is the large Terrace at *Bushy* Park, belonging to the Right Honourable the late Earl of *Hallifax* . . ." (*IR* II 166) (see below).

In most schemes the main terrace will be joined by other terraces along the sides of the parterre or lawn, and often on hillier sites, such as Burley-on-the-Hill, there will be several of them. He discusses the half-terrace walk, or Ha Ha, and gives its proper cross section (in his composite figure on *IR* II 50). He praises that feature for enclosing gardens, and notes that it is much superior to using walls. He prefers a water filled ditch on the outside, but notes that though it is not always possible to obtain, it is the better alternative to the dry graff or fosse. He also notes, rather ponderously, that it was not used in England until recently, and was first introduced by a "Gentleman deservedly honour'd with some considerable Posts belonging to the Architectural Province", that is, his friend Vanbrugh.

With the Parterre Switzer at last comes to what most of his early readers would consider the real garden, the heart of the matter. It soon becomes clear Switzer would relegate it to a lesser importance. It is identified ". . . here in *England*, by that level Division of Ground, that generally speaking, that faces the South and best Front of an House, furnish'd, as it always has been with us, with Greens, Flowers &c. These the *French* . . . divide into several Kinds . . . and according to the Manner they are set off and adorn'd, *viz.* Bowling green, or plain Parterres, the method of which they own to have receive'd from *England*, and Parterres of Embroidery &c." And to avoid being thought "singular" Switzer includes examples of intricately patterned parterres, but at the same time makes it abundantly clear that he advocates employing the plain and decent kind. For him the parterre is the necessary horizontal frame, and horticultural accompaniment to the house, and at the same time the frame for the prospect from the house. And it ought to be bounded on either side by terraces and woods. He is at pains to ensure that there is a balance of axes from the centre of the house, with the parterre leading the eye forward, but with strong attractions to left and right, along the first terraces, too. The parterre's width is usually slightly greater than the main front, or, in really big houses, the central bays or main block. Its depth should be between two and a half and three times its width. For Switzer this should not exceed 350 feet (or 107 metres). See Caversham and Holme Lacy (below) for this advice in practice.

Next come Woods and Groves, which are "the greatest of all the Natural Embellishments of our Country-Seats" (*IR* II 196), and as one of his names for the kind of landscape design he is advocating is Forest Garden, this can hardly come as surprising. (As Switzer was a Hampshire man he will have known the New Forest, and thus be aware that *forest* does not equate to *woods* only, but is much richer and more varied.) It is at this point that he recounts the story of Wray Wood and the puzzling differences between those who "Pretend to Judgement", who would have had a large tract of noble forest cut down to be replaced by a regular star plantation. In such discussions, "the best and most general Rules that (in Words) I can possibly lay down, are to endeavour to follow and improve the Advantages of Nature, and not to strain her beyond her due Bounds" (*IR* II 197). But by that he also means that for plantations in parks and such wide and open grounds great figures of imperceptible regularity (made up of platoons and avenues) are appropriate and even desirable. These will usually be on the north sides of great houses, where they can be well appreciated as visitors approach by carriage.

Volume 3 of *Ichnographia Rustica* is the place where Switzer comes to consider the design of the whole place, and he begins it with a recapitulation of the qualities expected of the Good Designer. To follow nature, to take advantage of every opportunity for improvement a site can offer, to clear-fell only those woods impinging on the southern aspects of the main buildings, and only then after due thought and deliberation, and once the site of the house is selected, or humoured if it is already in place, then a good designer is allowed a Little Regularity near the main building, but "after he has Stroke out of Art, some of the Roughest and Boldest of his Strokes, he ought to pursue Nature afterwards, and by as many Twinings and Windings as his *Villa* will allow, will endeavour to diversify his Views, always striving that they may be so intermix't, as not to be discover'd all at once; but that there should be as much as possible something new and diverting, while the Whole should correspond together by the mazie Error of his natural Avenues and Meanders" (*IR* III 5–6).

For Switzer if intending improvers were to achieve these ideals there is one further requirement that they must fulfil, and that is that their imaginations should be suitably nourished, as critical for the designer as it is for the philosopher to cultivate his understanding. To that end they must make themselves masters of all rural scenes: ". . . if he is not well versed yet he ought have a general idea of everything that is Noble and Stately in Art, whether it appear in Statuary, in the great Works of Architecture, which are in their present Glory, or in the Ruins of those which flourish'd in former Ages." This was good advice, no doubt, and it was soon to be followed, but the additional requirement that improvers become men of taste before they can judge merit in the art of landscape making will cost his reputation, and dearly. For many will believe a nourished imagination is sufficient in itself and forget that the mastery of all the other requirements of designers of landscape remained essential also. Even by the mid-18th century such men of taste as the coterie of Horace Walpole, his Committee of Taste, or slightly later the vicar-critics, and then such like Uvedale Price, would become very knowing indeed about what makes a good landscape. When these men read Switzer's rhapsodic calls for designers to follow nature, they applauded a fellow man of taste, but when they then looked at his (by then old-fashioned seeming) illustrations, the result was laughter or derision. Fortunately, there were still a few ideal client-designers in the earlier part of the 18th century who took him seriously, illustrations and all.

There are three illustrations which show such designs at the landscape scale; the two for the Manor of Paston in volume 2 (essentially a scaled down version of Grimsthorpe) and his bigger plate 33 based on Castle Howard, the "Plan of a Forest or Rural Garden" discussed in volume 3. (The 1742 edition contains a further plan, based on a mix of Blenheim and Castle Howard, which was made circa 1728.) From these, and from his further commentary, we can illustrate more fully his ideas, and assess the effects they may have had on the improvers of his time.

Paston covers a notional 24 acres and is probably the smallest possible exemplar of a fully fledged estate containing the whole range of elements for a functioning country life. (Horace Walpole's Strawberry Hill, an early suburban essay, at its largest, was half this size.) Paston and Riskins are equivalent. However small it is, he has managed to illustrate the kernel of his theory. Switzer has already established the essential background, the supposed found topography of Paston before the design, in his worked examples of surveying, and these are referred to as establishing the structure of the outer parts of the example design. The scheme responds to the "mazy error" the topography had suggested, conforming to the 11 mostly irregular fields and enclosures found, yet now composed about the old Crooked Lane into *Rural Gardens*. That old Crooked Lane he has tidied into the long axis of the design, his "Bold Stroke", a middle walk of near 500 yards which will "be lik'd by every impartial Person that sees it on Paper, it being as Long as the middle Line in very large Gardens" (*IR* III 83).

His Bold Strokes are necessary because as soon as they are perceived he has already taken steps to undermine that strength and has begun to introduce alternative view points, and view zones, laterally. For instance the first of the three terraces just outside the main garden front invites views to the sides which are of the kitchen quarters; a few steps down, the next invites views, and by its strong horizontal shape tempts company to turn aside, and to what quickly becomes a seeming bastion overlooking a river! It is only when the third terrace is reached in a few steps, axially, that the geometry of the parterre and middle walk fully kicks in. Therefore, the Bold Strokes are comforting reminders of the underlying structure in exploring what is quite unlike great gardens with middle walks. First of all, the parterre is exceptionally plain, bowling green-like and furnished with "English Elms planted upon the top of the Terrace Walk, that goes around it . . ." In the commentary he makes it clear that these surrounding walks are only meant to be "but half a Terrace". This is an important detail, because it is thus clear that what looks on paper like a strong enclosure (a line of trees) is instead a "weak" enclosure. The rows of elms give vertical definition, while the horizontal is marked by grass slopes towards the parterre, and on its outside beyond the row of trees by a sunk fence (or Ha Ha). This means the adjacent quarters are lightly screened but still in full view, and in the quarters themselves are the kitchen and fruit gardens, with their own internal hedging as their culture requires. What appears a standard arrangement is deceiving, and the fact that the whole of this "interior" part is itself a very large hexagon fenced by ornamental fortification expands the variety of views even further. Despite its appearance on paper its architecture makes it a rather diffuse design . . . defined and crisp doubtless, but at the same time with views across and through the surrounding structural parts.

Following the attractive middle walk, by the time the basin with its fountain is reached, a third of the way along, it becomes obvious that the avenue itself has disappeared, to become a walk diversified by groves of forest trees alternating with lower hedge-rows over which are "Glances into the little Corn Fields that lie on each

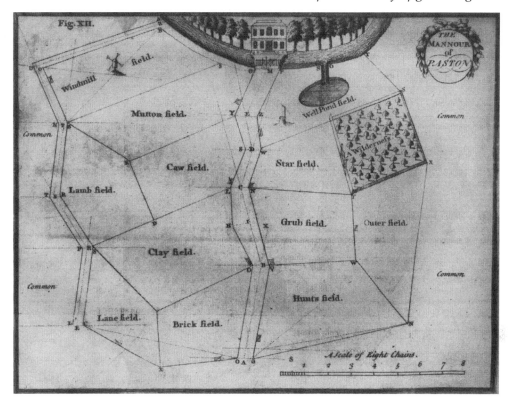

Figure 2.10 "The Mannour of Paston" as found. Reproduced from Stephen Switzer, *Ichnographia Rustica*, 1718, II 98.

side" (*IR* III 83). In these gaps, or through the groves, will be further gates leading to quite different kinds of walks. These are to be hedged too, but they meander into serpentines, or into straight or irregular crooked ways by turn, and along them are occasional gaps to look into the adjacent cornfields, or pastures, or even ploughed cultivated land. Where these walks cross are to be locations for basins, or cabinets, or statues, or simply further little gardens. Thus, in these outer parts "the Owner may Walk round it, and a-cross it, in his Night Gown, and Slippers; and visit all his Affairs, either late at Night, or early in the Morning; without either Dirt; or Dew. And seeing those are the chief times, either for Business or Pleasure, in the whole Day, I can't, but think that these imperfect Hints will be very acceptable to the World" (*IR* III 94).

Plate 33, "The Plan of a Forest or Rural Garden", meant to be bound in volume 2 at page 44, delivers the same message but is Switzer's attempt to increase his scale to that of a good sized estate, a landscape scale. Even so anomalies remain. The width of the walks and rides which separate the fields in the outer quarters is shown several times wider than in reality. Although his commentary warns of this, the diagrammatic nature of these illustrations needs to be reiterated. He calls attention to its similarity to Castle Howard, but it soon becomes clear that when writing he has left his designs elsewhere, or as he writes the description he begins to "design" afresh: thus, what he writes, and what is contained on plate 33, or indeed Paston, or the late additional large scale plan, varies in detail. This should not have undermined confidence in his readers; it is not that he does not know, or has forgotten; rather, it is likely because all these variables are interchangeable, which he often points out. The template that the illustrations show applies as a diagram, and just which of the elements go into it, and precisely where, will ever be a matter of judgement on the ground. His purpose was to show that all the elements of a country estate *could* be accommodated in his Rural Garden scheme.

By 1718, from the smallest scale of 25 acres to the largest, Switzer has demonstrated precisely how a *Man may make a Pretty Landskip of his Possessions*. At Grimsthorpe he had shown how an existing estate could be transformed into one. Similarly there was an example close to London where Riskins, the smaller version, had become the occasional resort of a young group of ambitious writers, soon to become influential ones, among whom were Jonathan Swift, and particularly Alexander Pope, who were able, and so minded, to spread the word in support of *Rural and Extensive Gardening*. And Bathurst had recently begun his very large scale version of Switzer's scheme at Cirencester. There is also an intermediate size of place, Whetham, belonging to one of Switzer's friends, whose beginnings may go back to the start of the 18th century, and whose extensive water-works had been noted as comparable to the greatest ones by 1712. Between then and 1725 it too was turned into a *Rural and Natural Garden* which thoroughly illustrates Switzer's method as taught in *Ichnographia Rustica*. Critically it also includes all those happy accidents and opportunities which arise from the site and the requirements of the place.

Whetham, Wiltshire

Figure 2.11 Whetham, Wiltshire: anonymous 1846 view from the south-east. Money-Kyrle MSS.

A rural and farm-like way of gardening 67

Early in her reign in 1703 on one of her sojourns to Bath for the treatment of the symptoms of gout, Queen Anne honoured the grandson of her father's Chancellor of the Exchequer, Sir John Ernle, by agreeing to visit him at Whetham House, a few miles north of Devizes. John Kyrle Ernle (1682–1725), who had inherited in 1697, had only recently come of age. Whetham was a comfortable gentleman's house, obviously fit to receive his monarch and her entourage but, unlike nearby Dyrham, far from a great or power house. Even the Chancellor himself had a grander neighbour, Sir Orlando Bridgeman, who had also been in office in government, and whose larger estate Bowood lies immediately north of Whetham.

Whetham is an estate long occupied by the same family. At the beginning of the 18th century its house was spruce yet in a rather old-fashioned style still with casement windows and a generally vernacular aspect. From the house's beginnings there were various gardens, and by 1700 an ample garden had been laid out on the west front. So in a sense Whetham was a typical kind of place, but presentable, and familiar to most parishes, perhaps the sort of place Addison imagined Sir Roger de Coverley inhabiting. It has hardly changed its nature since. But why should it claim our attention? There are several reasons, chiefly that Switzer praised it and his friend its owner, citing especially the water-works, which he compared favourably not only with Dyrham and Chatsworth but also with those of Italy and France. From other sources these exceptional qualities are corroborated. But its true nature lay long concealed, if in plain view.

Whetham, with Bowood, Spye and Bowden, occupies one of the hills of northern Wiltshire chosen by the fortunate for their estates where a straggling end of the Cotswolds meets Chalk. There is the trace of an ancient road sometimes called the Roman Road, or Wandsdyke, which marks the southern edge of the Whetham estate. The Whetham brook rises nearby and has formed a working mill pond, in its present form since the 17th century, and under Lancelot Brown's guidance feeds the lake he made at Bowood in the 1770s. A secondary stream rises out of Bowden Hill and Whetham Wood and flows east to join the Whetham brook some distance north of the house. These water courses have given a changeful, seemingly hilly form to the site of the house and the contiguous estate. Whetham House sits high on the west bank of the mill pond, and to the south its park lies also high, beyond a sharpish dip, and together they form a long north-south level which forms the axis of the designed improvements. On the west side of the house, beyond the Best Garden, on rising ground towards Sandy Lane is a smaller park. This falls steeply away towards Whetham Wood, where the secondary stream marks the division of these two elements.

At the beginning of his *Hydrostaticks and Hydraulicks*, after praising the natural beauties of the Wye, Switzer further boasts, "*Nor* need we in all Probability give Place to *Italy* or *France* itself, in some artificial Cascades and beautiful Falls of Water in *England*; those of Mr. *Blaithwaites* at *Durham* near the *Bath*, of Mr. *Ernly's* at *Whetham*, those of *Chatsworth*, belonging to the great and noble family of Cavendishes, are worthy of Account . . ." (*Hydro* II 12). When I was a young postgraduate student beginning my research on Switzer it was from such a reference that I took heart, especially so when I discovered further details of the Whetham water-works in a manuscript diary of a tour of 1712 by Charles Hope, 1st Earl of Hopetoun (1681–1742). However, although I anticipated getting further information about Switzer from the descendants of his old friend, on writing to Roger Ernle Money-Kyrle it transpired that no such water-works survived at Whetham, nor any memory

68 *A rural and farm-like way of gardening*

Figure 2.12 Whetham, Wiltshire: cascade-house analogy (north to right). Reproduced from Stephen Switzer, Introduction to a General System of Hydrostaticks and Hydraulicks, 1729, II plate 40. Private collection.

of them, or of Switzer, and the only information available then from the Money-Kyrle family concerned the collapse of the mill dam in 1918. There was also in those days a disinclination to accept the validity of evidence in contemporary topographical engravings, notably those of Johannes Kip and Leonard Knyff, nor was much credence given to any authors apart from the canon of greats. So Anthony Mitchell, then the National Trust's curator at Dyrham, and his colleagues even more so, was reluctant to believe Switzer's even fuller and more detailed praise of the gardens there (confirmed as it was by the engraved view of Kip and Knyff), not least because all evidence of them had disappeared by the end of the 18th century (Mitchell 1978, Jackson-Stops 1991 30).

Hopetoun was very precise in his notes about Whetham, a little less so about Badminton, Longleat and Dyrham, which he also studied, and it is clear that he is describing something in place and in perfect working order. He makes no mention of the design of the rest of Whetham, nor indeed how the water-works fit in, simply noting that they are sited with "Little walks in a wood like a wilderness and dropped in it, a handsome cascade". His account of the cascade-house is recognizable in Switzer's analogous illustration published some 17 years later, but his attention to detail suggests he had found something he wished to emulate in his own works at Hopetoun House, near Edinburgh. It was "25 feet broad and near as high & cornice proceeding a foot or two [with] 4 statues one top about 5 feet high arched door in middle . . . at foot of it a dolphin's head where part of the water falls into a basin sideways Part of it one every side goes by the basin into a pond . . . [and] then the building advances with a sweep one every side about 15 or 20 feet. In every sweep there is a niche arched on top." (All references to Hopetoun are from Hope MS 1712, Hopetoun House, with author's rendering into metropolitan *English*.)

Hopetoun House had been begun for Lord Hopetoun during his minority, and was designed by Sir William Bruce of Kinross, working closely with Alexander Edward. Its site west of Edinburgh and dramatically overlooking the Forth was exploited by Bruce and Edward with their characteristic imagination and wit, and is probably their best effort. Both had died in the first decade of the 18th century but had already established and overseen the grounds of Hopetoun House with their principal features in place. Bruce had incorporated prospects of historic and picturesque buildings and natural objects into his landscape compositions from the 1670s, and Edward, like the nearby improving neighbour John Erskine, 23rd Earl of Mar (1675–1732), had developed this notion further into views on the diagonal, and then into any view at hand. Such a method of composition resulting in a delightfully irregular series of avenues terminated by suitably interesting buildings and objects is best seen at Alloa, Clackmannanshire (Stewart 2002, passim but esp. 68 et seq). Their early master-plan for Hopetoun House apparently included hints which were developed into the famous Sea-Walk Garden of the second decade. So much would have done been during Lord Hopetoun's majority and under his direction. He remained in search of statuary and the detail design, and particularly the extensive water-works which are recorded by William Adam's survey of the grounds of Hopetoun in 1726 may be traced to this tour of 1712.

At Whetham he found the newly finished water-works, and noted them minutely. The most notable feature is the principal cascade. This began at the cascade-house and flowed eastward flanked by rows of yew (at three or four feet much too close to the water according to Switzer), and then it descended some 60 feet in height in a "sheet of water, the fall will be 8 or 10 feet then it runs level for 20 or 30 feet, & so falls cascade-wise for 10 or 12 steps & so continues for 500 feet in length", finishing in a circular basin of 25 or 30 feet where a sculpture group made up of three horse heads spouted water in the centre with three further fountains apparently set at water level towards the basin's edge.

Clearly he had found the water-works at Dyrham also worthy of emulation. Dyrham and Whetham estates are, at something less than 100 acres, of similar size, but their owners chose different ways of demonstrating their power and wealth. Both were, as Switzer noted, "only private gentlemen," and Ernle was content to live the retired life, while William Blathwayt chose a more public, fashionable and grander role for himself, and his house and grounds show it. This may also be partly to do with the character of the monarch he served. Switzer had commented on the change of taste at court to a simpler and less showy manner under Anne than in her sister and brother-in-law's time, contrasting the former's disdain for the fussier crowded gardens of William and Mary's "*Dutch* Taste", which Blathwayt's Dyrham certainly showed. It is quite crowded, but it is hardly fussy. One of its principal differences to Whetham lies in the house's internal nature and layout. Dyrham is very much in the current fashion with its large and numerous sash and case windows, its somewhat classical architectural manner, but strikingly in its furnishing and layout in the style as published by Daniel Marot and adopted all over Europe. The manner can be seen at Dyrham, where there are a number of suites, a series of two or three related and graded rooms

70 A *rural and farm-like way of gardening*

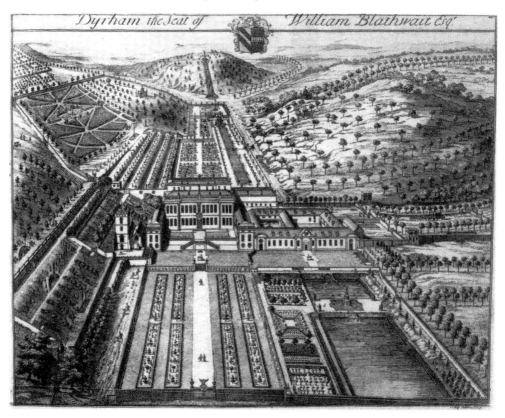

Figure 2.13 Dyrham, Gloucestershire (north to left). View by Kip and Knyff. Reproduced from Atkyns, *Ancient and Present State of Gloucestershire*, 1712.

of reception, plus several quite private ones at the far end of the range. These are also related externally to the design of the grounds, most completely and ingeniously at Dyrham, where the architect William Talman and George London worked closely together. But uniquely the really *principal* room at Dyrham was the Orangery.

Because of the peculiarities of its site the grounds of Dyrham are organized about the east-west axis (or more accurately a series of such axes), and this plus the topography upsets the convention of country house site planning. Blathwayt's architect at Wimbledon was also Talman. There he had also shown himself as responsive to unconventional designs for site planning as he had at Castle Howard (see above). Therefore, what might be thought of as entrance front and garden front are pleasingly confused. The Orangery, and also the Suites of State, faces east over the larger series of gardens. Blathwayt's own suite looked west from the upper floor. The topography of Dyrham also means that these gardens receive sunshine all day. (Even the most constrained steep slopes hard on the north face of the building are also sunlit.) Dyrham was one of the sites that early 18th century visitors to Bath frequented on excursions, and its beauties were well regarded and its water-works especially praised. However, its style had already begun to fade from fashion, and indeed Switzer led in his condemnations of the *Dutch* Taste; yet it is equally clear that he saw its exceptional beauties: he included a long and detailed description of it pointing out the ". . . beautiful Irregularity, here a Dale, there a Mount, here a winding Valley, there a purling Stream &c" of Dyrham in his *Ichnographia Rustica* argument (*IR* II 113–127). These are not the things one usually associates with the garden designs of William and Mary's reign.

Now we cannot look at Kip's view as published in 1712 in Robert Atkyns' *Ancient and Present State of Gloucestershire* without being struck by the *formality* of it all. That is our problem, not Switzer's nor that of anyone else in the early 18th century, who saw rather what he had just described, in its context of the mixture of all the beauties of the place . . . extensive open and lightly wooded parkland to the south and east with further hills and dales; to the west and north beyond more parkland and wilderness are orderly parterres and terraces, with Dyrham House in the distance. The terrace walks along the north slope stepped upwards through to a wilderness and finally to a loosely wooded mount with its Windsor Seat. But if Dyrham is the climax of a manner of design, Whetham decidedly is not, and although it fits more easily into the coming looser style, it is less clear that there is any other connection apart from fortuitously missing a brief fashion in interior design. However, we now can be sure that although the design of its grounds responds to and celebrates the same varied topography it is of a significantly different kind from Dyrham. But nothing about the design of Whetham's grounds is apparent at first view, nor does a comparison of plans through time show any signs of design . . . yes, there is a clear axial arrangement from the south, and perhaps also the north, but it hardly seems to be what Switzer called a *Bold Stroke by Art*. And there is a large rectangular area of garden on the west side of the house. These two are the only elements which appear to be designed. Since the once famous water-works have not been seen in nearly 300 years, apart from the generous natural seeming mill pond the rest is either wooded or planted with crops, as the topography might have suggested best. Thus, our understanding of the two places would have to remain so partial as to make further discussion pointless.

In his series of county studies of historic gardens Timothy Mowl called our attention to a hitherto unknown document at Bowood. This is the Tything Plan made in 1728, which records the divisions of the neighbouring estate of Whetham (Mowl 2004b 62), made as part of the legal dispositions following Switzer's friend's untimely death in 1725 and his daughter's inheritance of the estate. Analysis of this plan is presented in Wendy Bishop's excellent account of Whetham in the journal *Garden History* (Bishop 2010). Although it is not a garden plan, and certainly not a scheme for improvement, it is actually much more. Although it is intended as a simple survey, it indicates the size and use of each and every part of the estate in the mid-1720s, including the disposition of what was considered as garden. It also shows the site of the water-works, and gives clues to elucidate some of Hopetoun's less than clear remarks. The Whetham Tything Plan shows us, without meaning to do so, that what we would assume was a simple undesigned estate of little pretension, and with its constituent parts placed almost by nature, is in fact a very early *designed landscape*. It shows that Whetham was a designed estate where the useful parts, that is, the hayfields, the woodlands, the coppice woods and warrens for fattening game for use, are mixed together with more decorative parts, definitely in what Addison referred to as "a *Pindarick* Manner". The gardens – and gardens of various sorts, not only kitchen gardens and the Best Garden, but also gardens reaching out into the estate far from the house, designed for walking contemplation or pure pleasure, or even further away and detached – are still gardens. It also shows where the park is treated both as a park and as a designed feature.

Enough changes of colour in the washes survive to reinforce the textual references as to what was thought of as garden; otherwise, we might have been tempted to dismiss these curiously shaped areas reaching outwards from the areas closer to the house, but also quite detached and some distance away, as a misconception or scribal error of some sort. There can be no mistaking it: they are as shown and described as . . . *gardens*.

In other words, the Whetham Tything Plan is of exceptional interest because it indicates for the first time just what a *Rural and Extensive* or *Farm-like Garden* of the early 18th century looks like. It shows just how Switzer's ideas were actually put into practice. Although they are in themselves clear enough in *Ichnographia Rustica*, until corroborated by evidence such as this, they are apt to be taken as simply so much *theory*. Given the personal association between him and Kyrle Ernle, Switzer's residence and nursery nearby, his work for other improvers in the area, and most notably the fact that in this very early period the only advocate for such a garden-estate was Switzer himself, his authorship of the Whetham layout is a very near certainty. There remains much we cannot know as to the detailed furnishing of the place as an early 18th century garden. Still, much of that can be adduced by reference to other schemes, or parts of them, for which such evidence exists; or even relying on Switzer's published works to furnish absent detail will give a fuller picture of what the finished Whetham was like. From what we have seen at Dyrham, comparable, nearby and contemporary, and even taking into account the seeming personal differences between Blathwayt and Kyrle Ernle, Whetham will have been crisper, smarter and rather more neatly finished than its remains today might suggest, not entirely unlike Dyrham but likely a deal plainer than that then still fashionable show-house.

That Whetham has survived unaltered seems exceptional, but is probably more common than we might have supposed. Its creator died prematurely, and his only child, Constantia soon married the Earl of Kinnoul and moved north to Perthshire. The other Ernle kin, to whom Whetham ultimately came, lived comfortably in Herefordshire at The Holm, so Whetham became a somewhat secondary estate. The Bridgeman neighbours to the north at Bowood did prosper in the same period, and their estate received the improvements the mid to late 18th century is famous for, and acquired a new house by Robert Adam. The grounds were re-designed by Lancelot Brown. All the while Whetham remained, apparently, without further *improvement*, apart from a new road connecting Calne and Sandy Lane which cut the estate into two parts. Otherwise, it did not affect it, except perhaps to underline the impression that it was a place beyond modern improvement. How long its water-works survived we cannot say: those nearby at Spye (see below) were deteriorating already in the 1720s, whereas those at Dyrham survived much longer but by the 1790s were so neglected that they were removed and the place "reconciled to modern taste" (Jackson-Stops 1991 30). From the state of the site of the Whetham water-works it appears they simply mouldered away to ruin, leaving only curious lumps in the woods.

At his death in 1725 Ernle's Whetham had two main entrances: one near Sandy Lane, where a simple semi-circular space announced the estate, and the north entry, apparently the more commonly used, which turned south near Cuff's Corner (now part of the Bowood domain) to follow the high ground on the west side of the Whetham brook to the axis of Ernle's design, which begins slightly north of the water-works, and then proceeds all the way to the south edge of Whetham at the Roman Road, which lies beyond the more modern road connecting Calne and Sandy Lane

- Ⓐ Cuff's Corner Entrance
- Ⓑ Cascades
- Ⓒ Whetham Wood
- Ⓓ Coppice with reservoirs, stream and carriage
- Ⓔ Best Garden
- Ⓕ Whetham Pond
- Ⓖ Great Coniger
- Ⓗ Dyers Meadow
- Ⓘ Coppice and Gardens
- Ⓙ The Park
- Ⓚ Hayfield Wood
- Ⓛ The Ring
- Ⓜ Gardens and Ponds

Figure 2.14 Whetham, Wiltshire: plan of the estate in the early 18th century (north to top). Reconstruction by the author.

mentioned above. Within this domain there was nothing to disturb and intrude, and anything out-with it could be simply *called in* as adopted ornament. The estate is made up of the conventional elements of park, fields, woodland, ponds, farmhouse and secondary house, with the big house at its heart, along with its gardens, paddocks and home woodland.

According to the Tything Plan the core of the scheme, the House Platt, contained nearly 30 acres, and of that the Best Garden occupied roughly a third, making it a substantial element, about which we can say little more than that it lay to the west of the north-south axis, and faced into the rising ground of the Great Coniger. It will doubtless have been a formal exercise using parterres, much more likely *a l'Anglaise* than otherwise, perhaps ornamented also by sculpture, and perhaps also with conical greens. There would have been various sub-sections to provide variation, and these will have also given spatial variety by means of groves of standard yews. This Best Garden was separated from the Great Coniger by a Ha Ha, but also by the carriage-way from the north which led around to the entry court at the south front, with paddock stables and service further around the house to the east. The north-south axis is celebrated from the south front as a long walk on a terraced plateau looking through a thin coppice wood to the mill pond and the rising ground beyond of parkland called Hall Ridge. Woodland along the west side would be thicker, masking the Sandy Lane drive and the Farm which lies conveniently nearby.

The axial walk runs level for 100 metres or so, and then falls away sharply to rise again into a rectangular figure of over 30 acres. From the theatre-like north end of this three distinct ways are offered to the pedestrian company. The obvious way would be to follow the view into a Great Rectangular figure as the now celebrated axis becomes an out-size *walk* which carries on the eye southward until closed by a distant wood. But two further equally enticing ways are offered. To the left a short and easy turn leads through the coppice wood to an avenue called the Park Walk, and this runs parallel with the rectangular figure towards the wood on the south side of the estate. An equally easy short turn towards the right would approach a quite different kind of woodland walk through what the survey identifies simply as "Coppice and Gardens". This is the first element we meet that suggests Switzer's eye, and no other's. He earnestly taught in *The Nobleman Gentleman and Gardener's Recreation* the value of these cheap woodlands, how to prepare ground for them and how to exploit them, not only in the "new Seats but in noble and ancient ones" like Whetham, and how to make a coppice wood into a garden. "But when I mention *Gard'ning*, 'tis not that which has been commonly us'd and understood by that name; I mean, Flowring Parterres, Box-work, Clipt Plants &c but Wood, Water, and such-like Natural and Rural, yet Noble and Magnificent Decorations of the Country *Villa*" (*IR* I 271) Thus, this turning from the main walk, at the beginning of the park and its Figure he introduces this new element as an alternative to the avenue, and it leads informally past the Farm on the one hand and the Park on the other to another surprise, or group of surprises. These southern and western coppice gardens are the first signs of the *enfilade* or circuit walks: here they remain sometimes as discrete woodland gardens. They may well have been in place in 1712: if so, Lord Hopetoun did not mention them. It is more likely that these southern works were added between then and 1725, in the period when he married Constantia Rolt and they had begun a family. In any case these are still very early, and are the first for which we have evidence so full and contemporary. But even so we must speculate. The only indication we have of the manner of making the junction between these gardens and the adjacent park is a line, and it is most likely that these are half-terraces, with a wall to the outside and a walk with slopes to the inside, as described for Paston and used also at Cirencester (below) at the same time. (This coppice garden became the site of the later road from Calne to Sandy Lane.)

Also from this feature the visitor would become increasingly aware of a big formal element called The Ring, which will have been glimpsed to the south through the thin of enclosure the coppice wood provides. This figure, of slope-work, or plantation perhaps, or cut out of the grasses seasonally, was at the south-west edge of the park: it abutted a further detached "garden and Ponds" in coppice wood to the south-east which became Hayfield Wood to the west. What it was, and what if any use it was intended for, we cannot say. Its shape is circular, but also with balanced amphitheatrical ends on its east-west axis. There were similar figures of forest trees proposed in early schemes for Blenheim, and later to be found at Nostell Priory, where there are the great Sweeps in the north Park, and a slightly more rectilinear version lay in the park in front of the house at Ditchley. As The Ring is so close to the old Wandsdyke, or Roman Road, and the more open Chalk landscape to the south towards Devizes, it may well have an antiquarian character. Switzer's friend Stukeley had recently been in the district for his research into Avebury and the other *Druidical* sites, and they would have discussed such matters at length, but did such discussions lead to The Ring? Alternatively, it may well have been the earliest of examples of a ground for the game of cricket. We can say for certain only that its southern edge melds into the noted coppice of gardens and ponds running east-west and leading back to the avenue of the Park Walk, and also adjacent to the Roman Road.

If The Ring had not attracted them to explore further our visitors might have paused at Hayfield Wood, or have been tempted to cross the Drive northwards from the Sandy Lane entrance into another kind of park, the Little Coniger on the right, or straight on to hayfields (with curious incursions of cut grasses depicted on the 1728 plan), or into Dyers Meade, across which is yet another coppice wood . . . containing an early water garden complete with serpentine stream. This was the largest of the outlying gardens, at the southern edge of Whetham Wood itself. This afforded a shady walk with views of the house, and of the Great Coniger. It contained its own serpentine stream and ponds, plus vineyards, and led back to the north-south axis of the scheme, by way of the famous water-works. From the Tything Plan we have a very good idea of the shape and disposition and just how these water-works fitted into the now more obvious design of the whole place.

From this wood and across the entry lane is the water-works coppice, and following the serpentine stream visitors are first aware of three very narrow cascades falling down from the left, but it is only when the Horses Heads Basin is nearly reached that the Cascade proper is seen, although its presence will have been heralded by its noise long before. To appreciate its full force the visitor needed to walk at least a quarter way around the Horses Heads Basin, and look upward 60 feet to the west to the cascade-house. Here the visitor is not invited to climb up beside the Cascade, as at Dyrham with its double sided stairs and resting places. Rather, the water is further defined by the yews planted close alongside. Neither Switzer nor Lord Hopetoun mentions how, or whether, the company was expected to enjoy the Cascade along its lengthy fall. Presumably it was not mentioned because to both it would have been obvious: closer inspection must have been much more informal, and through the adjacent coppice wood kept clear of under-wood either along prepared paths (which are not shown on the survey so clearly they were not made up) or more likely at will through the woodland. This seems to be confirmed by one of the very few documentary references from Ernle where he notes his birthday party on 7 May 1712, when ". . . seventy neighbours dined here, & the Poor People reliev'd, who dined in the great Walk of the Wilderness, and walked about it with the Musick" (Bishop 2010 74). Hopetoun had noted that the water-works were "dropped" in a "wood cut out like a wilderness".

At the end of the north-south axis, and quite close at hand to the water-works, is a curious notation on the Tything Plan, a sort of Gloriette, a largish circle identified simply as *A Grove* (and it looks as if it may have had a small basin at its centre). Since this lies in a large woodland (denominated as Coppice) it must have had a quite different character, one supposes a much denser nature which might suggest evergreens, like yew. That would allow it to function as the full stop, or at least semi-colon, that its placement seems to call for.

One way to see the cascade that would never have been guessed by critic or historian before the hint by Ernle discovered by Wendy Bishop (Bishop 2010 74), in which in July 1712 he records that three squares of glass in the door of the cascade had been broken in the night, and had to be replaced, costing 10 shillings [£150]. Anyone would assume this meant a door in the cascade-house, but no, and this is confirmed by Lord Hopetoun's heretofore puzzling reference in his visit, in the same summer, when he mentions, "At the foot of the Pond [and he clearly means the Horses Heads Basin] is another piece of grotto work. [It] opens with two leaves of a door & a glass that represents the whole cascade" (Hope MS 1712). Therefore, the cascade was designed to be seen also as a reflection in a mirror! There has been much in the design of these water-works which is surprising, and subtly so, verging perhaps on the theatrical, and surprise wettings in a garden were still to be expected and even looked for (so long as it was someone else of the company), but this is a surprise of a different order. And just how it worked, and how the piece of grotto work was designed, remains at issue. As it is not shown on the 1728 plan, it possibly had been removed between 1712 and 1725.

With regard to Switzer's choice of illustration of the Whetham cascade-house, admittedly only as similar, or of like kind, his choice of Jean Le Paultre's work from Versailles suggests a classical composition, and Hopetoun's account bears this out, except that when he mentions the other piece of grotto work, with the looking glass, one wonders if the cascade-house at Whetham might have been a trifle more bucolic, as more in the style of those at Spye, or at the Upper Lodge at Hampton Court. When Hopetoun indicates that both buildings at Whetham are roofed with *sage* or *moss* it is really difficult to reconcile such materials being used to keep a classical construction safe and dry. This is especially so if it is be assumed that he meant thatch, but if that were so he would doubtless have used different terms. The manner of the cascade-house's siting might clarify this somewhat. To work well and easily it would more than likely have been built into the bank at the top of the cascade, where the entrance from Cuff's Corner passes by. From the entry side, or outside, and especially there, one can see the sense of, as it were, hiding the back of cascade-house, which was doubtless mostly filled with tanks to facilitate the flow of water. The showy side, as we have observed, is only seen after much preparation and long approach. So if this be true, then the roofing could well be flat, or a gently sloping plane which could easily have been covered with sage, in the manner in which sedum coverings are sometimes used now.

As to its dating we must conclude that the water-works were completed in 1712, most likely in the spring, and certainly by the summer. In anticipation of his 30th birthday celebrations, on 6 May 1712 Ernle moved the "great Head at the Cascade into the Arch with much labour and difficulty" (Bishop 2010 quoting Ernle's diary SWRO 1729/742). The pond which we can see on the Tything Plan is a large oval pool, on its long axis about 15 metres. This is almost as wide as the complete frontage of the cascade-house, including the curved wings or the "sweeps" to either side. From Hopetoun we learn there was an arched niche in each of these, verifying its similarity to those in Switzer's illustration. The final details from Hopetoun's account are "Two kind of niches", presumably on either side of the central arched door, and just under the cornice "there are three other niches with kind of statues in them", and, as we have noted, "the building is covered with sage or moss".

The head of the Cascades surveyed a large wooded slope towards the south, and to the east where the principal cascade, a little wider than its companion at Dyrham, fell in some ten stages or steps, the first beginning close to the oval pool by the cascade-house. On the broad and rounded hill southward are the three narrow cascades (noted above) arranged fan-wise, and seemingly disconnected from the big oval pool. These are open to a distant prospect to the south, past Whetham House and the Best Garden. This might have included a view of the chalk figure (if indeed it were then in place) or perhaps the distant hill-fort of Devizes. These secondary cascades are much narrower than the seven foot breadth Hopetoun records for the main cascade, but just how much narrower he neglects to note. From the Tything Plan it would appear they were about a third of that width, perhaps just over two feet wide, and therefore more of the nature of rills. As their runs are significantly shorter they will doubtless have been managed by a regular number of stepped falls and without the intervening straight canal-like runs of the broad cascade. These do not debouch directly into the Horses Heads Basin but join it indirectly and by way of the serpentine stream which runs along the bottom of the hill, where it joins the axial basin underground.

This all constitutes what we might have called the major, or principal, part of the water-works. But for all their interest and subtle design they make up a bare half of the scheme. All cascades and similar water-works depend on elaborate and often large scale accumulations of managed water, usually from some distance away. These do not normally figure in descriptions, and thus presumably were rarely shown off to company. This does not appear to have been so at Whetham. The water-carriage which fed the cascades started its journey in the west by a large pool in the wood adjacent to Dyers Meade, and adjacent to one of the vineyards at the far end of Whetham Wood. The ground falls away rather steeply from there eastward, so that the Great Coniger to the south is increasingly seen as a steepish slope, and since it was used for keeping game for the table it was enclosed by paling. This woodland, as a garden, with a serpentine stream provided its own charm and sufficient interest to entertain any visitor. The stream here is of course the same as is encountered at the foot of the narrower series of cascades, where it will have been given a crisper and smarter dressing appropriate to that place. But further away, in the wood, it would have been more appropriate for it to be, in Switzer's phrase, "a well govern'd pursuit of Nature" (*IR* I xix). He would have provided also in the actual water-carriage which started from the same far off pool, but made its own way further to the north side of the narrow woodland garden, and it would doubtless have been provided with a neatly channelled carriage rill whose dimensions Lord Hopetoun has furnished for us: ". . . the current that makes the cascade play will not be above two feet wide & the water runs about half a foot deep . . ." He also notes a trick bridge, probably over the more bucolic serpentine stream. "In the wood is a little bridge of one plank of timber 5 or 6 feet in length, that is fast on one side & has two iron bolts on the other side that when they are out if you go to one side of it it falls down with you & you fall into a little drik that wets one a foot or two deep . . ." (Hope MS 1712).

His widow lived on at Whetham until 1755 and brought up their daughter there until her own marriage in 1741. Her sister-in-law had returned to Wiltshire as a widow in the early 1720s to improve the neighbouring Spye Park (see below), and Switzer's work there may well have resulted from the Ernles' recommendation.

3 Early landscapes

At more than three hundred years' remove, and given the subsequent history of taste in garden making and designed landscapes, we are apt to downplay the strengths and attraction John James' *Theory and Practice of Gardening* must have had for 18th century British ideas about design. That it ran to several more editions, and updated ones too, before mid-century, and that it informed the design aspects of Philip Miller's more famous *Dictionary of Gardening* for more than 30 years, in other words well into the primacy of the landscape style, attests to this strength. It also shows the boldness of Stephen Switzer to propose, within just a few years, that the ideas James presented were not only out of date but really beside the point. When his grumbling rivals such the Rev John Laurence observed in 1716 that ". . . few can understand Mr Switzer's way of writing" they were understating the situation. In such a climate Switzer not only wrote his books but also established himself as a consultant designer of gardens and landscapes, and as far as we may judge, had to live by the income from such a new and, given his views about design, precarious profession.

Apart from Grimsthorpe in 1715 there were few gardens which could then be called landscapes . . . Cassiobury perhaps, Badminton was certainly big enough, and Blenheim, even without a large supporting estate, was also unfinished, possibly. Even Castle Howard, well on its way, was hardly there as yet. All these are certainly incipient landscapes. Of large gardens there was Wrest Park, big enough to have become a designed landscape, as it had its supporting estate, and might have become an early landscape, but it did not. Although Whetham appears to have been well on its way, its size is marginal. The term "a pretty landskip" had only recently been introduced. The drift of James' translation of D'Argenville would have led improvers to make larger gardens, without in any way changing their natures from the best, and mostly Continental, examples, and, led by the skilful and fortunate James Brydges, Duke of Chandos, most improvers did just that. Despite Switzer's glowing reference to that work, then just beginning at Edgeware, doubtlessly in the hope of securing Cannons as a design project after George London's death both Switzer and John Vanbrugh (Dobree and Webb 1927, 126), who had hoped to be its architect, were disappointed. Chandos chose James himself, and then relied on Richard Bradley, the most successful and prolific writer about gardens at the time, and also a professor of botany at Cambridge; it appears that Cannons was one of his few forays into consultancy. Similarly, the great scheme that London had recently initiated for the Childs at Wanstead apparently went (like Wrest) to London's nephew Thomas Acres to carry forward. There were other talented juniors in the Brompton Park enterprise, and one, Joseph Carpenter, was chosen by Henry Wise as the surviving partner to carry on the business with him there.

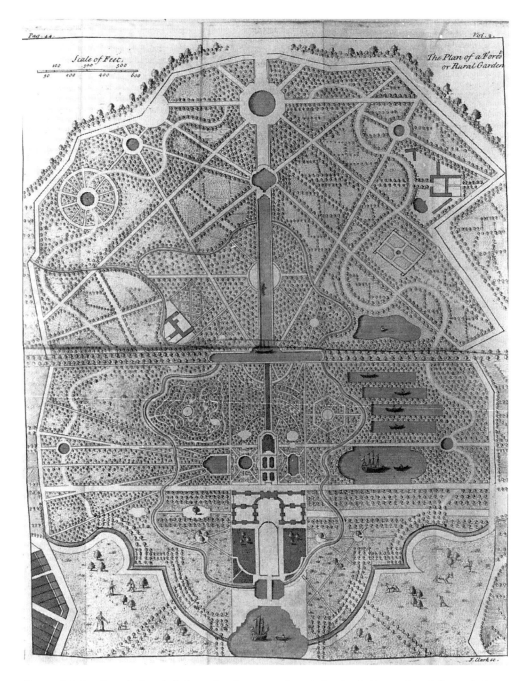

Figure 3.1 Stephen Switzer's "Plan of a Forest or Rural Garden". Reproduced from Switzer, *Ichnographia Rustica*, 1718, II plate 33. Private collection.

Early landscapes 81

Charles Bridgeman also worked with Wise for a time at Brompton Park, and joined him as his deputy before succeeding him in Crown work as the Royal Gardener in the later 1720s: in the 1710s Bridgeman had also become a consulting garden designer, working, among others, for a series of "new men" involved in the financial matters leading up to the South Sea Bubble and crash, and happily more consistently in the long term project for Lord Cobham at Stowe, his greatest work. The times were fluid, the talented advisers were many, and there were many men from many and varied backgrounds who were keen to be *improvers*.

Although London and all his partners had their beginnings as gardeners, albeit gardeners to very large estates, owned by powerful men of lively intellect, by 1714 the capabilities of the Brompton Park successors had outgrown even the large *gardens* they had created in England, and which were not uncommon on the Continent, and encompassed more than enough skills to satisfy the most elaborate of stretches of designed countryside, of *landscapes*. Of course it was not long before there were projects to justify and exploit these skills, but thus far Switzer was the only one of them who had shown how such ambition might be achieved. In the second decade of the new century the scope of these successors, whether as client or gardener, had grown bigger, and specializing in one or more aspects became not only possible but perhaps inevitable. So it seems to have been with Switzer.

Cirencester

Figure 3.2 Cirencester, Gloucestershire: garden front of the house. Reproduced from Samuel Rudder, *New History of Gloucestershire*, 1779. The Bodleian Libraries, University of Oxford.

As we have already seen, 1st Earl Bathurst had a taste for small scale gentlemanly farming at Riskins. However, his seat was at Cirencester, Gloucestershire. That was his estate, and he realized that it had to keep him and his family. As he was a powerful politician, his position, if not then positively dangerous, meant that was he clearly out of favour. So there would be no lucrative offices or favours from the government. Possessing such a large part of the Cotswolds cannot be seen as any kind of a disadvantage, except perhaps to an early 18th century potentate such as Chandos or either of the Marlboroughs, who had easy access to public funds and who happily used such access not only to extend their families' interests but also to support all sorts of improvements. Bathurst was not one of these; his circumstances, coupled with, as Switzer put it, ". . . a soft and sincere address, and a pleasing chearfulness . . . and an undissembled courtesy . . ." (*KG* dedication 1727) and what used to be called outdoorsy character, made him ideal to pursue the idea of making a pretty landskip of his possessions, acknowledged by Alexander Pope a few years later when he asked with his often quoted rhetorical flourish, "who builds like Boyle, who plants like Bathurst?" (Pope *Epistle to Burlington* 1732).

The making of Riskins would have been sufficient credit to Lord Bathurst as a garden maker, and it already had its nascent fan base, the informal *Scribblerus Club* of Alexander Pope, John Arbuthnott, Jonathan Swift and a few others who visited and enjoyed its charms. But Bathurst had a proper estate to manage, and to cultivate to provide needed income. It seems that from about 1716 onwards his attentions were increasingly directed west. The design, or master-plan, for these works, which were carried on from about 1715 into the 1740s, and beyond, has not survived: there was doubtless one made, and alterations or additions drawn up from time to time. We know Pope gave advice often and freely from the later 1710s on and during the 1720s, and we know it was not always taken (for Pope's role as a designer of grounds see Martin 1984a). However, in the mid-20th century it was not unusual simply to assume that such early 18th century works were somehow produced by the owners themselves, unaided by professional help. Thus it was that James Lees-Milne proposed that Bathurst was indeed his own designer. As a resident landowner dependent on the estate for his only income he would of course be most closely involved in all decisions affecting it, and as he was notable for his fondness for extensive planting it is equally obvious that his attention to that was also fully engaged. While the grounds of Cirencester have no hint about them of being amateur, and indeed exhibit much subtlety and surprise in their qualities as a designed landscape, it is no denigration of Bathurst's skills to suspect that this is evidence of the imagination wielded by a professional to whom these qualities should be ascribed, and that that professional is Switzer. Cirencester exhibits the very qualities Switzer elaborated in his *Ichnographia Rustica*, and its plan form looks like the realized version of one of his illustrations, or, as he put the matter in explaining his published engraving of Riskins, they were but a "Regulated Epitomy" of it.

Bathurst served Queen Anne as Member for Cirencester in the House of Commons in the first decade of the century, and was raised to the House of Lords as one of a group of Peers created to secure the passage of the Treaty of Utrecht. With her death, the coming in of King George and a Whig government Bathurst's time in power was clearly finished, certainly for the short term, and as he judged correctly likely for the longer term, and like a good old Roman he retired to his estates. He spent the rest of his life, an exceptionally long one, improving them. His father had only recently

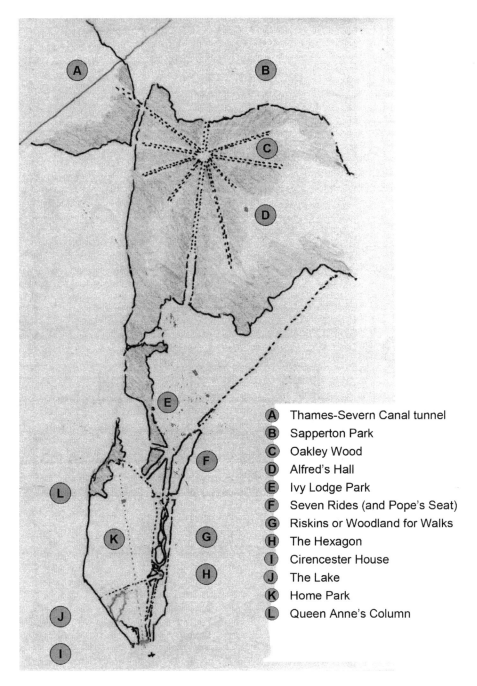

Figure 3.3 Cirencester, Gloucestershire: diagram of the layout of the grounds (north to right). Image by the author.

acquired the Cirencester property from the Dugdales, the most distinguished of whom had founded the Botanic Garden in Oxford. The house, Oakley Lodge, lay hard on the west side of the town and near the church. Later in 1716 Bathurst bought the Sapperton estate some five miles to the west from the Atkyns, the last of whom had been the historian of Gloucestershire, and thus made the very long holding of some 5000 acres. As the house was literally at its eastern edge in a major town all this made for a curious variation on the conventional disposition of a country estate.

That it was originally two estates is reflected in its topography. The eastern part, especially Oakley Lodge, was a smallish and comfortable mixture of garden, orchard and small enclosed fields, whereas the distant Sapperton is rather bleaker and more Cotswold-like with open and rolling countryside, and also perhaps a prominent existing woodland: Pope writes of "high timber" and much admires it, but precisely where it was is unclear (Hussey 1967 80). Certainly Bathurst concentrated his extensive forest plantations in this western half of the extended estate. Between these is a largish area of more open land with a valley, and a road, crossing it roughly in a north-south direction. The estate began in the east at the sharp point in the plan, and widened slowly towards its middle. The western part was the widest, and also the highest: through it runs the Edge separating Cotswolds from the Severn country, though curiously only perceptible as such at the beginning of the Frome valley at the far west end. The Sapperton-Thames canal tunnel uniting Severn and Thames lies on the south-west edge of the Cirencester estate. The lack of water of a suitable size for such a large estate was noted while the design was being carried on, and there were ideas of uniting the two great rivers of England somewhere within the estate. Pope reported such a design to Mary Wortley Montagu in 1721: ". . . the future and yet visionary beauties that are to rise in these scenes . . . the meeting of the Thames and the Severn which (when the noble Owner has finer dreams than ordinary) are to be led into each other" (Pope, correspondence, quoted in Hussey 1967 81). The design for this is lost, and it may be doubted whether it was seriously attempted.

The design history of Cirencester appears to have begun immediately on King George's accession. It is assumed that the great plantations of the 1720s followed a lost design scheme. There are also references to building works, the assembling of the materials from old Sapperton House for the "Castle of Oakley Wood", but the evidence for the ornamental buildings occurs in the 1730s, as indeed does the only water-work, the Lake. Perhaps these last works were funded from his recent sale of Riskins to the Hertfords. By the early 1740s Cirencester Park had assumed its present form and extent. With one major exception it has retained its original design through centuries of very significant changes to other estates, and not least changes that came about in pursuit of the design ideals first explored, if not quite perfectly realized, at Cirencester.

These are among the puzzles that are encountered in trying to write a history of this place. The most obvious exception to the early 18th century conception, which perhaps characteristically appears at first sight to be no change at all, is the decision to extend the east-west axis a further two miles or so towards the town, and there to meet the very handsome wrought iron gateway and screen. These opened the designed estate, and the newly created section of the Broad Walk, to the town. This design addition occurred sometime at the beginning of the 19th century, and though it has every appearance of being part of the *original* design it is no such thing. Thus, it would be the work of Henry, the 3rd Earl Bathurst. It almost appears as if the third Bathurst had taken Switzer's plate 33, assuming it to be the design for his grandfather's estate

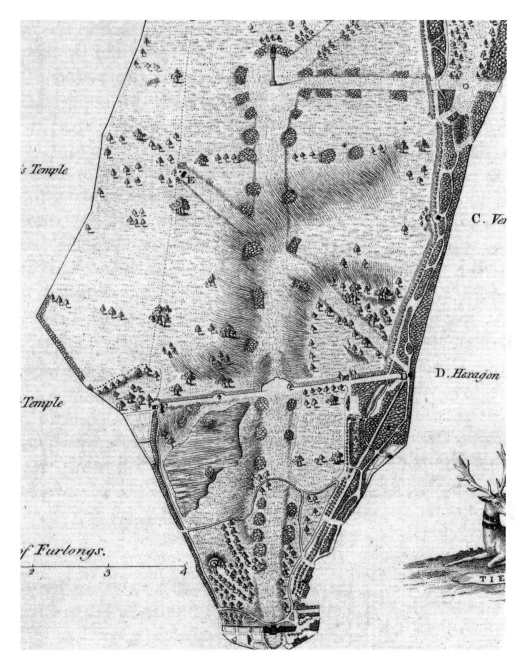

Figure 3.4 Cirencester, Gloucestershire: grounds, eastern section (north to right). Reproduced from Samuel Rudder, *New History of Gloucestershire*, 1779, "A Plan of the Home Park at Cirencester". The Bodleian Libraries, University of Oxford.

rather than the Regulated Epitomy for Cirencester, and simply added the missing eastern parts. As has been demonstrated (see above), plate 33 was never as simple as it might appear to be. In taking it as a guide the third earl seemed to accept an underlying formality of the design as being characteristic of the whole. But by opening the seemingly generating axis to all, and at first viewing, he robbed Cirencester of its nature and much of its subtlety. His addition saved the third Lord Bathurst the trouble of curious visitors presenting themselves at his front door, and it may have been a motive to divert such visitors to his park past his own house and the adjacent pleasure grounds, and as far into Cirencester Park as possible. It succeeded in doing that, and admirably so. But this sleight of hand has confused subsequent assessment and appreciation of the early 18th century design.

It appears, then, that from 1715 or 1716 work following a design was begun, with much planting of forest trees known as Oakley Wood, to the east of the old Sapperton estate; at the same time Oakley Lodge and its grounds at Cirencester were remodelled and extended westward. The intervening interruption of the topography by Rough Hills, called Lodge Park (or Ivy Lodge) from the late 1720s, joined Oakley Wood and the extended eastern plantations at Seven Rides.

Oakley Lodge became Cirencester Park House, and remains as such. As Oakley Lodge it was well fitted to adjoin the ancient town convenient to, but decently detached from, the church and marketplace. In 1712 its U or E shaped plan was sufficiently modern to be comfortable, yet established and familiar. Bathurst complained from time to time about its lack of style, even calling it "peculiarly bad", but he never did anything about it and seems to have been content to remodel as necessary. In the 1730s he built much, but never a new house, nor is there any evidence that he wished to change the relationship of the house to the town and to the park. And it is that alone that might justify him thinking it "peculiarly bad". A house for a great estate did not need to be great in itself, but it did need to be in the heart of the estate to be taken seriously. For it to remain sited by the front gate announced a singularity. Bathurst appears to have been content to live with such peculiarity. Nor is there much evidence that he wished to depart from convention. He inherited a conventional courtyard to the front, with kitchen quarters and orchards to either side with gardens (parterre-like and minimally plain) according to the view by Johannes Kip and Leonard Knyff in Atkyns' *Ancient and Present State of Gloucestershire*. These remain in order and in place, but brought up to a fashion suitable for the second or third decade of the 18th century. The most notable of these fashion updates of course is the new forecourt, whose shape follows that of Switzer's lake in plate 33 [3.1], with its great smoothly curved and three storey high yew hedge. It appears to have been the subject of the frontispiece of *The Nobleman Gentleman and Gardener's Recreation*. The parterres on the west front were also re-planned and extended.

But the enlarged and updated Oakley Lodge formed only a small part of Bathurst's estate, and it is the estate part which held, and drove, his attention, and deserves our own some three centuries later. It is his work and the lessons it holds for us which makes the Cirencester designed landscape so interesting, and historically important. To become Cirencester Park Oakley Lodge expanded westward and formed the first, the more *garden part* of the estate design. Structurally this is made up of axial elements arranged conventionally as a series of *patte d'oies*, or goose-feet, familiar from London and Wise's work. The parterres of the old house can still be recognized in the greatly elongated parterre-like *parade* which forms the centre of the main goose-foot and was finished with a column and statue of Queen Anne erected in 1742, as it happened the last of Bathurst's additions. The southern third of the goose-foot, a relatively small and subsidiary angled line of development, really a strolling garden with wilderness qualities, still exists. It also makes a (relatively short) terrace walk leading from the house to the Lake. The northern side of this goose-foot has been largely obliterated in the works of the 3rd earl, but its form is shown in Rudder's Plan of 1779, and enough parts remain to give its character as also a wooded terrace walk. It is this third part which is critical to the design and development of Cirencester as a whole.

In truth, the enlarged Oakley Lodge grounds, henceforth called Home Park, are of sufficient size to count as Bathurst's complete estate, and indeed it stands in for that, at least initially. The Lake lies in its south-west corner, roughly a third of the way along its apparent length, and the Lake's edges are marked by two lateral terrace walks, the east-most of these added, for convenience, sometime in the 19th century. The original and greater terrace runs across the axial scheme and "encloses" (defines rather) the more garden-like parts of the first *stanza* of Cirencester Park. At this terrace's centre, where the main axis from house to Queen Anne crosses it, is a semi-circular bastion. The inner side of the *stanza* was most likely to have been planted plain parterre-like nearer the house, with rougher, more park-like, or lawn-like, fields towards the west. The edges of this are splayed in plan, defined by forest trees, and supplemented by terrace walks or the "outsides" of half-terraces.

Already we have commented on a sufficiently large scheme for any serious early Georgian garden, and one very much alive to the beauties of *nature* and *simplicity*. Bathurst had every reason to be happy with it, as he doubtless was. But it was really only an introduction. If a big garden has to have a heart, before 1715 it would have been the parterre. For Switzer and for Bathurst the heart of Cirencester appears instead to have been one of these edges and an extraordinary new element: it is a walk, but *walk* hardly gives the right sense of it. A garden, certainly, but even that will mislead. It is more than a viewing platform, although it is surely that too. It has much in common with Castle Howard's Wray Wood if that can be imagined as a surreally stretched out thing. It is, viewed structurally, the thing that makes sense of the whole, that pulls all into one comprehension, yet it is without name. Perhaps calling it a *Riskins* might serve. Switzer had described what it contained and what its purpose was in full detail, and indicated a usually serpentine figure to link all the parts together; he called it an *enfilade*. At Cirencester this element is straightish although made up of irregularly placed straight runs on the north face, overlooking fields and pasture, whereas there were attenuated and lazy curves on the south facing terrace walk: between are a mix of straight walks and curved ones, generally leading east-west, but also meandering from side to side with the occasional glade or perhaps more regular space. Where the larger north-south Home Park Terrace joins the *Riskins* is the site of a seat, in due course, seemingly after 1736, the site of the Venetian Building or Hexagon. This "commands" its own goose-foot, where the centre line is the transverse terrace, with its right section terminated by the *Harley's Temple* and its left section aligned on the south front of the house.

The Hexagon marks the half way point of the north terrace walk, the *Riskins*, which Rudder shows continuing westwards as a series of linked meanders with views to fields, pasture and park. These terminate in a large semi-circular glade or space which becomes the beginning/end of the Home Park spoke of Seven Rides, where at 90 degrees to it is a cut through the wooded terrace edge towards Queen Anne, clearly a revision of the early 1740s. This is carried over the parkland as an avenue of platoons. These of course read as an avenue or pointer when the alignment is perfect, and otherwise will read as a series of clumps without geometric significance. Quite how these parks (for there are

Figure 3.5 Cirencester, Gloucestershire: details of north woodland walks, the "Riskins" terrace walks (north to right). Reproduced from Samuel Rudder, *New History of Gloucestershire*, 1779, "A Plan of the Home Park at Cirencester". The Bodleian Libraries, University of Oxford.

three, perhaps four different and distinct areas) were planted is unknown in detail. One assumes parks are furnished with grasses and trees, as these doubtless were, and remain. The question arises for these particular parks because they have always had an extra role to play, that is, as also parts of the *garden*. Real evidence about such furnishing becomes available only in the late 1740s (and at Wilton, see below), but the suspicion is strong that decisions about which grasses, or what "crops", were appropriate would have exercised Bathurst and his consultants from the beginning. But especially in these "captured" pieces of nature or farmland within his gardens at Cirencester the question of just how these choices were furnished remains open at present.

A first visitor to Cirencester Park, even one knowledgeable about the estate's character and design, will assume the axial prospect from the reception rooms across the ample parks to Queen Anne is the famous great axis, or Broad Walk, of the whole scheme, and that beyond the old Queen's monument will lie the bulk of the estate. Thus, like Versailles, one seemingly has a view of the whole place. In fact, as long as this view is, there is yet another and the major axis to discover. It appears that one sees the whole place at once, but that is far from being so. This dubiety or element of surprise had been introduced from the beginning, and it is the means of achieving this *trompe de paysage* element which is *new* both in being begun then but also in the sense that it was a radical departure in garden making which allowed the landscape to be comprehended and thus designed. It is the wooded walk, the *Riskins* (or the north terrace walk), which invites our visitors to explore the grounds, with southerly views over the axial arrangements seen first, but at an angle now, as well as the varieties of planting, shape and space the woodland had to offer, plus at various points views over fields and pasture to the north. The extreme length of this walk, never an issue with Bathurst, who loved a good long walk, will have become plain to his less robust visitors, such as Pope, who complained of it when he began visiting in 1718. But if a visitor could bear an agreeable, diversified and often surprising long walk he would find himself then in sight of Seven Rides, the first great roundel still half a kilometre to the west, and the new axial prospect towards Sapperton.

When Seven Rides is reached, there, tucked into a point between two of these, is Pope's "Sylvan Bower", since the late 1730s the graceful stone building known as Pope's Seat. Seven Rides is a familiar design type of which there are many examples, and many of those are in France, where the pattern has been almost universally renewed in subsequent centuries. At Cirencester its principal purpose is not to make hunting game more efficient. Rather, it is the first of the forest sections of the design, and not for walking in: it marks this beginning as a piece of landscaped *place*. Most of the rides are aligned on a church tower to secure this character. Primarily it marks the line of the Broad Walk, which leads westward towards seeming infinity. But fairly swiftly a major topographical change becomes apparent: there is the roughly north-south rent in the otherwise plane-like expanse of the estate called Rough Hills, which disturbs and disorients the design. It is only some 15 metres drop, but that is enough to lose the line of the axis. East of this topographical disturbance is Lodge Park, through which, presumably, woodland and its central avenue was carried, in the same manner as in Oakley Wood.

At Cirencester is the first intimation of a landscape designed. It is not just a question of serpentine lines, or variety, nor indeed of Andre Le Notre's trick of *trompe l'oeil* or *trompe de geometrie* which he had played first at the Tuileries; all these Bathurst's visitor would have already encountered at Cirencester, from the monumental entry onwards. The toying with conventional expectation in the prospect from the

90 *Early landscapes*

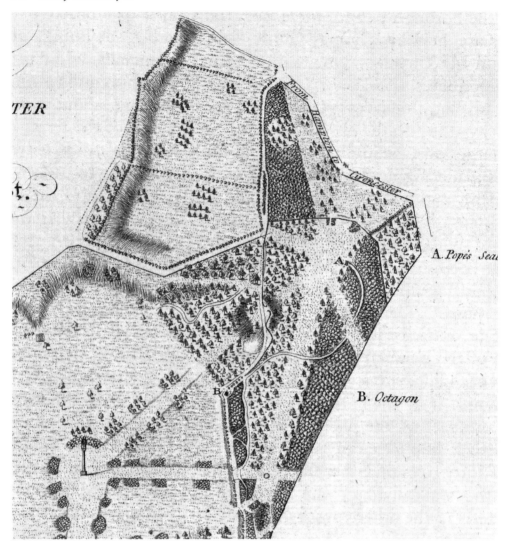

Figure 3.6 Cirencester, Gloucestershire: plan of Seven Rides (north to right). Reproduced from Samuel Rudder, *New History of Gloucestershire*, 1779, "A Plan of the Home Park at Cirencester". The Bodleian Libraries, University of Oxford.

reception rooms and parterre gives perhaps a flavour of surprise. But the new thing he and Switzer bring off is the manipulation of scale. The elements, whether the grand courtyard at the beginning, or an almost absurdly elongated parterre, should have given warning, but as they are familiar, if on the large side, they do not; similarly, the apparent endless prospect is "forgotten" in the varieties and changeful views within and without the *Riskins*, that wooded and terraced garden for walking. And at the end of that . . . then a new great prospect is offered to view, the real, or main, prospect as it happens, and at another, even vaster scale. From there further exploration, even for Bathurst, has to be done in an appropriately larger scale manner, in a trap, or coach, or at least on a mount. In both artistry and structure we encounter a significant new departure (see Lodge Park below).

Marston

Marston lies just over the Wiltshire border with Somerset from the Longleat estate. There Charles Boyle, 4th Earl of Orrery (1674–1731), improved the place from his inheritance of it in 1714. Switzer acknowledged Orrery's patronage in his dedication of *The Practical Fruit Gardener* in 1724. Orrery was born with great expectations. His Boyle kin were both successful as soldiers and politicians, and his uncle Robert is one of the giants of the history of science. His mother's family were the Savils of Knole, where another uncle was Duke of Dorset. However, his parents were ill matched, and they separated before Orrery's tenth birthday, leaving him to be brought up by his mother at Knole in Kent. He made a brilliant career at university in Oxford. That he was the only peer actually to take a degree from his college in the later 17th century is true, but his distinction is real and more personal than that fact would suggest. He worked with his tutor Francis Atterbury on translating ancient Greek texts, and showed skill and promise as a scholar. They both fell foul of academic politics and became embroiled in what Swift largely has left us with in his story of the *Battle of the Books*. Later they were more dangerously embroiled.

Although he served both William III and Anne commendably, and as a soldier was distinguished, he is remembered more as a patron, not least of the mechanical model of the solar system which bears his name, and as a bibliophile. Orrery had been assembling his great library since his student days, and it would have remained at Marston if it were not for his falling out with his son and heir. He had been a widower since 1708 and had grown closer to the wife of his secretary, with whom he had four children. His secondary house nearer to London, Britwell, seems to have become the household also for the new family. In addition to this, he was arrested and confined in the Tower of London for suspected complicity in the Atterbury Plot, and he had been recently bailed at the great sum of £50,000 (equivalent to £15,000,000 in current sterling value). Orrery was loyal to his friends and a trifle stubborn perhaps, but his bravery cost him much.

Sadly for the historian of gardens and designed landscapes, no plans of Marston nor design drawings for it survive, and there are no descriptions of it to allow us to assess their achievements there. We have parts only, provided by the plate in *Vitruvius Britannicus* of 1739 and a section of the water-works from the *Introduction to a General System of Hydrostaticks and Hydraulicks*. For these we must be grateful, and indeed for many schemes they would be more than sufficient. But one suspects Marston was a more complex design, and would have inhabited parts of the large estate, even if it were not a design for the whole, a complete landscape scheme. The Ordnance Surveys, from which we can usually find fragments of degraded landscapes, give no clues, so Marston was perhaps not so extensive a design. It remains a pity that the elder Orrery did not share his cousin Burlington's almost prolix fondness for having drawings and paintings of his domains made, nor that of the even more generous Cobham at Stowe.

As the family held Marston until the beginning of the 20th century the evidence of early Ordnance Surveys will indicate works only they undertook. The house and immediate gardens survived then, and can still be detected, as did Marston Pond, the only water-work to survive. There are structural plantations still intact to show where major blocks of woodland were, and where the large divisions of fields or of Marston Park lay. From this we can adduce a circuit walk, or more likely a series of walks, around the park dividing it from arable. This division lies, roughly, between these

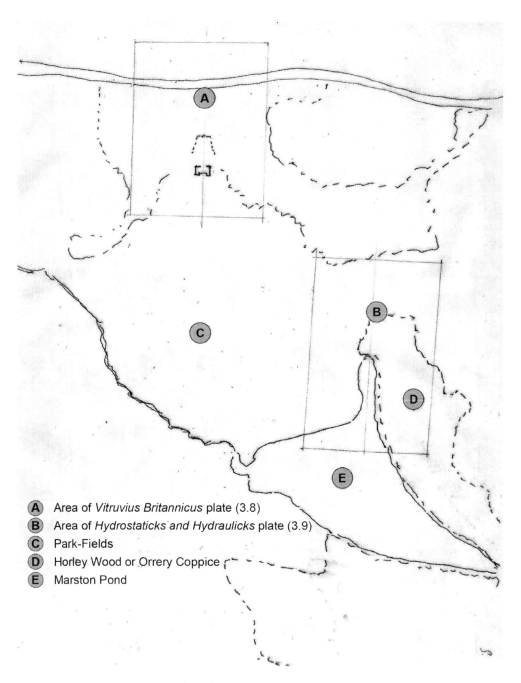

Figure 3.7 Marston, Somerset: plan of the estate in the mid-18th century (north to right). Image by the author.

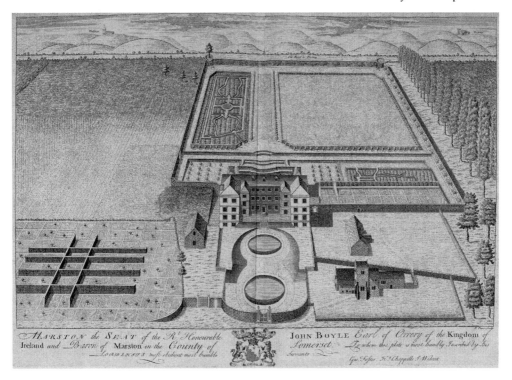

Figure 3.8 Marston, Somerset (north to right). Reproduced from *Vitruvius Britannicus, or the British Architect*, Volume the Fourth 1739, plates 69 and 70. Oxford Bodleian Library, Vet. A 4 a.3. NB pp 69–70.

two major and equal areas, so that a visitor following that circuit would have park or woodland walk (to include the only illustrated feature within the design at the head of Marston Pond) on one side, balanced by views across fields to distant prospects on the other. In other words, no part of the Marston landscape would be hidden or excluded from easy sight, or from reach. Given its size, roughly four kilometres square, such a circuit would be all that was needed.

The house lies near the north edge of the estate, conveniently close to the church and the road to and from Frome. Its form is regular, a three storey, seven bay *corp de logis* with two short wings (or bays) at either end, perhaps a reworking of an earlier 17th century house, and presumably the work also of the family, but under whose direction we cannot say. It does not present any strong stylistic character. As the younger Orrery's works were in the woodland gardens in the 1730s, this shows the works commissioned by his father, and probably records work mainly from the 1710s. Here the entry was from the south, the church then quite close by to the east of the entrance courts. These are in two parts rising up to the entry and formed in a figure-eight about two circular lawns, embanked by turf slope-work and finishing in a broad terrace. As each stage is significantly higher the terrace and main rooms of the house give a good open view southward over the park and estate. The Best Gardens are to the north. Presently there is a broad space immediately north of the house for entry (a change from the later 19th century); given the nature of the rest of the grounds on this side the more likely elements hidden from view will have been of the plainest, perhaps a bowling green type parterre and simple flanking walks. For the whole of these parts seem to have been given over to kitchen and fruit gardens, and to make a curiously private series of such gardens devoted to producing foodstuffs. The exception to this is a big lawn set off in the north-east quarter, and the parterre series made up of turfed banks in imitation of amphitheatres, curving ramps to either side, first in one direction, then the other, which imparts a livelier finish to the more geometric parts, which are plain like the earthworks on the south front. Even the wilderness turns out to be a fruit garden, and all else is devoted to kitchen crops.

In the south-west quarter, and quite outside the walled parts of Marston, is a most extraordinary type of kitchen garden, rendered in a seeming stylized fashion but obviously realistic. Here the walls, so conventionally presented in the gardens proper, are dispensed with entirely, and marshalled rather into the centre of things, in an otherwise checkerboard division of beds for kitchen stuffs, even more minimally conceived than the new style kitchen gardens Switzer proposed in *The Practical Fruit Gardener* and employed as we will observe at Hampton Court (and also at Spye Park, see below). It is unclear whether these are "walls" with plants trained on them, or whether they are a kind of treillage used for the same purpose. I have seen only one other such kitchen garden, a late 18th century one at Newton House, Aberdeenshire. It was most productive. The Marston one was built over when the house was enlarged.

The character of Marston, perhaps a trifle more pointed in Parr's rather abstract engraving, was decidedly masculine with minimal planting beyond the edible or that necessary for structural definition. Perhaps the rest of the grounds – the park, fields and woodlands – gave this quality and took the place of the garden parts. Therefore, it appears that the normal contrast was reversed at Marston, as the smaller scale, intricate elements commonly associated with the parterre or wilderness near the house are to be found in the distant woodland gardens instead. But about most of these outer works we can only be indicative rather than descriptive, relying as we must at present on the earliest of the Ordnance Survey evidence, confirmed incidentally by the earliest trial Ordnance Survey drawings from the late 18th century. From these it is clear that the park, tilting gently to the south-east, had a neat almost elliptical structure as it was perceived from the house and the terraced ground immediately south of it. From there we can trace notional walks in either direction which would have followed the boundary between the park's edge and arable. A counter-clockwise tour would take the company west passed St Leonard's Church (re-sited here later in the century) and then quickly towards the south along what had in the 1870s still a semblance of an avenue. From this excellent views were to be had of the park, and beyond it to the east, with the Marston stream serpentine to a large piece of water, Marston Pond. There were clump plantations in the southern park near the fields further south-westwards suggesting the turn of the walk to the east and towards the large Thickthorn Wood, itself suggestive as the site of rustic garden works of the kind found in Wray Wood. This expectation becomes the stronger as Thickthorn leads along the east side of the estate, always with at least glimpses of Marston Pond, into Horley Wood. All these south-eastern elements in the Marston landscape would have been part of the big water-works design Switzer included as plate 37 in his *Hydrostaticks and Hydraulicks*.

Early landscapes 95

Where Marston Pond still shows a deep and narrow inlet as the watery end of the feature he illustrated, as he said the upper part is a "Sketch of the fine Amphitheatre . . . the Design of the very Ingenious Mr Bridgeman", with the rest, especially the bottom half, "where the Water Spouts out, is an Addition of my own, from a Work of that Kind that I have done for the Right Honourable the Earl of Orrery,

Figure 3.9 Marston, Somerset: plan of part of Marston Pond and wood (north to right). Reproduced from Stephen Switzer, *Introduction to a General System of Hydrostaticks and Hydraulicks*, 1729, II plate 37 ("Claremont" plate). Private collection.

at Marston in Somersetshire" (*Hydro* II 405). This formed the meeting of pond and earthen architecture, and recalling the forms he had used in the gardens north of the house, but here in a large woodland garden overlooking the pond and the wider designed landscape. The margins appear to be paved, and the pond's edge coped with stone, giving a surprisingly crisp finish. The pond is also edged by walks planted as avenues. Marston Pond is now roughly triangular in plan shape, still very close to a natural pond, but with long and lazy curved sections hinting at perhaps some kind of part geometric and part natural original. The pond is open on the south and west sides, with Marston House and the gardens along with the church set along the terraced boundary with the park. The pond is closely wooded towards the south-east half, and even more so along its long east curving flank. It is here that we find the heart of the place, the woodland garden, for the Orrerys and for Switzer too. This element, as we have seen elsewhere – at Riskins, Grimsthorpe or Cirencester – is the key to his manner, and also the practical means of tying gardens, woods, parks and estate together into a designed landscape. Here it stretches north and then west to join the extended grounds specific to Marston House and its gardens to make a crescent shaped series of woodlands and gardens in a crescent shape plan.

The absence of evidence leaves us to guess just how the connections were made. Because of the lie of the land and the rest of Switzer's design, the top of the waterworks would have been a more linear arrangement than he shows and more like that which prevailed at Chargate (renamed Claremont), perhaps a long rectangular cabinet, or a complex grouping of spaces whose effect would be to lead rather than to stop. At the north end of Horley Wood fragmentary remains of early work are still discernible, and indeed have been re-gardened in recent historic time . . . Edwardian and more likely 1920s in style, where the succeeding owners continued to live into the 1960s. This is where the younger Lord Orrery made his additions in the 1730s. These he reports to a friend in 1733 with regard to his works in these eastern gardens, and mentions finishing the three hanging terraces, plus three fountains "at three several distances", with "ten thousand designs for other parts . . . to be finished next summer". His views over his "beautiful prospect in the distant Vale" and, he fears, the other "charms of Marston make me forget to hope one day to be an inhabitant of the Kingdom of Heaven" (Orrery to Southern 1 Nov 1733, in Countess of Cork and Orrery). This area is at the top of Horley Wood (then newly planted as Abdel or Orrery Coppice) and its water-works, and is also a convenient easy walk eastward from Marston House. We assume that a terrace walk south of the house must have been one of their first amendments to Marston in this later period, that is, in the 1730s and early 1740s. Thus the circuit is easily completed.

Hampton Court

The second volume of *Ichnographia Rustica* was dedicated to Thomas Coningsby (1656–1729), who was the Member of Parliament for Leominster, a Whig and a supporter of William III, with whom he had served in Ireland. He was quick tempered and litigious; in his youth he had crossed swords with James Brydges, later Duke of Chandos, and made an unfortunate marriage with a Jamaican heiress. His family were rivals to their great neighbours, the Harleys, Members of Parliament for

Early landscapes 97

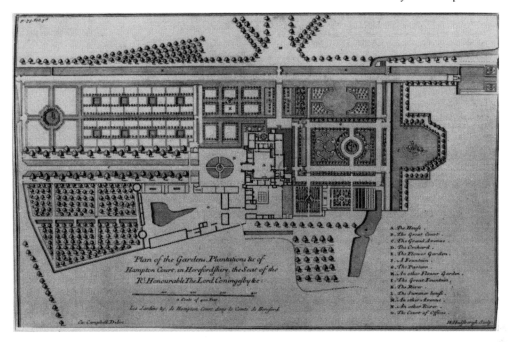

Figure 3.10 Hampton Court, Herefordshire: plan of the gardens (north to left). Reproduced from Colen Campbell, *Vitruvius Britannicus, or the British Architect*, 1725 (ed 1731) III, plate 75. Private collection.

Herefordshire and Tories; not unsurprisingly, Coningsby was rather ignored in Queen Anne's reign. He was raised to peerage by King George and made earl in 1719: his title passed to his daughter, Margaret Newton of Culverthorpe, in 1729 (whose husband was one of Switzer's *improvers*; see below), who also shared his interests in gardening. Coningsby's estate was Hampton Court in Herefordshire at Hope under Dinmore near Leominster in the Wye valley, and it overlooked a tributary, the River Lugg. He had already laid out extensive gardens and water-works, probably by London, and these were illustrated by Johannes Kip and Leonard Knyff, and painted also by John Stevens before 1722.

These three early 18th century paintings of the grounds are our evidence for their design. There was also an atlas assembled during Coningsby's lifetime which had many images, mostly maps, of the grounds and estate: by the time these appeared for sale in the 1960s they had been sadly depleted in content (Sabin 1973). They were saved from export by the Arts Council. Hampton Court appeared also in an east view in *Britannia Illustrata* in 1708. So it is on these paintings, plus the plates from *Vitruvius Britannicus*, that we must rely. The Stevens picture is not dated but has been listed as circa 1705 in most references. But as it shows work done after Knyff's view it must be later, and as most of that work was done about 1718, surely a date for the picture should therefore be nearer 1722, the year Stevens died. The canal to the south side of the house is shown as such in 1708, and this must record London's work by that date. But a painting by the same artist was later altered (perhaps by Knyff himself, though probably not as the changes are so ill disguised); it shows the canal widened into a large pool of semi-octagonal form. In Campbell's plan it has received its Neptune sculpture group.

So Hampton Court came equipped with its smart, modern grounds, a well-sited, productive estate, and as Coningsby had also an old house which was the very image of the *Castle* already, there was no need and little call for architectural romance. Switzer was engaged in the mid-1710s on two quite different tasks at Hampton Court; the first was to add a new style kitchen garden and, perhaps, to tidy the gardens in the simpler taste the early Georgians adopted from Queen Anne. These improvements are shown in the plan published in the third volume of *Vitruvius Britannicus* of 1725; according to Campbell these ". . . are esteemed very Curious, and the large Decoy is remarkable" (*Vit Brit* III 11). The parterres seem little altered, though less crowded. The gardens on the east front, the flower garden and the kitchen garden north of it are rendered in almost 20th century modernist checkerboard simplicity. Likes are marshalled with likes into orderly and very tidy arrays of small beds, small square basins contrasting with the large octagon basin at the end. A version of these kitchen quarters appeared in Switzer's *Practical Fruit Gardener* of 1724, where he explains that the small basins are linked by conduit to supply the contiguous beds with water ready for their nourishment.

The Great Fountain, so-called on Campbell's plate of 1725, is also a new addition, and it was in relation to this very significant feature that a good, strong supply of water would be needed. This appears to have been Switzer's real job at Hampton Court. This problem he remedied by a major landscape work north and east of the house and gardens. There he constructed a new river, some three kilometres long, north and west of, and following roughly the route of, the Humber Brook. Switzer's river is about three metres broad, and two metres deep, and its profile is semi-circular to parabolic and when seen, empty, in remarkably good condition. It intercepted a number of tributary brooks rising in the higher grounds to the north, and there were a number of pools he formed as reservoirs, the last of which is a large circular pool high above Hampton Court and a kilometre north on the axis of the entrance avenue.

This was doubtless the connection between the old garden site and the new works, accomplished by the tree-lined avenue shown on Stevens' painting. None of these had survived into the period of the early Ordnance Surveys of the 1870s. Along this hypothetical north-south major avenue and slightly to its east was the big decoy from London's time, whose remains did survive. From the circular basin, which is the western end of Switzer's river, there remains a woodland of varying shape and width, occasionally opened up, which meanders through the parks and arable fields of the estate, with views northward to rising ground, and southward towards the house, the Lugg beyond and thence the Wye valley. Thus was a water supply furnished, and also an extension of the gardens into the contiguous estate, as the illustrative plates in *Ichnographia Rustica* had directed, but here, as elsewhere, made particular and local in consultation with the genius of the place. Thus, the necessary water-carriage becomes also the means to extend the gardens into the estate, and throw them together, as Switzer might say, and as we have observed happened at the same time, if not before, at Whetham. Switzer's New River exploited as *garden* had the effect of turning London's Hampton Court into a *pretty landskip*. By simple addition the whole place is transformed, and any picturesque qualities the wider Wye valley possesses are seen across parkland and arable, with a castle of the old fashion, if

Early landscapes 99

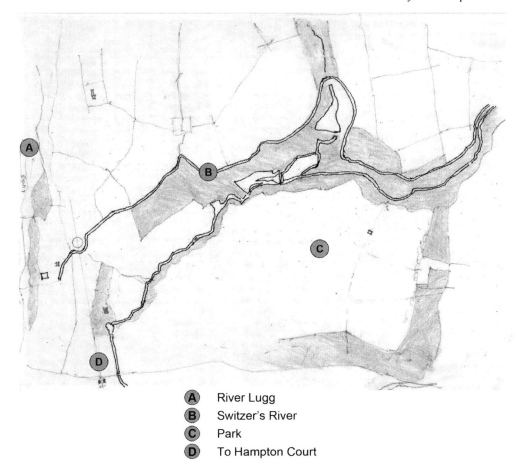

A River Lugg
B Switzer's River
C Park
D To Hampton Court

Figure 3.11 Hampton Court, Herefordshire: plan of the estate in the early 18th century (north to top). Image by the author.

comfortable enough to suit a Whig earl, set in its smartly dressed gardens . . . precisely as Addison had imagined. It was the destruction of this venerable Avenue that Price so regretted as indicative of Brown's *excesses* (Hussey 1927 176).

Like Lancelot Brown a generation or so later, Switzer was wanted for works in Ireland. Indeed, the grounds for Dromoland, County Clare, were laid out in imitation of some of his mannerisms in the 1720s and 1730s, probably by John Aherne for Sir Edward O'Brien (Irish Architectural Drawings 1965 plate 47), a kinsman of Lord Inchiquin (see below). But Switzer, like Brown, resisted, although it appears in a letter from Robert Molesworth (1656–1725) to Coningsby to have been a decided possibility. In the long newsy letter in 1719 Lord Molesworth speaks of Switzer's plan to travel to Ireland, and of his encouraging him to do so. Reporting his own fairly extensive water-works at Brackenstown, just north of Dublin, he writes,

> . . . I do not intend to lye idle this summer but shall be deep in mortar & other work too chargeable for a purse like mine, wch gett's nothing to speak from a

100 *Early landscapes*

> Government I have served all my life. However I can not refrain doing, tho I spend my whole income, & could wish for Mr Switzer to joyn his maggots to mine, & I am vain enough to think he would learn as much here as he would teach us. I have & shall manage a little water to as great advantage as any man in Britain, tho I want proper workmen & instruments for the execution of my designs, this Kingdom affording none good . . .
>
> (Malins and Glin 1976 16, quoting Molesworth to Coningsby 26 May 1719 PRO (Belfast) MS D 638/82/2)

Personal remarks about Switzer are very rare. Molesworth may be the source of an insight into Switzer's personality as he perhaps hints at his character in passing. He means that he wishes Switzer's (and his workmen's help) in engineering scale works. As *maggoty* was also used then to denote, and not quite in denigration, a quickly moving and not very attentive cast of mind, could he be referring to a quickness bordering on absent-mindedness in Switzer? This became evident in the early 1730s, usually in consequence of taking on too many projects.

Leeswood

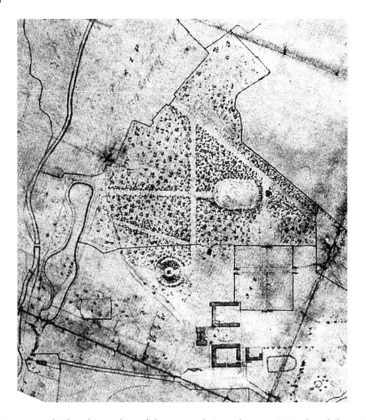

Figure 3.12 Leeswood, Flintshire: plan of the grounds (north to top). Undated (late 18th century) survey reproduced from J E Furse and D L Jacques, *Report of the Historical Interest of the Garden and Grounds at Leeswood Hall, Clwyd*, 1981.

Sir George Wynne (1700–1753) came into great wealth through the discovery of lead in land he had inherited from his mother. Although the lead was discovered in 1715 it was several years later that he secured it, and began first to build and then to plant. His contemporaries gossiped about his extravagant tastes (Hester Thrale 1726), but they do not seem to have been unusually so: his house and grounds at Leeswood (apart from the two sets of iron gates, on which he happily spent the equivalent of close to a million pounds) are on the modest side. He did, however, spend prodigiously to get and keep himself elected to the House of Commons, where he loyally served Sir Robert Walpole. Since most of his neighbours were opposed to both him and Walpole, they fought him at every opportunity, effectively cancelling the value of his £30,000 spent to stay a Member (the same amount his gates had cost). But it was not the expenditure that was against him, but rather the sad fact that his lead mines soon ceased to produce, and by the late 1730s he was in financial trouble. One of the creditors he was unable to pay then was Switzer. Fortunately for Switzer and for garden history most of the works at Leeswood had been finished and already paid for.

Leeswood, near Mold in Flintshire, lies in rich country close to Cheshire and on the main route to and from Ireland. Wynne at first had William Smith repair the old house, Leeswood Hall, and then in 1724 build a new one on a site further west . . . three stories of eleven bays flanked by two blocks of offices. He also engaged Switzer to make a design for his gardens and estate. These are extensive but essentially modest, even plain, and are in Switzer's style of *Rural and Farm-like Gardening*. They consist of woodland, lawns and a small lake, connected to and mixed with adjacent arable land and meadows. His method of composition is somewhat surprising. There are strong axes, mostly east-west, and one important one roughly north-south, and these are used to structure, or really to connect the centre of the new house to its policies. Thus, the grand frontage is answered to the west end of the Parade by an equally grand corresponding set of wrought iron gates, the famous White Gates. The main design element in terms of impact, amount of work, size and conspicuous understatement is this Parade. This great lawn is the breadth of the house (excluding the flanking blocks with their long axes extending the frontage by a further 13 bays each) and is entered by the grander of the iron screens. Between them is the meticulously levelled Parade of short grass, a piece of earth-architecture uniting stone with iron . . . crisp, sharp, seemingly absolutely empty of embellishment or ornament. This is Leeswood's Bold Stroke. A similar element survived at St Giles House, Wimborne, Dorset, into the 1770s and provides a good indication of the style and original nature of the Leeswood parade [6.13].

All else is looser, and although mostly structured as a series of large triangles in plan, each is responsive to its particular site, and its relationships to neighbouring ones. For example, north of the Parade, and taking that as the southern boundary, is a park-like triangular Lawn, ornamented with a scattering of trees, bounded on its east side by a dense woodland, whose edge to the lawn is feathered and slightly broken to imitate a seemingly natural boundary. On its west side is the Lake. The Lawn is also furnished, perhaps surprisingly, with a Bowling Green defined by thin lines of shrubs and trees and lying parallel to the Parade. On the other, wooded side of the Lawn and peeping out of it (since it is largely enclosed by the woods) is the large Mount. This still retains its four stone seats and table, and is one of the few built ornaments of the grounds. The Lake side of the triangular Lawn presents itself as artfully serpentine in the manner we associate with a slightly later period of the mid-century: it may have been originally crisper and recognizably geometric. The earliest representation of the grounds is late 18th century where it is shown as serpentine, but close to natural. This led Jane Furse and David Jacques (1981) to propose its origin was a circular pool at its north end. This may prove to have been so, but its late 18th century form is not dis-similar to other contemporary designs of Switzer, and a circular end (or beginning) to an otherwise serpentine lake can be seen at Mereworth in Kent (see below) and at St Giles House, Wimborne, and appears as an addition to London's Wootton Buckinghamshire, so highly praised by Thomas Whately (Whately 1770 84). On the other hand, it might well have been designed in this form. (See Nostell Priory below for a similar designed lake of about five years later.) This is one of the designed elements . . . what to call it? *Compartment*, yes, but it is rather big for what that normally suggests. Perhaps *episode* will serve? Although it has three distinct sides, and one of them very strong, it is not all that easy to define the Lawn by them: in terms of visitors' experience of it they might easily conclude that it is that open part lying beyond the Mount, the space between the Bowling Green and the Lake. In other words, as a regular triangle of space it might not be read as such. We have, then, a space with a measure of transparency, signifying both-and, or neither. Yet it also indicates purposefully the way Switzer has laid out his grounds.

On the other side of the Bold Stroke, where the answering pair to the episode, or series of elements, just discussed is expected, we find something rather different. At first it seems the same, or at least similar enough to signify that symmetry has been observed. Here is another "lawn". This is also a triangle of sprinkled trees, but a much sharper, narrower one where the trees seem to define the far edge, but imprecisely, before greatly opening up into a much larger field (or indeed two) which is no longer lawn but pasture (arable or meadow), as are all the enclosures, elements or episodes on this side of the estate. In fact, it soon becomes clear that the Parade-Lawn-Wood episode is the one and only *garden* element of Leeswood: all else is some form of "useful" space . . . park, field, pasture, arable . . . of the order of 20 in all, and each of similar but different size and shape and occasionally interspersed with woodlands, or wooded margins.

There are garden-like design gestures such as extensions of broad walks reaching out through woodland to further fields beyond. There is also evidence of a sort of assemblage of elements which suggests garden design but very much within the more workaday parts of the estate. For example there is an axial walk/prospect from the centre of the Mount which runs eastward across the extended Terrace of the house through a sort of coppice wood to the gate of the walled kitchen garden, through to the paired gate on the opposite side, thence through more lawn-like ground with fields to one side, woods to the other, and finally beckoning onward as a walk (or ride?) into the rest of the estate . . . forming one of the longest of the various axes, but hardly the primary one. Despite the Bold Stroke and these various axes there is no expressed hierarchy in the layout. Yes, the house is clearly dominant, and easy to find. For the rest it all hangs together by its own mazy meanders. Most of the generating lines run east-west. The axis of the gardens and the house's Terrace is orthogonal to these. From the garden front on the west side the obvious eye-catcher is the set of spectacular White Gates, straight ahead at the far end of the Parade. The eye moves easily slightly to the north to the gentler Lawn, or south to its more rural companion. The shorter run of the Terrace to the south connects quickly to this suite of meadows and fields, which are the southern side of the estate. The wooded gardens, Leeswood's Wray Wood, lie to the north. The broad Terrace runs through these for a good distance to an open and informal cabinet before being closed by a spur of the wooded garden. A short walk from the house leads to a widening (is it the start of a triangular cabinet, or simply a natural opening?) which introduces the Mount a short distance to the left with its paired sculpted walks rising on either side to the outside reception *room* on top, furnished with a stone table at the centre, and the four double seats, each with its own elliptically arched top. From there the Lake, and the fields and park beyond, can be seen, as can the Bowling Green in the Lawn, and beyond it the Parade and White Gates.

Shortly another walk leads at an angle also towards the Lake, while its opposite end leads to a Garden House, probably for rest and convenience. A more important cross axial walk, east-west, soon occurs. A short walk eastwards leads to a largish regular cabinet, with a shallow curved western end but otherwise rectangular, perhaps a further bowling green, more likely a theatre, for lying beyond it on axis almost as a stage setting is a further building (which it turns out faces also onto another walk). This

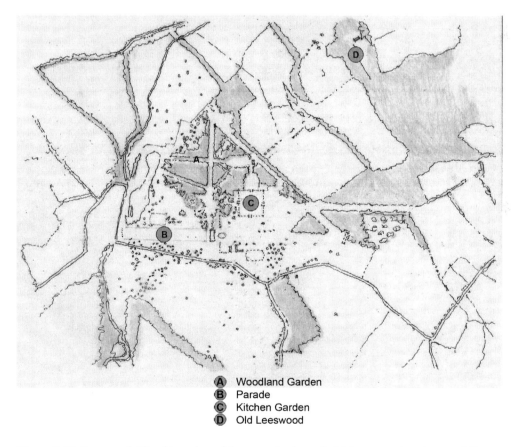

Ⓐ Woodland Garden
Ⓑ Parade
Ⓒ Kitchen Garden
Ⓓ Old Leeswood

Figure 3.13 Leeswood, Flintshire: plan of the estate in the early 18th century (north to top). Image by the author.

feature may well have been more elaborately formed, but its appearance in the later 18th century plan indicates its geometry only. Its axis is the same as the cross walk which also leads westward to end at the top of the Lake. There its long views can be appreciated, or alternatively views across the entrance Park to another set of wrought iron gates, the smaller Black Gates on the main road.

The woodland garden is edged by a terrace walk overlooking the park which leads from the mill end of the Lake eastwards, and back to the main Terrace. Here are three surprises. A visitor approaching from the terrace walk would encounter the broad Terrace on which he or she began, but here hardly recognized as such since it is enlarged into an informal glade . . . too big and unformed to count as a cabinet while too small to read as a park or captured countryside. Of its planted furnishings we have, sadly, no evidence. Second, it is also at this northern space where the three walks meet (or seem to commence) that there is a hint of a structure for the whole place. These seeming goose-foot of walks correspond to the middle and two sides of a big equilateral triangle whose base is the east-west axis through the house. Such recognition might well add a pleasing sense of structure revealed: it might, and probably would, have gone completely unrecognized. It is hardly essential to the experience of the place, rather more a reassuring footnote to those interested in such things. And, finally, there is also an entirely new walk. This is set at 90 degrees, and is clearly the principal walk, being as broad as the Terrace. This new walk is also a terrace walk, and it overlooks fields and woods in the eastern part of the estate, where old Leeswood Hall in the middle distance provides architectural interest. Thus are visitors beckoned to explore the longest of the walks at Leeswood, perfectly straight with woodland along its right side and now overlooking pastures and arable on the outside.

A visitor following this long walk would encounter a series of discrete elements along the wooded side while the open prospects of the eastern side provided a rather slower moving unfolding of the well-managed country life. Just beyond the straight edge of the informal glade, and a short stroll along the new walk, an easy opening to the right reveals the supposed theatre building, last encountered through a screen and as if on-stage, but the short end is seen as the walk passes in front, and the visitor finds himself on the stage. A further short walk, off-stage, would lead to a new large cabinet focused on the north gate to the Kitchen Garden. If our visitor had returned from his or her stage appearance to the long walk, another substantially large informal glade soon appeared in which the Kitchen Garden, then the broad Stable Block and its pair, the Kitchen Block, showed itself in perspective, and finally the entrance front to Leeswood behind its forecourt and oval turning green. If the axial walk aligned on the east gate of the Kitchen Garden and leading out into more woods and fields is resisted, still the long walk continues to offer the view in perspective of the terminal building to it, and as terminal also to the east-west axis of the whole scheme. A return from there to the proper, or common, entrance court is reassuringly straight and easy.

Apart from for the iron gates (which Switzer had already warned against using as little more than a snare to capture improvers in *IR* II 141), Switzer's modest wooded scheme in an improved agricultural context, and with only a few garden ornaments, gave Wynne full value in variety and interest, as well as the necessary grandeur wealth had commanded. One of the unlooked for boons of Wynne's early impoverishment was that these grounds, and some of the ornaments, have survived the subsequent changes in fashion.

Cliveden and Taplow Court

Figure 3.14 Cliveden/Taplow Court, Buckinghamshire: painting at Cliveden House of prospect from the south, undated (ca 1760). © National Trust.

The benefits, and the perils, of patronage and changes in circumstances within the early 18th century can be seen in the relationships of two families whose works will offer an illustration. Switzer dedicated a book to members of each. As alluded to above, when *The Practical Fruit Gardener* was published in 1724 Charles Lord Orrery's affairs were as far from the best fruits of his gardens as might be imagined. By then he had been discharged from the Tower of London, as the government could not really keep him there nor bring him to trial. Robert Walpole was still convinced that Orrery was a Jacobite and that he had used his house near Taplow in Buckinghamshire, Britwell House, to plot against the government. That he was a Jacobite seems to have been true: it is unlikely he plotted against the Crown. He was a scholar and a most distinguished bibliophile; he was most loyal to his friends; he was, as Switzer wrote, the great encourager of artists and scientists, personally agreeable, and in business of "quick dispatch"; nor was he a stranger to dysfunctional family life (as we now call it), having first encountered it as a child at Knole.

His politics and what his neighbours thought of them were not his only worries. It had become clear recently that the agent for his estates in Ireland had mismanaged affairs there, and his income was thus reduced, probably the result of fraud. Orrery's wife had died in the 1710s and in the following years of widowhood he had become involved with the wife of his secretary. They had children together and lived fairly openly as a family.

In the mid-1720s his heir, John Boyle, proposed to marry Henrietta Hamilton, one of the daughters of the Orkneys, who lived nearby at Cliveden. George Hamilton (1666–1737) was one of the younger sons of probably the greatest man in these islands, the Duke of Hamilton (ne Douglas: his wife had conferred the superior title and name on him on their marriage, as she was Duchess by birth-right), seated at Hamilton Palace in Lanarkshire. General Hamilton had sought his fame abroad in the army in the later 17th century, for which he was ennobled in 1696 as Earl of Orkney. He served also in the early 18th century, and was noted for his campaigns with Marlborough, where he was "probably his most distinguished and effective lieutenant" (Hanham *DNB*). In 1695 he had married a cousin, Elizabeth Villiers (1657–1733), who was "widely acknowledged as one of the most engaging and intelligent women of her time" (L B Smith *DNB*) and possibly also a mistress to King William. The estate of Cliveden came from her kin, the Buckinghams. Orkney and his wife remained good and useful courtiers through four reigns. They were never quite rich enough and wanted the extra boost from sinecures to keep the state of their ancestry and titles. They were on close terms with the new royal family and entertained them at Cliveden. His recent biographer has characterized Orkney's role as that of an "influential spectator" (Smith *DNB*), and noted his hesitation in speech as a possible reason for Swift's remark that he was "modest and shy to meddle", although good judgement could be an equally true guess and shows his character to more advantage. Lord and Lady Orkney were as Whiggish as Orrery was Tory, only probably more so.

There are garden connections with the Orkney daughters, too. Lady Frances married the heir to both Lumley Castle (see below) and the title Earl of Scarbrough, Thomas Lumley-Sanderson, in 1724. However, it would be 1740 before Lumley Castle came to them, and then without the income to improve it further. But Frances and Thomas were courtiers also, to Frederick, Prince of Wales, recently immigrated from Herenhausen in Hanover. They were very much part of the Prince's life throughout the 1730s, and his court figures prominently in developments in landscape design until his death in 1751. The third daughter, Anne, Lady Inchiquin, figures even more significantly. She was heiress to the Orkney honours and titles, and as owner of Cliveden became Frederick's landlady in 1739. She had married William O'Brien, Earl of Inchiquin (1700–1770), in 1720. His Irish estates brought him £6,000 a year (as much as the Orkneys' income before top-ups by sinecure), and he was a cousin, being a nephew to Anne Villiers Hamilton. He was also a loyal Whig and a Member of Parliament for various constituencies: in due course he too becomes part of the official household of Frederick, Prince of Wales. And of course Lord Inchiquin claims our attention as the recipient of Switzer's dedication in 1729 of volume 2 of *Hydrostaticks and Hydraulicks* and as such must be ranked as a patron.

It was Henrietta, the youngest of the three Hamilton daughters, who wished to marry John Boyle, son of Lord Orrery of Marston. When the Orkneys forbade their daughter to visit Britwell, Lord Orrery, considering Lady Hamilton's own well-known background, took this very ill. He blamed his son for agreeing, and he and his son fell out over it. Although they were reconciled before his death Lord Orrery had meanwhile willed his great library to his college, and it remains in the new wing of Peckwater at Christs Church, Oxford. Even more dolefully still, less than a year after becoming Lady Orrery in 1731, Henrietta died, leaving the new earl bereft, on top of the loss of his father's library, the settlement of much income on the irregular "family" and the knowledge of his late father's agent's skulduggery in Ireland, which meant that his ability to continue to improve Marston was much curtailed. It is only in the later 1730s that he is able seriously to take up his improvements there. Thus, we find a group of improvers carrying the burdens of three generations: the elders, with family standards to keep up (and of the highest order), coupled with a good sense of their own accomplishments and capabilities, and the younger ones inheriting these characteristics, plus the restrictions their living parents place upon them . . . the circumstances of youth and obligation. And into this mix of family life we must assess their roles in garden and landscape designs. Marston we have seen, and Lumley will be discussed later, but what of Cliveden? And more particularly probably what of the contiguous Taplow Court?

These both enjoy one of the most spectacular sites for a designed landscape to be found anywhere. John Evelyn had noted in 1679,

> Clifden, that stupendous natural rock, wood, prospect, of the Duke of Buckingham's buildings of extraordinary expense. The grotts in the chalky rock are pretty: 'tis a romantic object, and the place altogether answers the most poetical description that can be made of solitude, precipice, prospect, or whatever can contribute to a thing so very like their imaginations. The stande, somewhat like Frascati as to its front, and on the platform is a circular view to the verge of the horizon, which with the serpenting of the Thames is admirable . . . the cloisters, descents, gardens, and avenue thro' the wood, august and stately, but the land all about wretchedly barren, and producing nothing but ferne.
>
> (Evelyn 1827 iii 13)

At Taplow is the bridge to Maidenhead across the Thames, here flowing north to south. Between Cliveden and Taplow, its east banks fall and rise some 300 feet to the plateau on which Cliveden and its immediate surroundings sit, commanding a truly extensive southerly prospect of the Thames (as if it were their axial canal), with rural Berkshire laid out below to the west, balanced by the lands of Buckinghamshire to the east. At the south end is the other, slightly smaller and lower plateau and the site of an older house, Taplow Court.

It appears that Orkney improved these throughout his life there. A history of the works there has been dependent on two sources. The first is a group of drawings in an album assembled in the late 19th century for Lord Astor, the third very rich man to acquire and rebuild Cliveden in the 19th century. These include designs by Alexander Edward, Thomas Archer and Giacomo Leoni, and others attributed to Claude Desgots and Charles Bridgeman. These are all discussed by Gervase Jackson-Stops (Jackson-Stops 1976, 1977 65–78 and 1991 33–40). There is also occasional but very useful correspondence from Orkney to his brothers (National Library of Scotland, Fraser MS 1033).

The house the young Orkneys moved into was exceptionally tall, like Ashdown nearby, and also by William Winde. By removing the attic and top floor Archer remodelled it in about 1706 into a more conventional pattern and, with the later additions such as the quadrant colonnades about 1717 (Colvin 1978 69) completing it, it was as close to ideal as possible. Campbell illustrated these works in the second volume of *Vitruvius Britannicus*, published in 1717. Although the grounds are not illustrated the nature of the house and especially of its courts and terraces shows that a very ambitious scheme integrating the house and its gardens had been designed. His double plate of the garden front displays an exceptionally wide elevation, augmented by doubled wings of building, and equally important pauses, wings of space. All this seems supported on a breath taking tall and broad arcade-colonnade which lifts the whole composition, and commands the parterre to respond. Of course this is all elaborate *trompe l'oeil* to try and reduce the still absurdly tall house. It all requires an equally robust response from the gardens below. The garden front of Cliveden is the most elaborate of the type of design that Campbell calls the *Theatric Stile*. It is really the culmination of that means of uniting grand house and garden on its principal frontage, its face. Who the architect of these works was remains unknown: the flanking blocks have a kinship with James Smith's work at Orkney's parents' great house near Glasgow. Smith is an architect of considerable worth and importance, but his work programme in the second and third decades of the 18th century remains an almost complete blank (see Colvin 1974 and 1978 757). His protégé was, of course, Campbell.

For the gardens they would likely have consulted London or Wise for such a site, but equally possible is Alexander Edward, who is, given the work then being carried on by other members of the Hamilton family, perhaps the more likely consultant. It was Edward who made the design for the grounds at Hamilton Palace in 1708 (Brown 2012), which the family faithfully followed after his death. Edward was then very much active as a garden designer and architect, and designs by him for furnishing parterres at Cliveden survive. He had contracted with a number of Scottish improvers to advise them on the current Continental best practice, and he sourced plants for use at their sites from suppliers in London and district too. Therefore, his role at Cliveden might have been a significantly larger one. But Edward had been dead ten years, as likewise London since 1714. So for the development and elaboration that leaves only Archer himself, but, whoever he consulted, Orkney was very well advised on the gardens and landscape setting of his house: it corresponds to the Theatric Stile, exploits its grand site, but also provides the conventionally modern arrangement needed. Could Switzer be his unknown consultant in the later 1710s after London's death?

There is evidence of activity in the gardens in the mid-1720s, and then is the first indication also of works at Taplow Court. Taplow Court was the older and larger of the two houses, and it was the more comfortable. It was doubtless used by the Hamiltons from time to time, and perhaps this had been home to the Buckinghamshire Hamiltons and the centre of their family life while Cliveden was being remodelled. With the Inchiquins living as a married couple since 1720 it is reasonable to assume they lived at Taplow Court while the Orkneys occupied the now grander "main" house at Cliveden. With the setting up of three of the four Pedestals installed in 1725 at Taplow and the final one at Cliveden, we may also assume that the great

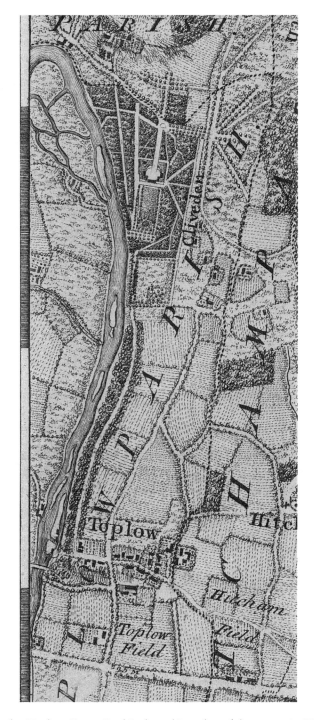

Figure 3.15 Cliveden/Taplow Court, Buckinghamshire: plan of the estates in 1752 (north to top). Reproduced from John Rocque, *Berkshire*, 1752. National Library of Scotland.

Long Ride linking the two houses was likely begun at that time also. This element is the first sign of the two estates being conceived as parts of a single entity. The Long Ride, or Taplow Terrace, uniting the long narrow estate-landscape recalls contemporary works at Cirencester. It also has resonance with Hamilton Palace in Lanarkshire, where Edward had designed the similar great avenue, there three miles long, without doubt one of the Boldest of Bold Strokes.

From that period survives evidence of a scheme for furnishing the parterre, and adding a big earthwork mount south of Cliveden, in a hand which appears to be French. There are qualities about the design of the slopes and earthworks at the south end, however, which suggest Bridgeman, or indeed Switzer. It resembles Switzer's contemporary Mount at Leeswood, and Bridgeman's later one at Kensington. However, there is a very simple notation on this drawing, across the earthwork . . . "ugly". In a letter to his brother that season Orkney notes that the earthworks were then "quite struck out". Jackson-Stops takes this to mean that it has been staked out ready for construction. But as Orkney had already noted it to be "ugly", it equally, if not more likely, means that it has been abandoned. It is more likely that Orkney is referring to the amphitheatre due west of Cliveden, where Thomas Arne and James Thomson's *Arthur* will soon be performed, and not to this aborted feature of the parterre. Orkney had written of the "great difficulty to get the slope all that side of the Hill where precipice was [that is the west side], but Bridgeman mackes difficultys of nothing. I told him that if I had thought to had been the one Halfe of what I see it will cost I believe I had never had done it, he says the beginning is the worst . . ." (Orkney to Panmure 2 Oct 1723 quoted in Jackson-Stops 1991 37).

Given the unhappiness then between the Orrery household and the Hamiltons Switzer's decision to publish his fulsome praise of Orrery in the dedication to *The Practical Fruit Gardener* cannot have endeared him to Orkney, and could well have occasioned a peremptory dismissal. Switzer could be somewhat contrary himself, and gardeners then, and subsequently, were famously robust in their opinions. As he writes in his rather subdued dedication to Inchiquin a few years later, "I know not well, my Lord, what kind Luminary it was directed me to the Felicity, I am now acknowledging . . .", but they were of repeated ". . . Marks of Favour and Friendship" (Dedication *Hydro* II). Doubtless, documentary evidence will appear in due course to clarify these speculations about Cliveden. About Taplow Court there seems to be a surer fit between this dedication and what we can recover about the design of the place that makes Switzer the confidently presumed designer of them.

Certainly by December 1725 Orkney had decided to have a severely plain scheme at Cliveden, of plain grass parterre ornamented only by rows of forest trees, and finished, not by the amphitheatrical earthworks, but by a simple low circular platform. As he wrote again to his brother, "I call it a quaker parter for it is very plain and I believe you will think it noble". Its manner as it appears in images shows more a scheme of sublimity than of niggardly plainness. In 1725 Giacomo Leoni was consulted about a house, and there are designs by him for the pedestals and garden pavilions. A dining pavilion, called the Blenheim Pavilion, was designed and built in about 1727 to the north-west of both the house and the parterre. Then in 1735 Orkney added the Octagon beside the parterre at the beginning of the slope down to the Thames. It contained a Prospect Room above and a grotto below. It figures prominently in the painting of the late 1750s (see Bouchenot-Dechin and Farhat 2014 320–321). This was finished just before Orkney's death, and in 1734 we have a description of the place by the attentive visitor John Loveday (Markham 1984 177–178). The sublimity I have ascribed to Orkney's "quaker parter" for Loveday was plain and wind-swept: ". . . The trees in the Garden are forced to be upheld by Ropes. Otherwise the Winds would tear them down", doubtless a prudent precaution for the recently planted rows along the edges of the parterre. In the same pre-Burkean appreciation Loveday found the banks of the Thames, ". . . in some Places the Descent is almost a Perpendicular and very terrible", but he nevertheless praised the unbounded prospect from the grounds to the Thames and "[t]he good large village of Cookham (where the Church is also large) . . . just upon it" and a view of Windsor Castle "from the noble Gravel-Terrace". He noted the woodlands on both sides of the parterre with "several Walks in it and Vistas cut through it". On that early visit he did not go on to see Taplow Court, but did note, "The Wood with-out the Garden-Pales towards Taplow is said to have fine Walks in it, whence a rather finer View than from the Garden".

This part of the place, which as we have assumed was given over to the Inchiquins, occupies the slightly smaller half of the estate and was laid out by design, but a design of a different kind from that seen by Loveday, from what he noted as "the Garden". This was Taplow Court, which consisted of conventional gardens and the wooded walks and fine views he reported, plus a large pasture and several good sized meadows. This is shown on a survey of the grounds by the Eton builder-architect Stiff Leadbetter, made in or about 1743. Hard by Taplow Court were the drive and turning circle, courtyards and a parish church on the south and east, the village sides. To the north was the large bowling green and two other good sized rectangular gardens in a row between the house and a large field. Beyond this field the ground falls away northwards, to a valley where a stream runs into the Thames, then rises again towards Cliveden, giving good open views to the woods, garden and house; in other words the reverse of the view noted by Loveday.

Therefore, we can recover something of the design of Taplow Court formed from the later 1720s as it appeared in the early 1740s. Thus is indicated two great houses and garden schemes within the context of the ensemble that the elder Orkneys had established in their time. The nature of this double estate already allowed it to sit comfortably into the 18th century alongside for example Cirencester, or Grimsthorpe. Cliveden has always been the grander; it is the great and late "baroque" house with a commanding prospect and *Theatric Stile*, and when Frederick, Prince of Wales, moved there it began to have the allure of celebrity as well, which will have polished its reception with visitors, increasingly less alarmed by the bleak newness Loveday had found, and much more receptive to the extensive views from its woods and Noble Terrace walk. All the while Taplow Court provides its lesser completion, and to a degree its antidote.

At Taplow Court we find a suite of gardens in conventional form and manner, but there are aspects which initially seem anomalous. They lie parallel to the house and on its north side, and where we might anticipate a parterre on the west side, only the "Back Yard" is noted and occupies three-quarters of that river facing frontage. The south front almost adjoins the ancient church and churchyard, and is also walled off. As Taplow Court is a late 16th or early 17th century house of four stories where important public rooms would be on the upper floors, these "vagaries" at the ground floor level may have been of little importance. The favoured views at the elevated Taplow Court were southerly. Over the church and two largish fields, the Babsey Meadows, was the prospect of Windsor Castle with the Thames in the foreground. Here the circular pond, at the extreme end of a series of ponds, hints at a former canal-like feature, roughly on the axis of the south front. Uniquely, the nature of the whole Cliveden estate meant that the views to the north were perhaps of equal attraction from Taplow Court. Here beyond the Bowling Green was the big Cherry Tree Field, then pasture and woodland to Cliveden itself. The wooded verges of the Thames mark the entire west side. So the Inchiquins had the most favoured and theatrical view of the big house, whether occupied by the parents, or by the heir apparent. So how best to manage this abundance of views with its somewhat peculiar arrangement of existing gardens and its location of the immediate site between Windsor and Cliveden? As the Best Garden, the big Bowling Green opened from the shorter north front, and this will have served as the parterre. Here, as at Longleat, a raised walk encloses the Bowling Green, whose dominant east-west axis soon offers entrance to the two further gardens to the east, or further around the entrance to the broad Green Walk, a sort of delayed Terrace, running alongside the Cherry Tree Field and its neighbouring open grounds to the north. This distant prospect is flatteringly lighted by the sun from the foreground to Cliveden House, and would be cross lit all afternoon. But the Green Walk is a prelude only, and leads shortly to the Bold Stroke of Taplow, the Taplow Terrass.

This feature runs parallel to the Thames along the escarpment on the west side of Taplow Court. Its south end, as it is appears on Leadbetter's survey of the immediate site of the house, stops (rather abruptly) south-west of the house at the churchyard, and there it overlooks the Babsey Meadows and the view to Windsor Castle. Although the line drawn on the survey is quite bold, it is clear that it is a line for demarcation, and not indicative of a fence or other object. In other words, the Meadows and the Pasture immediately to the west simply join there. Taplow Terrass was created to make a place to enjoy all the views conveniently close to the rest of the gardens: thus, that view to the south, but also the long series of views along the banks of the Thames west, and north-west over Berkshire, and, to accompany these and to give variety and enhance the sense of balance, the more pastoral "home" views to the north and north-east are incorporated. This is all a very short walk from the house. We can measure its width, but how long was Taplow Terrass in 1743? According to John Rocque's survey of 1752 the Terrace extended all the way to Cliveden. Roughly half way along, at the Old Quarry, until 1950 the Root House occupied this site on the west edge of the escarpment. A building of semi-circular plan originally occupied this site, and would have overlooked the Old Quarry, roughly at the mid-point of the shallow curve it made of the escarpment here. This mid-18th century folly would have made a place to appreciate the prospect over Cookham and Berkshire, or the adjacent paddock. It may be seen, if indistinctly, on the 1747 Prospect. Its form and architecture would also make a pleasurable contrast with the grotesque nature of the quarry. That point is also what the Prospect of 1747 indicates as the end of the tabled part of the topography, which forms a natural domain in the southern part of the estate in sight of Cliveden woods. There have always been other paths indicated in that long middle stretch between Taplow Court and Cliveden with several seeming to dip down nearer to the Thames itself.

There are other terraces similar to this one which might offer clues to its furnishing and detailed design, not least the smaller Parade at Leeswood, but also Shardeloes, also in Buckinghamshire (*Vit Brit* 4 plates 100–101), or Oatlands, Surrey, attributed to Thomas Wright (Walpole 2 100, *Vit Brit* 4 plates 67–68). These are both one sided and lie against a wooded margin, whereas Taplow is open to both sides equally. The contemporary Fir Walk at Stourhead (which I also attribute to Switzer; see below) ran along an escarpment between park and view, as does the anonymous Ravenfield in Yorkshire (*Vit Brit* 4 plates 108–109), which is also planted with fir trees. Leadbetter indicates no plantings of any kind in his survey, and thus cannot adjudicate. But since the Taplow Terrass was the site of the Cedar Walk it is most tempting to assume that it started its existence as such. It will have had some barrier to the adjacent pastures, perhaps a Ha Ha, or low terracing such as at Cirencester. Otherwise, we must assume it to have been plain.

Thus, we have a hypothetical division, and two rather contrasting designs: the larger, grander (and in the late 1730s soon to be princely) part to the north, and an equally designed and identifiable section to the south . . . the extended grounds of Taplow Court with the *Taplow Terrass* its generator, designed by Switzer and formed in the period from the mid-1720s to the early 1740s. This would be on the order of 50 acres or so, with pleasure gardens at the south end, the small park or paddock of about 30 acres embraced by the wooded bank of the Thames and the Cliveden-Taplow Road on its east side, and open towards Cliveden itself, forming a kind of pocket landscape or *ferme ornée*, certainly a *rural and farm-like garden*. Cliveden remained in the tenancy of Frederick, Prince of Wales, until his death in 1751. During this time it was much frequented and a focus for an alternative court, and through his interests and his own efforts, especially in employing William Kent, he and the place exerted influence on the then swift changes in taste and designed landscapes. The custom of visiting grounds for ideas for improvement in this period often included visits to Taplow and Cliveden. The Dillons of Ditchley made such a tour in 1750, taking in Hardwicke House, Whiteknights, Taplow, Windsor Castle, Oatlands, Painshill, Claremont, Esher, Woburn Farm, Whitton and Hampton Court (Cousins 2011 161–162). When Anne Hamilton, Lady Inchiquin and Orkney, died in 1756 the gardens and landscapes of both places were well established. If there remained a whiff of the old style, notably in the parterre and terrace walk at Cliveden, it was not mentioned. Yet its time of fashion had passed. Inchiquin remarried in the 1760s and lived on at Taplow Court with his interests in politics still alive, notably through friendship with Edmund Burke and William Pitt. It was only at his death in 1777, when Taplow Court passed to his son-in-law and nephew Murrough O'Brien (1754–1790), that further works in the grounds are noted. In 1778 Lancelot Brown was consulted by O'Brien about Taplow Court, apparently about further plantation along the escarpment by Taplow Terrass, and was duly paid his fee of £100 to cover the visit, the survey and presumably his initial advice (Phibbs 2013 252). Dorothy Stroud had noted a letter, undated but in 1777, from O'Brien, still the novice improver, to Brown seeking his advice: ". . . as I am entirely unacquainted with the method of proceeding, when, and how to begin . . . shall be obliged to you let me have a person to set us well to work" (Stroud 1950 [1975] 182). When J C Loudon visited Taplow Court in the 1820s he found these hanging woods still wonderful, if rather neglected, and teased the Orkney of the day by commenting that he preferred to interest himself in scientific matters.

Stourhead

Henry Hoare (1677–1725) commissioned a design for gardens from Switzer in 1720 for which he paid him 15 guineas (equivalent currently to just over £4,700.00). Hoare had recently bought the estate of Stourton through intermediaries from the family of the same name, apparently with the express intention of establishing his family as landed. Henry had already acquired Quarley, Hampshire, where he and his wife, Jane, had lived from 1709 and brought up Henry II as a young squire. Jane was the sister of William Benson of Wilbury. Henry I and his brother Benjamin had prospered in the early 18th century, and although closely involved with the South Sea Company they did not share in its opprobrium. The Stourton estate and another at Boreham in Essex, acquired by Benjamin, are likely the products of their acumen in those boom times (Woodbridge 1970 11 et seq). Although there was a house at Stourton, Henry and Jane chose to build anew, and very likely consulted her brother about it. His protégé was indeed their choice, and Stourhead, as it was named, became the first of a distinguished type, the square plan essentially one storey villa style house derived from Andrea Palladio's seemingly similar works for the similarly placed Vicentine well-to-do of the 16th century . . . who were also often merchants taking up civilized life as farmers.

Campbell's design for the house was, despite its Palladian inspiration, no more adventurous in its exploitation of setting than the first effort of Lord Burlington a few years later at Chiswick (see below). Those lessons were slower to be realized, or perhaps even formulated, and, apart from rare earlier examples like Nostell Priory (see also below), really belong to the period after mid-century. Stourhead is now famous as an exemplar par excellence of fusion of house and landscape. However, just how it became such requires re-telling. It was in Campbell's design only like a Palladian villa from the front elevation. And its plan has been significantly extended to cope with the needs of subsequent gentry Hoares. The same fate overtook Cousin Benson's more revolutionary concept for Wilbury, which has been swamped by additions into a very conventional country house.

These seeming lacks of direction or decision might be applied to the early design of the grounds, or what we must assume was the design for the grounds. The only contemporary representations of them occur on an early estate plan dated 1722, and in two one point perspective drawings in the Library of the Royal Institute of British Architects, of the entrance and garden fronts, undated but also of the 1720s. Although Henry I died in 1725, Jane lived on at Stourhead, and, very importantly, Henry II continued the works there while his mother remained in residence. For example between 1726 and 1734 he spent some £10,000 on building and garden works and a third of that amount on furnishings (that is, £3 million and £1 million respectively). Henry II bought Wilbury for himself from his uncle in 1734, while he continued to enrich Stourhead in the same period with works of art. It was only from 1742 that he embarked on the embellishment of the Stour at Paradise Bottom as his famous Lake, for which Kenneth Woodbridge has clearly traced the design history. However, it is the nature of the works before then that claims our attention here, and these are not without interest in themselves, for it is in these that we may find the hand of Switzer.

The 1722 plan shows the new house embraced on the north and west sides by a series of meadows, either let or in hand. These are part of the Salisbury Plain and are relatively high, open and extensive, although none is large in itself and all are defined by hedges. To the west is the Great Oar Pasture, and towards the south are the village of Stourton, the Mill and a parsonage farm, all rather more crowded into the topography along the edge of the plain as it falls down towards the Stour, where the river has already been formed into a series of ponds. Stourton also straggles across the course of the river; there, ten or more cottages and their plots lie to the east and the west along an irregular lane. There are also large and walled gardens on the east and south sides of the new house. These lie regularly to each face, with kitchen garden and secondary yards accommodated between them, and the stable yard lying irregularly beyond the south-east corner, clearly a relic of the old house of Stourton. The east, or entrance, garden is laid out as an oval lawn with a drive around it and augmented on its east end by an apse-like extension where the gates lie opposite and on axis to the house. The first of the drawings shows differences using the same parts. The entrance side is a simple iron screen on dwarf walls terminated by big obelisks, with the apse-like element now used against the front of the house, giving it the needed frame of curves and extra width. The main garden on the south side of the house axially connects it to the Barn Meadow, which also fronts the edge between the plain and the Stour. At the house end its walls also curve forward in small quadrants, mimicked by a fairly complex sunken and sloped parterre of plain grass. Later this was extended southward to include a large circular basin further south. At its centre was a large female statue (most likely the original place of the Stourhead Diana) on a combination fountain and pedestal. On the plan its end is indicated as simply straight, whereas the drawing shows it as two shallow curves of low hedge, with a generous opening on axis. Both these enclosures are otherwise unfurnished, but there are blocks of close planted woodland or shrubbery indicated adjacent to each. The immediate setting of Stourhead is thus established in a cool and decidedly architectural manner. But what of the surrounding grounds?

Our evidence is rather meagre, in the sense that no drawings of these parts have survived, and after Jane's death in 1741 Henry II's imagination was taken up with the next ring outward from the house, and his works there were transformational and deservedly famous. What had happened in the previous 20 years was of less interest to Woodbridge, who was never able quite to accept my assertions of their importance (see Woodbridge 1970). However, the question remains about the forms and intentions of that second ring of improvements about the house, and the even larger question of whether their character in any sense led to the manner of the completion of Stourhead. I think they were a critical step in the ongoing design of the place, and that without an understanding of them we shall continue to suffer that lack of completion and totality which still nags at sensitive visitors to Stourhead.

Given the sum Henry I paid Switzer his response must have been rather more than what is shown on the 1722 estate survey. Both in terms of the fee itself and, even more, in terms of the nature of the man to whom it was paid, we expect something rather bigger, and certainly more extensive. The formality of the walled sections is not the issue: it is precisely what we should expect from Switzer at that date and in light of what he had recently written and practised. What seems to be missing is the looser frame of meadows, woods, walks and fields, and their connections to both the architectural core, based on the house, and the wider topography or landscape beyond. The elements which could easily have been employed in 1722 were the contiguous meadows in hand. These were the Great Oar Pasture, at some 28 acres, with the smaller New Meadow beyond it to the west; to the south were the Black Meadow (later the site of the Lake), at about 16 acres, while closer to the house was the 8 acre

116 *Early landscapes*

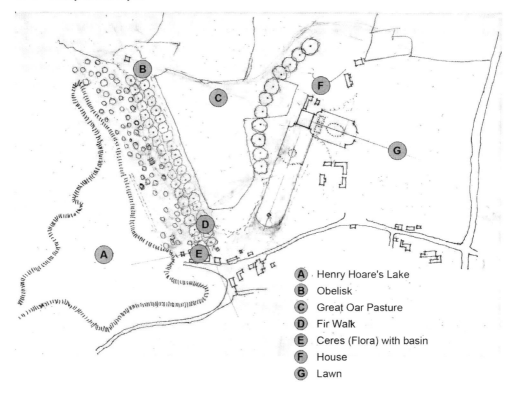

Figure 3.16 Stourhead, Wiltshire: plan of the estate in the early 1740s (north to top). Image by the author.

Barn Meadow lying south of the south garden; and finally eastward was the site of the old house of Stourton, the Slade Meadow pasture of 17 acres. Therefore, (leaving aside the Lake area at present) we have roughly 50 acres of level ground adjacent to the gardens discussed above which are in hand and favourable to Rural and Extensive Gardening.

Clemens Steenbergen and his associates at Delft University have proposed that this ground indeed was developed in the 1720s and 1730s as a *ferme ornée* (Steenbergen and Reh 2003 328). They have published a very plausible plan of it, based on archival reference from Hoare's own account book, and also by reference to elements suitable to the earlier period but recorded later by the meticulous Swedish surveyor and artist Magnus Piper. Thus, we have a hypothetical design which in the absence of Switzer's original will need to serve for our commentary. As he had instructed in his explanation of the design for the Manor of Paston Switzer takes the major elements, here the shapes and dispositions of the meadows, as the directors of the composition, including retention of any significant singleton trees or groups. An axial extension from the house westward is supposed, and confirmed with the later construction of the Obelisk, where it also lies on the axis of the Fir Walk in the 1730s, laid out as a terrace along the edge of the grounds overlooking the Stour lying below in the Black Meadow. The other end of that axis is managed by a sort of natural bastion, itself reorganized as part of the Terrace planted and formed in the Barn Meadow, also in the 1730s. There was a Venetian Alcove there also, and, more importantly, the parterre has been lengthened, and ornamented by a "new" statue, a copy of the Apollo Belvidere on a low mound. There are traces of the half-terrace walks, or Ha Has, making the edges of Great Oar Pasture into a continuous terrace walk, of the kind still in existence at Cirencester, and also (as Steenbergen points out) in Bridgeman's earliest parts of Stowe. Piper shows a broad walk of large forest trees disposed (roughly) in symmetrical form, curved as part of a great segment in plan and arranged to either side of the western central axis. This can have been perceived as such only dimly, but as an exercise in an incomprehensible regularity it would fit into Switzer's family of formal elements. The edges of the parts had been defined even in the Stourtons' times by trees, and that is not changed but rather regularized into the design for this side of the grounds. A rather different mode of composition was used on the east front, the old Slade Meadow pasture. Here a notional central axis on the entrance front to Stourhead is observed, when at some time probably in the later 1730s the walled forecourt with its obelisks is replaced by a shallow splayed figure for the parade element: this is composed of two lazy serpentines giving the whole space a bell shape, open at its wide mouth to the old Slade Meadow. The resulting Lawn is ornamented only by surviving single trees, and augmented by three clumps. These changes might be from the 1730s or 1740s.

The nature of the place as found in the first ring around Stourhead is maintained, but spruced up, or civilized, to make pleasant walks along the edges, with varied views across the Oar Pasture, or outwards, especially along the Fir Walk adjacent to the Lake site. Lined by "Stately Scotch Firs of Mr Hoare's own planting" (*London Chronicle* 1757, quoted in Woodbridge 1982 12), then thought exotic, it made an agreeable object in itself, and sufficiently distant to afford good exercise. As an avenue, then still the core of what any garden should contain, but curiously the first at Stourhead, it provided structured semi-enclosed walks. At its beginning was a broad terrace-like area acting rather like the parterre had recently done, providing company with a comfortable space to observe all parts of the now extended grounds, and affording varied prospects of all parts. As well as the Venetian Alcove there was the Ombrello recorded by Piper. Throughout Henry Hoare's life this series of prospects remained (Harrison 2015 130). Soon, in the 1740s, they would provide the introduction or prelude to the famous part of Stourhead, the Lake and its many ornamental buildings. And on the entrance front the old pasture is abstracted into a suitably formal approach to Stourhead, and then only noticed when the axis is tweaked. Thus, Stourhead of the 1730s should be seen as a handsome up-to-date but small place such as Leeswood, Rousham or Hanbury. The addition of Henry Hoare's Paradise Bottom to this already subtle and inclusive composition completes the picture.

These areas Henry Hoare began in 1744 with the Temple of Ceres (soon renamed the Temple of Flora) facing into the short rectangular basin already in place. Hoare had planned other buildings along the wooded slope between the Fir Walk and the Paradise Bottom, where the Lake grew as it was made up of enlarged and joined ponds. One of these, perhaps related to the Diana statue and now lost basin, was a circular open temple with a dome to be in the Ionic order. This was to be sited almost certainly somewhere in the upper works, perhaps adjacent to the short dog-leg spur leading to and from the original garden and the Fir Walk, or even in the wooded bank associated with the "several irregular Walks of Different Breadths leading into the Valley" (*London Chronicle* 1757, as above). Although this building was designed and pretty well advanced it was not proceeded with, and the later ornaments in this part of the gardens really ought to be seen in association with his later embellishment programme. The works of the 1730s were sufficient in themselves, and made an excellent introduction to, as well as probably an inspiration for, his Paradise. They also provided, and still could provide if properly managed, a critical mediation between the immediate surroundings of the house and the outer landscapes. These additions appear to me to be works designed by Switzer.

4 "Nature to advantage dress'd"

Caversham

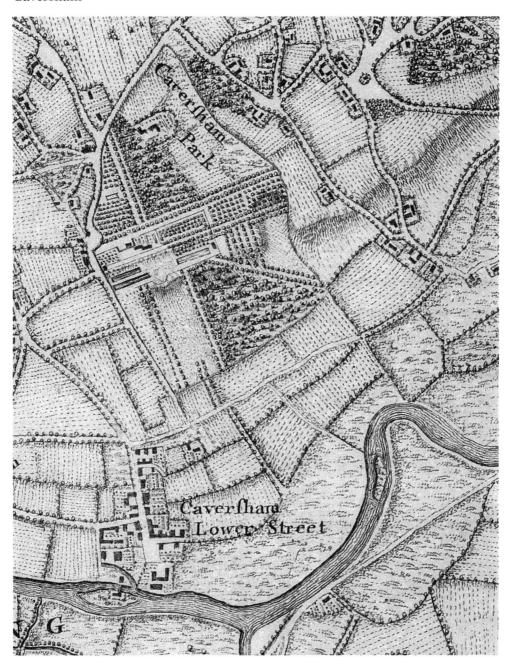

Figure 4.1 Caversham, Berkshire: plan of the estate (north to top). Reproduced from John Rocque, *Berkshire*, 1752. National Library of Scotland.

As we have seen at Grimsthorpe, forms of field fortification were used to make the elaborate enclosing terrace walks around Lady Lindsey's enlarged woodland, and there remain in the family archives at Lincoln Castle images of Vauban-like fortification patterns clearly used to explore the best and most authentic shapes for design. Such field fortifications would be familiar to soldiers who had served in the recent Continental wars, or even earlier with King William there or in Ireland. So it is perhaps less surprising to find fortification derived features at Blenheim, or at Castle Howard. As many of these old soldiers can be found as commissioners of improvements such forms will have been readily accepted, and maybe even desired. As well as fortification forms there will have been a general acceptance of such large scale earth moving as not quite commonplace but certainly not extraordinary. Therefore, it is an easier step to include such engineering scale works as part of what would have heretofore been simpler, much more proscribed, where costly works were horticultural, or occasionally as sculpture. Thus, it will be less surprising that a contract drawn up between Stephen Switzer and the Earl of Cadogan for works at Caversham in 1718 is largely for these infrastructural works of earth forming . . . of landscaping. The works consisted of terraces, canals, banks and slopes, none specifically military in form, yet all of military scale, as Lord Molesworth had it, to be achieved by sapper-like *maggots*. Cadogan had been quarter-master with Marlborough at the Battle of Blenheim slightly more than a decade before. He had also, like Marlborough, withdrawn into "exile" when the Tories formed a government in 1711, to be rewarded by the new Whig government which followed. One of the rewards was his peerage, and he bought a new estate at Caversham near Reading. It is made like a field fortification, but without formal military reference.

Caversham lies north-east of Reading in open, flattish country dominated by the Thames, which runs between them. Lord Cadogan's house and grounds are just east of the village on a site slightly tilted southwards to the river. He built himself a new house from 1718 on. Its architect is, curiously, unrecorded. But as Colen Campbell had already illustrated a design for him in 1717, and not the one built, he may have preferred to simply remain silent about it. Campbell did illustrate the gardens layout as a double plate in the third volume of *Vitruvius Britannicus* in 1725. From its outline there it is clear that the house was very substantial with a five part entrance front with a pair of quadrant colonnades linking to service wings. The garden front, known only from a late 18th century print which may reflect later changes, was of nine bays and three stories and exceptionally plain. The terminal ends stepped forward as pavilions. Although Campbell does not mention the house, he is fulsome in his praise of the grounds. Their design suggests the military man not only in the tidy and regular array of forest trees planted quadratically as a very large grove on level ground occupying the north-west quarter of the estate, but also in its composition of strongly regular generating lines running resolutely east-west or north-south. Three single avenues define the large Thames-side parks, and mark the estate's centre to the south, whereas a parade runs northward, defined by treble rows of forest trees. Parkland, seemingly emparked by Cadogan himself, makes an ample buffer around house and grounds, and the Thames offers a suitable and substantial boundary to the south, with the town of Reading providing visual interest towards the south-west.

The garden grounds occupy the south side of the scheme and run from the west to the east ends of it, and they exhibit the same regular, precise and architectural quality as the whole layout, including the satisfyingly classically proportioned parterre, whose centre line responds precisely to the house and its Terrace, of course, but also generated seemingly from its centre, the ruling east-west axis of the two canals laid out to either side. Its military regularity is set off somewhat by the big semi-circular end of the parterre jutting towards the Thames a bit like a great bastion. This would be a most advantageous spot for company to gather to enjoy the heart of the gardens, for all would be easily and comfortably to hand, from a good prospect back to the house with the framed parterre set off in front, as well as the sweep of the whole ensemble towards the river. According to the detail shown on the published plan, re-drawn by Campbell and probably a change from the original intent, beds for flowers are rather crowded into this feature. The bastion shape is echoed in the near park, and the two other "halves" of the missing semi-circle appear as quadrants providing a secondary connection from the Terrace and the canals. The contract to execute this scheme was drawn up between Cadogan and Switzer in 1718 for works that summer. It is a very detailed document full of information rarely found. It is precise in terms of the specification of the works, also quite specific as to costs, and the issues of what is to be provided by the estate, and what by Switzer, how payments are to be made to workmen, and how managed.

There are several aspects of Caversham that claim our attention, apart from its nature and intrinsic merits. It exhibits the best nature and quality, and the very ideal of the regular design of the heart of an early 18th century garden. No scheme for improvement in this period can be without such a suite of elements. So Caversham's are therefore both representative and typical of aspiration. That we have through the contract such detailed information about these parts gives a strong understanding of the more technical aspects of the hearts of these gardens, their costs and their importance to their owners. And at a time when fundamental matters of taste are at issue the formal

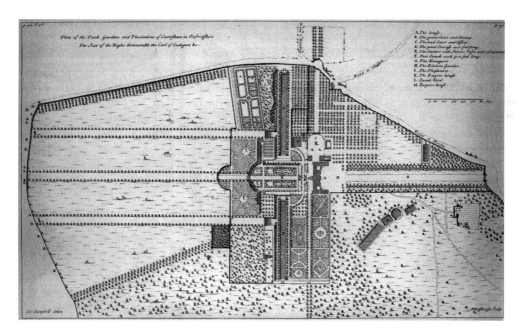

Figure 4.2 Caversham, Berkshire: plan of the gardens (north to right). Reproduced from Colen Campbell, *Vitruvius Britannicus, or the British Architect*, 1725 (ed 1731), II plates 96 and 97.

nature of these elements is worth clarifying. Finally, the circumstances of its execution raises interesting issues about attribution, professional practice and historical evidence.

A southerly aspect towards the Thames in an orderly and essentially regular topography near London is of itself an ideal. The position as politically favoured military hero, with wealth to build a very handsome new house and to embellish its grounds, raises that ideal even higher. And its occurrence so recently after the appearance of John James' clearly authoritative text on how to manage these matters assures critical interest, and Switzer's rendering shows that he is capable of rising to such expectations. The Caversham parterre in its setting of banks and related terraces may stand for the best centrepiece of the conventional and preferred type. At Caversham we have the ideal garden of 25 acres, or thereby, accomplished elegantly and appropriately, and, as we shall see, with more subtlety and skill than most exercises in ideal productions manage to achieve.

Clearly the first view to catch any visitor's notice is the prospect just beyond the main reception room doors . . . the Thames valley, laid out straight in front according to Campbell as four beautiful lawns, across the Terrace and down the broad steps (of the best Portland) into the parterre. This is embraced by tree-lined walks at a higher embanked level, but is focused on the river prospect at its "best" view point, the semi-circular bastion. Caversham's design aspires to be among the best symmetrically designed schemes, most famously perhaps Andre Le Notre's Vau-le-Vicomte. Therefore, the first rule must be . . . break the rules. The first thing a returning visitor notices, or perhaps a discerning one from the beginning, is a distinct imbalance, here towards the south-east. The entry to the Terrace, some 370 metres long, rather than marking the centre of the south front, begins there and so invites the eye eastward into a very long garden walk. (It was later extended a bit further to the west.) Therefore, the obvious vista has an alternative. Which to choose? It hardly matters: already the symmetry is, as it were, tamed and made comfortable. The terrace walk extends eastward beyond the grounds, and along its way its own symmetry is relieved by the changes in level to either side. And as it is largely wooded, the walk gives that part of the design the added role of wilderness, or garden for walking in.

Even if the more obvious direction is chosen alternatives are provided by the raised and embanked flanking walks. If either of these is preferred, then one of the canals soon beckons away from the axis of direction. Seemingly dominant on plan the canals initially appear obliquely, and through screens of forest trees, and are encountered head-on only at the ends at the walks flanking the parterre. They can be accessed also from the little quadrant walks from the Terrace, when their great length is appreciated only once one is under their geometric spell. Therefore, the clarity of the plan and its very tidy regularity are apparent only in plan: as a garden experience, or series of experiences, it will reveal itself more subtly. Each of the big elements – canals, parterre and Terrace – is sufficiently large, arresting and embellished to satisfy. These are the issues which are taken up, and critically, with Alexander Pope's strictures on symmetry in his Villa of Timon in the *Epistle to Burlington* nearly 15 years in the future.

Cadogan for his part has assured that the content, the furnishings of the gardens (what most of his visitors will notice), is to the very best standards. According to Campbell's commentary these furnishings were costly and fine, and worth the effort of examining rather as if Cadogan saw his grounds as also a sort of gallery. Included were four "Originals in Statuary Marble, of King William, King George, Duke of Marlborough and Prince Eugene [of Savoy, with Marlborough the principal director of the Continental forces against Louis] all so very like, that they are known at Sight; besides many valuable ones cast from the best Antiques" (*Vit Brit* III 12). All these, and the plantings in the parterre, are reserved for Cadogan to provide. And the parterre was further finished "nobly with fountains vases and statues". There were also ornamental buildings; at the ends of each canal was to be a Doric Portico.

Switzer advised that one should follow nature. To some following nature was a good thing only so long as it is the currently admired version of nature. Even Pope occasionally exhibits this childishness. Shaftesbury and the other Neo-Platonists had a more grown-up idea of what that might mean. (Until recently Shaftesbury has been generally credited with originating the idea of following nature; see Myers 2010.) A mature view of the consultation of the genius of the place, like that advocated by the 20th century architect, critic and teacher Louis Kahn, would counsel trying to determine what the place wished. If the habit of a plant tends to the circular, or spherical, then it can be argued that it ideally wants to take that shape, and as Shaftesbury indicated in the portrait he commissioned of himself in his garden at St Giles House the parterre trees have their aspirations rewarded, and do appear as spheres on regular trunks, in tidy order, and on a seemingly perfectly flat ground. To take a quite different example of the same thing, as Switzer had written recently . . . if one encountered an ancient woodland with varied ground form which offered a surprising and agreeable aspect, and if the wood commanded a high hill with views round about, then it should be humoured and formed into its best self. It should not be clear-felled and replaced with some other ideal. Therefore, since Caversham is in a river plain, gently tilted southward and otherwise open and tending to the flat, its nature may be argued to favour the regular, rectangular and orderly design it received.

The design meticulously described and specified in the contract was carried out, with the exception of details in the parterre and the amphitheatres designed to go at the ends of the canals, but not in 1718, nor, according to Campbell, by Switzer. Campbell's commentary concludes, "These Gardens were form'd by Mr. Acres, where he has left lasting Monuments of his Capacity, Anno 1723" (*Vit Brit* III 12). This refers to Thomas Acres, who seems to have carried on Wrest Park and Wanstead after his uncle, George London, died in 1714. Acres is otherwise unknown, apart from his part in the successful attempt to unseat Sir Christopher Wren from the Surveyorship of Royal Works and replace him with William Benson and, as his deputy, Colen Campbell, in 1717. It became clear fairly quickly that Benson was incompetent in the role, not necessarily the disqualification it might appear to be, but clearly Campbell as deputy had been unable to cover for him sufficiently. In the same onslaught on the Board of Works Acres had been proposed as the successor to Henry Wise, largely on the grounds that the annual charges to keep the Royal Gardens were too high. As these gardens had initially been founded on the costly style favoured by William and Mary, there had already been questions about these, and reductions in Queen Anne's reign. Wise busied himself in answering the charges brought by Acres and his associates, and this defence and his own political strengths were enough to fend off the attack. Wise retained his position, and Acres lost his bid.

There is perhaps a hint in Campbell's comments that Acres may have inherited the execution of the designs at Caversham on the grounds of cost. According to Campbell, Cadogan, ". . . from a Place that could pretend to nothing but a Situation capable of Improvement, with vast Labour and Expense, has now rendered it one of the noblest Seats in the Kingdom" (ibid). According to the agreement with Switzer the works were to cost just under £1400 with about £840 extra for labour, nearly £2250, roughly the equivalent of £675,000 in current sterling value. The moiety retained by the contractor, whether Acres or Switzer, was up to them, and Acres may have been prepared to under-value his work here, as he had been happy to do for the Crown contract which he had attempted to secure with Campbell and Benson the year before. Although we know that Switzer had other demanding work in 1718, notably at Hampton Court, Herefordshire, he was still based at nearby Newbury and could have doubtless managed both contracts. But Cadogan had good reasons to put off his works: he was then leading negotiations with recent allies to establish internationally the stability of the Hanoverian succession; he had an ongoing dispute with the Duchess of Marlborough over shady dealings with investments, which cost him dear; and he had to answer an investigation by a committee of Members of Parliament about his alleged mismanagement of funds pursuing the Pretender in Scotland. Of course with the house then under construction Cadogan might well have simply found it prudent to wait a few years to proceed with the landscape work. Thus, it was at the conclusion of the Treaty in Vienna that he took them up again. By then Switzer had removed to Devizes and was busily engaged with Spye Park and other works nearby.

Holme Lacy

Holme Lacy in the Wye valley of Herefordshire was the long term seat of the Scudamore family, which was politically important locally but had waned in the later 17th century although their wealth had continued to grow. John Scudamore, who inherited in 1671, was closely allied to his Whiggish neighbours, and especially the Coningsbys, but had rather veered away from these tendencies when pressed to action, and his neighbours took this ill, believing he had been influenced too much by his Tory-leaning household. His son, James Scudamore, 3rd Viscount Scudamore (1684–1716), was a minor when he inherited so that Tory tendency was continued by his tutors. The family's chance to prosper, politically, with the revolutionary change in monarchs was thus lost: he was abroad in those times, and then at Oxford. He married Frances Digby in 1706. He was gravely injured in a riding accident in 1710, but went on to become a Member of Parliament, as a Tory, so was at least in favour with the Harley faction in the county. Their only child, also Frances, was born in 1711, but Lord Scudamore died at the early age of 32, leaving Lady Frances to bring up their daughter, manage their estates and, we believe, continue the improvements to the grounds. She also became known for her patronage of literary men like Alexander Pope, John Gay and Thomas Southerne. She died in 1729 just before her daughter's wedding to the Duke of Beaufort.

Holme Lacy had been rebuilt with Hugh May as the architect in 1674, and the house bears comparison with his Cassiobury but is actually architecturally even grander. It has three major fronts, the entrance to the north, Wye to the east and the garden front facing south. There are very good interiors as well. The house is most advantageously sited, with an easy bow of the Wye below in the middle foreground eastward, and an ample park to the north. The south aspect might have been thought problematic as it sloped shortly to a series of ponds and the park rose up perhaps a trifle too sharply beyond to admit the kind of prospect then in fashion. It should have had the design from one of the Brompton Park partners also, but the gardens appear to be of later date. These may be a remodelling, but the grounds, in my judgement, have the stamp of the early Switzer.

"Nature to advantage dress'd" 125

Figure 4.3 Holme Lacy, Herefordshire: view of the house from the south, ca 1780. Pen and black ink with monochrome wash. © British Library Board.

The design of the gardens is similar to that at Caversham and also Marston, and exhibits the conventions still desired in the second decade of the 18th century. Although there is suggestive evidence of a companion terrace next to the park on the north front, as well as the inherited large "courtyard" open to the Wye eastward, there is the same broad terrace walk Switzer advised as critical to include along the southern, garden, front. This does the job as described in *Ichnographia Rustica* and seen also at Caversham. Here its asymmetry runs "backward" towards the kitchen gardens and compartments to the west: its east section addresses the Wye valley and the adjacent prospect of the southern hilly parkland. From the centre of the garden front, retired slightly between the two terminal wings, the expected garden axis is carried across the terrace and down into the parterre, in almost text-book perfection. But as the park is so close and rises so sharply it becomes the object of view, a fact made even more prominent by the theatrical setting of the parterre itself. Therefore, the main prospect becomes a "picture of nature", framed by the parterre ensemble. Conversely, the house is similarly framed when seen from the park beyond. The parterre itself is grassed with strong but few slopes leading down into it, and supporting the two walkways to either side. These are managed as directed in the Paston commentary, with standard yews providing the enclosure, and at the same time offering lateral views to the gardens and walks beyond them. There is no basin; rather, the old pond has been broadened to take its place, and is introduced by two broadly curving arms of sloping ramps from the side walks.

Figure 4.4 Holme Lacy, Herefordshire: plan of a kitchen garden, related to the layout of Holme Lacy, ca 1716 (north to left). Reproduced from Stephen Switzer, *The Practical Kitchen Gardener*, 1727, between pages 368 and 369.

The marriage of the heiress of Holme Lacy to the Duke of Beaufort sadly ended in divorce, in those days and in those circles exceptionally shocking. Its implications, which were long term, had the effect of stopping the further changes that fashion would have otherwise pressed on the family, and both house and grounds have survived in their early 18th century form, largely as created. *The Nobleman Gentleman and Gardener's Recreation* (Switzer 1715) had seriously introduced the early 18th century fashion, and gone some way to describe its benefits, and with its expansion in 1718 in the second and third volumes showed worked examples. Plate 33 is the aspirational design which seeks to show how the qualities of James' and D'Argenville's can be achieved, while the Grimsthorpe prototype is more meticulously presented; with the many qualifications necessary for such a complex and new design type it will have taxed many to understand him. But it has to be recognized that with those two examples Switzer had in a sense produced his life's work . . . and he has since been judged by these designs. And for any who wished to do so he had shown precisely how a man might "make a pretty landskip of his possessions". At Caversham and Holme Lacy it is the heart, the close setting of the house and its immediate adjuncts, which survives, and this was perhaps as much as was intended.

As Switzer wrote in 1718 "a Gentleman in Shropshire" had done just that, and on the basis of Switzer's writings had commenced to survey and lay out his own estate. How he thrived is not recorded. When in the 1720s Lady Betty Hastings' gardener traced these same designs from the plates and presented them for her approbation she chose, perhaps wisely, to go with Charles Bridgeman's design instead. Since Sebastiano Serlio and Andrea Palladio it had been possible for gentlemen to use such works as templates for designs, and even James Gibbs' *Book of Architecture*, in many editions from the 1730s, made the same sort of claim. Occasionally this method succeeded. Like the generation before them who sought out advice from London and Wise, and later from Lancelot Brown, most improvers preferred, however, to seek and then follow, at least to a degree, professional advice, for these very expensive and time consuming works. But for the same reasons they would have kept a very sharp eye on progress, and will doubtless have questioned every proposal closely . . . As Frank Lloyd Wright observed of his clients in the early 20th century the more opinionated, picky and tough they were, the better they were as clients, and thus the better the design became. In the more sociable 18th century a landowner's friends and acquaintances will have offered much advice and many alternatives also.

Ebberston

Figure 4.5 Ebberston Lodge, Yorkshire: prospect of the gardens from the house. Anonymous painting, ca 1730s. Reproduced from *Country Life*, courtesy of IPC Media.

Switzer and Campbell were associated as garden designer and architect at Stourhead, and Switzer may have provided Campbell with the layout of Wilton and others published in volume 3 of *Vitruvius Britannicus* such as Hampton Court, Herefordshire, and perhaps also Thoresby and Lowther. Plans for the gardens of these houses are an additional subject for this third volume, and often, as they relate to places already published, Campbell glosses them only briefly in his commentary, as at Wilton or Hampton Court. Although Campbell praises Bridgeman's Eastbury design, and has noted Acres' work at Caversham, both of whom were subscribers, his failure to mention Switzer at all is marked. Even so the design of Ebberston Lodge of 1718 is one of Campbell's earliest, and also the smallest and most concentrated essay of the architecture of simple things, and he and Switzer were likely associated there. We know from quite other sources than Campbell that Ebberston also was the subject of an equally interesting garden design which includes its landscape as prospect.

There is no documentary evidence to identify its designer, nor is there contemporary reference to it. Happily, however, it was the subject of a suite of topographical paintings, also by an unacknowledged artist, for another Yorkshire house for a relative of Ebberston's owner. The pictures show the same features and design which have survived in place, but with some added detail and, of course, an added 18th century crispness, also to be seen in Ricci's picture of the similar scheme at Upper Lodge at Bushy Park, which passing time has extinguished from the place. These pictures, and Ebberston, were brought to our attention some years ago by Christopher Hussey and published in his *English Gardens and Landscapes 1700–1750*. In trying to establish who the designer of the landscape might be, Hussey, noting Benson's current association with Campbell, and also the recent advice Benson gave to George while he was still Elector at Herenhausen immediately before his elevation as King George of the United Kingdom, suggested, "Though Benson can be considered as possibly having a hand in its design, stronger probability attaches to Switzer . . ." (Hussey 1967 68) on the basis of his expertise and writings on water-works, but also the now abandoned assumption that Switzer and Bridgeman had divided landscape work between them, north and south of England. Thus, a slender attribution commends Switzer to our attention as being the Master of the Ebberston Landscape.

Ebberston is a secondary house, not quite a villa in the sense of Riskins since it was located only three miles from Thomson's principal house in north-east Yorkshire, but really almost a playhouse or casino, and it may well have been built purely for pleasure. Thomson was a very successful lawyer busily employed in London and a sometime Member of Parliament, a close ally of Walpole and a leading judge at the Old Bailey. He became rich from his professional activity, and had also married Julia Blackett, the widow and heiress of Sir William Blackett of Newcastle, in 1710. The house is sited most skilfully, and the characteristics of its location are exploited not least by a flouting of the typical conventions of disposing gardens and entries, which are reversed from normal. The garden, insofar as it actually is a garden, lies on the north side with the long entrance from the south. Furthermore, it overlooks the Vale of Pickering from a somewhat elevated position, and the ground behind it rises quickly upwards to moorland. From there stem the springs, as Campbell calls it "a River", supplying the water-works via a canal of 370 metres (the same length as at Caversham), which fall into a series of basins or pools by means of cascades. The one nearest the house is set back from the north front in a sort of parterre of grass, or parade, about three times the expected length. This is overlooked by the main reception room, decidedly modest at 16 by 12 feet, on the raised ground floor, and is (at least originally) a recessed *loggio* (rather like the stand overlooking Greenwich Park in the Queen's House). The sunlight from over the house strikes the cascade just as it empties into a secret drain to apparently run under the house. So from the little *loggio* the full view of the whole garden scheme, a canalized and planted valley, is a sort of homage to the villa Aldobrandini at Frascati. Switzer also used that trope at Spye Park in the 1720s, and elsewhere, and published both in 1729. The valley is defined by plantations of forest trees on either side, but comfortably so with a broad margin for turfed walks. On the south side of Ebberston, the entrance front (raised up over a service floor and accessed from a broad plain terrace) had two flanking and very small service buildings. These define a broad turfed court which is extended further south by two large pools which receive the overflow from the canal by way of underground pipes from the ends of the last cascade. Ebberston here has the whole of the Vale of Pickering as its prospect. Thus, Ebberston delivers the greatest pleasure from the least means possible.

Shotover

Shotover House, near Oxford, was built in 1714 by Sir James Tyrrell, the historian and Whig political theorist. As he was then 72 perhaps it was in celebration of the settlement favouring the Elector. The accompanying garden followed soon, from 1717 into the 1730s. His son, General James Tyrrell (ca 1672–1742), finished both. He was acknowledging his father's work and continued his intentions into a period of changing fashion, and doubtless had supervised them jointly with his father from their beginning. The grounds were engraved by George Bickham in 1750, the bird's-eye one point perspective looking back to the earlier Kip style, while the slightly rougher rendering of the plantations is more up-to-date. Insofar as the grounds at Shotover are characterized by the formal ponds and canal they resemble those at Ebberston. The scales, however, are quite different with Shotover being more akin to Caversham. The authorship of both the house and the grounds is unknown. William Kent built the handsome circular Temple south-west of the house in either 1732 or 1737 (authors vary widely in their datings of this building; Weber 2014 13 has it as 1724–1725), and he is also credited by some with the Obelisk as well, and even the layout of that section of the gardens. That part of the gardens is of the standard one expects of Kent, but it does not seem to me to be Kent-ish, and as they seem easily to be at one with the grounds as a whole I believe they are rather earlier. Kent is more likely to have added the building there to an already established bastion on the edge of the earlier design, and perhaps also marked the axis with an Obelisk, in a design for the grounds in no way amateur, and thus possibly by James, less likely Bridgeman (Willis 2002 66–67), or Switzer. Of all these Switzer seems the most probable author.

Structurally Shotover is a long section of ordered spaces set off by rows of forest trees between swathes of arable land. It lies north-west of Wheatley with hills to the south-west and to the north. There is a large pool at the west end, a somewhat elongated octagon, and it all lies on an east-west axis of a kilometre in length. This axis, and indeed the design, is defined to either side by lower hedges in the western section,

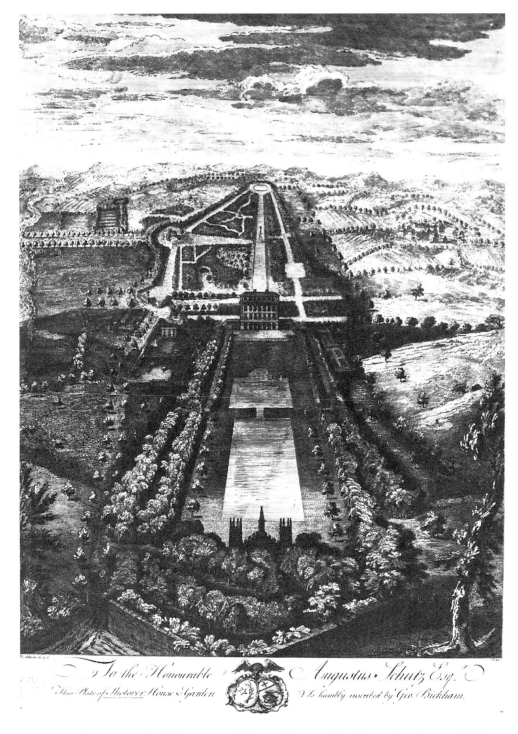

Figure 4.6 Shotover, Oxfordshire: view of the gardens and landscape, by George Bickham, 1752 (north to right). Oxford Bodleian Library, MS Gough Maps 26, fol 71.

the wilderness or walking part, whereas the eastern half is given form by walls of forest trees. The wilderness is similar to the wood at Grimsthorpe with its walk open to fields across a Ha Ha on the south side centred on "Kent's" bastion, and finished at the juncture with the carriage entrance by a more soldierly Vauban-like piece of fortification. Along the north side there is a simpler series of walks and cabinets. The new house is at the centre of the design, with the entrance front to the west and the garden front eastward, where, still on axis, it looks down beyond a simple plain embanked parterre onto another slightly bigger octagonal pool which is spatially overwhelmed by its much bigger neighbour, the broad, still and lengthy canal-like lake. On the far side of the lake is a terminal feature of fair size and squarely facing back towards the house.

This is the feature that has made Shotover famous, mainly because of its style . . . and its date. As early as 1717 (authors vary somewhat; Mowl 2007 gives it as roughly 1720) the Shotover pavilion is Gothic in very marked contrast to the house, which is a classic box of seven bays and three stories, raised on an arcade. Both are in a pale ashlar construction that reads as white, in pleasing contrast to both the forest and the water features. The house is classic, but as it still boasts good, big, English windows, hardly yet in the surprising modernist look that Palladio inspired house will soon have. It is a pleasingly conventional box, and could be the work of Gibbs, of James or even of Smith. Similarly, the Gothic of its companion building does not have the faintly stylish camp aspect we associate with the early 18th century essays in local antique which has always been denominated as "Gothick". It is too straight for that, and could easily be from the same authors as the ongoing enlargements at All Souls College, and indeed one of the builders there, the mason William Townsend, has been put forward as the architect of this pavilion (Mowl 2007 66). The two manners of these major objects in this spacious, cool, masculine and slightly surreal landscape add the resonance of the possible message such a choice of style might have. Given its place, date and especially the character of its commissioner the style is almost bound to be a significant extra issue. But what?

To jump forward a bit: From Horace Walpole's time in the middle of the 18th century a contrast between Gothic, as emblematic of the liberty loving barons of English history famously established at Runnymede with Magna Carta, and Classic, representing more Roman virtues, has been an idea underpinning appreciation and criticism about design in these islands, and especially the design of gardens and of landscapes and the buildings within them. This dichotomy accounts for much in our culture, and it reached its most extreme form in the high Victorian attitude expressed so forcefully by John Ruskin, who could believe that Gothic was spiritually pure whereas the Classic was Godless. The earliest intellectual-political foundations for these philosophical ideas were agreed to have occurred with the Hanoverian settlement, and the establishment of Whig government under Horace's father, Sir Robert Walpole. These foundations had been given much thought and credibility by the writings of Sir James Tyrrell, with due debt to his mentor and great friend John Locke. So to find a manifestation of them at Shotover as his seeming last act accounts for the power of the place.

Or does it? Such a narrative has been current for some time to explain Lord Cobham's essays in landscape with Bridgeman, Gibbs and Kent in the eastern extensions at Stowe (see below), designed and executed in the 1730s as a mute but built and landscaped riposte to Walpole's government. It was the emblem and the expression of the first real opposition of his Whig colleagues, and the beginnings of modern parliamentary government.

Timothy Mowl and others have cited the pavilion as the first herald of the coming Arcadian style and acknowledged its role in that its non-classical form curiously triggers an agreeable association of ideas. But just what might they be? Surely not the same as the later Stowe; perhaps, even probably, not even an overt attempt at satire or censure. As a place of contemplation, which Bickham's choice of view point supports, the pavilion may have given the elder Tyrrell sufficient allusion in its similarity to All Souls and was to be a place for an elderly scholar to contemplate a serene and idealized landscape, and one of his creation with his own brand new and smart house in full view. Of course, the reverse view might have agreeably reminded him of his past and his role as a historian in contemplation of a revered place. This is speculation, but such speculation is the very point of such follies. Their appeal should never be literal . . . plausible, yes, but always allusive.

Studley Royal

Can Studley Royal be the example par excellence to illustrate what an amateur can do unaided? (Newman 2015, 70 et seq) I think it most unlikely, and yet many are content or even happy to accept that it (and other places too) is just that. It has to be conceded that there appears to be no one else who can be the likely designer: Switzer, who otherwise would be a contender to be thought the master of the Studley design, simply alludes to Mr Aislabie's great works in the north, as if he had never seen them. John Aislabie is famous for being the Chancellor of the Exchequer when the South Sea Bubble burst. If Switzer had lost his fortune in that frenzy, and very many were adversely affected even if they did not lose all, he might have thought ill of its chief personification. Many thought Aislabie culpable. Technically that is true as he was in charge at the time, and was certainly no less eager to enrich himself than any other contemporary Whig minister, nor indeed less eager than very many of the investors who also got their fingers burned. The South Sea Company had been a Tory idea in Harley's administration, and it was conceived as a means of reducing, or even liquidating, the alarming national debt which had newly arisen on account of the Continental wars. National banks had only very recently been created too, the conceptions of plausible Scots, and neither was really trusted, yet in Paris and London their funds grew through investment. The South Sea Company was no more nor less likely to prosper, and amazingly did prosper, until 1722. John Vanbrugh lost a small fortune, and thousands of others did similarly, so Switzer might have been among them. A few, like the Marlboroughs, sold up in time and transferred their funds into the Bank of England, but only just in time, and many doubted it was only good fortune that saved them.

Aislabie escaped with a depleted fortune, and a lost public trust, but kept his liberty and remained an undiminished character in his part of Yorkshire, and the North more widely. He now had the time to devote himself to his estate, which he did. Campbell was a protégé already and had doubtless benefited from Aislabie's patronage when he mounted his attempt to take over the Board of Works. The ornamental buildings, and the later house as well, are from Campbell. The grounds are made up of rising woodland and seemingly level and low turfed and embanked lawns of various shape. There are broad pools of water, reflecting the sky, and all these elements are composed together by a canal-like river. The river seems to be two or more. It breaks at the south end at an angle and cascade, and this leads by another cascade into a widened section resembling one of the placid pools to the north, but bigger. The woodland to the east rises and covers a hill-like slope, whereas the other side, where the house stood, is close woodland on an apparent plane. To the north of the garden is a large pond whose broad cascade marks the junction, between a pair of fishing pavilions. The River seems regular as a canal would, and each of the compositions related to it are also regular, the main one of the east, a small Doric temple, has a round pool on axis, flanked by two fan shaped pools to balance like wings. The compositions on the other side are not opposite, rather more related but just out of direct sight, and the principle of these is a Banqueting House arranged at the head of a rectangular lawn framed by high and steep turfed banks, and then close woodland. The formally unrelated house was nearby, and out of sight. The ruins of Fountains Abbey, then still in other hands, were added later.

Lumley Castle

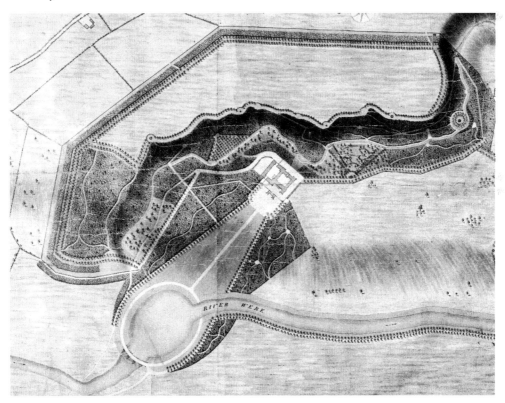

Figure 4.7 Lumley Castle, County Durham: anonymous plan, ca 1720 (north to right). Private collection, photograph from Durham University Library.

We know of Switzer's business in the north-east of England through the discovery of some of his correspondence which fortuitously appeared at the Castle of Newcastle at the beginning of World War II, but that snapshot does not tell us when this consultancy there began. Lumley Castle was known to Switzer as his passing remark about very large mill-wheels indicates (*Hydro* I 274). And Laurence Whistler, among others, has suggested him as the author of the landscape works there. These have been known only from a later 18th century view which shows them only in very sketchy form, and so they have been thought rather enigmatic. However, it is clear from the site, and from even later views, that they were decidedly romantic, if for no other reason than the view to the Castle seated on its precipitous ridge as seen south-east of Chester-le-Street. However, since Peter Willis published (Willis 2002 412 and plates 210–212) the recently re-discovered design drawings for the grounds, the nature of the scheme has been much clearer. It is also clear that it is a most interesting and masterly exercise. These drawings, which are undated and unsigned, he was happy to add to his attributions to Bridgeman. I think they are more likely to have been by Switzer.

Richard Lumley (1688–1740) asked Vanbrugh, who recently had been working north of Newcastle at Seaton Deleval, to prepare plans for improvements at Lumley, adjacent to Chester-le-Street. Then still referred to as Lord Lumley, he became 2nd Earl of Scarbrough the next year and is a little known Whiggish soldier and member of the Kit Kat Club, and a friend of Vanbrugh's. Vanbrugh, in a letter to another soldier, Brigadier Watkins, notes from York, ". . . I have been near three weeks finding a vast deal to do, both at Delavals and Lumley . . . Lumley Castle is a Noble thing; and well deserves the Favours Lord Lumley designs to bestow upon it; In order to which, I stay'd there near a Week to form a general Design for the whole, Which consists, in altering the House, both for State, Beauty and Convenience, And making the Courts Gardens and Offices suitable to it; All which I believe may be done, for a Sum, that can never lye very heavy upon the Family . . ." (in Dobree and Webb 1927 IV 137–138).

He also noted the nature of the countryside round about, and compared it most favourably in opposition to the tamer country near London. These improvements, including the layout of the grounds, presumably began the next year, as Vanbrugh writes on 24 April 1722 to Lord Carlisle, ". . . My Lord Scarborough [sic] tells me he certainly go's to Lumley Castle the end of May, and has desir'd me to propose some things for him in order to begin Works there . . ." (in Dobree and Webb 1927 142). Some of the major elements of the design drawing survived to be shown on early editions of the Ordnance Surveys. The circular pool below the Castle is not shown at that date and of course may not have been carried out. Equally likely it was carried out but did not survive the periodic flooding the river Weir is subject to, to which it, and especially its pristine form, would have been most vulnerable.

The design was a very simple one. This is in line with Vanbrugh's implied frugality of the whole scheme of improvements. Essentially it consisted of the valley made by the Lumley Beck laid out as woodland gardens. This lively stream flows to the east of the Castle before joining the Weir north-west of the grounds. Its west side, which makes a precipitous ridge near the Castle, is the primary site for garden elements, with cabinets, amphitheatrical banking and a circular fruit garden sited seemingly at random, but actually where the ground will permit, and with curved walks joining all together. The other side of this extended woodland is simpler in its treatment, but it has a rather sinuous terrace walk with occasional bastions, and this provides a variety of views along and across the valley and also the open parkland to the east, The

Hags. A similar walk lies on the west side of the grounds: there it runs along a ridge with steep slopes down to the Lumley Beck, and a much gentler slope over parkland to the west to the Weir. And it is on this side also that there is the Bold Stroke. And this formal gesture is all there is to remind us that the scheme belongs to the 1720s. Here, aligned on the north-west front of Lumley Castle . . . looking towards Chester-le-Street, and of course making a framed view of the Castle from its neighbour . . . the gentle slope to the Weir is arranged parterre-like. A plane of turf splayed on each side outward from the castle front and defined simply by forest trees presents a real picture from its Terrace top. Chester-le-Street and County Durham lying beyond are the subject's background, with the Weir making a serpentine and diagonal line in the middle ground, and elaborated into a seemingly circular basin where it bisects the parterre element, the foreground, which joins the Castle to the picture. The picturesque of the composition is no less apparent when the view is reversed.

The incidents to be found in the wooded valley, the actual gardens, are also varied and provide mostly closer views, and of smaller things which are of (or tend to) geometric shape, arranged at first view also by conventional means. Once the sapper-like landscaping had been accomplished, with footbridges, and the plantations established, the gardens would have been exceptionally cheap to make, and to keep spruce and tidy. There are few, if any, ornamental buildings indicated. The most elaborate element, and the one closest to the house, is the Amphitheatre. It may have hoped to have a circular temple at its top, where the banking comes to a point just adjacent to the east terrace walk. With its outward view across the park to the Weir on the outside, the Amphitheatre would tempt the company to stroll down into the gardens and the Beck. This could be done by easy slopes along the spayed sides of the element, or by traversing the banked ranks of pretend seating between: these formal platforms dotted with trees informally planted follow a sort of meandering path themselves, and in easy stages to the almost semi-circular course of the Beck at the bottom. Beyond this, closer planted woodwork (a special kind of early 18th century woodland) rises steeply up the opposite slope.

Further south, again following the west terrace walk to its end, is a sharp turn left into close woodland, or, sharper still, to the left into a broad serpentine path. This leads to a semi-circular ante-room or foyer, where the Beck is screened by a close coppice plantation through which appears the plantation of fruit trees on the other side, arranged in circles around a basin. An easy way back would be to follow the curving course of Lumley Beck on its far side along the turfed walkway at least as far as the dramatic view of the Castle, looming above a splayed and turfed glacis foundation. The far side of the Beck, below the Castle, is planted with trees, as it were, sprinkled on an open lawn. If this were followed around another sharper turn in the Beck the principal element of the south-east woodland is seen. This is a grove, triangular in plan, planted quadratically and contrasted to denser woodland beyond. On the Castle side a very broad serpentine walk beckons the company to return.

Belvoir

There are numerous references to Belvoir in the second edition of *The Practical Fruit Gardener*, which dates Switzer's involvement there to the 1720s. These were occasioned by amendments to the sloping walls on which fruit was grown, established originally in the belief that it would be thus improved. Switzer was not persuaded.

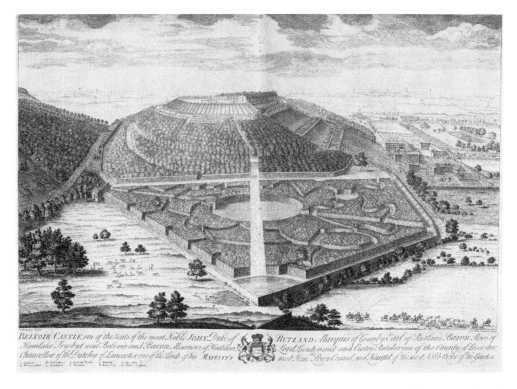

Figure 4.8 Belvoir Castle, Rutland: prospect from the south, by Thomas Badeslade. Reproduced from, *Vitruvius Britannicus, or the British Architect*, Volume the Fourth 1739, plates 47 and 48. Oxford Bodleian Library, Vet. A4 a.3.

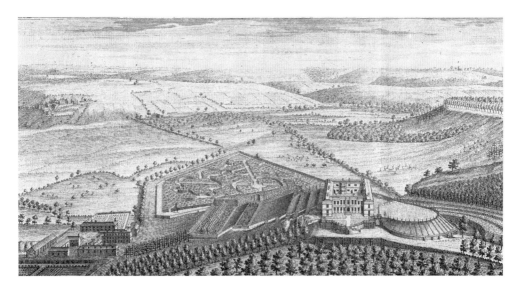

Figure 4.9 Belvoir Castle, Rutland: prospect from the north, by Thomas Badeslade. Reproduced from, *Vitruvius Britannicus, or the British Architect*, Volume the Fourth 1739, plate 49. Oxford Bodleian Library, Vet. A4 a.3.

However, in experiments to improve the performance of these plantations much digging was involved and the notion of introducing heated air was tried, but with little success. It was then Switzer's ". . . good Fortune to come that Way . . .", and he offered the advice to concentrate the heat on the roots rather than the leafy upper parts. That "answer'd beyond Expectation and has confirm'd me in the Opinion I was always in: That the Fire in a Kitchen Chimney lying low and being generally under the Roots is the greatest Occasion of the Maturity and Acceleration of Fruit, especially Grapes . . ." (*FG* 1731 319–320). And according to Switzer the Duke of Devonshire concurred.

It is in that period that the extensions illustrated by Thomas Badeslade were designed and planted. These Switzer does not address in his comments. But given his fulsome account of the experiments, it is probable that he re-designed the inherited grounds in that period also. These appeared in 1739 in the supplementary volume of *Vitruvius Britannicus*. They call attention to the peculiar nature of Belvoir's place: how would anyone make a *rural and farm-like garden*, or a pretty landskip of a seeming mountain? For that is the character the site presents: the Vale of Belvoir is a flattish rolling country dominated by the very prominent hill of Belvoir. Prospects are there in plenty, perhaps too many, as are slopes, but where can one find a flat space? And if a mountain is a pleasing prospect from afar, is the landscape from an eminence also pleasing? Badeslade's views are prospects; two show the grounds from a distance, and the viewer is impressed by the lofty mountain-like situation. The third, while also an aerial prospect, is much closer in its point of view and gives a truer idea of the relationship between the garden, the immediate sloping grounds and the contiguous landscape, both the elements close by such as the large new wilderness on the flat ground to the south, and also the planted and farmed grounds spreading out beyond. These, when seen in reality from Belvoir, are in no way diminished by distance and appear as integral to the gardens. Thus, the views, being elevated, are richer and more inclusive than they would be from the De Caus terrace at Wilton, or the newer-fashioned ones at Grimsthorpe or Castle Howard. The *utile et dulci* are very pleasingly mixed at Belvoir.

Wilton

If Caversham can represent the early 18th century perfection of "Nature to advantage dress'd" (Pope *Essay on Criticism* line 297 1711) then Wilton House gardens are among its earliest essays in these islands, and also its exemplar. Wilton had its fame in Elizabeth's time when the great house was built, with its connection also to the literary excellence of those times aptly symbolized in the marriage between the Pembroke heir and Mary Sidney. Their son Philip, 4th Earl of Pembroke, created the great gardens in the next dynasty, and in these the family is shown as reaching the taste and accomplishment of the best European standard. Both the new wing to Wilton House of the later 1630s and the grounds it fronted are examples of design of the highest quality in merit, and also arguably among the most fashionable anywhere. The son of the creators of this marvel was Switzer's first Pembroke patron, to whom he dedicated the third volume of *Ichnographia Rustica*. Thomas Herbert (1656/7–1733) was the 7th earl, having succeeded, in the year of Switzer's birth, his drunken scape-grace uncle, confirming that all families are apt to misstep from time to time.

According to his recent biographer, Pembroke was distinguished as "a patron of the arts and sciences, a collector and a virtuoso" (*DNB* 2004). He had been a student at

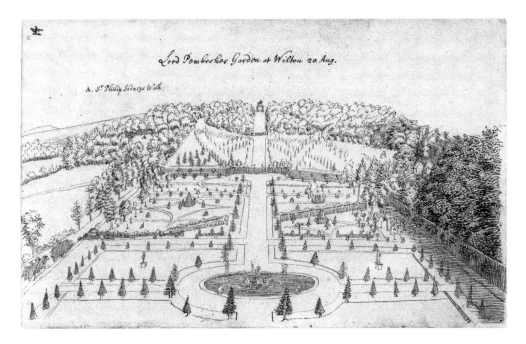

Figure 4.10 Wilton, Wiltshire: prospect from the north, by William Stukeley, 1723. Oxford Bodleian Library, 4.10 MS. Top gen. d.14. folio 10v.

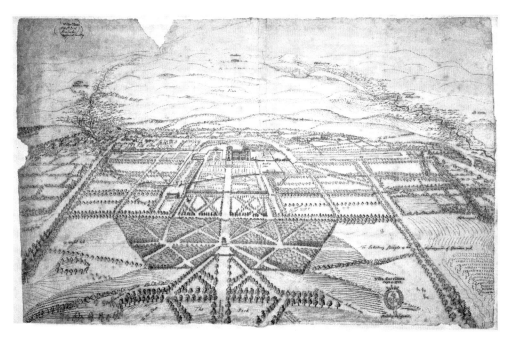

Figure 4.11 Wilton, Wiltshire: prospect from the south, by William Stukeley, undated (early 1720s). Oxford Bodleian Library, 4.11 Gough Maps 33, folio 19v.

Oxford; travelled abroad, where he met John Locke; and served King James. He did not vote for William to be asked to become king, as consort to James' daughter Mary, although he served under him with distinction. He served also under Queen Anne: his politics are described as mild Tory. He was also an early, and keen, fellow of the Royal Society, and to him is owing the extraordinary collections of artworks still at Wilton House, including the Van Dykes and the Arundel Marbles. There was no place in Wiltshire, and very few elsewhere, which could bear comparison as a library, museum or setting in which to have some standing, or occasional share, so Switzer was fortunate to have his patronage. Added to that Pembroke deserved the role of Maecenas of his time, as George Vertue attested. But even under him Wilton was not then the same show-place that had been illustrated by Isaac De Caus' *Hortus Pembrochianus*. The Civil Wars and their aftermath, and two dodgy earls in succession, will have sapped the family finances, and also their will to keep up such a splendid place. Its state was recorded when it was visited by Cosimo de Medici in 1668, and this record shows it dis-furnished, that is, with the plants and ornaments all gone, leaving a simple and almost bare enclosure, but with the walls, and the terrace at the south end, in place and in good order.

One of the tests of any Maecenas is confidence of taste, especially in times when taste and fashion may be at odds. Clearly Pembroke knew his house and his garden provided a setting which called also for works of the standard of Van Dyke's pictures or Arundel's sculptures. On the present evidence, the double plate possibly prepared by Switzer for publication in Campbell's third volume of *Vitruvius Britannicus*, published in 1725, it seems that Pembroke was happy with Wilton, even in its imperfect state, that is, not as its original designers intended it to be. Thus, it is left relatively under-furnished, but still in tripartite division, with each turfed between gravel walks, where the divisions are marked by conical greens at the corners and along the edges, and standard greens planted on the major axis. Whereas De Caus had humoured the somewhat serpentine Nadder as it flowed through his second division, not so much disguising it as making it appear not too discordant in the otherwise geometric setting, the two different elements simply exist within the same setting. (Nor, it has to be said, does he allow the serpentine to flow through open lawn: perhaps this even simpler acknowledgement of disparity was over-ruled.) The major change to De Caus' design is to replace the southern terrace walk and the grotto housed under it, in favour of an iron screen gate in a simpler wall. This was done to open the axis to the south, to make the gardens seems much larger and to show off one of Pembroke's recent acquisitions, a Marcus Aurelius on horse-back, raised on an arcade and sited on axis on the ridge at the highest level in the grounds. This new quarter is composed of regular avenues of forest trees arranged Saltire fashion and wooded to either side of the ridge.

That change suggests a new attitude to the place itself. There was always an acknowledgement of a happy relationship between garden and park. De Caus had made the terrace walk the element where that relationship was displayed, even celebrated, and the promenade along it, in full view of house, park and garden, was the very place one went to see these things. This was much less important to Georgian taste than to the Jacobean taste of almost a century earlier. The enlargement of the scheme to include the adjacent park with its splendid ornament is key, and in light of the subsequent changes in the next generation (see below) it is clearly a contingent one. The grotto house and the other ornaments associated with it, as might be expected, were in need of repair, and perhaps replacement. Whether for that reason or others they are re-sited

140 *"Nature to advantage dress'd"*

to the end of a short walk on the west side of the original garden enclosure. De Caus' ornaments are recognized as valuable, and are never given up, but like the pictures and sculptures they are re-arranged, and more than once. That appears to be the attitude the Pembrokes took to the composition of the grounds as a whole. These are nurtured, repaired as needed, rather fussed over perhaps, but always seemingly in search of the idea of a perfect Arcadia that great-uncle Philip Sydney had introduced to this place, and to the world.

Castle House, Marlborough

Algernon Seymour, Earl of Hertford (1684–1750), was another soldier who had served with Marlborough and was his ally in Parliament and a staunch Whig. He was also the son of a duke and heir to the Percy estates, probably the largest landowners in England. His wife, Frances Thynne Seymour, had been born at Longleat, the site of Brompton Park's famous garden, and one of London's most accomplished designs. They were thus natural and most valuable patrons for Switzer. But as the son of the Duke of Somerset the full value of his wealth was a very long time in becoming his to command, because the Proud Duke lived for an exceptionally long time. The duke was very much aware of his station and good fortune, and according to James Lees-Milne he was also "preposterously snobbish" (Lees-Milne 1970 49). The legitimate scope for improvements by the son of such a high-flying improving builder would be somewhat proscribed, and always in his father's shadow. Despite the son's own prospects and wishes to make improvements himself, there is only so much that even a great family

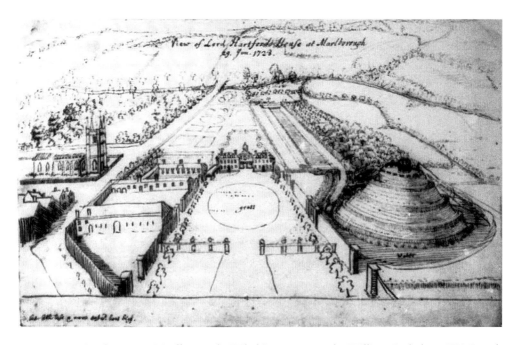

Figure 4.12 Castle House, Marlborough, Wiltshire: prospect, by William Stukeley, 1723 (north to bottom). The Bodleian Libraries, University of Oxford.

and their estates can carry. A proud duke would not have been looking to his son to make such contributions to culture: so long as he lived that would be his role. In the early 1680s he had already rebuilt Castle House at Marlborough, the family seat, and as his marriage brought him Petworth in Sussex this became his favourite. There he built an even greater house, then remodelled and renewed it after it was ravaged by a fire in 1715. With the duke thus preoccupied by Petworth the Hertfords moved into the Marlborough house by 1718.

Switzer's dedication (*Hydro* I) hints that Hertford was of a character a deal more approachable than proud, and he acknowledges friendship, and their mutual love of water-works and gardening, as the basis of their relationship. Certainly the warm personal character of Lady Frances Hertford comes across in her correspondence, and in her own independent patronage of poets, such as James Thomson and Stephen Duck. As we have seen above at Riskins, which the Hertfords took over from Bathurst in the late 1730s, they were very much alive to that place's qualities and happy to be part of what was becoming recognized as a new way of gardening. Lady Hertford, like others, will have been aware of the praise, publicity and even celebrity that was soon accorded to some new gardens: as Queen Caroline's Lady in Waiting she was especially well placed to observe these changes in fashion. And yet one detects the same kind of surprise and perhaps also mild annoyance that Switzer would also feel to find great praises being lavished on places, things and people because of their taste in gardening, as if it were a thing she and he knew nothing of, and had not already accomplished. Thus, in a letter in 1739 she observed that "the grotto we have made under the mount [at Marlborough] . . . is much prettier than that [Pope's] at Twickenham" (Marlborough College website).

For a new house (Colvin gives a date of early 1680s for the rebuilding) there would most likely also be renewed gardens. At that date they would be too early to anticipate the involvement by London or any of his partners. But at present there is no evidence on which to base a judgement. The earliest representations of the grounds at Marlborough are by William Stukeley. Switzer had chided his old friend in a letter for visiting the neighbourhood and not getting in touch in 1724, and as the drawing is dated the year before, when Stukeley was gathering material for his *Itinerarium Curiosum*, perhaps he was then staying with the Hertfords. His illustration is in the Kip and Knyff mode, still current and with new editions to come, despite the "newer" style of representing houses and their grounds that Campbell was experimenting with (*Vit Brit* III 10), and he shows the whole scheme in bird's-eye one point perspective with the house on axis. Marlborough House is on the west side of the town between St Peter's Church and the Mount, also known as Merlin's Barrow, the 20 metre high pudding bowl shaped antiquity constructed in the third millennium BC. The site is on otherwise level ground with the River Kennet marking its west and south edges. The 1680s house stood behind a large square forecourt with stables on the town side, the Mount on the west with gates to the north opposite the house on axis fronted by another grassed court and drive. The arrangement of the house is in a curious staccato like composition rather like the contemporary Bethlehem Hospital by Robert Hooke, that is, a smallish pavilion-like centrepiece, here recessed, flanked by pairs of wider house-like blocks.

The Best Garden lies behind in three parallel sections, as one would expect of the 1680s, with the centre section itself divided into three, where a parterre with elaborate shaped large figures of presumably low plantings is followed by simpler parterres finishing at the river's edge. A similarly disposed suite of quarters occupies the town side,

142 *"Nature to advantage dress'd"*

conveniently behind the stable court, where the composition is made up of kitchen and fruit gardens. The opposite side is occupied by a broad walk and a canal diverted from the Kennet. There is a close woodland beyond that. The canal becomes a moat as it passes the forecourts and curves its way around the Mount, now planted as a shrubbery with walks in spiral form leading to its summit. It is at the Mount's base, facing south, that Lady Hertford's Grotto was made, at the head of a walk in the canal-side woodland. These are part of the further ring of pleasure grounds, made up, as we might expect, of a series of small meadows (perhaps fields?) and a more serpentine diversion from the Kennet, and then broader meadows to the river proper, and further fields to enclose all on the far west and south sides. This outer ring finishes in a large woodland south of St Peter's Church and east of the kitchen and fruit gardens.

Spye Park

Half way between Marlborough and Bath is the hamlet of Sandy Lane, then on the main road to and from London and also routes north and south. Northwards is the hill, or hills, the southernmost of the Cotswolds, which made an attractive site for a series of estates, the most notable being Bowood, but also including Whetham and Spy Park. Spye (sometimes Spie, always Spy for Switzer) occupies the south-west slopes of Bowden Hill and offers good southerly views, and further west these become

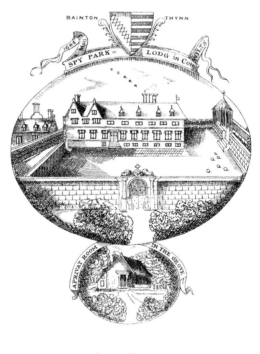

Figure 4.13 Spye Park, Wiltshire: house and grounds in the 17th century (north to right).

more prominent but still on the comfortable and pastoral side of spectacular. In the mid-17th century the Bayntuns relocated there to a lodge-like residence a short distance north of their place at Bromhall, which had been ruined in the Civil Wars. Spye became their principal residence. John Evelyn visited it in 1654, and commented on the folly of the house and its situation, noting that it was ". . . a place capable of being made a noble seate; but the humourous old Knight has built a long single house of 2 low stories on the precipice of an incomparable prospect, and landing on a bowling greene in the park. The house is like a long barne, and has not a window on the prospect side . . ." (Evelyn 1827 78). Evelyn was a trifle peeved with his host, whose cheer had spread as far as the coachmen, making them as drunk as the company, but his remarks remain just. Not only had Sir Edward Bayntun ignored the view, but the house was sited so close to the edge as to make any kind of amelioration by extension on that side near impossible. Apart from the fact that it was a single pile, that is, one span or one room only in depth, we do not know what the plan of the old house was, and the lack of windows on the west front does seem extraordinary. Some 70 years later Switzer undertook to overcome this disadvantage on behalf of Anne Bayntun Rolt (1689–1734), the great-granddaughter of the builder.

Her father had married the heiress of the infamous Lord Rochester, but his own premature death in 1696 left a much expanded but mortgaged estate. Her mother's death then put Anne and her brother, Henry, in guardianship. Both were left as heirs: all was to go of course to Henry first, as elder and male; then Anne was to succeed to full ownership of the estates, so long as she either married a Bayntun relation or had a son who took the Bayntun surname (http://bayntun-history.com). Anne's marriage to Edward Rolt in 1708 and their move to Sacombe Park in 1710 promised her a comfortable and settled life in Hertfordshire. Rolt's sister Constantia married Switzer's friend John Kyrle Ernle at roughly the same time, and moved to Whetham (see above). Rolt was briefly a Member of Parliament in the Tory interest but otherwise did not have a public life. Edward and Anne had begun a series of improvements to the almost 100 acres of grounds at Sacombe by 1715 (Milledge 2009). Initially they approached Wise, but he seemingly passed the commission on to Bridgeman, then at the beginning of his independent career. A design for Sacombe by Bridgeman has been published by Peter Willis (Willis 2002 plate 46b); this design combined the site for a new house with a forecourt and large furnished parterre, and beyond was the long axis of the scheme, designed to be continued into the far distance by a canal. A good sized woodland ran across this axis, and Bridgeman proposed cutting that out into cabinets, with walks and an amphitheatre. There was also a park, apparently in place, where the walled garden was sited. Although it was begun it was unfinished at Rolt's death in 1722, and just how far this scheme had progressed is unclear.

Rolt had inherited Sacombe and a rental income of over £750 a year (£225,000 current value) from his father, who had prospered as a merchant trading in Persia and India with the precursor of the East India Company. And Anne Bayntun brought a good marriage settlement. Such an income would have allowed them to garden and to build, but still relatively modestly. Vanbrugh seemingly designed a house for them, and the large walled garden is credited to him. They could put a big house to good use for they already had four children. For some reason his house was not proceeded with, and Gibbs also provided unrealized designs. In 1716 Anne's brother's died (Wall *DNB*), leaving her the mistress of a great estate and income. She wisely kept it separate, for Rolt, like many at the time, had invested in South Sea stocks, and it seems that he lost heavily

144 *"Nature to advantage dress'd"*

(see Willis 2002 59, Milledge 2009 49). When he died, of smallpox, in 1722 his bank accounts were found to be exhausted, and Bridgeman was left the major creditor. A fifth child had been born in 1721, and the sixth died shortly after her birth in 1723.

Henry Bayntun is not known to have made improvements at Spye. At his death in 1716 his sister Anne was free, and indeed obliged, to improve her estate with its substantial rental income as she pleased. She was also much engaged with projected improvements at Sacombe at the same time. Possibly the cascades east of the house, being as much for the good of the estate as for any other purpose, could have been carried out then; their being made of "very poor materials" might be on account of imposed frugality. This can only be a guess, however. The documentary evidence we have for Switzer's work there is his letter to Stukeley, in part about the water-works, and the reference, dated 22 May 1722, by a neighbouring landowner that ". . . Mr Switzer who is busy at Spye park . . ." was coming to help him with his new garden designs (J I Talbot to H Davenport Lacock MSS).

Mrs Rolt's move back to Wiltshire cannot have been a happy one, but at least an aunt to all those children, Constantia, was next door at Whetham. Switzer thought very highly indeed of Anne Bayntun Rolt, calling her a "Lady of extraordinary Merit", and her behaviour under adversity showed substantial character. She had installed herself and her children at Spye Park House, took up residential oversight of her projects in garden design with Switzer and, as luck would have it, found a new husband at Bath, all in 1723. That marriage, to John Somerville (1698–1765), was the talk of the season at Bath. He had recently won his case in the House of Lords to revive the title due to him, which since James VI's move to London had been in abeyance. Thus, the 13th Lord Somerville and the widowed Anne Bayntun Rolt were married by special licence in the abbey. John Gay, staying with his patrons, the Queensberrys, and their friends, reported the stir their association, courtship and quick marriage had caused to the company at Bath.

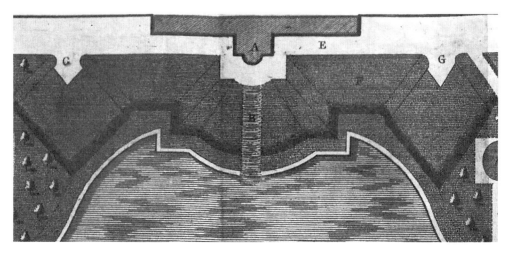

A Porch/Grotto   **B** Cascade   **C** Bastion   **E** Terrace   **F** Slope of Glacis   **G** Bastion

Figure 4.14 Spye Park, Wiltshire: plan of the terrace, grotto pavilion, west cascade (north to left). Detail from Stephen Switzer, *The Practical Fruit Gardener*, p. 307 1724.

The site at Spye Park was largely parkland lying on a smaller hillock with a flattish top on the south-west edge of the larger mass of Bowden Hill. It had become home first to a lodge and then to Spye Park House, with its walled Bowling Green making a complete composition perched on the edge of the escarpment. South of this are the stables, which remain now as the only part of the original ensemble to survive. The original Spye Park House was enlarged in the later 18th century by the addition of a new frontage with a portico on the east side. This was replaced with a new Spye Park House to the east, built in the 1870s, and itself demolished after a fire in 1972. There was a large basin at the highest point of this space, shown on the survey of 1849, a likely survival of Switzer's scheme as a reservoir to feed the cascades he created here and also on the western slope beyond the old house. Unusually, Switzer illustrated both these major parts of the works at Spye. The western half appeared in 1724 in *The Practical Fruit Gardener*, and the eastern part became the subject of plate 50 in *An Introduction to a General System of Hydrostaticks and Hydraulicks* in 1729.

At Spye there are individual ". . . Falls of the Water being over Steps and rough Work of different Kinds and different Heights, of about 30 or 40 Foot Fall" (*Hydro* II 413), that is, the complete fall, rather than the seven individual falls. (Switzer used elements from at least two designs in this plate, so his remarks, and its appearance, need to be addressed with due caution.) It was sited immediately in front of Spye Park House, probably just east of the old Bowling Green, with which it may well have been incorporated. Here the dependence from the reservoir noted on the 1849 survey is a little more than 10 metres, and so it fits. It also fits with his description of an ornamental reservoir which also provides water for the household and gardens as well. Viewed in that light, then, his illustration may be taken as pretty near what was made at Spye Park. Even so it is an element unlike any seen before. It takes the place of a parterre. It also has the qualities of a parade. And, of course, it is a mix of water garden and wood, but tidy, crisp and garden-like. It has much in common with the scheme at Ebberston Lodge and Bushy Park's Upper Lodge (see above). Its breadth, and its openness, is parade-like, and getting close to a lawn, while the cascades and pools and the extraordinary rock-work (here almost pure *rocquille* work) belong to the Best Garden. There are crisply banked edges to the water, and these change direction to form complex frames to basins, and connecting water channels. The changes of level, the actual cascades, make the decorative addition, being in rough rock-work for their visual as much as their auditory qualities. Many jets of water also play from the pools. In contrast, the ground (in fact and as the medium for his design) is level and plain and decidedly crisp. Set into this tidy lawn feature are trees with any lower limbs removed, so that they too seem tidy on their straight standard trunks but then branch out in natural growth above. This broad swathe of "parterre" gives the walk sufficient breadth to become another thing. Its edges are crisply defined by low and clipped hedges and furnished with benches to rest on, and closely planted forest trees beyond. The Spye cascade, although made ". . . with very poor materials, yet admits of such a Variety, as some good Judges who have been Abroad seem to like, and think equal, at least, to any in the *French* Gardens . . ." (*Hydro* II 412–413).

The upper part of the design (corresponding to the eastern park at Spye) shows a trio of more conventional walks laid out in goose-foot fashion behind a larger pool (indicative of his reservoir) with a resident Neptune lounging in front of a grotto big enough to give shelter when wanted. One of these walks leads across Wandsdyke, or the old Roman Road in the park, to further woodlands, and a valley with a major brook and further water supply for the estate. Thus, Neptune, his Basin and the

Figure 4.15 Spye Park, Wiltshire: prospect of the east cascades (north to left). Reproduced from Stephen Switzer, *Introduction to a General System of Hydrostaticks and Hydraulicks*, 1729, II plate 40.

Grotto, and then the cascades lie above the main house, and not only were designed to be ornamental in themselves but also were to furnish the house itself with sufficient water: "... after the Water had shew'd itself in this sportive manner, it was design'd to supply all the Gardens and the House which lie below; and this Supply of Water was to have been from a large Reservoir on the Side of the Hill, collected from Engines, Rains, &c." (*Hydro* II 413).

The siting of the western half of his scheme is surprising, and it might seem to some that he had abandoned his precepts of following nature. He proposed constructing an enormous basin, more like a lake, 50 feet below the blank west front of Spye Park. As it lay half way down the slope towards the Avon this naturally required much cutting and filling. This is laborious but not in itself "unnatural" so long as the amounts of earth cut away balance the amounts needed to give stability and the resultant banked forms follow the angles of repose for the materials in use. And to give himself even the possibility of any works on that side meant that he had first to exaggerate the condition as found. That is, he made the precipice sharper to allow for a Terrace ("of the narrowest", as he put it) to run along the prospect side of the house. This critically important feature was where household and visiting company would stroll to admire the view, and marvel at the surprise of it. It was given more prominence still by the construction of two outlying bastions. These pushed his earth-architecture to its technical limits. Lying to either side of the old house a comfortable distance to north and south, these bastions (although quite small in themselves) gave the appropriate scale to the earthworks and transformed the edge with the old house into a seeming castle-like base. Therefore, he created a hanging Terrace roughly 600 feet long (about 185 metres), and this dominant, arresting, yet natural element would have a significant visual impact. This means Spye Park House would "read" at a distance and from below on approach, and from glimpses from the broad river valley beyond, as a much grander establishment. Blenheim, Grimsthorpe and Castle Howard had employed a similar design idea.

From the rest of the grounds, focused on the presumably retained old Bowling Green as the Best Garden, reaching this Terrace was easy and attractive, but from Spye Park House itself there was apparently one entrance only, and that was by way of a grotto housed in the addition, squarish in plan with a semi-circular bay pointing

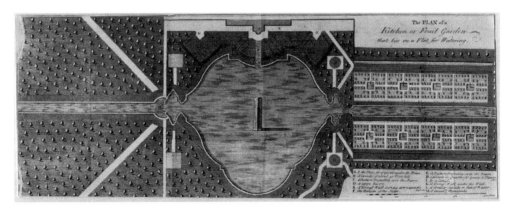

Figure 4.16 Spye Park, Wiltshire: plan of the house, west cascade, basin etc from "The Plan of a Kitchen or Fruit Garden" (north to left). Reproduced from Stephen Switzer, *The Practical Fruit Gardener*, p. 307 1724. Private collection.

westward on axis. It measured 30 feet in breadth and 25 feet in depth, including the 10 foot diameter apse projection, and it seemingly acted also a porch. This was attached to the old house at the mid-point. Switzer notes that it contained "a Grotto under the House". This clearly refers to the two rooms Anne is reported to have added to this side of the house (http://bayntun-history.com). Its size is sufficient for a modest reception room, and its placement and form cry out for an easy opening from the house (and also from the chambers floor to a platform on its roof). It most likely consisted of a sort of large bay for appreciating the view, and opening from a principal reception room on the (slightly) raised main floor. This would have fitted easily with the style of the place. The surviving Spye Arch, apparently made up at least partly from the remains of old Bromhall, was constructed to serve as the gatehouse to the park, and both additions were likely designed by Switzer. Below the Viewing Chamber would be the Grotto, reached from the lower floor of the house and opening also onto the Terrace.

The ostensible reason for including the folding plate of the Spye works in *The Practical Fruit Gardener* in 1724 was to illustrate Switzer's idea, or, as he put it, "invention if you like", of an easily watered kitchen garden. The form of this garden was a series of square kitchen quarters each with a small square basin at its centre. These were arrayed in ranks to either side of a canal. This form is close to the kitchen garden at Hampton Court, Herefordshire (see above). The beds were to be watered simply by turning a stop-cock which allowed the beds to be gently flooded, and thus watered. Essentially the small square basins were a constant source of ready water, and also useful as fish ponds, but they would not supply clear water. "The Ponds themselves when drawn down a Foot, will near Water the Quarters adjoining thereto; but then there is a Canal that is communicating with the lower Part, and a Reservoir that communicates with the upper Part for the Garden . . . which lies on three different Levels" (*FG* 1724 309).

The kitchen quarters lay towards the south at Spye, conveniently adjacent to the stables and yards. Through its middle there was a canal supplied from springs in the parkland higher up Bowden Hill. After the kitchen array there was a small cascade emptying into a complex shaped pool adjacent to the big basin, and opposite it on the north side was its pair, emptying through a larger cascade, semi-circular in plan, into a further canal in woodland, identified as the *Menagerie*. This lower and productive part of the gardens was reached from the Terrace by a diagonal walk from the south bastion which led first to a broad lower terrace walk along the kitchen garden, or to the edges of the basin. There were broad grass walks along the edges of the canals and the edges of the basin. These opened into further walks, gravelled, into woodland to a variety of "Cabinets or Quarters for Greens and Flowering Shrubs". From this series of lower walks the shapes and forms of the great grassed slopes supporting the Terrace and the house could be better appreciated, and further views of the big Cascade, the *jet d'eau* and the basin itself could be had, as well as more views west across adjacent fields. There are remains of earthworks on that side near the site of the old house, but when it was demolished in the later 19th century any remains then of the terraces and bastions were likely much altered, although there are now fragments surviving, and also the carcass of the terraced edge and its associated slopes remain in place. The modern ménage occupies the site of the basin, and is roughly the same size.

These works on the west side of Spye were on a much grander scale. Since the similar infrastructural works at Caversham would have been some £1,200 plus a hefty additional amount of £850 for labour, they cannot have been much less at Spye. At £2,000, perhaps more, perhaps less, their value in current terms was £600,000 or thereby. After Anne married Lord Somerville, she lived with him at Spye, where their daughter Anne was born in 1725, and their son James the next year. This period will have been the time also for these more major works to be carried out. In 1732 (and noted in the later editions of *The Practical Fruit Gardener*) Switzer makes it clear that not all of the design had been finished by then. For example the ". . . Menagerie, with Orcharding or Groves on each side . . . is not yet begun upon" (*FG* 1752 335). Also, in writing about the basin below the west side of the house, he makes rueful use of one of Virgil's quotations from *The Aeneid*, "*Sed Deus dedit hos quoque finem*" (*FG* 1752 331).

The Somervilles had another major project to occupy them, and in that Switzer would have likely been involved, if marginally. As the heir to Spye was now nearly of age, the Somervilles had decided to move to Lord Somerville's old home near Edinburgh, and to leave the elder boys in England. The late 16th century House of Drum was rather like Spye, in that it was long, barn-like and irregular. Whether they had initially hoped to make the old house fit for their occupation or not, it soon proved too small. In 1726 they decided to commission a new house incorporating the old one. They chose a local architect just coming into full flower professionally, William Adam. Adam had just finished nearby Mavisbank with his client there, Sir John Clerk of Penicuik, and was continuing his work on his major and long term effort for the Earl of Hopetoun a few miles north-west. The new Drum house, sometimes called Somerville House, is one of the Adam's earlier and one of his better, if not most academic, works. It is of a size similar to Gibbs' earlier design for the Rolts at Sacombe, and its structure was completed fairly quickly. It has exceptionally good interiors, but these date mostly from the later 1730s. Its grounds were designed at the same time, and are very simple, but boldly so. As they are structurally very similar to Spye they may well have been designed by Switzer. However, Adam would clearly have been given the task of making them. These consist of the very large woodland, cut out into large walks at the far end, and with the parade avenue on the "garden" axis, here to the north of the house. There are also clumps of plantations of forest trees into the neighbouring parks, very much in the style of the *Scots Improvers*. The parade element is the only one common to both Spye and The Drum. Spye remained in use, although not continuously: the Somervilles began the agreeable habit of dividing their life between Midlothian and Wiltshire. Indeed, it was while at Spye, then with young Edward of age, and with the other children in attendance at a picnic overlooking the new works, that Lady Somerville died in 1734.

Lacock Abbey

Lacock Abbey was an ancient pile of English religious architecture in delightful decay. From the 13th century to the Dissolution it was an Augustinian nunnery, not so enclosed as most and dedicated to good works in the community. Since then it had been a house belonging to the Sharingtons, and from the late 17th century to the Talbot family. It has had a happy history in being neglected for long periods, and then repaired with inspired additions in the briefly fashionable but nevertheless best taste: finally, it has been presented for us through the very early and elegiac experiments in photography. It lies in the plain of the River Avon south of Chippenham, and its

150   "*Nature to advantage dress'd*"

Figure 4.17 Lacock Abbey, Wiltshire: *Beeches at Lacock*, photograph of trees in the gardens by Henry Fox Talbot, 1844. Science Library.

character was also appealing to the 18th century, attractively old yet oddly out of its time: allusive, romantic, capable of raising all kinds of associations of ideas, but its topography was flat. How can nature be pursued to advantage in such a place? The obvious answer, offered both by Pope and later by Horace Walpole (and seemingly even by the old Chinese scholars), is to rectify the disadvantage of flatness by introducing a hill, such as the one provided by the ancients at nearby Marlborough. Many mounts were included in 17th century gardens for just such reason. Might there be a subtler yet equally effective response? If the nature of a place is to be flat, then a sensible designer, and a sensible improver, will contrive something which will suit the nature of the site, and that something will necessarily be congenial to the genius of the place. It will be most likely something flat, perhaps linear, geometric and regular, certainly something horizontal and planar.

There is a survey of the grounds of Lacock dated 1713 which shows the disposition of the place then: an accretion of elements, all of similar configuration, on the whole small, and all clustered together, and connected to each other, and importantly also connected to the house and its courts. It is this doubtless agreeable state that John Ivory found the next year when he inherited, through his maternal grandfather, the last Talbot, whose name he added to his own. John Ivory Talbot (1687?–1772) was born in Ireland and educated at Christ Church, Oxford. He was a Member of Parliament, first from 1715 for the constituency of Ludgershall and then from 1727 for the county of Wiltshire. He was a convinced Tory and even identified as a potential Jacobite at the time of the Atterbury affair. His connoisseurship is attested by his commission in 1753 of the new hall for Lacock. This was the work of Sanderson Miller of Radway, the important architect of structures and designs arising from their topography, closely allied to aesthetic theories deriving from the then strong, but too little developed, notion of Association of Ideas. These were for designs in landscape, or as architectural ornamentation (actually more of elaboration of aspects) of landscape design . . . place-resonant follies. His work at Lacock testifies to the power of such an approach applied to old buildings. His hall, while it is clearly of the mid-18th century, persuades us that it is somehow ancient as well, and very much part of the Abbey it was added to. Such essays in "Gothick" were rare, and often cheaply executed, mainly for want of craftsmen capable of realizing such work, and also the lack of building experience on the part of their amateur designers. However, they are an important contribution to architectural design theory, and still too little explored. And, of course, their origin can be traced to the advice Switzer gave in *Ichnographia Rustica* about how buildings in a landscape should be done in "imitation of some Antiquated Place" because of a resonance that brings poetic quality to a place, and their cheapness. By Miller's time, and certainly in his limited practice, the architect's skill was beginning to catch up with the theory behind it. Such is the case at Lacock Abbey.

But how might all this relate to the design of the landscape of Lacock? Of Ivory Talbot's activity as an improver we know relatively little. That he was known to Switzer is confirmed by a mention of him in *The Practical Fruit Gardener* in 1724, and he also appears as one of the subscribing improvers in *The Practical Husbandman and Planter* of 1733–1734. In a letter from Ivory Talbot to his brother-in-law Henry Davenport (for knowledge of the letter's existence and its importance I am indebted to Sandy Hayes, who has been researching the Lacock archive on behalf of the National Trust) he mentions, along with other family news, that although he has been delayed he hopes soon to "prosecute his new design in his garden" (J I Talbot to H Davenport 22 May 1722, Lacock MSS). The evidence for this garden is contained in another survey at Lacock, a rather fuller and more professional one dated 1764. From this we may get a picture of his seemingly limited and at first blush rather old-fashioned efforts. Of course the survey shows an obviously old-fashioned garden: it is made up of a series of straight walks and is roughly rectilinear in itself, and in no way indicative of advanced ideas about garden design. Closer inspection reveals this to be true, but more as well.

What the 1764 survey shows is the Abbey now with a broad lawn to the south and east, and a wooded garden of some 15 acres to the north. This girdle of grounds is defined by a seeming platform made up of half-terrace walks enlivened by bastions at the corners. Lying beyond it is a second ring of bigger similar lawn-like spaces, each of about 15 acres . . . the Paddock to the south, March Meadow, and *Fating Leaze* bounded by the Avon, serpentine along large meadows, with others in an even further girdle beyond, and finally beyond the old Nunnery Farms, the ground rises to Bowden Hill on the east. Southward were many even larger fields and an old wood, Luwood, all bounded by the Wandsdyke. The town of Lacock filled the western side of the estate. To put it another way, we see the constituents of an extensive farm-like garden, or *ferme ornée*. The only curving, or "natural" element is the River Avon: all else is flat and regular, though in this place entirely appropriate, and thus natural.

The new garden to the north made a large extension to the place; by making the same Ha Ha-terrace walk in imitation of the fortification work at the corner bastion, it also suggests an ancient castle-like quality overall, now with the new woodland garden three times longer on the river side, with the old gardens all subsumed and abstracted into lawn. The entry from the Abbey, that is, the garden side, is at a sort of inverse bastion where the new work juts out into the valley accommodating the end of the old canal, and tidying that up is another bastion: an excellent view of the canal is provided (in that it is in perspective while giving a glancing end-on view of the whole). There are broad walks to either side . . . woodland to the left, river to the right. The new garden provided for walking, contemplation, water-works and all the interests which might have been assigned to their quarters in the earlier scheme. Like other such recent woodland gardens beginning with Wray Wood this walking garden at Lacock was defined by walls, not for exclusion and shelter, but for definition. Here they formed a rectangular precinct, and were raised slightly from the insides onto neatly gravelled and turfed terraces on walls sunken to the outside, pretty classic Ha Has, but retaining in these earlier manifestations as half-terraces also their roles to extend and make grander the appearance of the house. And to the east and south of the Abbey the lawns were similarly defined. There was thus a bold contrast between the two parts, doubtless built into the design from the beginning. The low lawns are absolutely open, and the wood closely planted and high, with the old Abbey lying between them: an open sunny clarity, and closed obscure enchantment, mediated by a comfortable old house.

Within the walking garden were many long walks, and these are straight. There were no *arti-natural* serpentines here (according to the 1764 survey), and, curiously perhaps, there was also no geometric figure in the composition either. The disposition of these walks is irregular, and would seem to be so in response to their being aligned to significant landmarks outside. Certainly the main walk is in line in the middle distance with a stretch of straight run of the River Avon near Reybridge, and this was doubtless deliberate. But horizontal figures obvious on plan or in maps may make an insignificant difference to a visitor, whereas vertical landmarks such as church spires are certain to give satisfaction and make, as an 18th century designer-landowner put it, "a tolerably good termination" (Haddington 1761). As no such landmarks seem to be identifiable, might their disposition be irregular for other reasons? Maybe it was to provide the variety that all writers in those days craved, and that plainly a flat site could not itself contribute. Like much else of value in landscape design Le Notre had also encountered such problems, and explored ways of dealing with them. At Montmorency he had magnificently demonstrated how the eye could be fooled within a site into believing it to be much larger, indeed almost magically larger than one knew it could be. There from the terrace immediately outside the main reception rooms he designed an axial series of spaces. Comprehended as a single space bounded to either side by close woodland, even this was more complex. At a large rectangular basin (whose long axis lay parallel to the house) it was necessary to move sideways to get by, which leads to another stronger axial walk, at whose end was a seemingly transverse avenue of forest trees, set at rather less than right angles from it. This transition leads to another turning to the left, now really 90 degrees, which presents the big surprise of the place. Where one expects something similar to the route just taken, instead there is a greatly larger, longer and more varied axial series. Le Notre had simply led the visitor sufficiently off the anticipated track not only at a different angle but, at

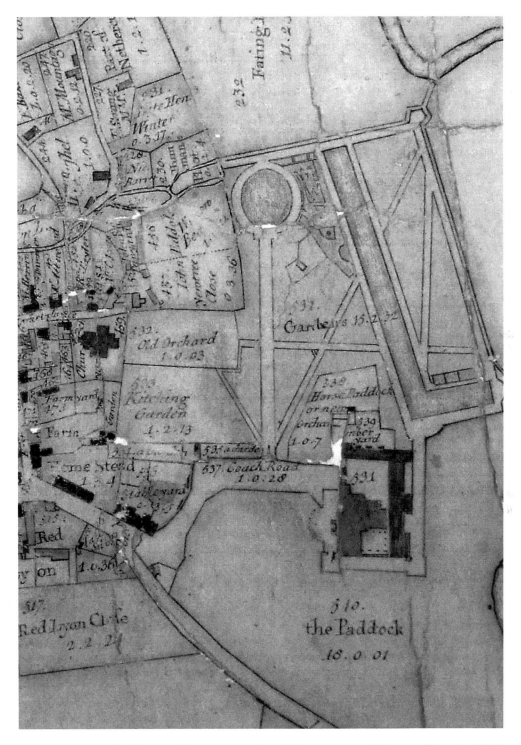

Figure 4.18 Lacock Abbey, Wiltshire: "Exact Plan of the Demean and Manor of Lacock 1764" (north to top). Wiltshire Archives Swindon.

Montmorency, at an angle sufficient to take the array of spaces past the house itself to end well beyond the entrance front, therefore packing in more varied and more numerous garden ornaments. And instead of the mere repetition expected he produced wonder and surprise.

The irregularities in the layout of major walks at Lacock would have had a similar pleasantly disorienting effect. Lacock is hardly Montmorency, nor Ivory Talbot anything close to so rich as the king of France's financier. Yet the pleasing effects of surprising irregularity in a well-managed 15 acres of woodland garden in Wiltshire will have had similar effects as the original had recently produced in Jean-Antoine Watteau's *The Music Party*, painted at Montmorency in 1718. Only a little imagination is needed to appreciate that the kind of reaction Switzer had so enthusiastically related about the joys of Wray Wood could also be produced at Lacock. This may be seen in one of Henry Fox Talbot's earliest photographs, one of this garden. Its antiquity as a photograph helps us to appreciate the kinds of pleasure the designers of Lacock aimed at.

At Lacock the walking garden's entrance is from a broad parade-like space along its southern edge. This was originally marked by a tall obelisk, but now a pair of giant pillars of classical architecture, as tall as ancient trees, leads into it. The main walk lies directly ahead and is centred on a large basin of water, of pond size, in the far distance. At a slight angle to the right is almost equally strongly signalled walk, slightly narrower, directed also to water and beyond to the distant Bowden Hill. Equidistant to the left is the much narrowest of the three walks; it leads along the side of the Kitchen Garden to the Old Orchard. All these elements are familiar and conventional, yet they are pleasantly skewed, by their relative sizes, destinations and characters, and surprising composition. Like the entrance the parts of the walking garden are put together in an irregular manner, partly through design and partly through the opportunities of working with found elements from the old gardens.

The most irregular of these elements is there very much by design. This is also the subject of the fortuitous snapshot of evidence that Ivory Talbot's newsy letter to his brother-in-law provides (J I Ivory to H Davenport 22 May 1722, Lacock MSS). Almost in passing he notes that he has not been able to get on with the design of his new garden, but that "Mr Switzer . . . comes over here for a day or two next week to lay out the ground." The purpose of that particular visit is to make a Menagerie. Only recently introduced to English usage in James' 1712 translation of d'Argenville's *Theory and Practice of Gardening*, the term *menagerie* had not yet assumed its more modern meaning but carried more of its (apparently) original French usage of a place for the husbandry of small domestic animals, such as chickens. It also has something in it of the decoy. Switzer had learned about how to design and lay out such a place when working as a very young man with Wise in St James' Park back at the very beginning of the century. As Ivory Talbot makes clear, this one is for ". . . ducks and wildfowl. The place is 3 acres to be thrown up in Islands and withy beds with water between, it is a rushy piece of ground and lays behind the mill upon this brook."

The site of this curious feature is south-east of the big oval basin, and is bounded also on its east by the canal, and to the north by the enclosing terrace walk. It is thus isolated from the rest of the walking garden and bounded by water and landscape (that is, the 11 acres of *Fating Leaze* and beyond it the Avon), backed up with close woodland to its south. In the interior the water is formed into mostly irregular shapes by islands and peninsulas of sharp and jagged outline, all designed to be visible from the terrace walks nearby, and backed by close woodland. With regard to wildfowl, it is attractive and natural enough to tempt them to settle, and at the same time to be visible in the garden. The large aviary part is arranged along the north terrace backing onto the refuge peninsula. Its considerable breadth lies along the terrace in contrast to its shallowness towards the refuge, which allows for the greatest observation of the birds within. Aviaries were a feature of ancient writers on agriculture, particularly in M T Varro's *Rerum Rusticarum Libri Tres*; a modern edition with an illustration of his aviary appeared in the 1720s. This is of a circular form, but its relationship to the gardens surrounding it are part of his specification, as much to humour the birds and make them feel settled, as to become an ornament itself to the gardens. Ancient wall paintings (then of course still unknown) show how important this aspect was to the Romans. It was an idea well accepted by the moderns, as, for example, the St James' Decoy in Westminster, still recalled by nearby Bird Cage Walk. Switzer's aviary makes much of the inherent transparency. As it is approached either from the canal-side walks or from the principal walk from the entry the cage and birds are seen first beyond woodland, and on closer view they are seen against the open outer meadows and the Avon . . . in other words, against landscape.

Transparency is one of the qualities that Switzer had introduced in the Manor of Paston plate and its commentary, and that we observe in Kent's work in garden design, especially at Chiswick from the later 1720s, where he quickly learned to exploit what could not be avoided (see below). Glimpses through one garden into another, and the melding together (to some extent anyway) of one garden space with another, can also be found with Le Notre or London. Here we see it used in the design of the Menagerie at Lacock. Although transparency comes more into use during the period of the English Landscape Style the other lesson Lacock offers is studiously ignored. The use of straight lines or other geometric forms to extend a house or building into its garden context, or such use in gardens and landscapes, disappears from the 1750s, only to return to fashion with Humphry Repton. But Brown, when consulted at Lacock (and it might have been about buildings), left no mark of change, and clearly recognized a design already attuned to nature.

Ferriby House

Of course, not all of Switzer's projects were local to his West Country base. In 1726 there is evidence of a chance commission, a commission that was difficult to refuse, and yet almost impossible to manage successfully. Seemingly out of the blue he was approached by letter, and as only four letters of their exchange survive we cannot really know quite how it began. In Switzer's first response he tentatively proffers the name of one of the great Pelhams, as a local friend, and as it is in the event ignored, it is unlikely Switzer had been approached by recommendation. Thomas Broadley lived near Hull in the East Riding of Yorkshire. He was not a man with great estate, nor a soldier, nor a courtier, nor even a Member of Parliament. Broadley's father had begun the family's rise to wealth in the 17th century, as had Thomas Rolt's father, but the Broadleys' rise was entirely within England, and specifically at Hull, where they began to acquire property. The family's advance and Hull's advance occurred together and were mutually enriching.

In the early 1720s Broadley bought grounds in the village of Ferriby, and sought Switzer out as the man to lay out his new gardens. It is worth reminding ourselves again just how quickly good fortune may come, and how soon depart. Although a number of owners of estates were anciently settled on them, very few indeed had been so fortunate as to be consistently rich, and powerful, to keep them in a grand manner. As fortune departs it usually leaves room for new men to take over, and certainly in the early 18th century they saw no reason why they should stint themselves, and cheerfully began to build and to plant as soon as possible. Broadley appears to have been starting quite from the beginning, and proposed the improvement of his place, on a somewhat grand scale, overlooking the Humber. Our knowledge of this comes entirely from the noted short series of letters between Broadley and Switzer beginning in the summer of 1726. The group gives glimpses of procedures and attitudes which are probably more common than we might have supposed.

Typically, the project is begun without including essential information, such as the plan of the house. Switzer's first advice was to secure a good survey of the ground, of plan and angles with profiles showing the risings and fallings. On receipt of this, still apparently inadequate (very basic matters take a while to be disclosed), and no doubt fearing and perhaps realizing the project can come to no good, Switzer's first response is quite a cavalier one. He regrets the site is neither large enough nor well disposed enough to offer a promising result. The house is too near the street, and it is too much overlooked by a lane between Broadley's place and his neighbour. He proposes securing a court-order to move the lane, and provides a design (to be collected from his peruque maker's premises in Chancery Lane) for a scheme for about 280 metres by a (hoped for) width of 50 metres. This duly arrives (the design does not survive, and Switzer's and Broadley's references to it have obscurities), but it seems to have consisted of a plain parterre below a "little sweep" and then five compartments with a walk dividing them axially. These, which Broadley assumes to be terraced, are each divided in two. "All the Quarters next to the middle walk are designed for fruit Trees . . . except the middle Division which is to be of Evergreens and flowering Shrubs with Cabinets . . ." (SS to TB 23 Oct 1726, Wilberforce Museum). Beyond these Switzer called for the outer quarters to be planted as "Wood or Coppice Worke", and at the Humber end are two lawns.

He produced a perfectly unexceptional design, plain, bold, simple and well disposed, and conventional and like Caversham of the standard type. There are several things about it which indicate procedure, and hint at the kinds of developments, ideas and offerings from the commissioner of the design which make the conventional design into a site-responsive and particular one. From Switzer's point of view he has provided the standard elements with his best advice for comfort and grandeur with a decent reticence. He is clearly not specially committed to any of the elements, nor indeed to the composition of them. Of the figure of the cabinets, ". . . they may be made either of this or any other Figure, and as I have kept a Rough Copy of all the Divisions or Quarters I can send you any new Design on larger Scales for either of them as you goe on always keeping the main Design in View . . ." He expects the design may change "as you goe on", and this is most likely the case in all his designs. "I suppose you will goe Regularly and Leisurely on, and then by Letter I may have more Time and Leisure to give you an Answer to each Particular . . ." Doubtless at Lacock, for example, there will have been much scope for various ideas to occur to Ivory Talbot or to Switzer in the intervals between meetings. At a place the size of Cirencester this certainly happened, and of course there was also the benefit of further ideas from absent friends such as Pope. At Caversham the project was meant to be realized in one season, but that is unusual, and even there it was postponed. More often works would be done over a longer period, for whatever reason, and changes along the way could be accommodated, and were expected. But he is most positive that Broadley needs to bestir himself sufficiently to rectify the structural weaknesses of the site, ". . . and sorry shall I be if you cant turn the Road soe as that your House may not be in the Middle not only of your Garden but the Enclosures Contiguous thereto . . .".

Time for leisurely reflection was clearly seen by Switzer as a great advantage, but he did require that there was someone on the spot he could trust, and whose judgement was sound, and who could act as executant for him and ensure that little difficulties encountered were never allowed to blossom into problems. He had such a man in mind, and had suggested to Broadley that he engage him. If a reliable survey of the ground was the first requisite for success, then this was a close second, ". . . Since 'tis Impossible for me at this Distance to settle every Point that might occur in a Design of this Kind, and a man may with almost as much certainty Paint a face as give a Perfect Design for a Place he never saw."

Broadley's response to Switzer's plan, of which he wrote, ". . . I would like extreamly well if my Ground would admitt of itt . . .", was that he definitely could not move the lane, as it was impracticable (partly because it was so deep that it would cost £150 to fill [nearly £50,000 in current value], which, of course, was wildly exaggerated) and he did not own the ground on the other side. Unstated, but pretty clear, was the fact that he would not receive a good response if he offered to buy his neighbour out. As his business had become one of acquiring property he would wish to appear a welcome buyer, and certainly not the seeker of a property. Unlike in the Hoares' acquisition of Stourton, Broadley had not bought Ferriby House to settle himself as a country gentleman, but for other, not originally specified reasons. Not surprisingly, some of Switzer's assumptions had been faulty.

As he now told Switzer the house was a small one to be used really only as a Hunting Seat. It contained only four rooms per floor, and the best of these faced into the street, and it was leased (although he thought he could buy out his tenant's remaining time). He wished to use Switzer's design, but could not provide the necessary space for it. He could do without the fruit trees as he had a kitchen garden already. Also, there were other problems such as the thin soil near his house, but instead of seeking advice about how to bring the soil there up to a standard for any garden, he suggests substituting the parterre for an oval of limes around a summer house. Otherwise, he continues, unless ". . . my Ground will not answer the Charge & expense of anything else I must submit to have nothing but Vista of the same down to the bottom". But he still hopes Switzer can provide something for him within his less than promising parameters. Could Switzer come up with something looking as much like nature as possible, costing between £150 and £200 (in our terms between £50,000 and £75,000), to fit in his small space, and send him a revised design, black and white only, and enclosed in a letter?

It is clear from this that Broadley was not then prepared to spend the kind of money and effort to make a garden of Switzer's standard. His relatively miserable house might have been overlooked, but the stinginess apparent in his weak excuses about thin soil, and his cunning in trying to get further advice on the cheap, might well have reminded Switzer that he had other and more pressing matters to attend to. As the surviving correspondence breaks off at this point we cannot know how the project developed. In the 1760s another, and appropriately large, Ferriby House was built by the Hetheringtons, addressing a handsomely broad garden southward to the Humber, and with the offending lane removed. Perhaps Switzer's advice was followed after all.

5   A public figure

In the mid-1720s Stephen Switzer's patterns of life and of practice changed. While it is not entirely clear why this should have been so, he was then in his 40s, and married. There was a shift also in the potential people who might wish to commission designs from him. Their circumstances and their own attitudes seem to be noticeably different from those of the people who quite often were their own parents, certainly of the older generation. The kinds of houses and the kinds of gardens and estates of the 1730s are so different from those commissioned in the 1710s that to consider the 1720s as a decade of transition may be productive and help us to understand more fully the character of the adjacent periods. The great Duke of Marlborough is dead, the new king is established and soon his son will begin to figure, and government has imperceptibly assumed its modern form and the Union of Parliaments has created Britain. Of Switzer's patrons Duke Robert Ancaster died in 1723, and Lord Pembroke at the end of the decade, and Lord Orrery is gaoled in the Tower of London for nearly a year as a suspected traitor for his support of Atterbury: he also falls out with his own family to the extent that his great library, a most important source for Switzer's work, is put in doubt before it is housed in Oxford, and he even has to abandon his darling Marston for Britwell in Buckinghamshire and an irregular family life there.

What, then, might Switzer do to ensure a suitably secure middle age, in the public eye, if not in public employment? He needed to be in the capital, and preferably in Westminster. And if not in a post, and none for him really existed, then he needed a place and station to give him accessibility, a memorable address and proximity to any who would consult, govern or be active in public affairs. And lacking a stipend or sinecure it ought also to be lucrative, well within his capabilities, special, perhaps rare, easily managed by others, and compact. Thus, his seed shop at Westminster Hall became his new business and address. This would have been granted through Peregrine as successor Duke of Ancaster and as High Great Chamberlain of England. He had inherited this lofty title from his father in 1723. With the office came the privileges and duty to manage the Palace of Westminster, including the Hall (Colvin 1976 V; Brogden, Correspondence 9 July 1970 and 13 Aug 1970). (The actual management of Westminster Hall was in the hands of the Warden of the Fleet Prison [personal information from the late Sir Howard Colvin, who also informed me that all records of transactions about it have perished].) John Evelyn had noted it as one of the known places where seedsmen could be found (in London and Wise 1704 ii). There, "over against the entrance to the Court of Common Pleas at the sign of the Flower Pot" Switzer set up shop as a seedsman. From 1726 he had a national presence, easy of access, to act as his depot, show his books and designs and provide a good income, as well as be a focus for enquiries and exchanges of news about all aspects of garden design, husbandry and rural improvement.

St Margaret's Westminster became his home church, and in the early years he had a house and garden in Kennington Lane, just across the Thames, then largely occupied by market gardens. Later he lived at Millbank, and his son Thomas was a pupil at Westminster School. Of his old associates John Vanbrugh died in 1728, having married late and established his family at far away Greenwich. Richard Bradley died, rather prematurely, in 1732. Charles Bridgeman set up his household near Marylebone in the new district north of the Oxford Road; he too was dead by 1736. The Hawksmoors were neighbours. Hawksmoor continued to build at Castle Howard, but by proxy, and he was much concerned about the planning and design of the New Bridge at Westminster. Sadly, Hawksmoor was rather thwarted in his laudable efforts by Lord Pembroke, also a neighbour in Whitehall, who had adopted the project too but took a quite different tack.

There are two sources which help to identify Switzer's *public* and give an often surprising insight into who shared his interests in improvement. The list of subscribers to *The Practical Husbandman and Planter*, published in six parts in 1733 and 1734, contains well over 300 names, and ten years later the list of members of The Honourable Society of Improvers in the Knowledge of Agriculture in Scotland contains some 300 more, with only a little overlap. These organizations shared the same aims and were similarly constituted. The Society of Improvers was established from Muirhead's Coffee House in Edinburgh in the summer of 1723, resolving to meet fortnightly in the high summer months of June and July, and in winter months to discuss correspondence between the resident committee of 25 and the members of the society. This committee received queries from members, sought answers to them and recorded these in their book of proceedings, which was duly published in 1743 as *Select Transactions*, edited by their secretary, Robert Maxwell of Arcland. The method was easy but formal. "All Members of the Society, who want the Opinion of the Council concerning their Farms or Grounds, shall, upon sending to the Secretary the exact Situation and Nature of them, with Queries concerning Particulars, be answered by the Council, without any Expense, except Postage. That it be recommended to the said Persons, to return the Secretary a particular Account of the Success; and that this shall be immediately inserted in the News-papers, to certiorate all concerned" (Maxwell 1743 6).

These are early cooperative and experimental organizations depending on good will, clarity and a disinterested pursuit of knowledge. The sciences of soils and of vegetative processes were yet to come, but even so these improvers deduced a great deal by observation, trial and debate. The strengths, and weaknesses, are apparent in this and their methods. Success in farming also depends on a fair measure of good luck, and in canny responses to many variables. The problems put by Lord Kilkerran are typical. Forty of his acres of riverside ground present three problems of "light Ground, with a mixture of small Stones . . . a rich deep Earth, with a Mixture of a clay Nature, though not so as to be called a clay Soil . . . [and] Meadow-land, a sour Ground, which in general throws up a pretty plentiful crop of Hay . . . but part of it is of a very coarse kind . . . [whereas] Other parts of it bear a very thin grass . . . [to which the Judge asks] how I may manage this Ground for the future, so as to bring it to better account?" (Maxwell 9). The society's diagnosis was quick. In response, "As the Ground is wasted in its Strength" he is advised to follow a regime of ploughing, harrowing and resting "for some Years" with dressings of burned clay and beneficial soil enriching crops, of which "Drill-ploughed" turnips as recommended by Jethro Tull is one (and one of Maxwell's favourites) to be employed experimentally. A short discourse on the qualities and issues of some of these is included.

Repeated experiment based on secure knowledge is the key to success. Such advice is repeated throughout the *Select Transactions* and applied to many and varied situations. Switzer, as an authority quoted by Maxwell and as a member of the society, agreed with these principles. That there are many occasions for error and failure in complex and remotely supervised experiments is obvious, and of course there were also doubts about the nature of some of the supposedly secure knowledge. The improvers busied themselves in the 1730s and 1740s pursing these experiments, proposing new methods and disputing causes of failure, and misguidance in knowledge. Switzer was party to these, and usually in the midst of them, directing. Of the efficacy of drill-ploughing and other aspects of Tull's writings he had led in expressing his support, but in the very early 1730s he, and his colleagues in the London based Private Society of Husbandmen and Planters, found reasons to object, and their objections became increasingly numerous and shrill, appearing in 1733 and 1734 in its monthly papers, written by Switzer. Tull's rejoinders were delivered in equal number and similar tone, and appeared as notes or additions to his various later editions of *Horse-Hoeing Husbandry* in 1735, 1738 and 1739. They were collected together only in William Cobbett's edition of Tull's works (Cobbett 1829 vi–ix). It is clear that Switzer knew Tull, and the apparent enmity in some of his remarks is personal. Certainly his observation that Tull's *Prosperous Farm* in south-west Berkshire was very far from the name given to it was unkind. This no doubt rankled with Tull as much as their disagreements about Virgil and ancient husbandry did. It is doubtful that any improver of that period was ignorant of the *froideur* between them. As a farmer Tull was not a success, but he was essentially right in his understanding of how soils work, and how they can be improved through tillage and planting. Sadly, Maxwell of Arcland also ultimately failed as farmer, and should indeed have held the first chair of agriculture, as he had wished (Hewins *DNB*).

Colonel Charles Cathcart (1685/6–1740), Lord Cathcart from 1732, was a very keen improver, and a friend and correspondent of Switzer's from the 1720s. He had improved his estate of Auchincroff, Ayrshire, with the assistance of the garden designer William Boutcher of Edinburgh: there, ". . . we were very muddy but the work was done" (quoted in Brogden 1973 359 et al). And it was his experiments into and his method of burning clays to improve soils that he had communicated to Switzer. Switzer added this as an appendix to his pamphlet *A Compendious Method*, which appeared in numerous editions and revisions between 1728 and 1735. A just character and measure of the members of the Scots Society and the Private Society is Cathcart, who was, neither more nor less, typical. He was primarily a soldier, first in the Continental wars, and then he commanded the successful battle at Sheriffmuir against the Pretender, and in the 1720s he held political posts and was a courtier, being Groom of the Bedchamber to the King from 1727. He was Commander in Chief of forces sent to America in the War of Jenkins Ear, where he died en route. The Duke of Chandos (although acquainted with Switzer) does not appear as a member of either society, but he nevertheless took a lively and very personal interest in what they did, and just how it was to be best performed. He peppered Cathcart with a series of letters asking for further clarification in 1729 (Brogden 1973 468), even to the extent of prevailing on him to send over some of his own staff to instruct Chandos' people at Cannons, Middlesex. This Cathcart duly did, but as the duke had moved on to Tunbridge, the emissaries were left waiting at Cannons unrecognized for several days. Apparently someone at Cannons had already consulted Switzer's pamphlet sufficiently closely to get the method understood.

Meadows increasingly became an integral part of gardens in the 1730s, just as Switzer had urged since 1715 that they should, and he continued to do so. He was no longer alone, and he might well have concluded with some relief that his message had truly been received. Recently there had been others taking up his ideas in print, notably Robert Castell in his *Villas of the Ancients Illustrated* of 1728, and Batty

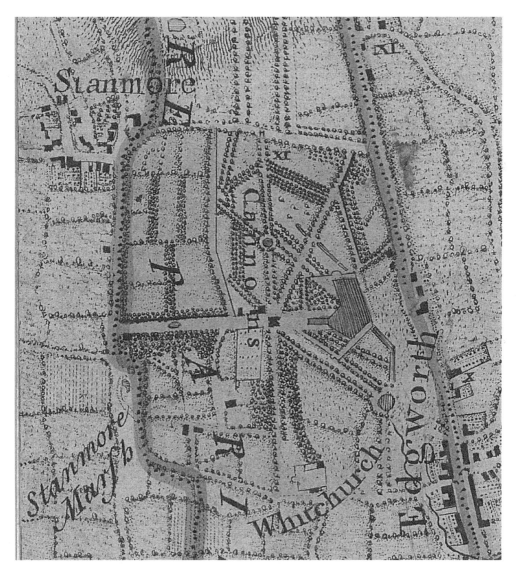

Figure 5.1 Cannons, Middlesex: plan of the estate in 1754 (north to top). Reproduced from John Rocque, *Topographical Map of Middlesex*, 1754. © National Library of Scotland.

Langley in his *New Principles of Gardening* of 1728. Younger amateurs such as Phillip Southcote at Wooburn Farm near Chertsey and Charles Hamilton at Painshill, also in Surrey, were being noticed for their designs of places made up almost entirely of fields. And one of Alexander Pope's Moral Essays, the *Epistle on Taste* to Burlington, leap-frogged over Switzer's liberal use of Pope's own early *Essay on Criticism* and now looked to become the very standard of how to judge buildings and the design of grounds. Switzer's decade or so of lonely proselytizing in favour of "Rural and Farm-like Gardening" looked as if it had been, if not quite fully accepted, at least taken more seriously by others. Even the Royal Family were creating their own *ferme ornée* at Richmond. There Bridgeman had introduced *utile* to *dulci*, if not quite mixed them together, in the grounds from New Park opposite Twickenham and adjacent to the bulk of Richmond Park. These included the grounds at Richmond Palace (recently Ormonde Lodge), its woods and the fields as far as Love Lane to the south to make a farm-like connection of meadows, arable land, woods and walks to the smaller grounds by Kew Palace at the south-east. As it seems Switzer was doing at Taplow (see above) Bridgeman formed and planted a Terrace, the tree-lined avenue opposite Sion Park, from Richmond to Kew. From there westward were the more rural close woodland walks separating the royal grounds from the farmed fields in various hands to Richmond Park proper. With these elements Bridgeman wove a series of walks along existing boundaries, adding garden-like elements from time to time, and making the whole into a sensible unitary one, much as Switzer had directed in *Ichnographia Rustica*. During the 1730s this series was further enriched by additional follies, and cabinets. But the new design was in place by 1733 (Marschner 2014 36).

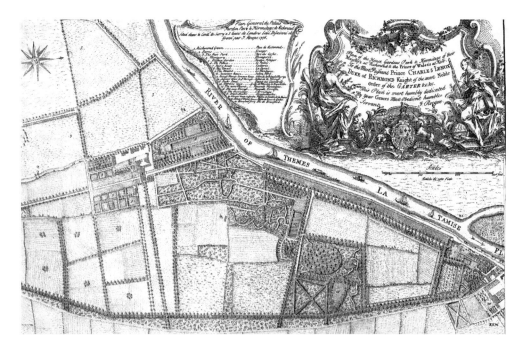

Figure 5.2 Richmond Palace, Surrey: John Rocque's plan of the grounds between Richmond and Kew, now site of Kew Gardens (north to right). Reproduced from, *Vitruvius Britannicus, or the British Architect*, Volume the Fourth 1739, plates 6 and 7.

And yet it ought to be remembered that John James' new edition of *Theory and Practice of Gardening* in 1729 had only had to acknowledge that French theory needed extra illustrations to show that it could easily conform to British practice: it remained the default manner for many, indeed for most. When Philip Miller published his *Dictionary of Gardening* in 1732 it took its ideas about design from James, not from Switzer. Switzer was most certainly alive to alternative pronouncements about issues such as identifying the ancients' *True Cythisus*, but that others had subscribed to his ideas about design does not appear to have troubled him for a moment. As Switzer had moved to Westminster and set up his business in the seed shop, and his many new publications required his time, he also was called on to give advice in all parts of England, and northern Wales, and perhaps also into Scotland. Increasingly he was sought out by improvers from those places as a natural part of their business when in London. Soon the directing of the *Private Society of Husbandmen* meetings at Temple Bar will show signs of hurrying and busy-ness likely to overwhelm, and occasionally cloud, his judgement. In no sense could Switzer think that he was being overlooked and passed by.

Switzer was so busy that he hardly had time to reflect on current matters. His contemporary William Kent (1685–1748) had been established in London since his return from Italy in the early 1720s and had lived in Lord Burlington's household in Piccadilly, working as a muralist at Kensington Palace, and as the editor of Burlington's collection of drawings by Inigo Jones, laying the foundations for his soon extensive practice in architecture. It is only in 1734 that any interest by him in garden design is noticed. That notice we owe to Sir Thomas Robinson of Rokeby's chatty letter with London news to his father-in-law, Lord Carlisle, about Kent's taking up garden design at Carlton House. And, of course, Carlton House was almost in sight. There he was "working without rule or line". Widely sociable and generous with his time, Switzer might also have had this news directly from Sir Thomas, one of his northern improver patrons, probably at his seed shop. But what Switzer made of such news we cannot say. The flat nine acres of the Carlton House site, between the Duchess of Marlborough's garden and the notorious ramble at the east end of St James' Park, had lately been sold to the Prince of Wales by Lord Burlington. It was hemmed in by houses along Pall Mall, and although its long side adjacent to St James' Park will have recommended it as real estate, it was hardly the most attractive garden ground. From such unpromising beginnings Kent discovered its, and indeed his, true genius. By the late 1730s his name crops up increasingly, and Switzer would by then certainly know of his success with that project, and also the works at Stowe and elsewhere. There is no record of any reaction from him, either positive or otherwise.

In the middle of the last century, when interest in the history of the designed landscape was being shown by landscape designers like H F Clark and young art historians such as Rudolf Wittkower and Nikolaus Pevsner, a pivotal and leading role was thought to have been played by Lord Burlington: much of that reputation is due to the early and quite fulsome praise given him, and Kent, by Horace Walpole in his *Anecdotes of Painting in England*, which first appeared in 1783. Walpole was a very perceptive critic, and was clearly able to see the balance of qualities in both men's works, and his *Anecdotes* still have their power (and I have had the advantage of owning Clark's copy of Dalloway's edition). Even so it was Walpole who amazingly proposed Burlington as the *Apollo of Taste* and Kent as his *proper Priest*. That fiction has been most attractive to Englishmen, and among many others James Lees-Milne

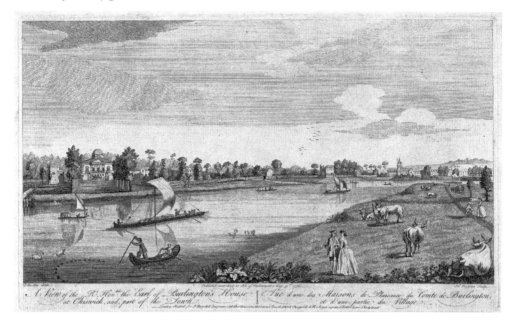

Figure 5.3 Chiswick House, Middlesex: south view from the river in 1750. Courtesy of Yale Center for British Art.

agreed and gave Burlington that role in his later *Earls of Creation*. He has retained that reputation since, but every attempt to go further into his roles, his actual contribution, has been, to some degree or other, disappointed. That he was intelligent and comfortably rich, was learned and critical and, if a trifle cool in company, was a most generous patron, and had the interest in his protégés that only really good patrons possess, has been confirmed. He also had a decided taste in architecture. He admired the clarity and simplicity of high Renaissance buildings, and such classical examples from ancient times which shared those characteristics. The provincial Mannerist Andrea Palladio from Padua seemed to Burlington to have all these qualities and few of the faults common to the modern Italians of the 16th and 17th centuries. Inigo Jones had also responded to Palladio in the same way. But it has to be pointed out that other architects also evinced these very same qualities, and most would agree that they sought them, even if they failed to achieve them. Getting it right, in a seemingly effortless manner, where all the qualities of commodity, firmness and delight are in happy balance, is what all architects strive for.

One of the most important features of Palladio's work lies in his acceptance of the fact that all buildings could share these qualities, not only expensive, public and important ones like churches or palaces, but also the simplest ones. Nobody else had taken the farmhouse and the farmstead seriously before Palladio did, nor had any done so since. He showed that these ubiquitous common buildings might become architecture, without losing their practical natures. It is true that his elder contemporary, Sebastiano Serlio, devoted one of his books to the design of houses, from cottages to palaces, but it remained unpublished in manuscript. Palladio's *Four Books of Architecture* brought the farmhouse (*villa* in Latin or *casa di villa* in Italian) centre stage. The examples to be seen in his fully illustrated book, and in the countryside of northern Italy for those who could travel, were also of a size and quality to make them very good examples for rich and powerful British builders to aspire to.

There is one further thing to note about Burlington. As architecture in those days was known to be a learned art but requiring no necessary skills in building, management or finances, someone who would act as a confident critic and advisor, someone who could save a potential commissioner from mistakes, needless expense and, much worse, the sneering ridicule of his neighbours, was very much wanted. Who better than an earl who was also a landowner, with the means and leisure to adjudicate? Therefore, when Burlington's neighbours asked him to oversee the building of the Assembly Rooms at York, his most complete and satisfying essay in design, they knew he was also good as a subscriber, and a trustee for the enterprise, and were content when he insisted that the narrow spaces beyond the rows of columns around the room stay as he wished, and not be made larger . . . although everybody else knew the spaces would prove hopeless as the place where the ladies sat out their turns on the floor, gossiped, chaperoned and otherwise got on with the real business of Assembly. In King James' day the king had simply refused to allow Jones to build such an encumbrance at the new Banqueting House at Whitehall, and what is more had instructed him to make the windows bigger to let in more light. Not so the York grandees, nor indeed Burlington's brother-in-law Bruce of Tottenham Park: in both cases Burlington's taste prevailed over common good sense. As Pope phrased it, there is "Something previous ev'n to Taste, – 'Tis *Sense*". Even so his readers were apt to be "Proud to catch cold by a *Venetian* door; / Conscious they act a true *Palladian* part, / And if they starve, they starve by Rules of Art" (Pope *Epistle to Burlington* lines 26 and 77–79).

Chiswick House

The same poem identifies Burlington with good sense in laying out grounds. There is no better example of Burlington's architecture and his landscape design than Chiswick House. A comfortable house with grounds, and fronting the Thames west of London, this was the site of his first essay in design, the Bagnio there in 1717. It is that very early date, and the supposition that a mature manner of the 1760s or 1770s is described in Pope's verses, that is the cause of much misreading of fact and consequent misguided history. These assumptions have remained prevalent until very recently. Chiswick was an admired example of building and gardening, and showed early use of the Ha Ha, and serpentine walks, and a close coming together of classical buildings and their settings, and it admirably illustrates also at least a version of Pope's very sensible advice to *Consult the Genius of Place*. Chiswick is also one of the most thoroughly illustrated of early 18th century works. It is possible, by reference to an extensive history of its design, particularly John Harris' in his *The Palladian Revival*, the critical catalogue of an important exhibition of the materials covering its development, to deduce its design history with some confidence. And therefore we can address the question of the relationships between the Palladian revival and developments in landscape design, and that of Lord Burlington's and, to an extent, also Kent's role.

At Chiswick Burlington inherited a 17th century house and moderately extensive gardens attached. These were recorded by Johannes Kip and Leonard Knyff in 1707: they are typical of the smaller estates of the time, like many on the edges of London. From 1716 to the late 1720s Burlington added to these, and reorganized them,

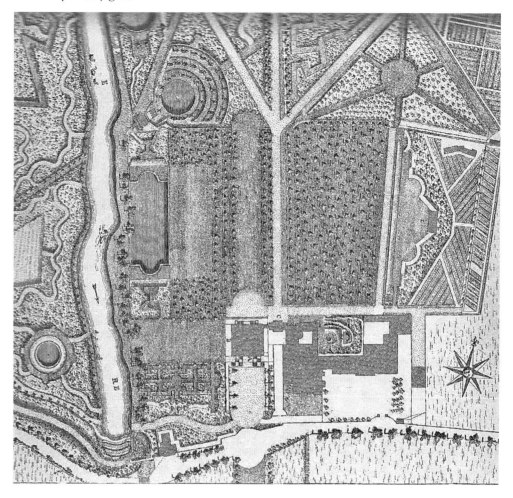

Figure 5.4 Chiswick House, Middlesex: partial plan of the gardens, by John Rocque (north to top). Reproduced from, *Vitruvius Britannicus, or the British Architect*, Volume the Fourth 1739, plates 82 and 83.

seemingly without a plan, but most probably with the advice of Bradley. And this "*ad hoc* gardening is characteristic of Burlington through his whole tenure at Chiswick" (Harris 1994–1995 47). The earliest of his additions is the termination of a north-south walk with a pavilion, the Domed Building of 1716 by James Gibbs, on the north side of the grounds. This existing walk does not connect to Chiswick House as such, but as the gardens then lay principally to west of the site, this, its *main* walk, passes the house neatly by on its west side. So far any integration of building and garden appear far from Burlington's mind, but its standing at the far end of a designed, and rather theatrical, setting will be typical of all his additions. Although Gibbs' building is perfectly classical, its author was soon replaced by his rival Colen Campbell, who designed Burlington's next addition, the Summer Pavilion. This little building was connected to Chiswick House and lay on an axis splitting the two quarters north of the house into equal parts, suggesting that there was, then at least, a desire to give the grounds a modern, conventional form. It was Campbell who encouraged Burlington's first "happy invention", the Bagnio, mentioned above. This was built in 1717 at the corner of the Chiswick estate, and also at the end of a different, and new, walk, a diagonal one, an easy departure from the orthogonal, and the best way give the impression of larger grounds; it was likely added on Bradley's advice. That building later becomes Burlington's studio and is thus the site of his architectural interests. The other northern corner becomes the occasion for a further diagonal, and then others are added, all from the same focus, and always in theatrical mode, that is, all aligned on an architectural or at least sculptural termination. Here is confirmation of a relationship between garden and building, but no attempt to create a *Bold Stroke* or make a unity of the scheme is tried. These additions are simply that, and his gardens and buildings are really parts of a growing architectural museum, what a contemporary called "so many buildings stuffed into a small compass" (John Macky's *Journey* 1724 quoted in Harris 2004 135).

Burlington marries in 1721 and has to update his house, and has the extra funds Lady Dorothy Savile brings to their marriage, but he continues to add small things, not to begin afresh. The old house gets a new "wing" at the front. In the garden a Deer House (two were planned) is added as a termination of the major cross walk, and it also makes a handsome show from three-quarters. This is added on the east side of the grounds with a Ha Ha separating the tiny enclosure for animals from a garden walk. The Rustic Arch at the end of the north-east diagonal and the Water Pavilion near the west edge of grounds come by the early 1720s. All are perfect essays in Palladio inspired buildings, of the smallest scale. In the 1720s also external spaces appear which are really gardens, but to Burlington's mind one suspects are actually more essays in architectural space, such as the new basin with exedra ends and a sloped lawn. Then he makes the Amphitheatre, with a circular basin and Round Temple in 1726–1727. By then Chiswick is quite crowded, and soon adjacent grounds are purchased from neighbours. There had also been a serious fire, and further attention had to be paid to his house, and when the designs for a new house begin, characteristic of Burlington this will be an addition.

But what an addition it is. It turns out to be a big pavilion based on Palladio's suburban farmhouse for the Capra family just outside Vicenza. Any visitor to the Villa Capra, of which Burlington was one, is struck by its peculiar relationship to its landscape, from its own small grounds, its intermediate surroundings and the longer views . . . it seems to embody the ideals the 18th century came to admire and to apply critically to similar projects elsewhere. Did Burlington transmit these basic lessons in successful site planning and landscape design to his new house? No, he did not. It is plain that what intrigued Burlington was the architectural *problem* Palladio's design posed . . . that of a square house facing equally in four directions. And he took the opportunity to explore that problem as one of his exercises in architecture at Chiswick. Like the other pavilions at Chiswick his Villa is a toy, recognized as such in the sharp observation credited to Lord Hervey that Lord Burlington's *bijou* is too small to live in and too big to hang on one's fob. But like his other pavilions it is closely related to his designed landscape, and the *genius of his place*, pre-dating Pope's dictum. That *place* was a flat and crowded one, and bore all the marks of its neighbours, and its own recent history. The site he chose was then his best garden, the parterres immediately west of Chiswick House. The north parterre in part became his ground plan, and the new Villa's forecourt occupies the rest plus the south parterre, which remained as much "garden" as parade. But his toy is a big one, and begged to be taken seriously as a new and important house in its own right. But as it was "merely" an adjunct to Chiswick House there is some justice in Hervey's jibe. But the Villa becomes attached to the rest of the house at Chiswick by the early 1730s by the addition of a further linking pavilion-like building to form a liveable and perfectly satisfactory whole. The Link is one of Burlington's most perfect miniatures, and it faces Gibbs' Domed Building at the other end of the axis as an equal. With all these additions Chiswick House has become a composition with at least three "centres", or none. It stands at the south side of the inherited grounds opposite the broad grove of now maturing trees divided into two unequal halves by the long axis. By 1727 the whole Chiswick landscape is a mature design, smart, even sophisticated and entirely commendable, and it was much visited and much admired. It is also conventional.

However, additional fields bought from neighbours add ground to the south and west, and scope for improvement. Judd's Close across Bollo Brook is big enough to count as parkland. Burlington, now fully working with Kent, is faced with how to exploit this extra space, and perhaps revise the inherited design they have already significantly added to. Their initial efforts seem like more ad hoc repairing and mending. They attempt to apply modern London conventions in their treatment of the immediate environs of the new Villa. Ignoring the mute lessons of the Villa Capra at Vicenza, where the villa was surrounded by open space, they opt rather to imitate another of Palladio's great square planned examples, the Villa Foscari, near Venice. This more up-scale prototype allows them to provide the "suitable" spatial adjuncts that houses of that importance conventionally provide. Therefore, the new Villa is given parterres for each front. The forecourt on the south side as the entrance is still richest. To provide a similarly suitable mirror on the north or garden side of the Villa is the first of Kent's forays into garden design. There the west section of the old Grove is felled, apart from the trees along the edge, and formed into a new parterre-lawn on axis with the villa part of Chiswick.

It is given an apsidal north end in the form of white sculpture, half figures or *terms* arranged in a big semi-circle making what was called the Exedra as a foil to the Villa's north façade. Additionally, there are urns on good classical pedestals between trees along the sides. Kent's first essay is a mixing of architecture and garden design, in imitation of Vanbrugh's recent furnishing of the parterre at Castle Howard. At the north front of the Villa, there is an answering semi-circle of iron railings, a new sort of invisible fence, an early example of the use, since ubiquitous around urban squares. These had also been used by the Duke of Chandos at Cannons, Edgeware, where Bradley had also advised on the layout of the grounds, and Chandos had seen them as one of the spurs to advances in industrial improvements as much as an alternative to the Ha Ha. Their use to make a barrier between the new Villa and the adjacent garden suggests perhaps that Chiswick already had more visitors than Burlington felt comfortable with, and he was rather plagued by them at the Piccadilly house. It, and a similar barrier on the west front, still strikes our eyes as a further essentially unnecessary encumbrance. The west front does not have an opening today (though a centre door is shown in the 18th century, for example by Rigaud), but that front is given a rectangular parterre, providing it with the conventional link between building and landscape. This side also has rusticated stumps of wall protruding a short distance, ornamented by the stone balls on a sort of inverted link-arcade, as Palladio had used at the Foscaris' house. This west parterre beyond the iron screen runs down to the Bollo Brook; its south side is formed by close woodwork cut out into walks and cabinets, which also forms a finish to the grounds, as beyond it lay Chiswick Lane. Its north edge was defined similarly by the already close planted ends to the older Basin and Lawn beyond.

These additions under Kent's direction, especially the Exedra, made evident a factor of the Chiswick design which has been observed by some as a precursor to some of Kent's stylistic qualities in his garden designs later in the 1730s: that is, an unexpected transparency brought about by two strong spaces (still formal), each of which was equally visible from its neighbour. This occurs simply because these elements have been crowded unusually close together. The problem had not been met with earlier because the necessity could never arise, and Switzer's positive uses of it, at Caversham or Holme Lacy, and in the Paston plate, are its lone precursors. At Chiswick it had arisen, first when the Amphitheatre and then the Basin and the Temple overlooking it were added in the earlier 1720s, where its formal division from the Bollo Brook was, at best, ambiguous. The effect, at least at the Temple, was not a disagreeable one, however accidental. The same effects occur with the addition of the Exedra, and its common boundary with the earlier Lawn with apsidal ends, overlooking another Basin, and Bollo Brook. Kent indeed heightened this seeming mixture of spaces by his further fragmenting of architecture to include the pedestals and vases lining the sides of the Exedra lawn-parterre. Thus were trees, tiny pieces of architecture and ambiguous spaces combined.

The addition of Judd's Close gave considerable room to expand. Here in the early 1730s the park-like addition is laid out, presumably to Bradley's design, but Kent likely supervised the execution of this large quarter of the grounds. The Bollo Brook marked the boundary between the two parts. It also provided the missing element, the *Bold Stroke*, to allow Chiswick to thrive, and make positive the ambiguities caused by the overcrowding in the inherited grounds. Bollo Brook became a New River by the very simple expedient of making it broader, most likely to be an idea from Kent. Perhaps in acknowledgement of its proximity of a real river, the Thames no less, where the old Bollo Brook encounters the old lane as a new *River*, the solution chosen to mask the obvious is to pretend that the *River* begins there and issues forth from a grotto. This is rendered in suitably Switzeresque form, here by Kent's grotesque three part rock-work of bridge-grotto-dam-wall. Beyond the brook to the west is ground open enough to become a small park, which is laid out with various tree-lined avenues criss-crossing, and defining small fields and meadows. With the *River* element in place, and the parkland as a broad buffer, the older parts of Chiswick could *borrow* space advantageously from both these new additions, and when later slightly simplified, the whole becomes a more resolved composition.

All this is important to note because of the reputation Chiswick has exerted on our understanding of the history of designed landscapes, but one further factor needs to be explored before it can all be explained. It is possible to be so particular about how this design progressed largely because of Burlington's role as a patron. Thus, he was proud of what he had achieved, and he was in the position, indeed felt he had the obligation, to be seen to be encouraging artists. Therefore, he commissioned many paintings of the grounds, and these became disseminated through the thriving trade in prints. One of this talented group of topographical artists is Jacques Rigaud, one of greatest of all, and as it happens French too.

Rigaud made drawings at Chiswick, and from these one thing is abundantly clear which no other source has given. He, on a short and to him ultimately rather troubled commission from Bridgeman in 1734 to record the grounds at Stowe, also made these drawings at Chiswick, presumably at the invitation of Lord Burlington. Rigaud recorded, and his drawings show, that he "saw" what Burlington and Kent had not "seen". He rendered Chiswick, as it were, from life, in properly constructed perspective drawings, but, importantly and critically, two point perspectives. These had been known and used in England in 17th century topographs illustrating county histories, but were not taken up further and had fallen out of fashion. Campbell had tried, rather half-heartedly, to revive the method, but one point perspectives were preferred by architects, and stage designers too. It appears that only an en-fronted view was thought serious enough, and it is arguable that Burlington, and Kent also, amazingly, could not bear to have their buildings displayed except in elevation: one wonders indeed if they could yet "see" buildings in the round.

It is only when the Villa at Chiswick is seen from the north, in elevation, that any necessity occurs to make it more open, to give it what in French academic circles is later called *degagement*, or room to be properly seen. Thus, Burlington and Kent were happy to remove the grove, and replace it with the Exedra. Certainly there is nothing "wrong" with the Exedra; it is simply unnecessary, and more to pity it postpones the ability to see the Villa in the round, in three dimensions, as one has to see the Villa Capra, no matter how strong the elevational quality of its design. Rigaud saw it thus; he also shows it perfectly fitting in with the grove, in his view, lying to the left. Similarly, in 1742 it is a view ascribed to George Lambert of the grounds from an angle, and atop of the Grotto-Bridge (transformed by him for the purposes of his painting into a classical one), that shows the potential sublimity of the scene, even though still unchanged, fussy and crowded, in a manner subsequent generations could *only* see, that is, Chiswick as an essay in the picturesque. Kent and Burlington were blind to this capability of the picturesque in the same scene in the 1730s, although topographically the views are identical. This is very curious. Harris' qualified assertion that in Lambert's image "Here by 1742 the effect of Kent's 'new Taste' and 'beautiful Nature' is apparent" (Harris 1995 249–250) is true, even though its authors had not yet "seen" it.

Palladio's Villa Capra is sited on top of a small conical hill, and that hill lies contentedly at the foot of the much larger and wooded rising of the Monti Berici to the southwest. East is a long view of the Brenta towards Venice, while below to the north and west is the town of Vicenza. The immediate approach is through a large gate, between ranges of agricultural buildings by a ramp and stair which rises to the hill-top, where there is open space surrounding the house. The house is square in plan, under a low pitched roof where the very low dome is just visible. On each side of the house are identical porches approached by broad steps which rise up to a full floor: each of these is rendered as a classical temple front. These are supported by classical columns, which are practically the only "architectural" ornaments; all else is rendered brick-work, plain and farmhouse-like. From each porch there are open views outward over varied landscapes. The only aspects of the Villa Capra translated to Chiswick are the square plan and the name, *villa*. There the site is flat, it has only one porch, its dome is prominent, its architecture splendid and courtly and very far from farmhouse-like, and the villa was, in fact, a wing only to a 17th century house. Sadly, therefore, in terms of landscape character the two projects do not bear comparison, although many have tried.

But if not from the lessons of a Palladian masterpiece, what accounts for Kent's manner? He was a painter first and a history painter too. In the early 18th century it was the branch of the art which carried respect with it. Through Burlington's good offices he had adorned Kensington Palace's walls and ceilings for the Royal Family. His interior decorating moved from murals to the furnishing and layouts of rooms. At

A public figure   171

the same time he began his studies in architecture, with Burlington, but these studies took the form, most unusual at the time, of preparing Jones' drawings for publication, and in doing so he also examined those drawings by Palladio which Burlington had acquired. The purpose of these studies was an edition of these, published in 1727 as *The Architecture of Mr Inigo Jones and Mr William Kent*. So Kent's analytical studies were of drawings ... plans and elevations, with some sectional drawings, and occasional details. It was an art historical kind of training, not that of a student architect. His limited experience in building was shared with Burlington, and was, as we have seen at Chiswick, small in scale. So a mature painter-decorator comes to the study of architecture in his 40s, essentially as an editor, acquires experience of building in a garden, if small still arguably of a landscape scale, and after five years further in practice, in the summer of 1734 begins to re-design the nine acres of grounds for Frederick, Prince of Wales just north of St James' Park. By this time he was nearly 50, an age when modern architects also come into their full powers.

Despite his training and experience as a painter Kent approaches designs in landscape as an architect. For him they are designs for buildings in landscape, and almost always they are shown, and likely also conceived, in elevation from the front, and being generally small they can be taken in at a glance, in effectively one point perspective. Spaces do not appear to figure in his imagination, and movement, if it exists, is hinted at by means of fragmentation and the transparency noted above, a lesson learned at Chiswick. Added to his preference for the small, concentrated architectural experience is his imaginative facility to find ways of heightening the qualities in an existing place, or of seeing minor architectural possibilities in a place which will bring out unexpected qualities. In 1734 Robert Morris, the kinsman of Roger Morris, who enjoyed a position with Lord Pembroke similar to that between Kent and Burlington,

Figure 5.5 William Kent, watercolour design drawing for an unidentified landscape scheme with deer house, ca 1735. Courtesy of Yale Center for British Art.

expressed in his *Lectures on Architecture* the thinking an architect would bring to landscape when he describes four sites of quite different characters at whose heart are such small buildings, for the use of one philosophical patron, or perhaps occasionally two at most. There the place, its landscape and the building at its heart form a sort of poetic unity. As he put it, for a sunnier, open disposition "a little remote from some noble *Villa*; and the Building I would place in some *Avenue* leading thereto" or, in a more melancholy spot, ". . . in the most unfrequented Part, surrounded with *Ever-greens*, and the Access to it by a declining spiral Walk, to terminate in a circular Theatre" (in Hunt and Willis 1975 234–235). These are the kinds of ideas that we can easily see in Kent's additions to landscape. Kent's contribution is to mix architecture and gardens or designed landscapes so closely that the distinction between them is blurred or disappears. He is the bringer of meaning, or the transformer, and rarely, if ever, the creator of the design at a large scale, the scale of designed landscape. Yet his additions had enormous punch when created, and these survive intact at places like Rousham, and could be readily sensed in less well-maintained places, such as the unrestored state of the Elysian Fields at Stowe.

At Holkham, where Kent played a significant role, perhaps that of the leading partner, in the progress of the design of the house, he also enriched the landscape, and at a landscape scale. Yet even there his contributions have the character suggested above: they are improvements on what was in place. For example the manner of terminating the cross axial south basin feature, which may pre-date his and Burlington's involvement, appears much improved by his ideas, for instance to add an Exedra, in alternative ways. And his essays in the disposition of the clumps of forest trees in the park add the consultant's finesse that makes his involvement in the project so valuable. That he became praised as a latter day Raphael may have amused him, but will not have turned his head. But to describe him as a bringer of the picturesque would be a surprise, both to Kent and to Burlington. I do not think it ever occurred to them. Clearly it occurred to Lambert in his 1742 image of Chiswick and perhaps also in his earlier painting of Ivy Lodge Park at Cirencester, as it did to Richard Wilson when he painted Wilton from the dam there a few years later: but both of these men were, after all, painters of landscapes.

Carlton House

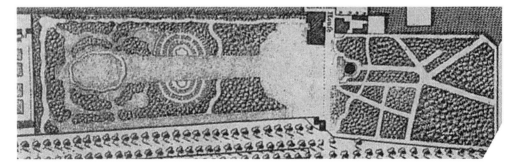

Figure 5.6 Carlton House, St James', London: plan of the gardens, by John Rocque, undated (early 1740s) (north to top). Private collection.

Kent's re-design of the grounds at Carlton House shows the range of his style very well. John Rocque recorded its plan in his topographical map of Westminster, and it was engraved a few years later in its maturity. Also, we have Sir Thomas Robinson's account of it. All of this, plus the supporting accounts and planting lists, is very thoroughly accounted for by David Coombs in *Garden History* (Coombs 1997). Carlton House was one of the private houses with grounds between St James' Park and Pall Mall leased by Queen Anne to her favourites, and on the death of Henry Boyle, Lord Carlton, it passed to his kinsman Burlington, who made it over to the newly arrived Frederick, Prince of Wales. He may have employed Kent as an architect at Kew, but the Carlton House project is the first (and perhaps only) new garden design by Kent. It had been a designed garden with parterres in the larger western part, and the old Wilderness left over from when it was part of St James' Palace remained at the east end. The parterres had been removed, leaving an essentially empty and flat site of about five acres. Its neighbours along the north side overlooked this part from their houses in Pall Mall (and they had built terraces on purpose to look over it to St James' Park a short distance beyond), as did the Duchess of Marlborough at the west end. The first issue for the designer was to provide some privacy while at the same time making sure there were ample open spaces left inside. This was done by adding trees, nearly 15,000 of them planted by the resident gardener as the site agent. Kent's design is structurally like its predecessor: a broad axial central section is balanced by a series of flanking wooded sections. At the west end of the scheme there is a large Basin, while opposite this at the edge of the old Wilderness Kent built the Octagon, also at the east side of a very large parterre-like space with Carlton House eccentrically sited to the north; this is big enough to accept very large gatherings in good weather, with just enough symmetrical formality about the east-west avenue entrance to pass muster for courtly convention.

The design is not at all revolutionary in appearance: it has the familiar parts, arranged regularly. But, as Robinson informs us, "There is a new taste in gardening just arisen, which has been practised with great success at the Prince's garden in Town . . ." (Robinson to Carlisle Dec 1734, quoted in Coombs 1997 153). The essence of this new taste is Kent's "notion of gardening, viz., to lay them out, and work without either level or line". As the site is nearly perfectly flat this seems a curious observation. What Robinson had in mind becomes apparent on closer inspection. The basin is apparently "round" (round like its contemporary at Kensington Palace, there actually complex, here oval) until one draws closer, when it is revealed to be edged by a series of shallow serpentines, rather like a pie-crust tea-table top, giving the "appearance of beautiful nature". Long before this had been reached, the strong axial avenue along the centre also on close inspection turns out to be bounded by two transverse Exedrae with pairs of semi-circular basins, made up of even smaller linked serpentines, backed by semi-circular beds rising by degrees to treillage arcades. As the avenue proceeds westward its sides, now reverting to closer planted woodwork, have also become serpentines, until at the Basin they become practically a-formal if still balanced, "according to what one hears of the Chinese, entirely after their models for works of this nature". When one turns around to look east, all snaps back into architectural propriety again to show the strong avenue terminated by the large and domed Octagon building, in *Palladian* purity and on axis.

174 *A public figure*

Robinson was not alone in being impressed with the successful design of Carlton House, and reported to his father-in-law that "a general alteration of some of the most considerable gardens in the kingdom is begun", mentioning Chiswick, Stowe (see below) and Claremont (see above) and predicting it would "grow a fashion". If not quite as Robinson might have anticipated, it did become the fashion, and a fashion associated almost entirely with Kent. According to Horace Walpole, writing at mid-century, "one Brown has set up, on a few ideas of Kent and Mr Southcote" (Horace Walpole to George Montagu 22 July 1751, in Walpole 1941 I 121). This appears just, if sharp, but is untrue. Kent's talent is inimitable really. If tried by others, Kent's seeming negligence, his almost magical waving of the hand, will do nothing except make such attempts at imitation look foolish. The attractions of the fashionable new manner took time to sink in, to be understood and find some kind of emulation by others. In his way Lancelot Brown was one of them, but his talents were also unique to himself. Certainly what others were already calling the *modern taste*, as for example John Loveday did at Wilton a few years later, was a quite different kind of design. Given his glowing report on Carlton House it would have surprised no one if Robinson had tried to follow this work, if not to engage Kent to carry it out. He did neither, nor did he appear to take much notice of the successes of Carlton House in his own works at Rokeby on the borders of Yorkshire and County Durham.

Rokeby

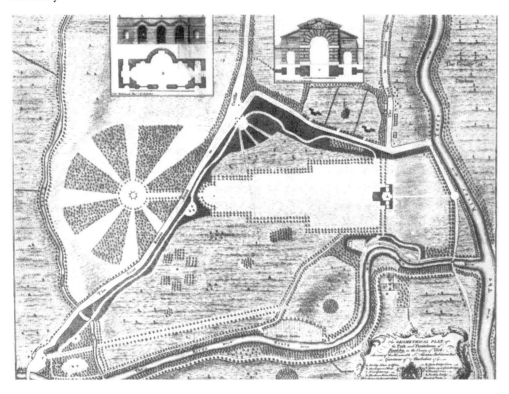

Figure 5.7 Rokeby Park, Yorkshire: plan of the grounds, 1741 (north to right). © The British Library Board.

Robinson (ca 1702–1777) was a man of some parts, talented (perhaps surprisingly so), sociable and not always wise, and his life followed contrasting halves. The first was as an architecture loving improver, grand tourist and Member of Parliament through the interests of his neighbour at Gibside, County Durham, and the marriage to Lord Carlisle's daughter, Elizabeth, recently widowed at Lord Lechmere's death. Switzer figures in the first half. The second half was just as interesting, but a bit darker: after his overspending on his house, and Lady Robinson's early death, he took the governorship of Barbados, where he discovered his colonial neighbours were a deal less obliging than his English ones, and he had to be recalled. Then he took an interest in Ranelagh Gardens, which he ran with great success as his own perpetual party.

Rokeby was designed by Robinson himself, and like Burlington's Chiswick it was something of an homage to Palladio; somewhat tiresomely for Burlington it was a better performance . . . chaste, severe to sublimity and more responsive to its place, and, if not picturesque, then bordering on it. Robinson was a frequent visitor to Burlington, keen to be part of his entourage of talented and busy people. This Burlington did not encourage, maybe sensing Robinson's strong talent, or maybe a trifle bored by his exuberance; staff at Piccadilly were instructed to keep him off, saying Lord Burlington was not "at home". Early on Robinson had decided to rebuild his house Rokeby and had engaged William Wakefield to design it, and that was published in *Vitruvius Britannicus* in 1725. Wakefield produced an interesting design, a sort of cross between a square pavilion and a house with wings: its façade was courtly with its centrepiece of engaged Corinthian pilasters standing on a half basement, but maybe more at home in town, or maybe Chiswick, than on its very rural country site. For whatever reason Robinson rejected it, and re-designed the house, entirely by himself. As Howard Colvin observed, Robinson ". . . built his design up out of established Palladian elements, he combined them into an original and highly effective composition that had no precedent among English country houses" (Colvin 1978 703). Unlike Chiswick, which was sited attached to an older house, within an enclosure, and with an ambiguous relationship to the north and west sides, Robinson sites his block proudly forward of the rest of the composition so that its square form reads from three sides equally, and its volume is simply capped by a big, square pyramid roof, further enhancing its geometric strength. Attached at its extreme north-east and north-west corners by a pair of towers are two almost identical, if smaller, blocks with their own pyramid roofs. These service "wings" are clearly independent. The fine rooms in the principal pavilion enjoy panoramic prospects southwards from east to west, and conversely the pavilion presents itself to view as (nearly) free-standing.

The landscape setting has an equally simple strength. Its site slopes gently from the Roman Road north towards the Tees, with farmlands to the west and rising ground on the east side beyond the small tributary River Greta. Essentially it is an enclosed park with four very large spaces defined by avenues of forest trees; these diminish in stepped stages to an apse (or Exedra) containing a monument at the west side of the grounds, not, as one would expect, open to the passing old Roman Road to Carlisle, but closed: indeed, the whole of the south and west sides of the park-garden is backed by close woodwork, which contains an *enfilade* or Circuit Ride with a gently serpentine drive in contrast to the strong geometric figure in the park. There is a major entrance to Rokeby at this south-west corner, from the Roman Road into a large semi-circle with strong linear views through the close woodwork, in quasi goose-foot fashion across a meadow and with a surprising diagonal first glimpse of the composition of Palladian *villas* and towers and the regular figure of spaces, and also, of equal value, a distant prospect of Mortham Tower, the consolidated fragment of English antiquity overlooking the wooded River Greta, which marks the east boundary of the scheme. Then the approaching visitor is conducted along the winding wooded ride to the first close view of the house, here from the west with the three big blocks in perspective, not even then in elevation. All the tricks which Burlington and Kent avoid for the Villa at Chiswick are here studiously exploited.

At Rokeby the visual strength and clarity of the house and its setting in parkland are picked up in the simple functional clarity of the other parts of the estate, and especially its "garden". A short walk by avenue east from the house leads to the valley of the Greta, dominated or, perhaps better, ornamented by the Mortham Tower, which will have been seen across the park already, as well as from the house itself. Here it is almost on the axis of the avenue, and will have been visible along it, but nearer the river the view of it is blocked by close plantation that turns the visitor into a curving walk down to the west bank of the Greta, seemingly enclosed, and here making a sharp serpentine curve and giving a long view due east, with Mortham Tower rising above it and seen through woods. This "garden" is a long terrace walk, with slopes and lawns from the Greta Bridge at the north end to here, its centre, then around to the Kitchen Garden out of sight, at the southern end. At this centre is a Bowling Green house, also by Robinson, built into the rising bank, and backed by close woodwork. In siting, it is not unlike Kent's contemporary Praeneste at Rousham: and the south-east entry to the estate passes just behind it in the park. The Greta Garden at Rokeby will have been like Studley Royal . . . crisp and abstracted, but it was also calculated to be romantic, and to draw character from both the rocky and rough river bed and the old Tower house opposite, which Robinson had repaired and made suitable for occupation.

Robinson was building Rokeby in the later 1720s, and the grounds will most likely have been in the making along with it. There is a lone transaction recorded in Switzer's account at Hoare's Bank in the spring of 1736 (Brogden 1973 220), by which time one would have thought the grounds would require only occasional visits. Robinson's enjoyment of the place was brief, as Lady Robinson soon died, and he then took up his post in Barbados. When Lady Robinson died in 1739 Sir Thomas did not inherit her fortune. That will have been a double blow to him. It went instead to Edmund Lechmere (1710–1777), the nephew and heir of her first husband. Possibly young Lechmere helped in the finishing and effective shutting down of Rokeby. There is a good sized transaction between him and Switzer, also recorded at Hoare's, in September of 1742, about sufficient to cover the preparation of drawings for publication. No design drawings for the scheme have survived, but the ground plan of the estate was published on Robinson's instruction that year. The house and the ancillary buildings were illustrated then as well. The ensemble of house and grounds is very well designed, but there it looks as though it could be left uninhabited for long stretches, as was the case. There is no sign of inhabitation from his prints, and indeed how could there be? If he had been able to live at Rokeby longer then perhaps it would have acquired personality, and fuller illustration and comments from visitors. The design itself doubtless dates to the later 1720s, and its dispositions confirm such a dating. The Park, the Meadows and the House ensemble are a clear unity, with the Greta Garden (acting as a wilderness or walking garden) lying close by, but hidden, with the woodlands, the entrances and the contiguous but distinct fields grouped around the edges.

A public figure

Mortham Tower was a substantial house dating from the time of King Henry III of England, and its form and state of dilapidation would have had appeal for Switzer, tutored as he had been at Woodstock to value such places, as he had recommended to others in 1715. The stables at Lodge Park, Cirencester, had been recently begun by Lord Bathurst with the intention in view to conjure up such qualities in his new buildings (see below). A site very similar to Rokeby was only recently begun for Captain Phillip Howard (1704–1741) at Corby Castle, near Carlisle, where it was made into a garden of this kind, which still survives as then described. It was seen by Tracy Atkyns on his tour into the North of England in 1732. He noted that

> . . . only one Grand Walk of about 300 yards in Length with a little Room at the End to drink a Glass of Wine in, on one side was Rocks covered with Wood of all Sorts, and Statues disposed in several Parts of it[.] on the other side of the River Eden which is a very clear Stream and a very rapid one, and Salmon leap in it close to the Garden: then will be a very fine Cascade when it's finished a Range of Rocks I believe at least 50 Yards, high, a large Lake of Water beyond that will be a constant supply.
>
> (Atkyns 1732 45)

Atkyns may have been a little jaded perhaps, and clearly he is not impressed with "one Mr Howard", his near contemporary. He allowed it might be thought "something Extraordinary so far North, but I saw nothing uncommon in it". As he omitted any mention of Wetheral Priory on the south bank of the Eden opposite the Cascade, he had signally failed to "see" the other half of the scheme. That shortly provided another visitor, Samuel Buck, his reason to notice Corby. For him Corby was simply the backdrop to Wetheral Priory. Unlike at Robinson's Rokeby here the two places

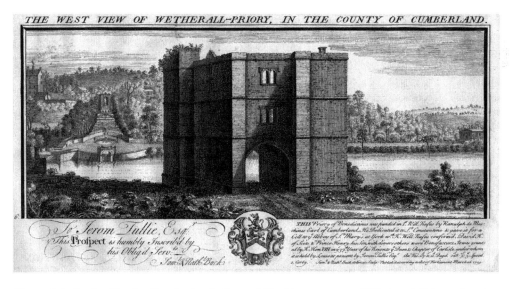

Figure 5.8 Corby Castle, Cumberland: Samuel Buck's prospect of Wetheral Priory showing the grounds of Corby Castle with reference to Rokeby, 1739 (north to left). Private collection.

were in different ownership, and perhaps only fortuitously made one garden scene. It was another 15 years or so before Arthur Devis painted his portrait of Phillip Howard and combined all into a suitably picturesque formula, as it were splitting the difference and giving marginal significance to both; Wetheral on the extreme right, and the cascade opposite at the extreme left. The "little house to drink a glass of wine in" now takes pride of place in the centre distance over Howard's likeness. Clearly at Corby the picturesque is announced (Strong 2000).

This was not so at Rokeby, where the almost identical "scene" made of the same elements became valued in a more literary or philosophical sense that Switzer certainly, and perhaps Kent and Burlington too, might have found immediately congenial and admirable. The landscape of Greta Garden at Rokeby was always calculated to conjure up an association of ideas, because of its history, and its state of ruin, allied to a masterly designed and planted exploitation of the place. Sadly for Robinson he had to sell up, and the place was bought by the Morritts. A great friend of theirs in the next generation was Walter Scott, a neighbour to the north on the Tweed. Scott was one of the first to see the moral values of the picturesque, because he was able to unite the literary and the visual in an association of ideas. But for him the story always comes first. It had begun to occur to him, working with William Stark on renovating his little country place near Galashiels, that buildings might be made to carry and express literary qualities, as he knew landscape might. Thus, his very earliest beginning on his creation of Abbotsford, as his renovated cottage became known, was enriched by his appreciation of Mortham Tower and Rokeby.

Having scored so successfully with the *Lady of the Lake* Scott hoped to make enough from *Rokeby* to fund the Abbotsford project. His romance was set late, in the period of the Civil Wars, and bore only tangentially on the place's real history. About its *gloomth* of setting, or the dress of its characters, or their heroic and heartfelt deeds, there could no doubt. J B Lockhart, Scott's biographer, noted that there was "an old Sybil" of Mortham who had recently died, having passed her century: she was glad to re-tell baleful stories (inspirited perhaps by the sad demise of Lady Robinson) about the Lady of Mortham, headless and in white, streaming garments, who had been seen haunting the place. Musing on the passing of heroes, or great events conducted on the site, or other *beneficial reflections* had become ghost stories. But the powers of places heightened by design to affect visitors, long established at Rokeby, had become a valuable part of designed landscapes.

Switzer's improvers

As we can pick up from his references in correspondence in the later 1720s and 1730s Switzer was often on his Circuits, to the North, or his Midland Tour, of more than two months each. Shorter journeys, for example into the Home Counties, would be for a few days between returns to Westminster, as confirmed when he instructs a correspondent in County Durham, "Direct all this to me under the Cover of the Rt Honble the Earle of Suffolk at Audley End near Safron Walden in Essex, where I shall be down again next week . . ." (SS to Sisson 20 Dec 1734, Gateshead MS). It is rare that we can glean more than fragmentary glimpses into the laying out and managing of the works then ongoing. The fragments point to a very wide practice supervising the layouts of landscapes, and, more often, the management of their kitchen gardens, or the equally lucrative forays into mining by his Durham client Sir Henry Ellison of Gateshead

Park, or George Bowes of Gibside, as well as the addition of features, such as the Menagerie for Charles Baldwyn at Aqualate, Staffordshire, in 1731 (Mowl and Barre 2009 78–79), or the supplies of seeds more generally. George London had set him on this method to ensure high standards of follow-up, replacements or changes of mind, typical of big and long term projects; and like London's his constitution must have been robust, as both carried on in this way well into their age. Sadly, these fragments only underline further the breadth of the works then on the go, and our loss in their disappearance, so often without any trace, and most rarely surviving in a recognizable original form.

A chance discovery at the beginning of World War II in the Castle of Newcastle of chests full of estate papers and related ephemera on their way to destruction happily came to the notice of Edward Hughes of Durham University, who mined that source for his *North Country Life in the 18th Century* (1952). A small part of that cache, known as the Cotesworth Papers, was retained at Gateshead Library, and from this there is a series of exchanges between Switzer and Henry Ellison, and Ellison's steward, Thomas Sisson. Through these we get a series of quite detailed insights into estate improvement, but the whole remains rather hazy, and with very significant omissions. Together with Switzer's list of subscribers, and fragments surviving elsewhere, we must make as much of these as we can. Ellison, of Park House, Gateshead, is typical of many improvers in a very swiftly changing environment, of which his estate and its design were only a part, and a very small part, of what happened around it. The coal deposits were already known, but their coming economic dominance, overtaking agriculture absolutely at Gateshead, and much of Durham also, soon swept it all away. Ellison married a Cotesworth heiress in 1728, and their new house was remodelled or replaced by one attributed to Gibbs, a handsome seven bay brick house of three stories with a segmental arch as its north front centrepiece. This, and the park, was consumed by Gateshead, with the park going first in the 19th century, then the grounds during the 20th century, with the house used as headquarters for a factory, and finally at the end of the last century what little remained of the house and factory was demolished.

From an Ordnance Survey of 1895 we can recover the layout of the grounds. These were laid out rather conventionally on a platform. To the north an ample oval turning lined by forest trees, as a forecourt, was flanked by woodland to the east and an orchard to the west. The house, on axis of course, addressed a broad terrace walk on the south front and beyond that a parterre, presumably always plain grass (as it clearly was in 1895) flanked by woodland, and terminating in an apse. Unusually the whole ensemble is splayed from its breadth on the north side to a centre point south in the park: this coming from the fortuitous alignment of the lane east of the property, which Switzer, if indeed it were he, used to advantage to create an efficient, and more interesting, scheme. The place is very much wider on the north side, because of the yards, canal, orchards and very large kitchen garden which was clearly Ellison's, Sisson's and Switzer's primary concern in the beginning. The splay of the whole somewhat disguises all this, and thus the terrace walk leads seemingly as quickly into the *utile* part of the scheme as it does the *dulci*. At the end of the 19th century the estate (apart from a discrete row of houses to the east along a wagon-way) is still ringed by large contiguous fields, so that Gateshead Park then continued potentially as a *rural and farm-like* design.

The first of the letters Professor Hughes discovered begins in the summer of 1733. Sisson, Ellison's steward, had dismissed the gardener from Park House and written to

Switzer to ask whether he could recommend a replacement, to which Switzer responds in August with apologies for the delay caused by his absence on his Midlands Tour: ". . . As for Wooley there is noe great wonder why you part with him, for though somewhat Industrious and Knowing in his Business is undoubtedly ill natur'd and false enough & won't stick at any Thing to fill his pockets as it is said by Those that come from Newcastle" (SS to Sisson, quoted in Brogden 1973 301). Switzer goes on to say, naturally enough, that good gardeners are all in post in summer, but "Being makeing a short tour round other Gardens near London this & next week & will assoon as Ever I can fix upon one proper for your Purpose send One down."

It appears that Ellison had been using Wooley as his gardener for several years, and that it was Wooley's suggestion that Ellison order plants for Park House from a firm of nurserymen in Chiswick owned by Henry Woodman. When Woodman was told that Switzer had been at Park House, he responded in February 1732,

> I am not at all surpriz'd yt Mr Switzer has bin with you & in all yr. Neighbourhood seeing he has nothing else to recommend him (having not a foot of Nursery ground & wt. he sells must take from others) but his elaborate draughts & designs & as every man is to be comended for his diligence & Industry I would not here be thought to say any thing ill natur'd of him but confess 'tis a practice I was always asham'd of to thrust me selfe in or indeavour to supplant any person yt has bin us'd to serve a Gentleman . . .
>
> (Laird 1999 32 quoting John Harvey)

Among the plants Woodman had supplied for Park House were "flowering Shrubs [which] are distinguish'd as low and more hire", evidence from which John Harvey had first tried to persuade the rest of us that the early landscape was very far from being only an abstract and green effort, an effort taken up then by one of his most apt and keen students, Mark Laird, who went on to give us chapter and verse most convincingly in his *Flowering of the English Landscape Garden*. But just where at Park House these plants had been used we cannot say for sure, although there was more than ample scope in the flanking "woodland" margins of the splayed parterre-lawn, which may well have exploited the tiered flowering shrubbery Woodman had supplied. An informal wooded section with a canal south of the kitchen garden would have been a perfect venue for this kind of planting.

The correspondence also reveals something of Switzer's manner of business, and that of Wooley and Woodward. It transpires that the latter two were working in combination, and that is what led to Wooley's dismissal. The division between wholesale and retail must have existed, as it is the very basis of business, but Switzer was acting as a professional in a manner similar to that worked out during the 19th or 20th century. As a designer he provided the design, and in its execution he sought the best deals available for his clients. Switzer would not accept any payment from the suppliers. His clients may have paid him something, or, as likely, gave him their patronage instead. When he sold seeds from his shop he invoiced the agreed retail costs.

As Switzer wrote to the steward in January 1734,

> When I found that Wooley had previl'd Sir on you to go to Strand in the Green I guess'd at the Reason, and that by a Private Understanding between the Nurseryman and him (which he knew I would never submit to) you was in a fair [way]

of Being well cheated. But it was not proper for me as I thot at the Time to intermeddle in it. I take Wooley to be as Great a Rogue [as] any in England that way, he has had the assurance to call and write to me for Place, But I never answer'd him. I suppose the bill the Gentleman Brings contains the hedge Plants, fruit trees shrubbs &c. that Planted the new Garden. I Remember they were all pretty smal tho: I dare say the Price will be large enough. There was a gardiner in Bishoprick [County Durham] yt. wanted to come in with me on the same foot as Wooly has undoubtedly done with your nurseryman. But I did not only refuse, But (as was just) told his master of him: this the Collonel [Sir Henry Liddell] knows to be true.

(Laird 1999 32 quoting John Harvey)

Switzer mentions also that he has sent the subscription proposals for *The Practical Husbandman and Planter* to Hugh Boag, Sir Henry Liddell's surveyor at Eslington, Northumberland, and hopes Sisson will subscribe to it. He did not, although Ellison did subscribe. And more than 20 other improvers did so too. Most of these are landowners, and range from Sir Robert Eden of West Auckland, a near neighbour of Sir Thomas Robinson, through Thomas Allan, William Carr, John Hedworth and John Hylton to Liddell (subscribing from Ravensworth Castle), all in Durham, and as many more in Newcastle and Northumberland. Which of these men gardened on a grand scale? Liddell was engaged in building anew at Ravensworth in the 1720s, but of the grounds we know nothing; similarly, John Hedworth of Chester-le-Street had employed Campbell for a new house in the 1710s, but of grounds to go with it we are ignorant. There were other designers to whom these men might have turned who were working locally, such as William Etty, who had also worked at Castle Howard, and with Vanbrugh at Seaton Deleval in the 1720s, where he was probably responsible for the grounds: he had provided designs for Sir George Bowes at Gibside in 1727 (Colvin 1978 301), which were not proceeded with. But Bowes had begun work there, it is thought in the 1730s, when for whatever reason he needed to borrow £35 from Switzer (in current values about £10,000!), which Switzer obligingly provided (reference kindly supplied by Margaret Wills when librarian at Newcastle University). The Forest Garden at Gibside, which is the kind of design we would expect of Switzer, was probably under way then. Stables and other structures were being built there in the 1740s by Daniel Garrett (Colvin 333), but the famous Banqueting House which completes the Great Terrace was not built until 1751.

The only major landowner-improver absent from these subscribers in north-east England is Sir Walter Blackett of Wallington, and it is his works there for which we have sufficient information to comment. Like many, perhaps most, of the improvers in the north of England, Blackett was young and recently come into his wealth. Wallington lies north of Newcastle in the heart of the county, and there he rebuilt his house as new, employing Garrett from about 1735, and his works in the grounds will have been contemporary. Two alternative designs for this work survive at Wallington, but neither is signed or dated. Either could be from Switzer, but I am hesitant to make an attribution. The elements he employed are all there, and in the right order, and both designs respond to the place. One appears very slightly earlier, simply because of the manner of designing the major feature in the western wilderness, or Walking Garden. It is in the form of a large, oval basin lying south of the entrance, an extension of the Terrace Walk: north of the basin are complex sloped banks in pairs, imitating amphitheatres. A design very similar to this, related to Audley End from about 1728, has been attributed to Claude Degotz by David Jacques (Jacques 1999). As Switzer was working at Audley End (see above) it could conceivably be his. However, the manner of finishing the large platforms on which the west and east gardens sit, which derive ultimately from Wray Wood at Castle Howard, is handled in the way of those at Newburgh Priory: that design appears to me to be by Etty, and he would be a likely candidate for this Wallington design also.

The second is slightly more in the fashion of the mid-1730s . . . into the brief *rococo*. Instead of an avenue southwards it employs a very strong and splayed lawn feature with an equally large circular feature, not a basin, at its heart. There are the two wildernesses as before, but the west one in this design has an informal, if equally crisp, basin, still almost symmetrical about its east-west axis, but definitely *informal*. There are also two quite artfully sinuous canals, one to the north-west, and another larger one serving as a reservoir for the kitchen gardens on the east side. The walks are equally artful in their layout. An addition (but very soon after completing the design) carries the north-west sinuous canal into a proper stream which wiggles through a woodland enclosing a meadow to join, almost, the eastern reservoir. From Harvey's research and his characteristically thorough and genial *Early Nurserymen* we know that William Joyce had recently set up as a nurseryman in Newcastle, and was consulted by Blackett. Therefore, we may assume he supplied this design as well, although it is rather more assured than, for example, the contemporary effort of the equally estimable Thomas Perfect, who provided an alternative design to Switzer's for Nostell (see below). Thomas Wright had early works here at Wallington, for example the Rothley Parks, and this even earlier design might be his. There is a third design, for beautifying the real river at the bottom of the south park. This, incidentally, shows that neither of the previous schemes had been carried out then, but elements appear to come from each . . . a sort of simplified splay to the front park, and a neither oval nor artfully informal basin in the wilderness but rather a square one, set diagonally with stepped edges. This Jackson-Stops (1991 78) dates to "c1750" and tentatively suggests might be by Robert Greening. It shows a more natural seeming river in three sections, and the long wooded circuit walk along its south edge would have made a most satisfying finish to the grounds.

Lancelot Brown was born just to the north of Wallington in 1716 and would have been approaching his majority when these designs were made and being discussed, if not actually carried out. Brown was then working nearby at Kirkharle, and Switzer would make for him a most admirable George London figure for emulation. As Brown's recent biographer Jane Brown has pointed out, "Switzer was enough of an iconoclast to attract a young man's attention, and time and again in Lancelot's working life echoes of Switzer's philosophy appear" (Brown 2011 17). She even suggested that he and Switzer might have met about this time, and through the good offices of Joyce: I wish I were able to confirm that as true, but sadly I cannot. However, it is almost inconceivable that they did not meet then, and Brown's first move south to Lincolnshire and Grimsthorpe is suggestive also. Her convincing surmise underlines also that the scene among improvers in northern England in the 1730s was just as lively as it was anywhere in these islands.

Subscription, or paying (in part or whole) in advance for the production of a book, as well as consenting to appear on a list of subscribers as further validation of the project, was not uncommon in early 18th century practice. Pope's translation of Homer was managed in this way. The investment of a guinea per folio copy (currently equivalent to £315) gave him an early surplus of funds which he parleyed into annuities underwritten by rich patrons who were often short of cash. Switzer had begun to collect subscriptions for his *An Introduction to a General System of Hydrostaticks and Hydraulicks* but early on had abandoned that method. That big book appeared in 1729, and in the same year he had numerous editions of pamphlets in press, and a new edition of *Ichnographia Rustica* planned. Raising the funds for publishing was not the determining reason to open a subscription list for the *Practical Husbandman and Planter*. Rather, it was to be an affirmation of commitment to improvement, in imitation of the Edinburgh *Scots Society of Improvers*, as was the Dublin based group. His Private Society of Husbandmen and Planters was to be a forum for encouraging, experimenting with, discussing and publish directions for improvements in what was still, and very obviously, the source of the three kingdoms' wealth.

The list of the subscribers published in 1733 indicates who these committed improvers were. As no subscription forms have come to light, we do not know the terms of the issue, but as the projected monthly papers, each of eight sheets (8vo, that is, a folio sheet folded four times), were to be sold to the subscribers at two shillings and to all others at two shillings sixpence, a fairly substantial outlay equivalent to several hundred pounds in current value was required. A significant number of these were booksellers, who usually invested in multiple copies. Gardeners, stewards, bailiffs and nurserymen accounted for another 45 subscribers. There were some 40 other professional men . . . ministers of religion, lawyers, medics, farmers and one painter. There were also governors of American colonies. The largest group, numbering more than 150, however, were the landowners. Of these roughly a third were titled, of whom six were dukes, the rest being knights, baronets and honourables (with many bearing courtesy titles).

The *Practical Husbandman and Planter* was dedicated to George Montagu (ca 1684–1739), Earl of Halifax, and Henry Lowther (1694–1751), Viscount Lonsdale. Halifax had inherited Horton, Northamptonshire (called *Houghton* by Switzer), from his uncle Charles Montagu in 1715. The ranger-ship of Bushy Park and with it the Upper Lodge there, whose water-works were then still not complete, came to him also. An interest in that property (along with the nearby manor Abb's Court) had been assigned to Katharine Barton (Handley *DNB*), the presumed mistress of his uncle Lord Halifax. Switzer wrote of Abb's Court as being in the second earl's charge in 1733, and as he had already agreed to complete the works in Bushy Park it is assumed that Mrs Barton's occupation of these properties was brief and had ceased with her marriage. Horton was a moderate sized estate with its house near the village at its north end, and the long and relatively narrow grounds were laid out on either side of the Bold Stroke of a big avenue running southward. There is evidence that George Montagu employed Garrett to rebuild the house there in the mid-1730s, and that architect was also involved in embellishing the grounds in the 1750s for his son, the 3rd Earl of Halifax, who also employed Wright then (Colvin 1978 334 and 939), whose works of the later 1730s and 1740s gave the place its *rococo* character. By 1759, however, the 3rd Earl had been obliged to turn "all his pleasure-ground into tillage which cost so much at Horton . . ." (Speck *DNB* quoting a cousin Montagu to Horace Walpole). How much (if any) of the design of Horton could be ascribed to Switzer cannot be assessed. Its ultimate "fate" of being turned to tillage would not have perturbed him, nor presumably his patron, the second earl. As Switzer had addressed him, "in the humble, yet not less useful Epithets, of a good Husbandman and Planter; in both which you have made such great Advances, that Posterity must recite it with Pleasure, and every one of the fine Fields at *Houghton* and *Abbs Court*, must in Consequence perpetuate the Memory of their Improver (if any reasonable Care be taken of them) to Generations yet to come" (*PH&P* iii).

At Horton there is no design or survey. Of Abb's Court Switzer is the only source of our knowledge of it. It lies due west of Upper Lodge in Bushy Park, but on the other side of the Thames just beyond Moulsey, and has been submerged under the eastern edge of Bessborough Reservoir since the early 20th century. However, there are maps from the Ordnance Survey dating from the initial survey drawing of 1803, from which we can get an idea of its layout. Covering some 20 acres at its core are a series of fields which are essentially rectangular but without any geometric perfection and hardly distinguishable from those of neighbouring farms. On its long north edge is a broadly curving wooded margin following the line of a lane, which itself mimics the Thames' shoreline beyond. This wood thickens towards its middle and forms a woodland, where it meets a clearly designed serpentine avenue; this in turn links to a more conventional composition of a rectangular enclosure containing the house and "gardens". Abb's Court is therefore more flowing and less wooded than Riskins; its fields are more varied in size, and the whole a deal simpler than Kew; and it is more farm-like than Dawley, where the Bolingbrokes' usage had transformed Sir Godfrey Kneller's tiny but perfectly formed residential estate into a farm. With its companions Abb's Court shows the varieties inherent in the type established prior to Philip Southcote's works at Wooburn Farm nearby at Chertsey.

Because of his bad luck at gambling, and in the South Sea Bubble, Lord Londsdale was thwarted in realizing his improvements at Lowther, Westmoreland. As one of the great landowners of the north of England he was well placed. He was ambitious, and a very good patron (according to Switzer), and he had many designs made, and some published, for rebuilding the house after its near destruction by fire in 1718. When Switzer dedicated the second volume of *The Practical Husbandman and Planter* to him he was in government in Walpole's cabinet, and intent on carrying on these works, and reviving his grounds there. He left government in 1735, citing his improvements at Lowther. The design for the grounds that was published in 1725 (*Vit Brit* III 76) was a severely simplified revival of his inherited landscape, as depicted by Kip and Knyff. It is possible that a grander scheme, not dis-similar to the contemporary scheme at Garendon (see below), was then proposed, and perhaps of Switzer's design, to which Francis Richardson later proposed changes. These can be seen on the next surviving piece of evidence, dated 1754 (Laird 1999, 121 et seq). However, the contemporary survey shows just how little Lord Lonsdale had achieved. Indeed, when Brown was later consulted, matters had hardly improved. The Lowthers were great improvers but on paper only (Colvin et al 1980).

We know Switzer's Midland Tour took nine weeks of the summer of 1733, and if we were to assume two days for each consultation he would have visited some 30 properties. On the list of subscribers there are some 50 owners or agents in that part of England who could be said to require such a consultation, but of these we have only glimpses, and very rarely fuller information: and many are otherwise entirely unknown at present. Some of his visits might be classed almost as courtesy calls, or calls to some place where advice might have been given years before. At these, and perhaps more formally at others, there will have been a kind of watching brief on progress, or difficulties encountered, or further changes contemplated. As the exchanges between the Duke of Chandos and Lord Cathcart show, improvers were (at least in early 18th century British terms) remarkably blind to rank and wealth. We may comfortably assume that those who subscribed to these tracts not only read them, but read them very keenly, and tried them out. Still, the great men retained their sense of themselves, so the Duke of Devonshire might well have warranted a courtesy call, and the Duke of Ancaster would expect Switzer to continue his interest in Grimsthorpe, and not to pass by without calling. The Duke of Rutland, and his neighbours at Belton, would also be called on, to monitor if not see to finishing touches to the big works at Belvoir of the previous decade, or to discuss the additions soon to be created at Belton (see below).

Chatsworth had grown over its long life since the 1690s, but its character and layout had altered very little. There were additions in Brown's time in the parks, and Kent is known to have made designs for alterations in the wooded hills, but the layout established under London's supervision remains even now. It had become more mature, and by the 1730s a great deal simpler as a result: the blocks of planting, and larger trees, were indeed more suited to a simplified palette, and the famous parterre had become less "furnished" over that period. For another great Midland duke, Kingston, we would expect Switzer's involvement, especially since it was the water-works there which were the famous aspect of Thoresby. But that place, also, had received its improvements early, under London and Wise. When the improving Duke Evelyn Pierrepoint died in 1726 he left a minor to succeed him, his grandson, also Evelyn (1711–1773), who had just begun his schooling at Eton, and promptly went on his Continental tour, which took a decade. On his return to Thoresby it was field sports which claimed his attention. He was not an improver, although his appearance in Switzer's subscriber list suggests that hope of his becoming one had not been quite given up. There is a good run of estate papers for Thoresby, in which water-works figure, but they are not revealing, and sadly Atkyns' visit to them in 1731 provides little clarification about their design.

Belton in Lincolnshire was the seat of John Brownlow, Viscount Tyrconnel. He inherited the place in 1721 from his uncle, leaving his aunt, Lady Alice Brownlow, in place and in charge. She presided in some state and ensured her daughters married appropriately. One of these was the Duchess of Ancaster, who is commemorated in William Stukeley's *Duchesses' Bastion* drawing of Grimsthorpe (see figure 2.2). Thus, Belton, one of the most thorough and splendid estates of the time, was effectively brand new although its received style would soon be surpassed by fashion (*Vit Brit* II plates 69–70). John Brownlow, 1st Viscount Tyrconnel's improvements are sadly, if typically, undocumented, but it appears that the grounds were maintained as inherited, perhaps with their minimalist abstract style enhanced. The orthogony of the layout remained, indeed remains today, but extended by him along the eastern axis later called Sandy Walk, as a Switzer-like *enfilade* walk suggesting a fusion of garden and estate. An extension of the grounds was undertaken later, from the 1730s, parallel to the south axis, incorporating a stream and making a river-garden. This is presided over by the magnificent Waterwork made in 1742 [8.1]. These additions are most likely to be the work of Switzer.

The evidence of these improvements is variable of course, but there is one significant grouping which appears in the additional group of mostly garden schemes that forms volume 4 of *Vitruvius Britannicus*, which was dedicated to Frederick, Prince of Wales and published in 1739, after Campbell's death. Many of these do not have known archival backup, so we cannot at present confirm details of just how and when they were formed. Belvoir and Belton were illustrated very fully, as were other large schemes, about which we yet know very little more. Their qualities and styles of presentation suggest these projects were assembled from several sources by John Badeslade and John Rocque. I have seen evidence in the Clerk MSS in the Scottish Record Office of the original drawing for Drumlanrig (whose rough but accurate plans were sent on by the good offices of Sir John Clerk of Penicuik). There is similarly a companion to the view of Admiral Torrington's estate at Southall which, for whatever reason, was not published but survives in the Bedford Record Office (see Jacques 1999).

There is a large group of smaller schemes, in landscape terms, which may often be thought of as *Rural and Farm-like*. Their very natures make them somewhat difficult to chart, as by design they were little different from unimproved nature, and they were invariably carried on and maintained by their owners. For example there is the earliest of these, Bunny Park, Nottinghamshire. There Sir Thomas Parkyns (1663–1741) was very definitely the master of the place, very like Henry Fielding's Squire Western in *Tom Jones*, but athletic to boot. He was clearly a favourite of Switzer's, who includes jocular references to his inventiveness at employing water-works advantageously. But of Bunny hardly anything can be said about its design. Its boundary was walled by a then unusual manner of construction: instead of laying complete foundations Parkyns had his park wall built on shallow arches instead. His house lay to the west edge of his smallish home estate, very near the church, so the improved and walled part lay altogether to the east, and appears from the earliest of the Ordnance Surveys to have been made up of a circuit of woodlands enclosing meadows and fields.

Sugnal in Staffordshire is very similar to Bunny in extent and management, and perhaps also in design. There the Earl of Glenorchy was a subscriber to *The Practical Husbandman and Planter*, as was his gardener, Mr Richard Brown. Also, his man of business and neighbour, Walter Noel of Hilcot, subscribed. It has, seemingly, survived in its 18th century form as a series of fields and meadows and other enclosures linked together by woodland, suggesting old walks with farm buildings of appropriate date from the higher ground of the west end to the ancient Cop Mere at the far east end. It has every characteristic and hint of Switzer's Rural and Farm-like Way of Gardening, a *ferme ornée*. I had visited the place, and convinced myself of this. When I was newly elected to the Garden History Society committee, and was asked to become the society's editor and to turn its journal *Garden History* into a professionally printed and illustrated one, and to build on its already high academic standard to make it a genuinely refereed one, Sugnal seemed to present the very best subject: our advisory board of distinguished garden historians agreed, and who better to ask to tackle the subject than another newly elected committee member, and scion of that place, David Jacques? Happily he agreed, and wrote the very pattern of what I had in mind: specific, thorough, informed by archival research and most sensitive to place, and to the practice of design. As he found indeed "Lord Glenorchy's personal papers show that he did actually undertake a scheme of Rural Gardening in the 1730s" (Jacques 1981 26). Switzer even supplied seeds from Westminster Hall on 20 February 1734 (Jacques 1981). Apart from Glenorchy's reading Switzer's books, and perhaps seeing him in London, that is the sum of the evidence in the archival sources for Switzer's involvement. And from that Jacques concluded that Switzer's involvement was "peripheral". Surely that was the whole point, was it not? Already Switzer's influence is manifest . . . what to do, how to do it, how others have done it, what to plant, why and where, and by the way here are some seeds to get you started: all that is documented. Whereas I would argue that there will have been a design done, almost certainly by Switzer, which is now lost, Jacques assumed that this meant it was Glenorchy by himself who designed it, as well as carried it forward. It could equally have been argued that Sugnal was happily so close to being a designed place by its nature and history that it would have taken very little to transform its unimproved state into a *ferme ornée*. Glenorchy married Annabel Grey of Wrest Park, and their daughter Jemima soon demonstrated her own interest in gardens by freely commenting on Brown's first works at Stowe in the late 1740s (see below).

Charles Baldwyn had been improving his place at Aqualate, also in Staffordshire, a few miles south of Sugnal, since 1729, and in 1731 he commissioned the Wilderness, or menagerie/decoy. This has many similarities to Glenorchy's Cop Mere. According to Timothy Mowl, acting on a reference from Paul Stamp and Keith Goodway, Baldwyn had been acting previously as his own designer in modifying his grounds (Mowl and Barre 2009 78 quoting NLW Ottley MSS 2744:1731), but on that occasion asked Switzer to come and to lay it out, which took him three days. Laying out in person is a significant improvement on making a design. As a sculptor will likely make a maquette of a very big piece for building by others, occasionally they will work at full scale, as Switzer did here, so the exploitation of site opportunities, the full consultation of the genius of the place, is assured. Even so the implementation of a landscape

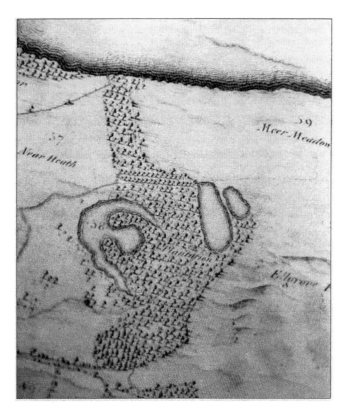

Figure 5.9 Aqualate, Staffordshire: the Menagerie, from a survey of 1767 (north to top). Courtesy of Staffordshire Archives.

188 *A public figure*

design requires others, and others working to message over time. Its collaborative, or even social, qualities are built in. At Aqualate this is documented:

> I am forced to spend the season turfing instead of planting that ground Switzer laid out for a Wilderness. Mr Sneyd who has been with me two or three days as well as my own gardener tell me [I] must have a yew hedge of 4 or 5 feet high if any so that I think will hide the little view that way more I think than an open grove of near 100 trees, which one may look through at a less expense when the Yews themselves will come between 20 and 30 pounds and cost much more in the keeping . . .
> (Mowl and Barre 2009 78–79)

What Switzer produced was an apparent fragment of nature, and without other evidence would not be taken as a piece of *designed landscape*. The earliest evidence for this design is from 1767 (Staffordshire Record Office D 4046): that decade is also the earliest map evidence for Sugnal.

Rhual

- (A) River Alyn Mill Race
- (B) The Grove
- (C) Paddock
- (D) Kitchen Garden
- (E) Woodland Garden
- (F) Court
- (G) Alleluia Monument

Figure 5.10 Rhual, Flintshire: plan of the grounds as in the 1740s (north to top). Image by the author.

Switzer had added further remarks about his *rural and extensive* gardens in 1727 towards the end of *The Practical Kitchen Gardener*. Its supplement, about more delicate or unusual vegetables, specifically melons, cucumbers, ". . . broccoli, potato's, and other useful roots and plants, as practis'd in France Italy Holland and Ireland" (*KG* 369), concluded with the observation that the plans he had thus far included had been "chiefly calculated for kitchen gardens that are enclos'd or wall'd in", but that there was an alternative method, "where its produce is rais'd promiscuously up and down in fields, where there is a choice of ground proper for all kind of vegetables, sometimes by plowing only" (*KG* 420). Although this is about the smallest scale application of his ideas first published 12 years before, they are essentially a restatement of those notions specifically at the foodstuffs scale of garden making, underlining the assertion that his method was appropriate for designs at any scale, save the very smallest, that is, the enclosed town flower garden. And despite the additional and inherent difficulties getting these ideas across on a plan of such small scale, he reckons it will "serve as a specimen of what this and some other noble Lords have and are so judiciously doing on this head" (*KG* 422). These were noted as "[t]he Lord *Bathurst*, at *Riskins*, near *Colnbrook* . . . The Lord *Cobham*, at his fine seat in *Buckinghamshire*, and the late Lord *Bolingbroke*, at *Dawly* in *Middlesex*". Although his observations and rationale duly appeared, the actual plan of Riskins was left out and was only published as an addendum to the 1742 edition of *Ichnographia Rustica*.

Lord Cobham's Stowe was already, in Pope's phrase, a "Work to wonder at", and its fame, and its size, continued to grow over the next 20 years of its development. It was the creation of one of Marlborough's generals, soon to rise to an even more heroic state, and the staunchest of rich Whigs. Lord Bolingbroke was "late" in Switzer's term, not because he was dead, but because he had been exiled abroad and stripped of his titles, having shown himself to be a leading Jacobite. At Dawly Park, or as it was called in his tenure Dawly Farm, he practised not only what Switzer had advocated in 1715, if not quite publicly, when he returned, certainly in a manner that was noticed but also approaching close to fashion, and most likely it was he and his French wife who gave us the very term for this manner of design (see Woodbridge 1981). As Switzer wrote, it had been "the Practice some of the best Genius's of France under the Title of *La Ferme Ornée*" (*IR* III Appendix 9). Lord Bathurst was a famous and avowed Tory. The fifth of Switzer's heroes of designed landscapes on the small to moderate scale, at Abb's Court, Moulsey, was George Montagu, 2nd Earl of Halifax, a courtier, if not a grandee, and certainly a Whig – so much for advanced ideas in gardening being allied to one, or the other, of the political parties.

Stowe would appear a curious companion to the other four, but it should be remembered that in 1727 only the western part of the grounds had been designed, and these were still without the lake, or the extensions southward and westward. So its form and scale certainly, and also its nature then, according to Switzer, was a mixture of his *utile et dulci*. Dawly was already a designed landscape, made for Sir Godfrey Kneller and illustrated by Kip and Knyff. It was how the Bolingbrokes managed it that made its inclusion appropriate . . . the distinction between garden and field had been abolished by then. Switzer's written work since the later 1720s, and also his practice, had re-visited his initial ideas of combining the useful and pleasurable in laying out grounds at the smaller scale. All the pamphlets about enriching legumes for improvement, even his *Practical Kitchen Gardener* supplement and much of the

Practical Husbandman and Planter were written to that end, so it is not surprising that his latest commission is for another *ferme ornée*.

Rhual near Mold in Flintshire was such a place. There, at the invitation of his client at Leeswood, Switzer acted in 1739 as a designer at a distance to produce a scheme for the Griffiths. Nehemiah Griffith was one of Switzer's improvers, and may have been so recruited by Sir George Wynne of Leeswood; he had recently died, and Rhual passed to the kinsman to whom Switzer wrote. Here, as doubtless elsewhere, he produced the easiest and most effective way into his now quite mature idea of the rural garden at a moderate scale. At Rhual the existing garden suite was extended into a wood laid out as a kind of shrubbery-wilderness for walking and contemplation. The other axis, also pre-existing, was to be modified into an eastern "garden" and would no longer serve its original purpose as an entry: it retained its Marston-like form, however. The rest of the Rhual scheme consists of linked fields, one of which contained the Alleluia Monument, an obelisk commemorating the fifth century battle between local Britons and the invading Saxons and their Pictish allies.

The house is connected to this wider scene by a terrace walk edging the west woodland, to define and also to enclose a large field. As the terraced *edge* leaves the wood it becomes more a wooded walk, no longer related to an avenue, but more like the hedge-rows, as Switzer had originally proposed, and had reiterated in the *Practical Kitchen Gardener* supplement. Their character at Rhual was laid out as recommended:

> . . . a little hedge-row of about six or seven yards wide, thro' the middle of which there will be a private path of five or six foot wide, or more; for as these hedge-rows, if to be planted, are generally of nuts, phillibuds [phiberds], chestnuts, or other ordinary, but useful fruits, there will be an agreeable pleasure in such a private retreat: but that may either be, or not be, as the owner pleases; 'tho a walk of this kind, a little detach'd from the middle one, I have observed to have a good effect, especially in the plantation of the Right Honourable the Lord Bruce, *Tottenham Park*, in *Wilts*.
>
> (*KG* 423)

At Rhual these extend as a long, narrow circuit of woods embracing meadows to the north, and also (as edge again) the wooded banks of a water course (a mill lade from the nearby River Alyn) on the far edge of the north woodland, before joining the house-dependency group. Thus, perhaps Rhual indicates the new default pattern of a *Rural and Farm-like Garden* design, and there, and at Bunny in Nottinghamshire for Parkyns, and many other places now "lost", this template may be traced. The resulting circuit woodland walk, which at Rhual is augmented by way of a significant spur opening to the west into an otherwise entirely agrarian scene, enclosed the large (nearly 20 acre) home paddock, or field, and also led to further and more bucolic prospects further out, but still within the small designed landscape/farm. The disposition and shape of the various parts, and therefore the whole of such extended designs, come from the place's nature and the needs of the owner: they were required to be locally suitable, and therefore most likely to appear natural, even to appear to be an undesigned element. The paradigm seen in the Rhual scheme was used at Hanbury, Worcestershire, for Bowater Vernon (Switzer 1734), where London had supplied the design for the gardens, which became greatly augmented by such a woodland and circular walk in the 1730s. Typically, that place was changed to accommodate a new taste without the necessity of entirely remaking the old gardens.

At its heart Rhual possessed the elements still deemed essential. He had noted that the tiny wood-wilderness already in place between the stable buildings and the old entrance court was too small and should be sacrificed and replaced with new and larger entry court. Thus, the original elliptical turning court was transformed from an entry into a garden, on axis with its enlarged companion court before the house, here rendered as grassed surface with slopes to higher "walks", more lawn than court. From the front door the estate is framed by these, and axially, but, perhaps surprisingly, there is no avenue to carry the eye further. There is no *Bold Stroke* here at Rhual. As the house faces east, the suite of gardens, the Best Garden of convention, lies to the south and in an axial array stretching westward parallel to the present main road. Immediately west of the house was one of Switzer's "problems" to which his short letter to Wynne and Griffith offers amendment. To allow a handsome and uniform slope between the west front and the Best Garden and its woodland extensions, Switzer directed that the bank should be built up at the north end, from spoil from his proposed sunken bowling green, sited at the beginning of the new wood.

With Rhual there is still an observable response to Joseph Addison's observation *that a man may make a pretty landskip of all his possessions*, and it does so by manipulating walks, no longer in the avenues at Magdalen College, but through and alongside woods and in elaborated hedge-rows. There and at similar places, as Switzer had put it, was the practice of a *rural and farm-like way of gardening*. Such responses are identical to early landscapes like William Shenstone's, soon to start The Leasowes in Shropshire, or even Hon William Hamilton's contemporary beginnings at Painshill in Surrey. But are these seemingly identical projects all early landscape gardens? H F Clark certainly thought so, and chose The Leasowes as his "first" Landscape Garden (Clark 1943). To assert that they are not might appear to take away something of their power and quality, which would be manifestly unfair. Still, these essentially *Arcadian* designs are different from the stylish landscapes of the 1760s or 1770s in one major regard, and that is not the vestigial axes of the old entry courts and suite of Best Gardens. Most notably they are different because they mix *utile et dulci*: they manage to be two seemingly contrary things at the same time. They are working, productive (even agriculturally advanced) farms yielding not only produce and wealth for their community but also the income to establish their owners as landed gentry. At the same time they bristle with an aspiration to being works of garden art. They succeed in being both.

Landscape gardens after mid-century, and particularly later, will make a very definite distinction between *utile* and *dulci*. When the Landscape Garden is recognized as a Work of Art, defined as such and criticized as if equivalent to a picture, or an epic poem, the very element that brought them about will be excluded. They will be works of art obviously and separately sequestered, ideal and definitely *superior* to the surrounding common farmland. I believe Switzer would have been saddened to have lived to observe that development. Paradoxically, by then he had done very much to bring it about.

6 Essays in the landscape style

Cirencester, Lodge Park

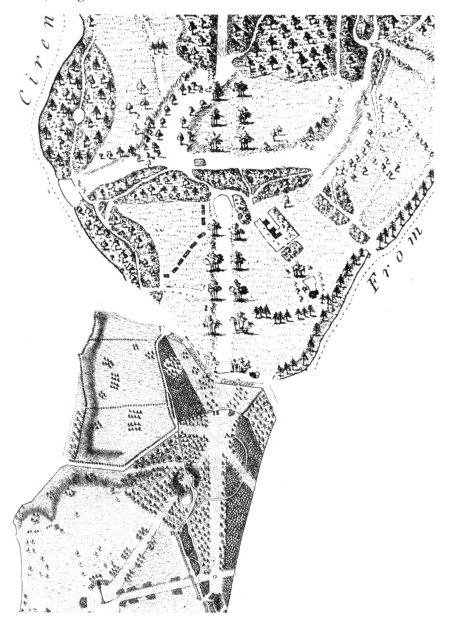

Figure 6.1 Cirencester, Gloucestershire: Ivy Lodge Park and Seven Rides sections, from joined plans of the whole estate (north to right). Reproduced from Samuel Rudder, *New History of Gloucestershire*, 1779, "A Plan of the Home Park at Cirencester" and "Plan of Oakley Great Park" showing in detail Ivy Lodge Park. The Bodleian Libraries, University of Oxford.

In the summer of 1728 there were major works in the middle part of the estate at Cirencester, works which addressed the improvement of the visual links by axis from Oakley Wood to Cirencester Church at Seven Rides. To do this, much of the wood in the Terrace Walk-*Riskins* element was sacrificed. Enough of it to bring the tower into view, roughly 500 metres, was clear-felled.

We know of this, happily in exceptional detail, through Alexander Pope, who had been accidentally denied Lord Bathurst's customary hospitality. According to Pope, the tower as terminal point thus exposed to view now lay "on one side", and because of this asymmetry, it now needed to be demolished. Pope was clearly cross, and had been put out of sorts because Bathurst not only was absent when his friend arrived but had left no word of when he would return, why he was away or where he might be. Hyperbole might therefore be looked for in Pope's condemnation, but he appears to have been in earnest: not only was his long letter of rebuke written after plenty of time for reflection, but it expresses his mature judgements, and it gives us insight into the kind of arguments which are often encountered in design projects, and especially design projects deemed important. Pope cared very much about the design of Cirencester, and was mortified to discover it had taken a turn about which he had not been consulted, and of which he much disapproved.

One suspects there is more to Pope's unhappiness than the slightly squint prospect the tower of the church now made from Seven Rides. It could of course be personal, but, curiously, fallings-out about design matters are often more keenly felt than purely personal slights. There were really two things about these new works that Pope disliked: the felling of *High Timber* he regretted, but his anger seems to have been raised more by the very idea of starting again . . . the seeming acknowledgement that mistakes had been made and that a revised design was needed to put matters right. We cannot be sure how much plantation was actually "lost", or how old or venerable the timber lost was. The disapproval, however, is very clear. What the new design for Lodge Park consisted of we can recover from Samuel Rudder's *New History* as its earliest plan, and its intended character we can deduce from the siting of the buildings then erected and, more importantly, the manner, or style, chosen for those buildings. The scene was also painted by George Lambert, apparently around 1730 (see Acknowledgements).

Ivy Lodge Park, or Lodge Park, was designed as a park. That is, it is mostly open ground laid to grass, with trees. In like manner to the surroundings of Queen Anne's Monument, and in the other outer parts of Home Park, many of these plantations were in platoons or clumps. And in similar fashion also, these clumps carry the Broad Walk axis from Seven Rides across Lodge Park to Oakley Wood beyond the dip at Rough Hills. The rest of Lodge Park appears to have been, even from the later 1720s, a mixture of open ground with the occasional tree, or group. We can assume that these were original survivors of the near clear-felling of the area, the strongest and healthiest of the older planting. So the clumps carrying the line of the Broad Walk from the "new" park, when viewed from any angle except the cardinal ones, appeared as fortuitously placed groups of trees. Therefore, we may have the first designed park looking like an old and *undesigned* one. But the buildings ornamenting it make the intentions behind it perfectly clear. These are for estate use, but they too are arranged seeming negligently, and their style or manner suggests old work as well. There were various lodge houses for staff, and there was also a substantial stable block, which was very much wanted here to provide transport for visitors, as well as power for forestry and other estate operations. These are located in the middle of the extensive estate; in other words, use and necessity dictated their placement. Their arrangement was geometric . . . originally there was a group of nine buildings that formed a street-like row on the south-west side, while on the other side of the park the Round and Square lodges follow the axis from the later Queen Anne's Monument, also called the Cross Estate Ride. The sense that they are part of a very large geometric figure may be discerned in both Rudder's plan and in Lambert's painting, where immense circular curves are hinted at. Yet these buildings also appear, as it were, dotted around the edges of Lodge Park, and it is clear they were meant to be as decorative as in fact they are.

Their architectural manner or style is far from classic, and while they are also hardly scholarly exercises even in Gothic, yet they are hardly *Gothick* either. They seem to take their cues from local vernacular works, and were, as Stephen Switzer had proposed, almost executed in the manner of "some Antiquated Place". Of course, the antiquated place to hand was the old Sapperton House, whose materials had been gathered together for the "Castle" in Oakley Wood from the early 1720s, and which was soon celebrated in print form as Alfred's Hall, with the approbation of authenticity from an Oxford antiquary by 1736. Not surprisingly, Alfred's Hall and the more prominent Stable Block were confused by early surveyors for the Ordnance Survey (see E B Metcaff's survey drawing of 1816 on the British Library website, BL.UK/onlinegallery/ordnancesurveydrawings/14). The architect of Alfred's Hall and the Ivy Park buildings and also the other, more polished (as we might say classical) ornaments of the estate is unrecorded. Alfred's Hall was Bathurst's joke, and a private one too, far away from anything else, in deepest woodland, yet a splendid and welcoming place for refreshment, for a nap or even for short residence . . . an alternative Cirencester Park house as a playhouse, in short, a Folly, and surrounded by its own Riskins-like woodland garden. Ivy Park is the earliest evidence of what will become a determining and typical feature of future designed landscapes.

Bathurst and Pope remained friends, and maybe to make amends the pivot for the Seven Rides part of Lodge Park is a soberly classic building, small but clearly commanding the views from its shaded site on the south side of close woodland, since 1737 known as Pope's Seat.

There are lessons in the Cirencester design for the skilful management of large parts in an even larger scale entity; really how to make a pretty *landskip* of one's possessions. These can be emulated by any to advantage, and they *may* have played a role also in the

Figure 6.2 Cirencester, Gloucestershire: views of the garden at Alfred's Hall. Detail from Samuel Rudder, *New History of Gloucestershire*, 1779. The Bodleian Libraries, University of Oxford.

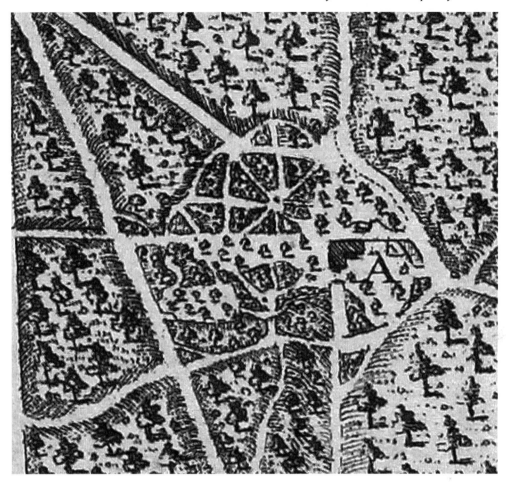

Figure 6.3 Cirencester, Gloucestershire: plan of the garden at Alfred's Hall, Oakley Great Park (north to right). Detail from Samuel Rudder, *New History of Gloucestershire*, 1779. The Bodleian Libraries, University of Oxford.

development of the 18th century transition towards the as yet to be identified thing it later called the Landscape Garden. However, this next phase of Cirencester, the design, or, more correctly, the re-design of Lodge Park, lying just west of Seven Rides, gives us a legitimate and significant change point as most likely the earliest essay in the forthcoming new style. It also has to be observed, as it is the only pastoral, seemingly Claudian part of the whole design, the impact of its variety will have been even greater.

As Riskins is *bijou* so the Gloucestershire spread is Brobdingnagian . . . and so large as to be barely comprehensible. Even if Bathurst's house had been nearer its centre there was little to guide him towards an appropriate figure to follow in laying out his plantations, and pulling all together into something sensible. The pattern he followed was that which Switzer had written about, and that we believe they had followed together in Berkshire. By good management, and perhaps trial and error, they produced an early landscape, or Forest, or Rural Garden, of surprise, subtlety and merit.

The scale and disposition of the parts at Cirencester not only beggared comprehension but also must have seemed impossible. There were others also attempting designs at this scale, but they were few, and nobody had yet demonstrated quite how it was to be accomplished. There were other large gardens with contiguous estates, such as Wrest, where no integration of the two parts had been attempted. There were other landowners attempting designs at a truly landscape scale. Lord Carlisle was in the same situation as Bathurst, if earlier in beginning his works. He, however, was still more preoccupied with buildings, not least his new house, one of a quite extraordinary scale. Lord Cobham had also begun his works at Stowe, contemporary with Bathurst and likely around 1716, and Lord Bruce's contemporary Tottenham Park, with which Lord Burlington was associated, has the scale and many of the forms of its neighbour Cirencester (Lennon 2011).

At first glance the Cirencester design seems to share much with Stowe or Tottenham Park. On closer examination it is clear that Castle Howard and Cirencester have more in common, especially when we remember that they exhibit the designers' concern to relate large scale elements to each other, and give some kind of sense of natural affinity and connection. As we have observed at Cirencester the concerns were to lead easily from one element or area to another, and usually with some surprise hoped for. Similarly, at Castle Howard, the Bold Stroke of the big Avenue rising and falling, and thus losing its geometric force, reinforces the newly regained geometry with each new view, almost like a new stage set . . . functional as a gate, or a wall certainly, but evocative also of extra and surprising things, like walls with battlements. Although technically static (they are after all a series of one point perspective stills) they are actually, if barely, picturesque. They were certainly sufficiently so to tickle Horace Walpole's fancy. Stowe's Ridings, which we have to imagine since they no longer exist, do give the impression of a hunting forest of a French sort, as do the ridings through the adjacent Savernake Forest at Tottenham Park. In other words, they appear as functional adjuncts not yet integrated with the *garden* parts.

And yet what would appear to derive from functional motives is a little muddied in some of Charles Bridgeman's schemes, and this is noticeable in another Lodge Park, the nearby addition to Sherborne Park. Sir John Dutton had inherited at the beginning of the 18th century and had begun to improve Sherborne Park in the period 1708–1712, and this continued into the 1720s, when he turned his attentions to an apparently new work a mile or so to the south in open country. These are both properties now in the care of the National Trust, and their history has been charted by K A Fretwell and published in *Garden History* (Fretwell 1995). There she based her account on the documentation, its distant view in the painting by Lambert of 1749 (Fretwell 1995 141), early Ordnance Survey maps, and surviving evidence, not then being aware of the design drawing in the Gough Collection at the Bodleian Library in Oxford. Peter Willis has since published this and has attributed it to Bridgeman (Willis 2002 431–432 and Plate 209). It seems that Bridgeman was consulted about the project as early as 1725 and produced the design by 1729; work on it was carried on in the 1730s until its completion (posthumously of both the designer and the commissioner) in the late 1740s. Unusually, the authorship, the dating of its execution and its nature are well attested.

There remain aspects which puzzle, however, and these may arise from its use and the way it was appreciated in the early 18th century. It is detached from the house, and from the rest of the estate. This is perhaps because it had always been associated with hunting, and there remained the chase, specifically the Deer Course, to connect Sherborne with the site of Dutton's New Park. At the south end of this rare survival was the Lodge, which was then and remains a most accomplished design of what the Italians would call a *casino*, and of a form perfectly at home there: it was studied and

Essays in the landscape style 197

Figure 6.4 Lodge Park, Sherborne, Gloucestershire: Charles Bridgeman's design for the park landscape, 1729 (north to right). Oxford Bodleian Library, Gough Drawings a.4, folio 68.

drawn by Henry Flitcroft, an architect much favoured and to an extent educated by Lord Burlington. It had been favourably compared with the Banqueting House in Whitehall by a mid-17th century visitor when recently completed, and it may have been a work of Balthazar Gerbier. It was to the west of this that the New Park was to be laid out, hence called Lodge Park. It also provides the focus for Bridgeman's design, at least on plan. By this I mean that Bridgeman used the site of the old Lodge at the east end as the generator of the Bold Stroke around which his park is laid out. A strong *axis* which runs to the west over the undulating ground of the park is given sense by a very broad series of blocks and clumps of forest trees in the far distance but only when caught on axis. A viewing platform plus siting mound half way across the park is obligingly supplied for this very purpose. From that point the picture composes into geometric coherence beyond the broad serpentine *river* in the middle ground: if missed, or when viewed from other angles, that coherence disappears.

The edges of the site are marked by very broad bands of forest trees, without walks, as if to de-limit while closing it. At Lodge Park we see Bridgeman cheerfully embracing the "Incomprehensible Vastness" Switzer was critical of (*IR* I 1742 12). Rather than attempting to extend the design into landscape, Bridgeman stakes out the large area to be designed and then excludes all without it. There are not so many landscapes that he designed, but they do all share that characteristic. For example in 1732 Isaac Ware published the plan of Bridgeman's proposed parks around Houghton House, Norfolk. These are ringed in a similar fashion, and also, as here, there are large divisions of "fields", vast sub-parks lining the outer range and giving an extra sense of depth to the designed domain: only then does the park proper begin more or less surrounding the great house, and its extensive grounds, said by some to be by Bridgeman too, but certainly the design published in *Vitruvius Britannicus* is not his, but as noted above was by Kingsmill Eyre (Eburne 2003 200 et seq).

As much as we may know about the circumstances of the design of Lodge Park we have no idea of what Dutton had stipulated to Bridgeman that he required, or even wished, to see in his New Park. Clearly neither appears to have seen any reason to knit the whole estate together into a unified design. Although Sherborne is close to Cirencester its landscape character seems far removed, as it lies in that open area in western Oxfordshire and into Gloucestershire, the high Cotswolds: in other words, its locality is essentially pastoral. Therefore, arable, or forest led designs, will not figure, or if tried perhaps not succeed. But as Dutton well knew his own patch, and doubtless Bridgeman too, they are more likely to be simply responding to their perception of the nature of the place. Thus, a piece of designed landscape here will be a different thing. Certainly here, but perhaps rather less so in Norfolk, but even there his vast "fields" can hardly be agricultural, except in the later 20th century sense of agribusiness: Sir Robert Walpole, unlike his neighbours Lord Townshend or Lord Leicester, gave no evidence of wishing to seem an improver; certainly he was too grand to wish to be thought a farmer.

Of the immediate surroundings to Sherborne we know little: wooded grounds with seeming gardens and parkland mixed appear on early topographical maps, but there are few clues to its design nature. Immediately outside these grounds, however, is open, almost prairie like country. There are field divisions but little wood. It is there that Bridgeman is asked to make a New Park. And of course there is the inherited special building, which Bridgeman as it were clothes in woodland, but was it always so? Certainly the Deer Course is as open as the surrounding country, as it had to be. And it is enclosed by walls but still making it a kind of horizontal work of architecture. Its impact on its locality is very strong, and made stronger by the metropolitan and stylish building standing at its southern end.

Similarly detached were Stowe's Ridings and famous gardens. The qualities admired at Stowe derive rather more from the garden part, and the Ridings do nothing to enhance these, or even impinge upon them. We may assume the same state for Lodge Park and Sherborne, only in reverse. Castle Howard constitutes a designed landscape almost in spite of itself, as if it all happened by happy accident, and as confirmed by John Vanbrugh's throw away comparison of his role to that of a midwife. Tottenham, too, may reveal qualities presently hidden as well. Cirencester is very much a both-and kind of design. It looks like a formal landscape suitable for farming, trees and hunting, and, of course, it is. It also reveals itself as a complex designed landscape, aspiring to art, whose purpose seems to be the discovery and enjoyment of all rural affairs, modern and ancient. And of course that is true as well.

Nostell Priory

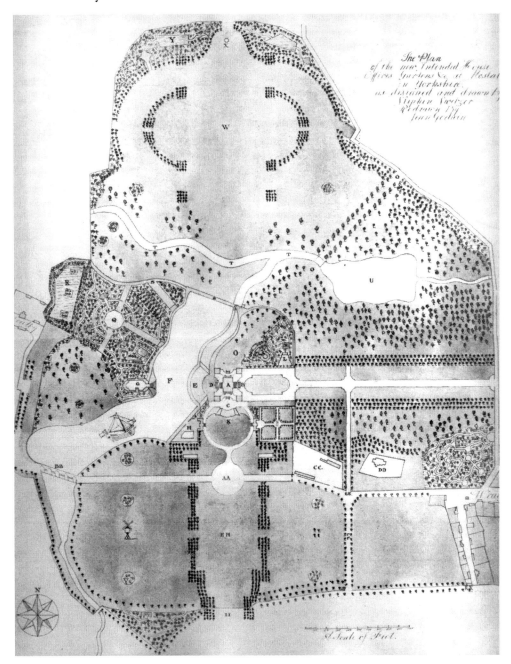

Figure 6.5 Nostell Priory, Yorkshire: design (north to top). Jean Godwin's facsimile of Stephen Switzer's "This View of the New House Offices and Park at Nostell, Yorkshire, with the improvements as made and to be made in the Plantation and in the Park and Wood as designed & drawn by Stephen Switzer". Reproduced from Maurice W Brockwell, *Catalogue of the Pictures and other Works of Art in the Collection of Lord St Oswald . . . at Nostell Priory*, 1915. © National Trust.

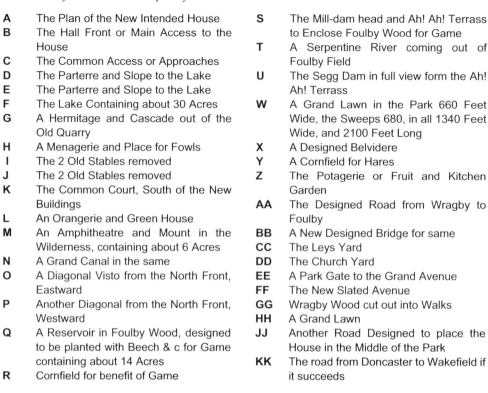

A	The Plan of the New Intended House	S	The Mill-dam head and Ah! Ah! Terrass to Enclose Foulby Wood for Game
B	The Hall Front or Main Access to the House	T	A Serpentine River coming out of Foulby Field
C	The Common Access or Approaches	U	The Segg Dam in full view form the Ah! Ah! Terrass
D	The Parterre and Slope to the Lake	W	A Grand Lawn in the Park 660 Feet Wide, the Sweeps 680, in all 1340 Feet Wide, and 2100 Feet Long
E	The Parterre and Slope to the Lake		
F	The Lake Containing about 30 Acres		
G	A Hermitage and Cascade out of the Old Quarry	X	A Designed Belvidere
H	A Menagerie and Place for Fowls	Y	A Cornfield for Hares
I	The 2 Old Stables removed	Z	The Potagerie or Fruit and Kitchen Garden
J	The 2 Old Stables removed		
K	The Common Court, South of the New Buildings	AA	The Designed Road from Wragby to Foulby
L	An Orangerie and Green House	BB	A New Designed Bridge for same
M	An Amphitheatre and Mount in the Wilderness, containing about 6 Acres	CC	The Leys Yard
		DD	The Church Yard
N	A Grand Canal in the same	EE	A Park Gate to the Grand Avenue
O	A Diagonal Visto from the North Front, Eastward	FF	The New Slated Avenue
		GG	Wragby Wood cut out into Walks
P	Another Diagonal from the North Front, Westward	HH	A Grand Lawn
		JJ	Another Road Designed to place the House in the Middle of the Park
Q	A Reservoir in Foulby Wood, designed to be planted with Beech & c for Game containing about 14 Acres	KK	The road from Doncaster to Wakefield if it succeeds
R	Cornfield for benefit of Game		

Figure 6.5 Key

The commission from Sir Rowland Winn to Switzer to provide him with advice for his estate at Wragby, near Pontefract, Yorkshire, is unusual in that the design drawing survives and is in very good condition. From it we may draw much about just how he proposed it should be laid out, and the considerable detail it provides allows us to recover its nature as if newly finished. As ever there remain questions we should wish to have answers for, but here we can be sure of his design intentions. Winn (1706–1765) was a baronet, recently returned from his Continental tour, and also recently married. In 1729 he decided to replace the old Nostell Priory with a new house, and sought architectural advice from James Moyser (ca 1693–1753), an ex-soldier who had served abroad as an *aide-de-camp* to Lord Sunderland, recently the prime minister. He, and certainly his client Winn, were of the younger generation whose improvements in the 1730s seem to set new standards and follow ideals clearly different from those of the Marlboroughs' generation.

There are several factors at Nostell which not only set it apart from recently designed schemes like Blenheim, but also suggest the beginnings of something quite new. It is a new house and located exceptionally close to a lake. The form of the house is unusual. It faces in four directions, seemingly equally, rather than having the customary two "faces" and two subsidiaries of all other houses of similar status. That formation appears to have been derived from a plan by Andrea Palladio for a villa for the Moncenigo family which had been published in *Il Quattro Libri dell' Architettura* but never been realized anywhere before 1730, although its principles had long preoccupied architects, as can be seen in the layout for the contemporary 16th century Wollaton

Hall near Nottingham. On Switzer's plan for Nostell the subsidiary dependencies are themselves cubic and also face indifferently in four directions. The only differences between them are so subtle as to evade notice: two are joined to the main block by wings or simple walls on convex curves, whereas the other two achieve this by concave curves. In Palladio's version the two convex curves "like arms . . . seem to receive those who come near the house" (Palladio 55); they are paired with two seemingly rectangular courts, thus recognizing customary usage. At Nostell in James Perfect's plan he indicates the east front as the formal entry, and the west front addresses (for him) the Best Garden (Brogden 1973 205–206). They are clearly still the superior ones for they show very large external steps to three bay wide platforms, whereas the south front, or Common Court, indicates paved walks, and entry to the main block at ground level only.

Switzer's plan for the grounds is undated, but as there is no reason to believe it is either earlier or later than the rival one by Perfect we assume it was also prepared in 1731. It shows a somewhat different response to the plan form of the house as designed already by Moyser, perhaps as early as 1728. On it the relationship between the house fronts, the pavilions and the purlieus of the house is much less demarcated. For a start it is not at all clear that Switzer intended more than a low wall (if indeed any) between the pavilions and the house. For Switzer there is connection to each front at the ground floor level, so that the distinction between *lesser* and *superior* courts is diminished. That would bring with it a lack of clarity in use, for these distinctions had grown up through the needs of the various groups frequenting a big country house, and their codification in recent times worked well. Equally obvious, however, is Winn's and Moyser's wish to explore differences in how to design a big country house and how best to set it into its site. We must assume that it was the client and his architect who had decided on the location for the new house, and on the attractive but ideal and frankly far from proven convenience of the Palladian prototype. Of course Lord Burlington, because of his being a neighbour at Londesborough, and because of his interests in architecture, has been suggested as a source for these ideas, and such a supposition has strength. But from wherever the client's notions did originate, or whether were tempered by Burlington and his associates, the decisions apparent in Switzer's responses to the seeming givens of the brief, that is, his design for Nostell Priory, derive entirely from his own ideas and works.

In Switzer's design proposition he not only makes the connection between the house and the pavilions convenient but also shows how Palladio's idea can be exploited to advantage in Yorkshire, to integrate house, purlieus *and* landscape more fully and easily. He adds an intermediate terrace on each front, and that allows the garden features to meld with the building features and at the same time allow a covered, secure and dry communication at ground level throughout to the whole house . . . that is, the main block and the pavilions. He maintains Moyser's distinctions: the *statelier* front to the east has a broad three bay set of steps, but he breaks it in half to provide respite and another opportunity to contemplate the house in more detail, and, of course, to enjoy the prospects to the grounds. Although the grandeur of the stately east approach is maintained, when it is repeated on the west front Switzer introduces a new and moderating element, equally grand and stately, but also in tune with the curves and the more varied shapes of the lake and garden side. The Common Court entry is also humoured: it will have been the normal way in and out for the family and neighbours, and being on the south side will have the most agreeable aspects. So there the turning circle is ramped upwards by a pair of garden-like amphitheatrical elements into a broad entry opposite the south front. Here Moyser had indicated convex curving walls

A	The Plan of the New Intended House	E	The Parterre and Slope to the Lake
B	The Hall Front or Main Access to the House	I	The 2 Old Stables removed
C	The Common Access or Approaches	K	The Common Court, South of the New Buildings
D	The Parterre and Slope to the Lake		

Figure 6.6 Nostell Priory, Yorkshire: plan of house siting (north to top). Grey-scale detail of Switzer's original design. © National Trust.

connecting the pavilions. This is not quite so embracing as Palladio had indicated, but Switzer's intermediate terrace re-instates the open-arm embrace idea, in pleasing contrast to Moyser's contrary curves, and from the top of his intermediate terrace Switzer proposed two *perrons* to lead into the first floor. On the opposite side, the north front, Winn and Moyser had presented an opportunity for which there was no conventional, or default, response. For symmetry's sake Switzer used the same forms on this side, where their amphitheatrical nature was appropriate (but see below).

Thus, from whichever direction the house is approached, or seen, it presents a handsome front, suitable to act as the show front. Nostell is the first house with dependencies to do this, and it is this factor that will make the *villa* form so very attractive within a short time. As a defining aspect of designed grounds, shortly to be conceived as landscape gardening, no view of the house need be less than best. Switzer makes sure that the opportunities of this Palladian design idea for a centralized villa are exploited in the prospects from the four fronts of Nostell Priory. The east front presents a suitably august and formal entry sequence. The classically proportioned forecourt is crisply defined between walled garden and wilderness, with its width the same as the extended east front, whereas the utterly plain grass platt in its centre echoes the body of the house. The broad avenue, which he designates as the Parade, leads straight to the east gate, and is formed of treble rows of forest trees with semi-open woodland glimpsed beyond on either side.

The south prospect begins with the common entry, and is a rather more playful design. It is a much broader affair with the flanking stables and coach house pushed back to make a big circle one and a half times the extended width of the house. Immediately south of the house is a big terrace-like standing for coaches as well as foot traffic, and this is served, taking Palladio's idea of welcoming arms, even further by the two ramps down to the stable and coach houses. These are to be re-sited and rebuilt in Switzer's design, integrating the stable court and entry court into the grander circular Common Court. Beyond this is an even wider Great Lawn defined by double rows of forest trees and articulated by blocks of trees planted four square and in rows of four by seven to form groves. Nearer the house is the crossing, in Switzer's round-about, of the road from Wakefield to Wragby, re-aligned and here suitably straight.

The west prospect is from a parterre, so named but yet so unlike that element, which also lies exceptionally close to the lake. That, of course, could not be avoided, and it may have been to re-instate the expected depth of field in such a formal prospect that Switzer aligns it on the far bank of the lake on a broad cascade falling from a shaped but still basically rectangular Bowling Green. The main reception room of Nostell Priory opens opposite this onto the flight of steps which leads to the intermediate terrace, which as elsewhere combines with the curved linking walls to make arm-like platforms to connect to the flanking pavilions, and with serpentine curves re-join the second half of the axial steps . . . here directly onto the grassed parterre, seemingly semi-circular in form but with wing-like sections north and south. Towards the lake and the cascade beyond is a very large semi-circular slope of plain grass down to the walk along the lake side.

The lake at Nostell Priory was mediaeval and at basis an ancient mere: its form when the new house and grounds were planned is shown on Perfect's design for the gardens. Its west side presented a gentle uninterrupted curve from the Wakefield Road to the mill dam. Perfect shows the east side as modified to accommodate his scheme for the grounds. Switzer, in his rival design, proposed a much more radical treatment of the lake. He intended to extend it by digging out much ground to the south-west. Not only would this be laborious, but it also required re-siting the highway, and a consequent court or parliamentary approval, and a new bridge, as it were to ornament the extended lake and carry the altered roadway. The new end was to be banked in part of an almost perfect circular curve at its west end. The spoil produced by this enlargement was to be employed in changing the shape of the lake on both sides. The west side by Foulby Wood was to be more artfully serpentine, and splayed out to take the new cascade opposite the main front of the house. The east side was also changed, partly straight, partly curved in the recognized glacis fashion, and then finished to the unaltered mill-dam head in a tapering bank of converging serpentines in plan form resembling a tadpole.

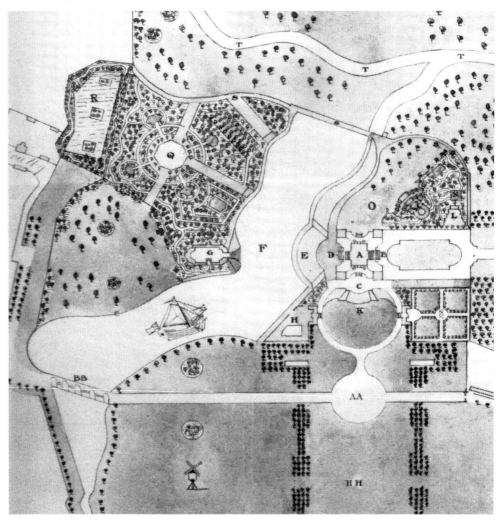

A	The Plan of the New Intended House	O	A Diagonal Visto from the North Front, Eastward
B	The Hall Front or Main Access to the House	Q	A Reservoir in Foulby Wood, designed to be planted with Beech & c for Game containing about 14 Acres
C	The Common Access or Approaches		
D	The Parterre and Slope to the Lake	R	Cornfield for benefit of Game
E	The Parterre and Slope to the Lake	S	The Mill-dam head and Ah! Ah! Terrass to Enclose Foulby Wood for Game
F	The Lake Containing about 30 Acres		
G	A Hermitage and Cascade out of the Old Quarry	T	A Serpentine River coming out of Foulby Field
L	An Orangerie and Green House	AA	The Designed Road from Wragby to Foulby
M	An Amphitheatre and Mount in the Wilderness, containing about 6 Acres	BB	A New Designed Bridge for same
		HH	A Grand Lawn
N	A Grand Canal in the same		

Figure 6.7 Nostell Priory, Yorkshire: plan of central section (north to top). © National Trust.

So although the proprieties of grand garden design have been acknowledged on the west side, the Best Garden, the effect was far from what would be expected. It is more a prospect than a view. By that I mean that its breadth ensures it cannot be taken in at one view, as in a stage set, and all other parterres. That works very briefly only when the whole is first seen from the Drawing Room. Once the company moves onto the terrace it becomes apparent that they have to look from side to side, in an unaccustomed manner, to appreciate the design. This would be far from disagreeable, as the shape of the banks of the lake itself would encourage such a sweeping view. There are two conventional goose-foot style diagonals to allow orientation, but the size, placement and design of the lake will have pleasingly unsettled this reassurance, and thus produced the surprising variety the early 18th century longed for.

Because of the unusual plan form Winn and Moyser had adopted there was the opportunity for another "major" garden front. Thus, from the north front of Nostell is another, but perhaps rather different, big view. It can easily be comprehended from one view point, thought appropriate perhaps for this side of the house as it was meant to contain the library and have a more contemplative cast. But it too is of a new kind of prospect, and equally has qualities we associate with landscape. Because of the strong edge of the lake, here running diagonally, the topography nudges the eye 45 degrees to the north-east. Switzer does not resist; indeed, he provides a flourish in the form of the big tadpole shaped bank between the lake and . . . what may we call this large grassed area? The parterre lies on the west front, the parade to the east, and *lawn* he has reserved for something else. This significant landscape garden feature without name is the centre-ground of the whole design: it allows, even encourages, the diagonal thrust while at the same time resolving everything back into the axial view that Moyser's architecture and the situation of the house demands. Thus, he makes a *scene* of the grounds on this side, and makes it both informal (for example in the disposition of elements like the dam head, the river in the park and the park plantations) and formal (the axis is tethered at the far side of the park by an eye-catcher, and its rather Newtonian *imperceptible regularity* is established by the great formal sweeps of forest trees in what Switzer designates as lawn).

We have noted the four important axes . . . both for approach, and as frames to accommodate the designed prospects. And of course these derive from the design of the house with its Palladian-Moncenigo centrality and welcoming open-arm symbolism. It is more complex than that. Switzer exploits the still potent memory of the goose-foot arrays of prospects with a mixture of Newtonian design notions of imperceptible or incomprehensible regularity, not only on the west front, but also for the north front prospects, where in a similar manner these lateral divisions of a big design are used. There the "axial" that is a straight-ahead view is primary, of course, and it is also more than sufficiently satisfying in diversity and resolution. Its more minor companions offer a short directed axial north-west across the edge of the reservoir wood, and a bit of parkland, into arable land. At Nostell Priory there were productive fields, naturally enough, but they are not part of the designed scheme. Although the large Foulby Field is noted, it is not celebrated, being covered by the legend bearing the identification of features on the design drawing. The only familiar Switzeresque farm-like element noted at Nostell Priory is the small "Cornfield for the benefitt of Game" just west of the Reservoir and beech woodland. Possibly by direction from Winn in his briefing, or maybe for operational reasons, the design for Nostell is for a large garden, not a *ferme ornée*, and it is of a size to be the coming new thing, a landscape garden. All its effects are the result of compositions to provide pleasure to the eye and imagination without recourse to any ideas of improvement of agriculture, that is, apart from this lateral view from Winn's library. Perhaps it was not so *minor* a prospect as it first appears to be. Its pair to the north-east is conventional: it runs along the line of the lake nearest the library with a rather fragmented sort of avenue, and then the eye is carried by a rough cut through fairly open woodland before being resolved in its final long half as a simple avenue pointed towards the edge of the grounds.

To these important compositional elements there are also several garden incidents which merit mention. The first of these lies on the north-east corner of the house. It is a Wilderness of six acres making a triangle in plan, addressing the parade to the south, open woodland to the east and a lateral combination of lake and park prospects across an avenue on its north-west, and principal, side. It is planted in close woodwork with hedged walks of straight and serpentine form, with an open Cabinet, a Grove and an Orangery facing south to the parade across a lawn with stepped quasi-theatrical edges. The biggest and most notable element of the Wilderness is the Mount and Amphitheatre which addresses the lake and park. The Mount is coloured red, indicating a circular structure of some sort, likely an open circular pavilion, or possibly of the kind previously noted at Leeswood. Its immediate enclosure picks up that form on the wooded side, but transforms itself into a series of three descending and increasingly complex slopes towards the lake.

Opposite the Wilderness on the other side of the lake, and joined by the dam head walk, is the 14 acre beech plantation arranged around the good sized octagonal reservoir. From this radiated a series of three major and four minor walks in a star-like formation. The reservoir was ringed by the close beech woodland, and an ample open

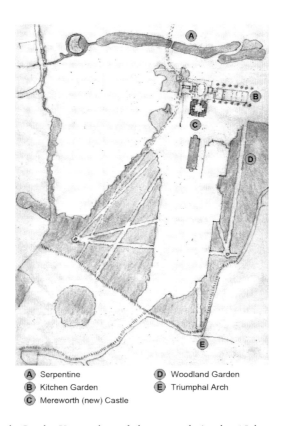

Ⓐ Serpentine
Ⓑ Kitchen Garden
Ⓒ Mereworth (new) Castle
Ⓓ Woodland Garden
Ⓔ Triumphal Arch

Figure 6.8 Mereworth Castle, Kent: plan of the grounds in the 18th century (north to top). Image by the author.

space divided by a circle of forest trees. A spur of this wood at its south end, and opposite the west front of the house, is an old quarry on the edge of the lake. This Switzer transforms into a Hermitage (recalling the site's early use as home to a band of Austin Friars) which overlooks a rectangular basin (or is it a bowling green?) to its south. The long axis of the "basin" is the same as the axis of the west front of the house, and Switzer celebrates that by connecting the basin to the lake by a cascade. The minor walks from the reservoir lead to four large cabinet-like clearings, each a variation of essentially rectangular form. The larger walks lead back to the house, and also northward to the park, and opposite this south to another park, significantly smaller, and yet still conceived as a park. This is one of Switzer's most identifiable early exercises in what a later age will call the Landscape Style.

This element, which, curiously, he does not name in the plan's legend, is separated from the north and east woodlands by a faintly discernible Ha Ha, which underlines its use as parkland. It is slightly smaller than the beech wood at roughly 12 acres, of the same size as the Paddock at Rousham. It is planted as pasture, with two large circular clumps and more than 25 artfully and informally placed forest trees. At the lake side to the south it presents a lazy serpentine edge. To the west and north are more vigorous serpentines, if not quite *arti-natural*, and these curves appear to have crisper edges defined by hedges, whereas the shorter serpentines along the eastern margins have groups of trees (and perhaps shrubs) in a kind of feathering to the denser edge behind the woodland. A larger designed element in the big park to the north is "A Serpentine River coming out of Foulby Field". This is suitably natural; that is, it could be a real river, and is much less *arti-natural* than its near contemporary pair designed for Castle Howard. Its siting is suitable for a real river, and it accepts the run-off from the mill dam, appropriately a little downstream so as not to take anything away from its novelty. Forest trees are artfully dotted on its sides, and with the circular clumps towards the west end it appears very much at home, seeming *natural*.

Quite apart from its intrinsic merits there are three major new things to note about Switzer's Nostell Priory design. It is a *garden* designed as landscape; it has several elements which are forward looking in terms of style; and it is the first *Palladian* garden. It is the first (and perhaps only) one to adopt, accept and celebrate the implications of the character of the Moncenigo prototype. At the same time it shows Switzer's use of axes to carry the scheme, both to *ground* it and also to remind us of the Newtonian lessons he accepts about the nature of creation, and he exploits the opportunity of composing a live picture in the prospect from the north front. These characteristics constitute the first evidence of something which becomes a standard test for the maturer Landscape Style of the 1760s and after.

There is another, and slightly earlier, house also influenced by Palladio which raises similarly interesting issues of siting and the design of the grounds. John Fane, 7th Earl of Westmorland (1686–1762), a soldier who fought at Malplaquet with Lord Cadogan, had Colen Campbell design a house for him at Mereworth in Kent. It was well under way in 1723, and is based on the Villa Capra adjacent to Vicenza, like Lord Burlington's addition at Chiswick, for which it clearly provided the spur (see above). Mereworth also combines the Italian's seductive architectural proposition of the simple cube facing four directions equally with the native idea of the English house surrounded by a moat: the new house occupies this site as Mereworth Castle.

It lies south of Tonbridge (about the same distance as that between Capra and Vicenza), but the English house is on a low rising in the middle of open south facing parkland which rises to low hills to the south-east: a classic and ideal situation for a country house. Campbell's house for Westmorland is tightly constrained by its moated position, yet still open to prospects on all sides; these have quite different characters. The Bold Stroke northward to Tonbridge is carried by the long avenue beyond the open ground immediately to the north, which is ornamented by a man-made *river* rather lazily serpentine in parts, one of which is a big circular basin with a crescent shaped wooded island, which reads as a clump. This axis is carried southward as a very large *parterre*, four times the width of the house-moat, and twelve times its length, which ends in a semi-circle. The west side is defined by a big planation of forest trees with a series of straight rides, and the east side, also wooded, is the *garden* part, in Wray Wood manner separated from the *parterre* by a very long terrace. Its more precise layout is hinted at in the earliest plan we have, which shows some of the major walks and one folly, the Triumphal Arch, probably contemporary with its twin at Garendon (see below).

Due west of Mereworth is an open prospect over parkland, contrasting to the orderly lawn on the east front, defined by the range of outbuildings and kitchen gardens and the entrance to the woodland garden. The immediate frontage southward, occupying under half of the *parterre*, contained a canal flanked by a lawn shaped by slopes; its presumed twin to the west had disappeared by 1789 (Ordnance Survey drawing 119). In its composition, its elements and its manifest mastery of situation, Mereworth bears comparison to Switzer's signed designs.

Exton Park

Lying south-west of Greetham in Rutland, Exton Park in the early 18th century was seated at an old house in the heart of its village and adjacent to the parish church. Like most of Rutland, Exton's topography is essentially flat, close to what Horace Walpole, rather surprisingly, described as "fine champain country" (meaning good for field sports). The only landmark of the county, Burley-on-the-Hill, the great proto-Palladian late 17th century house with grounds designed by George London, lies to the west. The proximity of Exton House to the church and village, though very far from obtrusive, raised a special set of issues for any extensive garden designs. These are the characteristics which determine the layout made in the later 1720s and 1730s, and illustrated in two double plates in the 1739 volume of *Vitruvius Britannicus*. Details of its making are otherwise lacking. In passing, Switzer noted the place and his being there in the early 1730s: also, its owner, Baptist Noel, Earl of Gainsborough (1708–1751), was an improver who subscribed to Switzer's *Practical Husbandman and Planter*. I attributed the design of the grounds to Switzer in my thesis (Brogden 1973). Gainsborough had inherited in 1714 as minor, and was still a young man when these grounds were laid out. His sister, Susan Noel (1710–1758), married their cousin Anthony Ashley Cooper, Earl of Shaftesbury (also a subscriber to *Practical Husbandman and Planter*). The improvements at St Giles House, Wimborne Dorset, also without a documented designer, have similarities to Exton.

Exton consisted of some 2,000 acres, for the most part parkland, but there was a planted woodland of 300 acres with a simple star at its centre east of the house near the two pieces of water, which we believe Switzer made. These pieces of water occupied over 70 acres. The house grounds and village accounted for perhaps as much as 200 acres, two-thirds of which were the extended gardens, and enclosed arable. Immediately north of Exton

Figure 6.9 Exton, Rutland: detail of view of the church and house, undated (mid-18th century). © The British Library Board.

was what appears still to have been common agricultural ground, which occupied nearly 150 acres. What were doubtless old gardens, from the 17th century, and perhaps earlier, lay immediately and axially south of Exton House. Those gardens' cross axis was extended westward, across Church Lane as a broad avenue. The grounds were separated from the churchyard by this lane on the west side, which also followed its way to the rest of the village of Exton alongside extensive kitchen gardens beyond the common courts on the north side of Exton House. These appear more like wilderness quarters in the main view, but that is doubtless a misreading by the engravers. These older features have the severe simplicity typical of the 1730s. They may well have enjoyed a more Williamite fanciness in previous generations, but the tenor of the illustrated Exton landscape was exceptionally (to our eyes) abstracted, made up of very large areas of close cropped turf within, and equally severe parkland without. And these are set within a seeming limitless planar topography.

The extended part of the garden grounds, those areas near the house, lay eastward with longish low ground at its centre, and this became the Menagerie (which like the one at Lacock was attractive to wild birds), and later in the century was naturalized. Its north side became a series of "captured" field-like enclosures defined by a half-terrace walk whose south and west facing walls were planted with espaliered fruit trees. The terrace was on higher ground and also backed up against the walls to the kitchen garden and village on those sides, and thus gave open views mostly southward over the little fields, essentially captured park and menagerie towards the other half of the extended garden. This side was composed into three parts, of roughly the same size. South-east of the house and next to the old garden was a very large lawn . . . part parterre and part bowling green (and big enough for cricket). On its entrance from the old garden is a complex of slopes, but still simpler than those which make up its west

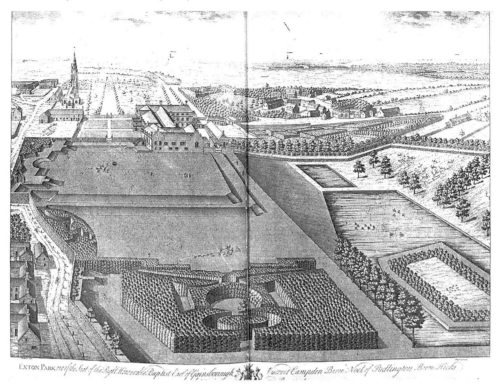

Figure 6.10 Exton Park, Rutland: south prospect of the house and grounds. Reproduced from *Vitruvius Britannicus, or the British Architect*, Volume the Fourth 1739, plates 59 and 60. © The British Library Board.

side. These are formed in the amphitheatrical manner but are of a greater breadth than he normally employed, and thus seem rather stretched out, and abstracted. These lead upwards to another terrace walk, broad enough to accept forest trees planted along its centre, which echoes the plan form of the amphitheatrical eastern side, but does not quite follow it. Ultimately, this whole margin is edged by the elevated wall hiding the village lanes on the south and west sides, where there was a "secret" entrance. Mostly this edge is defined by dense shrubbery, crisply clipped. The ground plan of this side of the extended gardens is irregular, allowing scope for a big curved block of plantation to define the west side of the second large lawn. This in turn is succeeded by the third division, in contrast planted as a kind of wilderness with very broad lawn-walks below the terrace walk of the edge. The margin between the second and third division takes the complex plan form of the theatrical slopes used elsewhere, but here rendered as clipped shrubbery. The eastern and western terraced edges are joined together along the south side of this enclosed extended garden, but tantalizingly just out of view in our source illustrations. Thus, we find a very large inner garden, enjoyed through the circuit of terrace walks, as well as in parts and at leisure by any number of alternative routes. This inner part is nearly the same size as Riskins, or the earlier parts of Stowe, and provides the same sort of variety. To that extent it might be thought a *ferme ornée*, had it been the only part. But it is only a part.

There is no connection by design to the outer parts of the Exton landscape. It might have proved possible, if difficult to manage. At best the western avenue could have been used to lead into it. The exclusion from view of one's tenants and neighbours is a feature met with in the later 18th century, but I believe it would never have occurred to the Gainsboroughs to be remotely desirable at Exton in the 1730s and 1740s. The inner parts of the design for walking, exceptionally spacious in themselves, are private and not overlooked by anyone. The outer parts dedicated to sport, mostly, would need to be appreciated mounted. The delicacies of the shrubbery were not yet in demand in the park, and the park at Exton was fully inhabited but hardly designed, although some sense of design is clear in the layout of the big Tunneley Wood. Big as this was, it was always overshadowed by the charm of the lakes and cascades, and by Fort Henry, as their chief Folly had become known by 1788.

The making and embellishment of the two lakes in the low ground near the eastern edge of the park showed the beginnings of a different kind of aesthetic applied to such very large scale places. There are two early views which show their state in Switzer's lifetime. William Stukeley sketched the scheme in the summer of 1744, and a few years later Thomas Smith (of Derby) and J Mason published their more detailed print of the same scene. While Stukeley's view is symmetrical, the plate printed in 1749 shows the same subject with a slight but very important bias to the side, a three-quarter view, and in the then newly adopted manner which soon became essential. François Vivares led in this new manner, and was in demand for his sympathetically picturesque rendering of recently improved places, such as William Hamilton's Painshill (Symes 2010), and Smith's Chatsworth also exhibits this changed and preferred point of view. Vivares was in partnership with Smith in recording improvers' schemes in topographical scenes. But Vivares' career in the early 1740s was as much in engraving the classic French history paintings of the 17th century by Claude and Poussin for the British market that contemporaries valued increasingly in *landscape* paintings. The apparently unconnected and contemporary landscape nearby at Formark has the same character (see below). So we must accept these essays as they appear. And, like much in what is called *rococo*, so a dominance of *space* is characteristic as much of early landscapes (that is, those designed in the late 1720s, 1730s and 1740s). The identification and then the acceptance of a *language* of the picturesque, thus begun in the 1740s, are not established until later.

The topography of Rutland and Exton Park hardly encouraged the sweeping curves one associates with lakes in ideal form. Both have long and essentially parallel edges, but the water is sufficiently broad for this not to impinge on visitors in its early days, and even if later censured by critics such as Thomas Whately (who does not note it), these shapes humour the nature of their place. What could not be disguised, even if it were a concern, is the man-made nature of the lakes, as the dams are very broad and straight, if not so high and prominent as their later contemporary at Wroxton, Oxfordshire, for example. There is one building shown in the *Vitruvius Britannicus* images, a fishing pavilion later to be called Fort Henry. But there is something peculiar in the views that might be explained initially by the newness of the scene that has essentially to do with the immaturity of the trees and the consequent rawness of the image. Scale is certainly very important as it is most difficult to reconcile the broad and flattish parkland, and the suddenly very busy scene made up of small scale elements. I think much of the disquiet comes from the standing stones: these are arranged along the edges of pools, as if they are in some way architectural ornament. But as the

Figure 6.11 Exton Park, Rutland: cascade, south view. Detail from *A View in Exton Park* by Thomas Smith of Derby and James Mason, 1749. © The British Library Board.

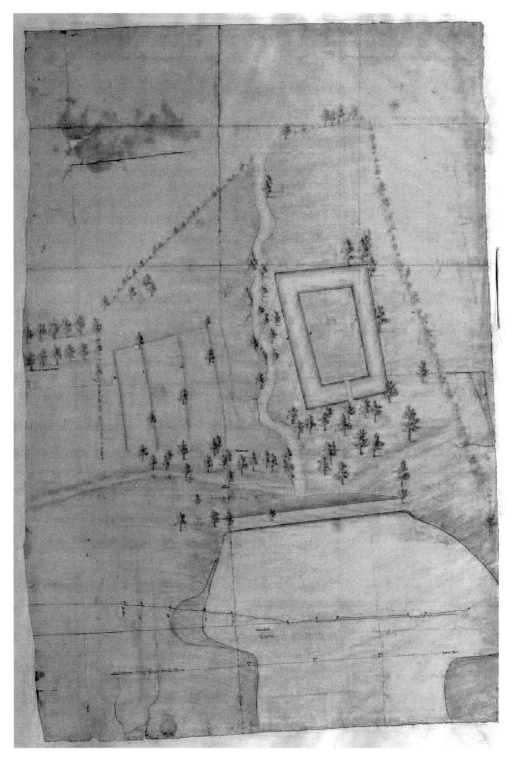

Figure 6.12 Exton Park, Rutland: plan by Stephen Switzer for the water-works, undated (1730s) (north to bottom). Oxford Bodleian Library, Gough Drawings a.4, folio 7.

18th century, any more than the 21st, could hardly explain the significance of such standing stones when discovered in Wiltshire or Aberdeenshire, of which Stukeley of course was the most knowledgeable, we cannot blame them for false assumptions. Is it the pure grotesquery of the scene that *disturbs* and makes it to some extent enchanted? The Exton cascades also have the character of a Salvador Dalí landscape: real, and exceeding strange, but only partly because they employ grotesques. The other quality they share is the predominance of *space*. The relative scales disturb, as do the geometries of the compositions used, but it is the seemingly dream-like *emptiness* that carries the punch.

The architectural character of both images is as grotesque as Switzer clearly wished his water-works to be, with not only rough stone-work in a misshapen, or very roughly hewn, manner, supplemented by many almost monstrous and sharp standing stones suggestive of the pre-Roman, a slightly more scholarly local reading of what *grotesque* should mean when used in England, an attitude he will have shared with Stukeley. The two lakes, each of just less than 40 acres, were formed by damming two streams whose more serpentine courses had joined together immediately north of the upper lake. From that point they took their natural form, which is very close to a regular rectangle. The only drawing of the works at Exton to survive is a working drawing which is clearly a part only. This dates to about 1730 and shows the lower lake, with its dam, and the cross section of the valley, and also the areas of run-off to the south: these fit the topography as shown in plates 61 and 62 of *Vitruvius Britannicus*, but were made several years earlier (see Harris 1979 for issues of dating).

The Exton cascades are in two parts. The larger lies between the upper and lower lakes in the centre of the dam. In two falls the cascades pass under a good sized Folly, itself of three upper floors, and composed into three bays, sufficient to provide a suite of rooms for entertainment, and accommodation above with ample service below. This upper part will also have been designed by Switzer, and is clearly derived from the work of his old friend Vanbrugh. The first fall follows the architecture of the Folly, so there are three streams of cascade under the recessed centrepiece, with two flanking falls through rusticated arched grottos under the two short wings. There is a pool to receive these half way down the dam, and this pool splays outwards in its plan form to the second and much broader cascade into the lower lake. This is flanked by grotesque rock-work making terminals to the pool, and also acting as the seeming basement for the whole composition. Opposite this the lower lake empties in four smaller falls by way of three interlocking rectangular pools whose corners are marked by the prominent standing stones in the pre-Roman style. The breadth of this lower dam also is marked by these stones. Below these is the serpentine run-off through a mostly wooded section, where the pre-existing fish ponds have been tidied up. This woodland and stream also provide an entrance to the lakes and the cascades, as an alternative to the entrance through the park, and Tunneley Wood from Exton House. This woodland, with its long and serpentine course through coppice woods to the edge to the lower lake, would capture the spirit of the place, and the scene as depicted by Smith and Mason perfectly.

As noted above, Lady Shaftesbury oversaw works in Dorset contemporary with her brother's works at Exton, although the perfection of them is dated to the later 1740s (Mowl 2003 72) (see figure 6.13). In the course of the current restoration of the house and grounds much has recently been discovered about the history of the grounds at St Giles. This has been assembled by English Heritage as guidance

(Cattell and Barson 2003), and a history of the place has begun to appear in print (Fleming 2007 and also in Eyres 2012). Sadly, and hardly surprisingly, there is still much to learn. No named designer for these extended grounds is known. But it appears that Lady Shaftesbury took a lively interest in developing the grounds, and Suzannah Fleming believes she played the leading role, especially in the early incorporation of at least two big fields added to the pleasure grounds from the time of the famous third earl at the beginning of the century. According to information kindly provided to me by Fleming a survey of these grounds was commissioned in 1734, but it has not been found, nor has the plan of 1750, which recorded the complete scheme including the agrarian additions, as well as the large lake and associated woods and walks.

There are, however, two engraved views by Vivares which warrant discussion here. They herald a significant transition of taste at St Giles House in 1774 which also illustrates the before-after moment when the enabling and essentially transitional formal elements were perceived to be redundant, *retarditare* or perhaps old-fashioned. There are two versions, and the second is most often used to illustrate the *rococo* design (eg Mowl 2003 plate 32). Both show a part of the house but concentrate on the serpentine lake with its Chinese bridge and the background of the embracing wooded walk, the feature from the 1730s which divided the lake and the two big fields. In the dominant foreground is the large, empty greensward. However, the companion view shows the designed state from its completion in the 1740s. The greensward had been occupied by a sharply and elegantly rendered Ha Ha and two very large earthen terraces, grassed and with sloped banks. These runway-like elements give a place to promenade, on the same level, from the house almost to the very edge of the lake, and quite close indeed to the Grotto (still hidden from sight, but convenient for inspection). There are figures

Figure 6.13 St Giles House, Dorset: engraved south prospect of the house and grounds by François Vivares, 1772. St Giles House, Wimborne.

216 *Essays in the landscape style*

also shown strolling by the lake that is within the park, but it is clear that company would not need to be quite so adventurous to appreciate the designed landscape as to actually enter into it. The broad, and also rather severe, earthen terraces at Exton played a similar role, as did the even bigger one at Gibside, but it is the uncannily similar broad and severe large plane between house and the White Gates at Leeswood (see above) that seems so like St Giles.

Garendon

Garendon Park lies immediately west of the town of Loughborough. It claims our attention because of the ambitions and the talents of its owner, Ambrose Phillipps (1707–1737). Phillipps, who is not to be confused with a man of the almost same name, but no relation, the now more famous poet and friend of his biographer, Samuel Johnson. Rather, his forebears had established the family on these Leicestershire estates in the mid-17th century. His father, William Phillipps, a Turkey merchant, was not interested in estate improvement but left his family much richer. On his inheritance in 1729 Ambrose Phillipps was on his grand tour of the Continent. Unlike many who took that trip he was a serious student of architecture, and one with an aptitude for understanding how he might, by inspecting ancient buildings, translate Roman architecture and principles into England, as his epitaph records. His studies in Italy recommended him also as a very early member of the Society of Dilettanti recently founded by his uncle Francis Dashwood. He entered Parliament in 1734 as a Tory, and began his works of improvement (he had subscribed to Switzer's *Practical Husbandman and Planter*) at Garendon. There he began to improve the old house, and followed a plan of development of the grounds likely made by Switzer, where, on the most advantageous parts of the estate, the highest, and the most favourable for views (both to and from), he built a series of landmarks. He started with the Obelisk, then quickly followed with the Temple of Venus,

Figure 6.14 Garendon Park, Leicestershire: anonymous drawing of the Triumphal Arch, 1826. deLisle MSS, Garendon, Leicestershire. Reproduced with kind permission of Peter de Lisle.

and one of the first Triumphal Arches in English grounds. And he had begun work on bringing the old house up-to-date with the handsome and sober wing towards the new gardens, centred on the portico. All this was accomplished in the period of a scant four or five years before he died of smallpox. It seems that his pursuit of the duties of a man with a new estate was so methodical, and so sensible, that he had taken an extraordinarily mature and long view . . . especially so for one of his age and connections.

To say that Phillipps' attitude to architecture was a scholarly one, although that is true, may mislead. His scholarship derives from his happiness to inspect, observe and become inculcated in the building's nature. Most students of architecture then sought examples and confirmation of what they already knew to be correct, or occasionally became enthralled with a particular manner which took their fancy. His short career shows a course of design and building based on study of prototypical monuments . . . the obelisk, round temple, triumphal arch, portico, all of which were so strongly grounded in their design characters as to be almost *natural*. Therefore, his role was to determine how to best realize the type, and he did so at Garendon. The setting into which these were built was equally straight-forward. An obelisk is an ideal object and is well set at the end of a line, and also allows itself to be well shown in its "own" small space, such as a cabinet, clearing or small *place*. The round temple also favours these simple settings, but it also invites being placed in larger spaces, whether round or rectangular, or as an object within a star arrangement of avenues: it also makes an ideal pivotal building, and can link spaces of otherwise very different kind or character. The arch favours the promenade, and especially the triumphal one signifies entrance: if grand and a trifle pompous, so much the better. The portico en-fronts space, of whatever kind, and it stands for a destination. Also, it makes an excellent transition. As porch, grand entrance place or mediation between the great house interior and its external self, the estate, it is the perfect form. Garendon shows how this simplest architectural grammar could be applied in 18th century Leicestershire.

But Phillipps died young. His brother finished the house, and lived in it as the laird, but made no efforts to carry on any further architectural exploration. The estate also remained, and grew older, and no one saw any need to make it more fashionable as tastes changed around it. By the early years of Queen Victoria's long reign, it and its rather idealistic owner of the time became emblematic, and the place briefly enjoyed a moment of fame, if somewhat coyly disguised. Benjamin Disraeli, himself a somewhat improbable Tory politician, idealized Garendon in his novel *Coningsby*. It became a symbol for the home of a sensible, kind and thoughtful man and also the emblem of Old England, from which its idealistic young proprietor, based on the recent Roman Catholic convert A G M Phillipps deLisle, could espouse the values of Young England, against the rather sophisticated inherited power and culture of particularly the Duke of Omnium's heir (based on nearby Belvoir) as an entitled and perfect Whig. And the landscaped estate at Garendon, by then more than a mature one, could be described by Disraeli from nature as both verdant and venerable. Sadly, that was also the beginning of Garendon's century of decline and end. Ambrose Phillipps was recognized as an interesting, and perhaps important, figure in the early 1960s (Girouard 1965), just as the house was demolished and its contents dispersed. Happily the designed landscape has survived unchanged, and the recovery of the contents has occupied the family since then. Therefore, the chance survival of a survey, faithfully re-drawn in the later 18th century, which shows the estate in Phillipps' day is to be especially welcomed.

218   *Essays in the landscape style*

The divisions of the Garendon landscape are clear. To the north and west of the house are fields, but whether arable or pasture is not noted, and these are exceptionally close by. The south-west is occupied by parkland, mostly planted in avenues with stars and ornamented by the Temple of Venus and the Triumphal Arch. There is also a large quasi-formal area of park, not only roughly rectangular, but also with large, square clumps of forest trees. These western parks march with the arable fields, and make a seemingly more formal correspondence between these two parts of country life, hardly what we might have expected of a *ferme ornée*, yet providing the kinds of connection we have seen already at Riskins. And given the spaces between the large clumps and the consequent sizes of the lawns between them, the distinctions between *utile* and *dulci* are pleasingly ambivalent, and would be difficult to predict.

The east side is also parkland, more informally arranged. It is bisected by an avenue from the Obelisk to the old house at its juncture with Phillipps' south-west facing wing. The two smaller parks thus formed are designed in a different manner. The northerly one is composed mostly of scattered trees. There is one quite large "clump", roughly circular, and it is broken into four parts to make a squarish "cabinet" at the centre. This big clump is balanced about the left axis of a vestigial goose-foot, and given its form by the four large corner clumps of forest trees. This can be read as such in one or two positions only, and otherwise will have appeared like so much unplanned parkland. Its cross axis has to be a more imagined one, and even a visitor

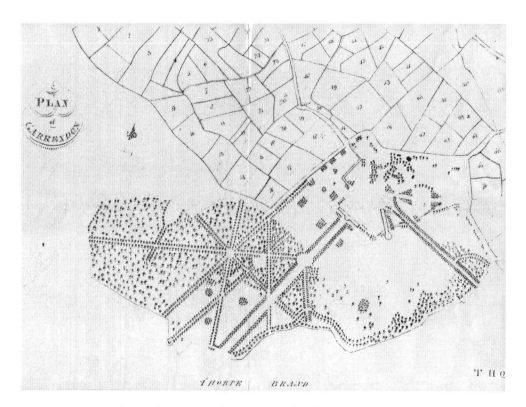

Figure 6.15 Garendon Park, Leicestershire: survey plan from the late 18th century (north to top). deLisle MSS, Garendon, Leicestershire. Reproduced with kind permission of Peter de Lisle.

suitably attuned would have struggled to identify it. The park to the south is fully informal in its plan shape, and is defined by forest trees following waving lines like the similarly sized contemporary one at Nostell Priory. Between it and the house, and aligned along the right branch of the vestigial goose-foot axis, is a canal. The east and west areas of parkland are divided by the broad "main" avenue, the "boldest of strokes", made up of double rows of forest trees, and a very large roundel, running diagonally across the design and marking the axis of the inner garden and house.

The inner garden, that is, the areas nearest the house, is, like the house itself, curiously left out of the survey drawing. Its edges, however, can give us some sense of its disposition and design. The main avenue meets this garden at a large body of water, itself part of a series of discontinuous canals which form the boundaries between parkland and inner gardens, Switzer's preferred manner of division, but with little evidence of its actual employment. This is marked as a semi-circular swelling on the main axis. To the north-west it is formed into an ell shape, and, as noted, there is a diagonal canal on the south-east side. The rest of the inner garden appears to have been made up almost entirely of an extensive lawn of roughly rectangular shape wrapping around three sides of Garendon House, thus making the portico obviously the terminal destination of the main axis, but also the centre of the whole design from which open lawn and wide parkland views are easily seen.

Garendon is a closed system in the sense that its main entry is not at all apparent; in other words, there are a number of equally important entries, plus a number of others just as convenient. Given the direction to the parish church clearly the entry on the west side is the principal one, close to the village of Shepshed and St Botolph's Church. It is this side that is marked by the Triumphal Arch. But just to the west of this is another alternative "signal", a very large open space formed by two large curves at the edges of the forest. In the middle of this great space is the White Lodge, already in existence when Phillipps began his improvements, and beyond it, on axis, is an equally appealing entry in the wooded part of the park. When Disraeli's party made their fictional way into Garendon a century later it was the venerable trees and the distant views south to the old Charnwood Forest that he noted, so perhaps the common entry for visitors was more indirect, and the arch was used more sparingly. Clearly the Obelisk avenue offered easy access to the east side from Loughborough.

Beaumanor

Phillipps' near neighbour to the south was William Herrick (1689–1773) of Beaumanor, whose estate lies between Garendon and Charnwood Forest. Herrick had inherited an old house too, a moated one which he lived in until 1725, when he rebuilt it on the same site, retaining only the old kitchen block. Unlike Phillipps, Herrick chose a young local man to build his house, John Westley (1702–1769) (Colvin 1978 880), and the form chosen was the square three storey block preferred in those days and used with distinction especially by William Smith of Warwick. Beaumanor is brick built and cubic, but not as plain as many: it had an engaged frontispiece with a pediment, corner pilasters and horizontal stone embellishments representing the full order. Some ten years later Herrick engaged Switzer to prepare a design for the grounds. Details of this commission are lacking, but happily the presentation drawing of 1737 has survived and gives further welcome details of his practice, as there are numerous sites where improvements were undertaken, and with connections between them and

220 *Essays in the landscape style*

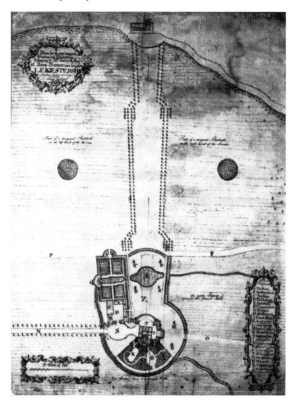

Figure 6.16a Beaumanor, Leicestershire: Stephen Switzer's design for the grounds, 1737 (north to bottom). Curzon-Herrick Collection, Leicestershire Record Office. Reproduced courtesy of Leicestershire Country Council.

Switzer about which we otherwise know too little at present to comment further. Although the design is professionally executed and abundantly thorough and clear, it is less finished than the one for Nostell, a trifle more workaday seeming; it also bears in the references block the "mistakes" executed by Thomas Switzer, then a schoolboy at Westminster. The design drawing gives us the much wanted details (missing from Garendon) of how the areas nearest the house, in a sense, the gardens were to be managed: these are very clearly shown here.

In his scheme for Nostell Switzer indicates a garden design of the landscape scale, whereas at Beaumanor it would appear that Herrick wanted more to concentrate his efforts nearer the house itself. Herrick seemingly had no park, and his very extensive estate was composed of enclosed fields, similar in size and disposition to those at neighbouring Garendon, and the whole was embraced to the south and west by the vestigial ancient Charnwood on higher ground. It is for grounds within this apparently already established agricultural estate with the new house in place that Switzer's design was sought. Beaumanor lies in a shallow and comfortable bowl which gives an impression of being level, but with woods rising in the distance sufficiently to provide a sense of enclosure. The fragment of moat surviving in the early 18th century was fed by streams from the north and east. Taking the square house as the centre Switzer makes a large, almost perfect circle as the figure for the "garden",

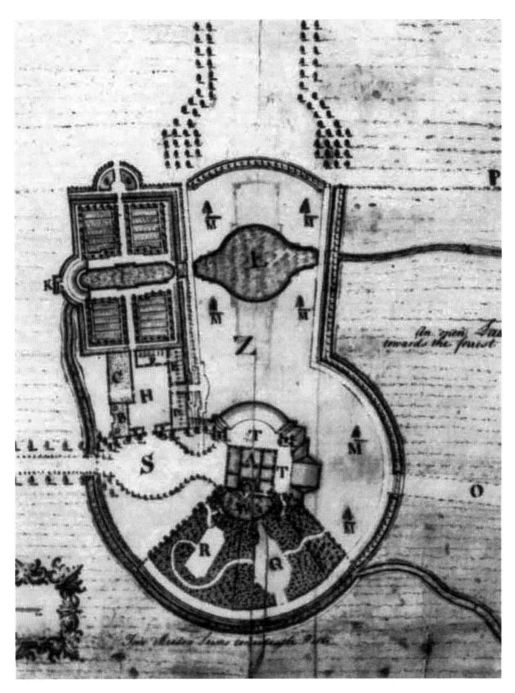

Figure 6.16b Beaumanor, Leicestershire: detail of Stephen Switzer's design for the grounds 1737 (north to bottom). Curzon-Herrick Collection, Leicestershire Record Office. Reproduced courtesy of Leicestershire Country Council.

and he uses the available streams to fence this "garden" (as used at Garendon and advised in the Paston plate). On the south side of the circle he breaks it with his Bold Stroke of an avenue flanked by two park-like "Padducks", and near the house behind the stable blocks is his new large kitchen garden, laid out also as a walled pleasure garden, and this also follows the line of the great avenue. Thus, the very strong figures of the circle, and the axial avenue to Woodhouse Church as an eye-catcher, set up the structure.

The purpose of these gestures is to establish the first of a series of zones of transition from the garden-like interior and farm-like buffer to the *landskip*, here more geometric because of the topography of the place. Its visible formal composition is made of gravel walks (crisply defined beyond turf), the extended moat, a small stream (two metres broad), then a line of regularly spaced trees with prominent trunks and then the Ha Ha and Paddock-Park. On the west and south-west sides of the garden this edge is seen at a distance of at least 60 metres, varying to rather more like infinite: therefore, its actual shape (the cause of the tension apparent on plan) is indeterminate if clearly purposeful. It is also, of course, visually permeable, and is in fact a natural screen or frame.

It sets up the far edge of another zone. On the west and near south sides these are lawns, turf with six widely spaced large trees with benches built around their trunks: these are disposed with symmetry opposite each major front of the house. However, the perceived reality of this zone of turfed lawn is complex, made up of a big, flattish bow beyond the west front, and a longer lawn southward, and leading into the avenue, with a significantly large section of bow at its near end. These tend to confuse the geometry. The Bold Stroke was to be further ornamented by a canal of three (or four) sections slightly splayed but axially arranged, or, as the preferred option, Switzer's late alternative of a broader piece of water, whose "axis" is a continuation of the kitchen garden axis and further disguised with edges of four regularly disposed serpentines.

The final zone is that of the house and its terrace-like parterres, whose slopes on the south side take their forms from the circle of the whole inner "garden", while the slopes of its extension around the corner of the house are more rectangular, picking up the geometry of the house plan. The quadrant of the garden circle balanced about the north-south axis is adjacent to the service side of the house, where there is the old moat and the retained old kitchen block, both at irregular angles to the rest of the compositions. But clearly observed from upper floors, and soon obvious even from ground floor rooms, are the three pie-sections of plantation making a fan-like foreground on this side. These are close quarters, planted with trees on the north-east side, low flowering shrubs in the centre section opposite the old moat and then trees for the north-west section. The terrace walk of the margin marking these zones noted above re-appears here at the far ends of the wedges of varied close plantation. On this side the far edges of the standard trees are replaced by a screen of iron fences (which had been recently introduced in London squares, and had been used very extensively at Cannons), perhaps as further protection for the quarters? This side of the house looks northwards into a narrower scene noted simply as "Fine Meadow Lawns towards the Woods".

The east quadrant forms the entrance to Beaumanor, and contains an elliptical turning defined by closely spaced conical greens: it splays out towards the house in convex curves to make a more vase-like plan form of the whole feature. To its south is the coach house court, and beyond that a walled kitchen garden. It can be entered from the court, of course, and can as easily be accessed from the terrace-parterres near the house by way of a gravel walk whose edges Switzer has designed into a recollection of the nearby slopes, running along the west side of the coach house block, doubtless with espaliered fruits planted against it, to provide extra treats. The kitchen garden has a canal running along its shorter axis with four large beds for produce, and terminated on the far side by an "Alcove Hall". Being so very close and convenient to the house, and its terrace-parterres, the kitchen garden is clearly intended as much for pleasure as for produce.

Wilton

Henry Herbert, 9th Earl of Pembroke (ca 1689–1750), became master of Wilton when he succeeded his father in 1733. He had become a courtier on the accession of George I and remained close to the Royal Family. Queen Caroline remarked of him, "He wishes well, but he is as odd as his father, not so tractable, and full as mad" (Connor quoting Hervey, *DNB*). He was only moderately effective in politics, and was noted for being litigious. However, his services to architecture were considerable. He championed the idea of a new bridge across the Thames at Westminster and assiduously attended the board which oversaw its design and construction. He had attended Christ Church from 1707 when its Master, Henry Aldrich, was preparing his influential book on architecture and when Peckwater Quad was being built, and followed

Figure 6.17 Wilton House, Wiltshire: part of the engraved view by Luke Sullivan 1759 (north to left). Courtesy of Yale Center for British Art.

this by a Continental tour. He has always been associated with supporting the adoption of ideas attributed to Palladio. He was the patron of Campbell, who designed and built Pembroke Lodge, Whitehall, for him in 1724. That design re-appeared in two subsequent projects on which he worked closely with Robert Morris: Marble Hill House at Twickenham and his own villa overlooking the park at Greenwich, Westcombe House, as well as the variant of it for the King at Kew, the White Lodge (sometimes also attributed to William Kent). Far and away his most distinguished effort was the Great Bridge which he built for himself at Wilton House in 1736 and 1737. Its quality was immediately recognized and also its powerful attraction. It was followed by a series of replicas, all now known as Palladian bridges but also known as "Pembroke" bridges (Whately 1770, 220). The type has become emblematic of the 18th century landscape garden.

The Great Bridge at Wilton was part of the contemporary reorganization, indeed re-design, of the grounds, clearly the most radical thus far, and by 1738 the new scheme was in place, "all laid out in the modern taste" as John Loveday noted (Markham 1984, 297). There is no surviving design drawing for these works. However, John Rocque's *An Exact Plan of the Gardens and Park at Wilton* of 1746 not only furnishes a detailed plan of the grounds but includes in a later edition a series of scenes of important sections of them. These together with contemporary accounts allow us to be pretty certain of the design. But who is the author of them? Pembroke himself took charge, of course, and as he had grown up there he will have nurtured ideas about their management from an early age, during which time his parents were actively engaged in restoring them and enhancing aspects of them. The old earl, to whom Switzer dedicated part of *Ichnographia Rustica*, oversaw those works. His third wife, Mary Howe, was an improver in her own right. And in the 1730s as the dowager countess she and the Earl of Peterborough (whose brother she soon married) subscribed jointly to Switzer's *Practical Husbandman and Planter*, and she borrowed a number of the gardening books from Wilton for use at Averham, Nottinghamshire, her dower house.

The documentary sources for Wilton are scarce, but there are references in Pembroke's surviving personal account book to payments to Switzer from 1738 to 1745. And Switzer renewed his dedication to Pembroke in the 1742 edition of *Ichnographia Rustica*. As these works at Wilton were in the "modern taste" Kent has been thought a candidate for consideration as their designer. He was engaged at Wilton in Pembroke's restoration of the fine rooms in the De Caus-Jones wing, and provided designs for furniture there, and also for the barge for the new lake. For all their merits, sophistication and modernity the 1730s designs for Wilton do not bear any stamp of Kent: rather, they are precise and crisp and incorporate axes and areas of slope-work and other "formal" features. These are all characteristics of Switzer, not Kent.

The inherited Wilton designed landscape was not only old but exceptionally distinguished. It was designed, as was the new wing it faced, by Isaac De Caus, nephew to Solomon De Caus, who King James and Queen Anna had engaged from France as a tutor to Prince Henry, and also Charles and Elizabeth. The other great protégé of that royal couple, Inigo Jones, had been consulted as well. Its structure had remained undiminished: the south front of Wilton House faced the remains of the terrace walk opposite. Connecting these were equally substantial flanking walls. Its furnishing, in three distinct sections, had tended to simplification, mostly the result of periods of neglect. The furnishings noted in Stukeley's drawings of the early 1720s (see figures 4.10 and 4.11) are evidence of the restoration of these, plus the big extensions eastward. But in the mid-1730s these earlier 18th century plantings were removed, leaving only a few of the larger ones in place (augmented into a grove-like plantation along the western edge). Also, the lateral walls and the remaining sections of the terrace walk were dismantled. Additionally, the axial view southward to Marcus Aurelius was severely thinned. To the east there were further great design changes involving

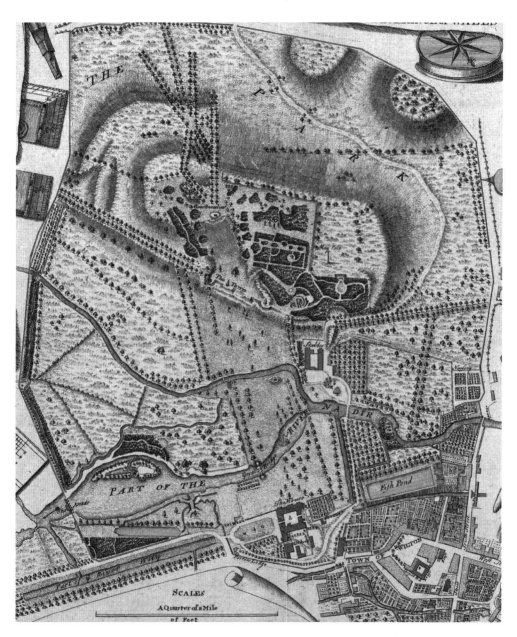

Figure 6.18 Wilton House, Wiltshire: engraved plan of the grounds by John Rocque, 1746 (ed 1752) (north to bottom). Courtesy of Yale Center for British Art.

abstraction and thinning, but more significantly a large addition of grounds to the gardens, plus a large incorporation of meadows on the south-east side, and a new wilderness. These additions increased the already extended grounds by roughly a third.

Yet for all these changes the grounds retained their original elements and in the same relationships to each other as had been the case from the mid-17th century: there was still the serpentine River Nadder (a smaller "river" than the adjacent Wylie, subsequently made into the axial canal on the east front). Also, the strong axis south from the "centre" pavilion of the De Caus-Jones wing of the house survived, and most of the buildings. The Nadder was and remained central to the gardens at Wilton. It has to be acknowledged, however, that the river as a feature raised problems which had never really been resolved satisfactorily. De Caus imagined a river, in form, nature and symbol, as most suitable to the wilderness. The wilderness had already been identified as a trope, notably by Henry Wotton and Francis Bacon as most suitably arranged as the last element (usually of three) in a garden design. Since the course of the Nadder was through the middle of the garden site at Wilton, De Caus had simply reversed the "preferred" order and placed the wilderness as the second element of his design. The extensions of the 1730s eastward towards Salisbury provided space for a much larger body of water than either of the rivers provided. Thus, the Nadder was formed by damming it into a seeming lake, and altering its banks within the area of the original gardens to provide a more placid, slower flowing river. A principal purpose of that was to provide a water course without the banks being parallel, seeming therefore more *natural* than its former actually natural course. That also provided a more appropriate foreground to the newly enlarged scene of Marcus Aurelius on the ridge in the park by adding an agreeable breadth to the river as it crossed the axis of the old De Caus garden. Additionally, the middle ground of that scene now was enhanced by the close woodwork on the ridge, a kind of new wilderness, and finally framed by a complex series of slopes celebrating Sir Philip Sidney's Walk, now called *The Tarrice*.

These alterations have to do with abstraction and enlargement certainly, but the transforming effect came from the consequent change in the point of view, or, more correctly, points of view, and this surely was the purpose of the new design. Although the spire of Salisbury Cathedral, the prospect of which Stukeley had recorded in the 1720s from the park, is brought into view from the gardens for the first time, important as that was, it too was really incidental, if happily so. For the new design was, like others contemporary with it, very much a closed scheme: however much it enjoyed views outward such as the one to Salisbury, it created its own *landskip*. The really important views are internal, beginning with the improved version of De Caus' original one. Others are similarly made collage-like out of existing elements modified sufficiently to work, but essentially accepted as given. Walks are an often used form, and usually straight: their junctions (ends or beginnings) are carefully arranged to coincide easily with the next. But they are very rarely united to the north-south axis of De Caus design: it remains but is teasingly played with. Larger areas, what could have been easily recognized previously as parterres, are assembled similarly. The Meadows as the wholly new addition derive their merits from their use and associational resonance, in other words the mixture of *utile* and *dulci* inherent in an agreeable agricultural prototype. The new wilderness on the hill is typical of its type in 1730s modern guise. Nowhere is there yet a hint of the mimicking of pictures, or of overt story telling . . .

no conscious picturesque composition of landscape. The key to appreciating it all is Pembroke's Great Bridge.

The extended landscape at Wilton, that is, the garden Rocque illustrated in 1746, occupies a large fan shaped area of ground that is largely flat, apart from the hill to the south. There are two perceived edges. The axis from the east front, later 17th and 18th century in origin, marks the north edge. The memory of the De Caus axis gives a lightly wooded sense to the west side of the grounds. The rising ground is partly wooded, wilderness fashion, and old Sir Philip Sidney's Walk has now become *The Tarrice*, with its axial entry marked by a complex of slope-works, surely the last of its kind. Between these are the fragments of old work and the new insertions and extensions. Between the northern edge and the augmented Nadder is the site of promenade, closely clipped turf next to the house, tidy, open and friendly . . . the perfect garden. This is composed of the first division of De Caus' scheme, plus the Bowling Green, and a further walled garden added in the earlier 18th century, now thrown together. This is the subject of Luke Sullivan's print issued in 1757: it assumes the role of De Caus' original design. The De Caus-Jones wing of Wilton is to the left, and the Great Bridge to the right, while straight ahead an open lawn offers the long view eastward to the lake and its arcade (called the Bridge of Communication by Lord Oxford and the editor of Defoe's *Tour* [1738 edition 293]) with Salisbury's spire glimpsed beyond. In the middle ground is a sort of mound made up of more sloped turf, in fact the Ice House, and to its left, along the edge of the grounds, are two canals. The larger of these is the River Wylie (marking the old entrance and east axis of Wilton House), and the smaller, set at an angle aligned on Salisbury's spire, marks the easiest approach to the lake and the arcade. This means the spire view appears only when the "axis" is left to follow the short section of canal, diagonal to all else.

At the lake are parts of De Caus' old buildings re-erected as the arcade. It has two new terminal pavilions which may be the work of Kent (whose barge is seen in one of vignettes around the 1752 edition of the *Plan*) but are more likely to be that of Pembroke with Morris. From the arcade the prospect back towards the house is the new kind of view that the new design for the Wilton grounds provides, a glancing sidelong view of the house and bridge with the extensive water in the middle and foreground and the woodlands used as a frame. In other words, it is a Landscape, and this very view was soon transformed into a landscape painting by Richard Wilson.

If the long walk around the grounds with large meadows on the right, a further rill in coppice wood to the left, to the end of Sidney's Walk is too tiring a prospect, then a turfed lakeside walk west towards the Great Bridge leads a visitor more quickly along a more serpentine path. Here there are meadows to the left, then a closer planted coppice wood and a larger meadow, laid out more like the little park at Nostell with its own serpentine rill crossing diagonally. That walk leads to the south side of the Great Bridge. There, the alternatives are to walk along a broad avenue of mature trees (left over from the early scheme when they shaded the outsides of the De Caus garden wall) on towards Sidney's Walk; or to go to the right through the Great Bridge back to the house; or to go straight on along the Nadder through the site of De Caus' wilderness towards the new one, a short way along a serpentine tree-lined avenue beside the stables.

The new wilderness is planted on the hill south of Wilton where the Marcus Aurelius statue holds pride of place. This straggles along its slopes through many mazy walks to cabinets, an amphitheatre, a big field with a Maypole in place and a thatched

Figure 6.19 Wilton House, Wiltshire: Bridge of Communication from the west with the Nadder as a lake. Detail of figure 6.18.

cottage from which to comfortably contemplate the spire of Salisbury Cathedral, which, according to Loveday, writing in 1738, was built specifically for that purpose (Markham 1984, 299). Of course there were views also back across the gardens towards Wilton House, and any of these, but especially an axial one, would show that another of the problems inherent in the De Caus design had been attended to. The intended south front of Wilton House was nearly twice as long as that actually built. That would have been splendid, no doubt, and would have matched the breadth of the gardens as laid out, but was well beyond the means of the Lord Pembroke of the day. In the 1730s revision some balance has been given to the façade by planting a nursery of Cedars of Lebanon to make up for the missing block of the building.

The Great Bridge can be seen, or glimpsed at least, from almost all parts of the grounds and from every angle. It is the pivot of the place. All other pieces of architecture lie on the edges of the scheme, not least Wilton House itself, exhibited rather more as a beautiful object than as the generator of the scheme: it had already become a preferred pattern for a country house, imitated by Sir Robert Walpole in Campbell's design for Houghton, shortly to be copied by Sanderson Miller for the Lyttletons' new house at Hagley, and by others later at Newnham Paddox or Croome Court. The Great Bridge is the only building totally within the gardens, and it is even more important as the place from which best to see all parts of the design. This aspect was lost on its imitators, who loved its beauty as an object without quite understanding its nature. Curiously, one of the earliest visitors, Loveday, perfectly understood its nature, and describes its importance and the joys it produced:

> . . . this present Lord has erected a covered Bridge; 'tis a very light and most elegant Structure upon 5 rustic Arches; besides the beauty of it, this building serves two

uses, that of a foot-bridge and that of a Summer-house on both sides the Water . . . the building is of the Ionic Order, under such an Arch you enter a square Room, passed which you are in an oblong Space supported on each side by four Ionic Pillars, not Arches; at the other End of this Space is such another square room; a Ballustrade of Stone (for such the whole is built of) runs on each side of the lengths of the 3 Rooms. The Roof is of brown Stucho in Panels, old Busts adorn the Inside and some Statues the Approach . . .

(Markham 1984, 299)

The Wilton bridge indicates a marked structural change in designed landscapes. We have seen the idea it answers developing at a number of places, but it is pleasingly clear here, and part of an orderly progression too. De Caus began it with a structured design in which a large section of landscape was made into art, and in which many agreeable activities were possible. Not the least of these was the stately movement up and down its principal axis to and from the house. To that he added the even more exciting prospects his terrace at the opposite end provided, with easy views back into the art of the garden and also outwards to the contiguous estate and "nature", where Sidney had begun his "walk to Arcadia". In the earlier 18th century this terminal terrace was modified by the replacement at its centre with the transparent iron screens which united the outer with the inner landscape, and elsewhere, such as Grimsthorpe, the terrace walk became a feature uniting the inner and outer parts of estates. In greatly enlarging their canvas by removing the last vestige of De Caus' enclosures Pembroke and Switzer made the external parts of the estate internal, and opened the possibility of each being equally picturesque.

Of course views had long been structured along axes, but even when they were, the lateral views are equally part of the visual experience, and sometimes equally if not more attractive. Other orthodox designs, like Caversham for example, show this, as does to a degree the earlier eastern extensions to Wilton. The effects of the dismantling of the lateral walls in 1733 could hardly have been a surprise to Switzer and Pembroke, although it must have been a thrilling tonic to others, as it provided an almost miraculous shift in perception: suddenly the parterre-garden had "turned" at right angles to produce the two (at least) new dominant axes of view and development: but as none of the axes could be followed on foot, the "centre" of the enlarged scheme is effectively concentrated at the Great Bridge. And this, as Loveday reported, is a building of *space* . . . it is also the architectural heart of the designed landscape.

An element of the Wilton grounds, and it could be said that it is the dominant one, has not been thus far examined. This is the design and furnishing of the *fields*. As these Meadows are integral to the scheme at Wilton this is surprising. Here is the part to which the scant documentation refers, and thus it appears that Switzer's last efforts at Wilton were in this area of the scheme, experimenting with his improved grasses. The Great Bridge is quite as close to the Meadows quarter as it is to the "gardens" quarter soon illustrated so memorably by Sullivan. This integration, to the point of becoming the very subject of the design, is perfected there. Rocque was meticulous in his indication of the varying natures of the fields of Wilton (and that includes clipped turf and meadow, and all between). These he shows as three distinct qualities of texture in his *Plan*. The uniting of rough and smooth, *utile* and *dulci*, had always been Switzer's message, and having already covered all elements at his disposal in his later years he

Figure 6.20 Wilton House, Wiltshire: engraved later 18th century, west prospect from the Bridge of Communication or dam based on Richard Wilson's painting at Wilton. Michael Symes Collection.

is concerned with *grasses*, rarely then, or subsequently, allowed to be a fond subject for gardeners. At Wilton, and at the Great Bridge, all is at hand . . . the Meadows, the improved river-scape, the elegant parterre-gardens, the invitation to remember the ancient greats and the incorporation, or at the least a glimpse, of Arcadia.

7 *Furor hortensis*

A designed landscape is not necessarily the work of studied informality based on natural forms and made in the mid-18th century in England. An English Landscape Garden is what normally comes to mind when such a work is mentioned, and Lancelot Brown's design from 1750 (Stroud 1950 [1975] 57) at Croome Court, Worcestershire, is most indicative of that type. Therefore, precisely when and how such works of art came to be created is central to our subject. This has been so since Horace Walpole's essay "History of the Modern Taste in Gardening" in his *Anecdotes of Painting* of 1780. There he credits William Kent as first having the wit to see and the talent to lead and cause all to leap the fence and to see all nature as a garden and from the twilight of imperfect essays establish the English Landscape Garden. This early testimony has been taken as complete, and for many it remains acceptable. In the context of its wide history and critical overview of all visual arts in England it was a cogent explanation of how the then current and fashionable manner of laying out grounds at a large scale had come about. It was simple, elegantly put and for its time entirely convincing. However in the period from 1730 it is increasingly rare to find a *canal*. This is replaced by a Serpentine or a River; *basins* similarly become Pieces of Water, Ponds or Lakes. With some curious exceptions *Avenues* disappear. Finally and rather reluctantly even the *Parterre*, having grown vastly in size gives up its primacy about mid-century. Fields have become the prominent element in design.

Robert James Petre, Lord Petre (1713–1742), whose career as a designer is confined to the 1730s, never gave up a commitment to formality in his elements and compositions. His parterres, still very highly elaborate at Thorndon, Essex, from the early 1730s, and at Worksop, Nottinghamshire, in 1737, were simpler and more like what was becoming known as *lawn*. Lord Petre's career, sadly cut short by smallpox, raises many questions while showing a designer of exceptional, and quite singular, talent. He was only slightly older than Horace Walpole and that group of young men who came to prominence in the 1740s and 1750s, and yet a cursory glance at his designs might suggest a man much older. Even more curious is that these large scale designs were combined with his use of plants at the smallest scale, rarely used as a mass, and always live to their individual qualities. Petre was utterly committed to plant materials, and what had heretofore been developed with a rather restrained palette of plants he exploits with as many new species as he could find. And as protégé of Philip Miller, and of Richard Bradley and John Martyn, professors of botany at Cambridge, he was tutored by the best and most advantageously placed plantsmen of his day. And, far from least, he was in close correspondence with both Peter Collison and John Bartram in the American colonies, who sent him prodigious quantities of specimens and seeds. As his open spaces were very large and in perception therefore diffuse, his closed quarters, or negatives, turn out on inspection to be botanically very rich: he appears to have been just on the point of exploiting that area of development when he died. Had he lived longer, given his talent, position and wealth, and the distinction of his teachers, designed landscapes may very well have taken a different turn in the 1740s.

As a botanist, and as a designer using plants, Petre shows exceptional talent, and as Collison remarked of his work it was like "painting with living pencils" (quoted in Chambers 2008). However, in his designs the open spaces are very great, and wonderfully complex and varied, and he appears to be master at this scale as well. This quality may owe something, perhaps much, to his amanuensis, or draughtsman, or possibly his partner Pierre Bourguignon, an alias of H-F Gravelot (1699–1773). Gravelot, a sometime pupil of Francois Boucher, was established in London between 1733 and 1745. When he left London he was suspected of being a spy for the French government. It is he who may be credited with introducing the *rococo* taste to London through his large output as an engraver for illustrated books and printed music. He also taught drawing in London, where he was a friendly colleague of artists such as William Hogarth. As Peter, or simply Sieur, Bourguignon it was Gravelot who made the plan of the large, and detailed, design of Thorndon, Essex, for Petre in 1732. Since it was first published as one of the earliest efforts of the Garden History Society (Clutton and Mackay 1970) the Thorndon design has always struck me as extraordinary and also slightly peculiar. That account was a most thorough one, and set the standard of what we expect such articles to contain. However, it was unable to give more information about its maker beyond "Sieur Bourguingion Surveyor", and his identity has remained without further resolution. Sir Roger Clutton and Colin Mackay suggested then that he acted as a draughtsman for young Lord Petre, and I am inclined to believe that to be true for the Thorndon and Worksop plans (Clutton and Mackay 1970).

In 1735 Gravelot made a similarly large and detailed plan for Sir Thomas Lister's landscape at Gisbourne, Lancashire. It is smaller but also considerably simpler. Whereas Thorndon looks as if it might have contained every possible element and variation then used, or imagined, Gisbourne has more the character of a fully digested and developed design. It too is clearly signed as "Designed by P Bourguignon 1735". In French *designed* means "drawn"; in English it usually means "conceived and gestated" and may also mean drawn: Stephen Switzer meant both when signed his plan for Beaumanor thus. What did Gravelot-Bourguignon mean? Is this an example of Gravelot-Bourguignon acting by himself, or has Petre's amazing exuberance cooled in two years? The question arises also because of that scheme's uncanny resemblance to Switzer's contemporary manner, and had it not borne another's signature I might have proposed it as one of Switzer's works, especially since Lister appears in the subscriber list of the *Practical Husbandman and Planter* as one of the improvers.

While the Gisbourne scheme has more crisp and courtly features in the outer, or "landscape", parts, it also uses elements and compositions in the way that Switzer had in the Nostell Priory design. But there is a further, and much more significant, matter to observe about Gisbourne, and that arises because of the happy survival of a pair of paintings John Harris has attributed to Robert Griffier (Harris 1995 68–69). The first of these shows the landscape before its improvement, while the second shows it with the "Bourguignon" design in place. It is an elevated, or bird's-eye, view, but taken from an angular rather than any axial view point. This shows just how at Gisbourne it

Furor hortensis 233

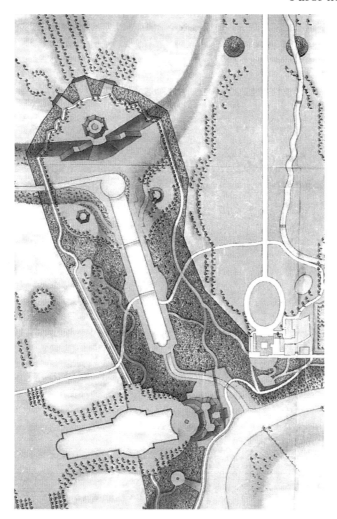

Figure 7.1 Gisbourne, Yorkshire/Lancashire: Peter Bourguignon's design for the grounds, ca 1735. Yorkshire Archaeological Society, Leeds, MS918.

is already the *landscape* that not only is dominant but is the noticeable, or perceived, aspect. There are the crisp earthworks, and the blocks of plantings in orderly groups, as the design drawing had shown, but the viewer needs to look for them, as it were to tease them out from the overall impression. These design elements have very obviously ceased to carry the visual punch we would anticipate. It has become not so much how the landscape has been designed as how it is perceived.

A design for Formack (now Formark) House, Derbyshire, by an unidentified designer, indeed tentatively ascribed as perhaps by Bourguignon in its official archival reference, has a similar resonance. It is entirely designed with geometric elements. It further undermines our idea of designs in the period developing away from formal elements towards more informal ones. Formark is clearly intended to be a landscape garden, but it is made up, with the notable exception of a somewhat informal and

234 Furor hortensis

very shallow "valley", almost entirely of elements which are unabashedly geometric. It is undated, perhaps as early as 1737 (Derby Archives), but possibly from sometime early in the following decade. There is a vestige of a major axis of parade and figure in parkland, and one expects its northern end to be a parade adjacent to the house: however, although close to the house, and an important element, it is designed to be formally unrelated.

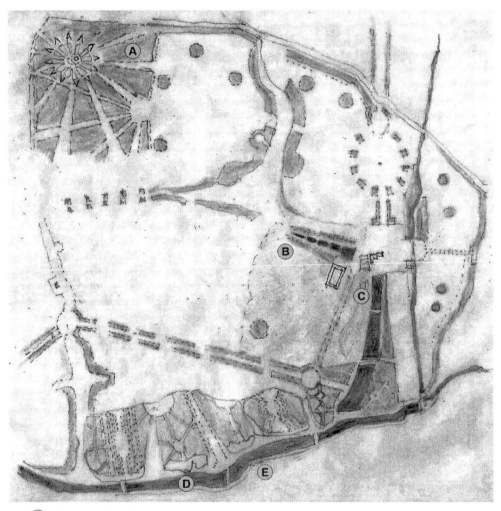

- (A) Fortress Woodland
- (B) The Alderie
- (C) Open Woodland and Wooded Garden
- (D) Anchor Church
- (E) New River (tributary to the Trent)

Figure 7.2 Formark, Derbyshire: plan of the grounds based on an anonymous design for the grounds, ca 1737 (north to bottom). Image by the author. Reproduced courtesy of Derbyshire Record Office, D5054/26/1.

It has similarities with Exton, but in a curious recollection of the problem in the design proposed by William Talman and George London at Castle Howard 35 years earlier it seems as if the lawn, like the forecourt a large roughly rectangular area, has become the centre of the design. Although it contains the house, that appears almost as an afterthought. The north-south axis noted above passes through (nearly on centre) to be carried on *both* as a large rectangular field-park *and* as a series of rectangular ponds making their irregular way towards the river-like canal skirting the northern edge of the grounds and leading to the Trent. A new house in the Palladian fashion was built in 1759 by William Hirons on this north-south "axis", so its siting might have been anticipated when the landscape design was made. However, a similar lack of clarity about the significance of an axis, and its employment in otherwise mature informal landscape designs, also occurs elsewhere.

The east "axis" is formed by another series of curved ponds and cascades which fall in their wooded enclosure from the informal valley mentioned above. The bulk of the Formark grounds is made up of parkland with lines of trees marking divisions and decorated with clumps, but these are circular, and their arrangement still betrays an orthogonal imagination. The existing valley is defined by wooded edges with walks and clearings. At the south-east corner of the park is a large woodland with numerous walks centred on an elaborate star-like feature. A series of six grove-gardens forms a boundary between the canalized tributary to the Trent as an extension to Formark's

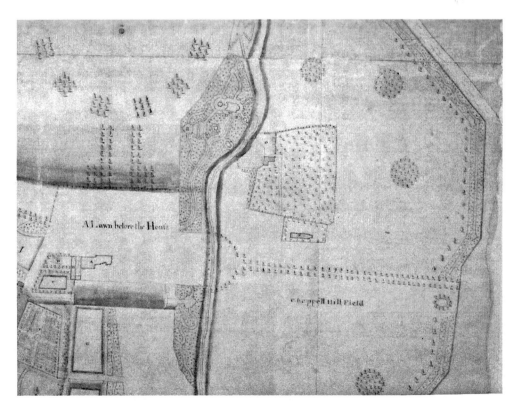

Figure 7.3 Formark, Derbyshire: detail from an anonymous design for the grounds (north to bottom). Reproduced courtesy of Derbyshire Record Office, D5054/26/1.

more canal-like waters. Each is laid out on individual bluffs, and each has its variation on a formal centre. The real surprise of Formark is here revealed, for these groves, very much part of the nature of the rest of the design, introduce a series of distant views over the flat estuarine-like landscape of the course of the Trent. This visual surprise is pleasing, and its associational values are many and strong. It is the site of cliffs of eroded stone making a very big grotesque "object" in which the famous Anchor Church is sited, and soon celebrated in the painting by Thomas Smith of Derby, and published by François Vivares as one of the earliest of picturesque views. But, just as with the contemporary estate at Hawkstone, laid out for another of Switzer's *improvers*, Sir Rowland Hill, it is as yet not integrated into the design as a whole.

All parts of the scheme are clearly designed to *humour its site* and would provide precisely the kind of delights to be seen at Stowe. The Formark design is clearly a landscape garden, and it can be said to follow the dictates Alexander Pope had urged in his *Epistle to Burlington*, but its employment of geometric elements makes it appear very curious. Also curious is the prominent serpentine valley, lower ground that is really little more than a swale, which divides the design into two pretty nearly equal parts. It is obvious, and has had much thought applied to its design, and yet it seems to be uncelebrated. The same is true of the marvellous rock formations among the northern edge, which are celebrated, but in such a very unusual manner. The major elements in the composition, typical of a landscape garden, are the fields, and these carry the design. They are here recognized for all their potential variety, as each carries its name – Lawn, Field, Park or Heath. Yet, like the serpentine and like the rocks,

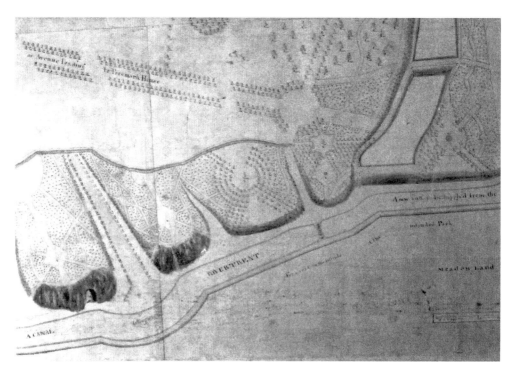

Figure 7.4 Formark, Derbyshire: detail from an anonymous design for the grounds, showing escarpment above the River Trent (north to bottom). Reproduced courtesy of Derbyshire Record Office, D5054/26/1.

Figure 7.5 Formark, Derbyshire: the Anchor Church, engraved view by Thomas Smith of Derby and François Vivares, from a painting of 1745 (north to left). Yale Center for British Art.

there is no recognition of the implications we would expect. The lines dividing the landscape come largely from the lanes connecting to neighbouring estates.

Fields

The most celebrated early *bringing in* of the countryside to a garden appears to have been at Stowe when the Home Park was first addressed by Charles Bridgeman's Ha Ha enclosing his early work at Stowe, then from 1726 bypassed and then "captured" as pasture, and finally by 1731 partly flooded with its Eleven Acre Bottom. This is the scene in about 1723 when it appeared in the foreground of one of Bridgeman's first views of it. The highly polished if wooded shrub-gardens were defined by terrace walks, incidentally, and doubtless with humour intended, "defended from attack" by beasts by the military form of the Ha Ha. These two inner lines met obliquely at a bastion, on which John Vanbrugh's Queen's Temple was soon built, and opposite to it Kent's Temple of Venus was added by 1732 on the south-west bastion of the extended grounds. As a pasture the Home Park and Eleven Acre Bottom was tamed and made a rough but still suitable adjunct to the more polished parts of the scheme. In these extensions Bridgeman takes his initial treatment of the grounds and uses his version of the half-terrace to define a new western edge and then a new southern edge of the enlarged grounds. Then Bridgeman sets up a wide and open but still very much directed view, essentially focused on the south-west corner of an extended garden. This scene has the pastoral foreground defined by forest trees in blocks, except for an avenue along the edge of the water, which is broken to reveal the wooded bastion in the distance reflected in the lake. It is theatrical, perhaps even picturesque, but so far as is known without any narrative message. Its theatrical visual power is equally potent in reverse, or from the variety of other "view points", and also in a new theatricality to be experienced *along* the terrace walks.

Like the gravel-pit in Kensington Gardens, Eleven Acre Bottom in Home Park was big, ugly and relatively useless, and it could not be ignored. As Switzer recognized the opportunities the gravel-pit offered so it fell to Bridgeman to work a similar magic at Stowe. The full implications of it took a while to be understood. The flooding part is doubtless the origin of Pope's compliment (noted above), which Bridgeman took exception to as a tease. There were also other opportunities to accomplish a similar development of what was central to Switzer's method and which he had advocated that everybody should adopt. Stowe was the "Work to Wonder At" (Alexander Pope *Epistle to Burlington* 1731 7). It was noticed, and it was expensive and marvellous, and so illustrated, and talked about enough to be celebrated.

It was a brilliant solution to what had appeared an insoluble situation. It had the effect of resolving Lord Cobham's grounds on the west side, but it also had an unlooked for effect. Despite Switzer's mention of Stowe as being one of the places where *utile* and *dulci* had been combined, it can be seen as the step which, although it brings the countryside into a garden, stops the development of great gardens in the direction

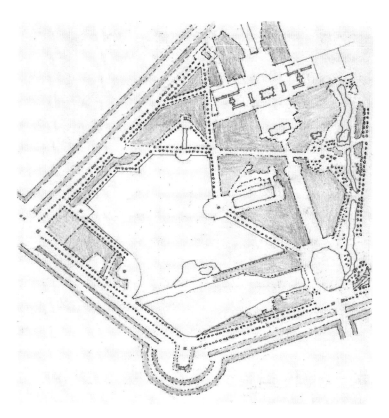

Figure 7.6 Stowe House, Buckinghamshire: plan of the gardens with Elysian Fields, based on Sarah Bridgeman's plan of 1739 (north to west). Image by the author.

Switzer had pointed out as most suitable for these islands . . . the easy and free mingling of fields and gardens together. Instead of *utile* and *dulci* being mixed in gardens, for the next 20 years or so Stowe will develop towards what appears to be acceptance of Switzer's *Ichnographia Rustica*, but the gardens become more and more natural, while remaining essentially gardens rather than the designed landscapes Switzer had advocated. These distinctions about very similar things become important when the new fashion has been identified, and becomes codified in the 1760s. Then a tendency to favour perfected garden ground and differentiate it from the common workaday farms and farmyards begins. But until about 1750 design trends continue in the contending experimental phase.

Although Switzer singled out these gardens for praise in 1727 as being similar to Riskins and to Dawley, where fields had been enclosed by hedges and made part of the gardens (*KG* 422), as it developed subsequently Stowe took on the character more of the large garden, rather than an estate mixed with gardens. Its owner was in no doubt that it was a large garden he wished to make. What Switzer had written about and advocated was an estate, not necessarily actually larger than a garden, such as Stowe, but still an estate – that is, a place where all the functions for comfortable country life were arranged, by design, to make an *Extensive Garden*, or a *Forest Garden*. The productive parts and the polished or ornamental parts, the *utile* and the *dulci*, were allowed their spaces and natures, but the whole was made to function as an estate, and perhaps hopefully it would become a "pretty landskip".

Rhual was such a place. Of a similar size, and initially similar also to the intentions of its owners, Colonel James Dormer, and Robert Dormer, was Rousham, Oxfordshire. Dormer had begun his improvements in the 1720s. The state of the grounds then is shown on a survey of 1721 (Martin 1984a 16). The New Garden shown at the corner above the River Cherwell was a large wilderness in the sense Switzer had identified in his Paston commentary. Another plan of the New Garden, showing much detail, is in the Gough Collection at Oxford: this has been dated to about 1725 and appears to record Bridgeman's additions. It is as Peter Willis has it "Bridgemannick" (Willis 2002 67). Then, from 1738 to 1741, Kent revised the grounds and added ornamental buildings to them, and wings to the house, as well as furnishings inside (Colvin 1978 493). This is the bare chronology of a most important site for the history of designed landscape. There is an abundant literature on Rousham's landscape: from Christopher Hussey (Hussey 1967 147 et seq) to the recent splendid summation by Susan Weber and her colleagues (Weber 2014).

A critical element of Rousham's collaborative design history, I think *the* critical element, is the treatment of the Warren. This 13 acre field has always been a fundamental part of Rousham, contiguous and in full view of the entrance, house and gardens, but it has never had the recognition it warrants. It has always been a (somewhat) civilized adjunct to the Rousham scene, but just when can we date its conceptual *inclusion* in the gardens? Before 1721 there was a line of trees there parallel to the house-gardens array, and most likely used as a walk: similarly, the spur leading to the New Garden, and the New Garden's border with it, had then what appears to be walks along the edges of the Warren (see above at Whetham). Certainly the Bridgemannick plan shows a half-terrace walk there, and by Kent's time the Dying Gladiator had been set up there to be seen against the backdrop of the Warren, and he is credited with the Gate, and the castellated refuge for visitors (perhaps remodelled from a doo'cot) has been added, giving a point of architectural interest to the far side. Thus, we may choose a prospective date from this 30 year period of "Leaping the Fence", which Walpole credited to Kent alone. It is the *inclusion* of this field that made the Rousham design possible, and its *celebration* by Kent indeed inevitable. His other contributions, the reworking of the ponds as Venus' Vale, the Cold Bath and Rill, Praeneste and the distant Mill and eye-catcher outside the grounds, all ornament this significant step.

Lord Cobham acquired the other half of his grounds from his reluctant but doubtless canny neighbour in 1733 and immediately set about exploiting the new areas by using the major cross axis, the Lime Walk, which crossed the principal, north-south axis near the parish church. The wooded ground immediately east of his main axis was already his, and the embellishment of this thin gut of stream and scrubby wood adjacent to the old highway is by Kent, and one of his earliest essays, apparently working in conjunction with Bridgeman. The much larger ground beyond it, Hawkwell Field, became the eastern companion piece to the Home Park, and Bridgeman laid it out in similar basic manner before his death in 1738. He provided three large bastions, clearly to receive ornamental buildings, and a wooded terrace walk around the whole, matching its companion from the 1720s on the west side.

The site of Kent's work was already occupied by the kitchen garden for the house, the parish church and the old road. At that point he made a new centre, a largish, irregularly circular cabinet at the end of the Lime Walk, overlooking the still straggling stream. This Kent developed into a kind of woodland glade water garden. At the heart of this part, just south of the church, to the south side of the new centre, he sited the Temple of Ancient Virtue, and from it the ground falls away steeply to the east, and rather more gently to the south. This is a serious building, one of the noblest by Kent, and its tall cella stands on a high base behind the colonnade, which supports a lowish dome. Its seriousness sets the tone for what became the Elysian Fields. It is here that narrative is introduced into the garden design.

The Lime Walk comes from the then well-known and cheerful part of the gardens, the large wooded wilderness that Bridgeman and Vanbrugh had started with, as it were the World, and provides an easy Broad Way. At Ancient Virtue, to the right, is an open view across water to another monument, the Temple of British Worthies, and beyond that Hawkwell Field, a suggestion of Paradise? To the left is the church (lightly screened) and the Grenville Monument, whereas to the right, in ruin (and long gone), was a monument to Modern Virtue, said by some to have been the rump half of Sir Robert Walpole. Straight ahead the way is blocked by close plantation. To reach Paradise (Hawkwell Field) it is necessary to take a Narrow Way whose circuitous path leads by the church to the River Styx (as the Alder is here named). As reminders of other, or pagan, spiritual guidance Kent provides there a composed long view up the *river*, passed an island towards the *Egerian Spring* housed in a grotto. Off to the right, beyond a Cold Bath was the Chinese House, standing (1737–1750) at the end of Thanet Walk on one of Bridgeman's new bastions. By the church and the Narrow Way at the River Styx visitors could cross to the Temple of British Worthies by way of the Fountain of the Seasons, and thence into the Thanet Walk along Hawkwell Field.

Whether this narrative came before the design of this part of Stowe, as it was developing, or later is not entirely clear. It balanced an equally full series of plantations and walks with many architectural and sculptural enrichments on the other side of the main axis. It is much looser as a composition, but it is still very much a garden. While the narrative fulfils its purpose and gives an added pleasure to the experience of visiting it, it is hardly necessary to it. In the period of its making Stowe was an exceptionally busy place with many visitors as strangers, plus many friends and family. Reactions and advice came from both groups, and no one seems to have been reticent to pass judgement on the works. Lord Cobham fell out with Robert Walpole over policy in 1732, and retired from his administration. Cabinet government was very new in those days, and in the centuries since such fallings-out within a party may be major news, but are hardly unexpected. It is difficult to gauge whether the falling-out was critical constitutionally. It certainly did not compel Cobham to back the Pretender in 1745, nor stop him from defending his part of the country when it appeared in imminent danger. Besides, the satire is pretty mild. The beneficial reflection gloomy places can bring forth had been recommended by Switzer, and used by him too, but always in a rather generalized if not positively vague way. The nature of the cabinets, walks and places of Stowe appears to have been always cheerful heretofore, so relative gloom would be welcome, simply as a contrast. And of course it is the vagueness that brings the power, as at the contemporary Alfred's Hall at Cirencester. One has to pause and reflect, and if one is suitably receptive then beneficial thoughts might come. Certainly the sight of a handsome memorial to heroes across water from a shady grove, with more open and pleasantly laid out fields beyond, would have been, and indeed remains, attractive.

If it were Paradise that is glimpsed from the Temple of Ancient Virtue it is hinted at only, and the way into it is not obvious. But once one has the way into Hawkwell Field such designation is replaced by the general feelings associated with a well-cultivated and well-planted, very large and formally indeterminate space adorned by handsome building. Hawkwell balanced the Home Park of the west side, and in the 1730s it is also similarly enclosed; that is, there were terrace walks around it separating field and walk by continuous Ha Ha. Only James Gibbs' Temple of Friendship occupying the south-east bastion is shown on the plan of 1739. It was soon followed by the nearby Palladian Bridge, actually part of the encircling walk and initially open only on its Hawkwell Field side. Gibbs' Gothic Temple (incidentally also credited with picking up elements of the narrative of the Elysian Fields, such as Gothic signifying Liberty and Thanet Walk in honour of early Saxons) was built on the east side in 1744–1748. The northern parts of Hawkwell Field were soon to be realized under the direction of Cobham working with Lancelot Brown.

The incorporation of fields into designs, or the reliance on them to carry the design idea, can be seen also in three famous early essays in what became called the English Landscape Garden, all in Worcestershire – The Leasowes, Enville and Hagley (Symes and Haynes 2010). They were famous because they were so often visited; so often visited, not least because of their qualities, but also because they were conveniently close together and because they were the subject of cheap and easily obtained guidebooks of the kind recently pioneered by Benton Seeley's *Stowe*; visited also because of the growing esteem for the poet William Shenstone, seemingly the sole author of The Leasowes. An examination of the genesis of their designs might help further enlighten this otherwise murky transitional period.

The aspect they all share is the reliance for their appeal, and the objects of their creators were the development of the design of *fields*. At Enville the park and arable areas detached from a sophisticated formal garden of the kind Switzer or Bridgeman might have proposed become the sole areas of improvement. In other words, with the grounds adjacent to the house satisfactorily in order, the farm begins to be ornamented. At The Leasowes, largely for personal and circumstantial reasons, Shenstone

242 Furor hortensis

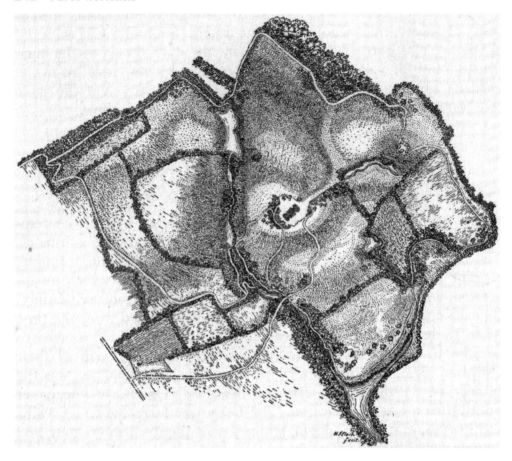

Figure 7.7 The Leasowes, Shropshire: plan of the grounds in 1745 by H F Clark, 1943. Courtesy of the Clark Family.

was able *only* to garden and farm in the same place and time, and on a moderate scale, and he produced probably the most famous *ferme ornée* of all.

Shenstone was of an age to be ready to seize any opportunity to design a landscape. His position in history is fortunate: coming of age in the late 1730s allowed him to appreciate what might be done, in the context of even by then a fairly general rural improvement, both from the point of view of public policy and good government and also from the point of view of what was becoming fashionable. He also had the best personal qualities to add to his good education; he was quiet, indolent, poetic and sociable. He inherited a farm of about 200 acres, and an income of £300 per annum (about £90,000 current value). Therefore, he was not rich, but not so far from rich as to make landscape making possible only as a garden designer, or a professor. He was rich enough to keep a farm, and improve it according to his taste, but not rich enough to do much more, certainly not to be extravagant nor to make elaborate monuments: if he had been inclined to marry he might have found his heiress to make greater improvements possible.

However, by the mid-1740s he had made his *ferme ornée*, using that term in 1746. His beginning in 1741 was at the edge. On high ground at the north-east corner of

The Leasowes on a kind of natural terrace he planted a wooded walk with a temple dedicated to Pan at its north end. From here a prospect of much of his place was open to view and contemplation. In the middle of that prospect was the house, seen across several descending fields on wooded ground rising above a stream. It had a pool at its wooded west end, but more noticeable is a larger wood along the eastern stretch of the stream in the bottom fold of The Leasowes. This area becomes the site of his Virgil's Grove of 1743. That view is characteristic of the many he managed to make, by embellishment certainly, but mostly by the establishment of a *point of view*, usually a simple stopping place, perhaps with a seat, inscription or further elaboration. A roughly circular walk is threaded through the farm, picking up many such points of view. Whatever route it pleased him to take would make its own senses, perhaps narratives, but Shenstone's circuit had yet to become systematized in his mind. That would come, of course, and sadly it came about because people wished to visit, had little time or were lazy and were anxious not to miss something, so, instead of looking, they followed the approved route. Visitors to Rousham suffered a similar snare, not surprisingly perpetuated by the gardener, whose preferred route for showing Kent's grounds soon became the *only* way to see them (see Batey 1983).

Shenstone's farm was hilly, good for landscape making, as he could easily have vistas, and the agreeable mix of woodland and arable field made it possible especially for an Oxford educated poet to conjure scenes from Virgil, or at least redolent of antiquity. His walks about the farm called forth reflections for him which he reduced to lines of poetry, and in due course had them inscribed giving power of association of ideas to scenes, perhaps otherwise taken for being simply a pleasant prospect. The woodlands which occur in farmed land, between fields, often in places difficult to cultivate could become, to Shenstone's learned imagination, places like Virgil's Grove. Urns, with inscriptions dedicated to friends or heroes, would enliven a walk otherwise without resonance, as could small pieces of sculpture, perhaps a Faun to remind him and his visitors of a passage from literature. Of course associationism, despite good trials, could never be precise beyond a general mood, and even then it was a limited way to give meaning to landscape. And some visitors to The Leasowes after Shenstone's death regretted that without the genius of the place, it was hardly better than a walk in the woods. His place, with Hagley and Enville, was much frequented in the mid-18th century, and genuinely admired, for Shenstone's inability to use the power of architectural ornament that Cobham employed at Stowe obliged him to provide it himself. And that is basically what he did, passing on his method in his very well-regarded *Unconnected Thoughts on Gardening*; he was also in demand from his neighbours and friends for help with their own grounds, and approbation for what they proposed.

We know about The Leasowes because of Shenstone's *Unconnected Thoughts*, because of the comments of his friends and because of the fame of his place, and the consequent publications and comment which followed. His best work, that is, The Leasowes, became the subject of codification by Thomas Whately, who in his *Observations* attempted to define what it was so that it might be imitated. Attempts to define just what a *ferme ornée* is, or was, continue to concern those searching for an answer (Symes and Haynes 2010). What Switzer meant by it is abundantly clear, a weaving together of garden and farm to make a new kind of place. His voluminous writings from 1715 to 1742 covered the matter from all aspects. To what extent he was understood by his contemporaries may be somewhat less clear. He had various

Figure 7.8 The Leasowes, Shropshire: *The Grove*, by William Shenstone, ca 1753, from his *Poems*, inscribed in 1754 and presented to Mary Cutter, MS with watercolours by author. Wellesley College, EPC image 50, Special Collections 63612080. With permission of Special Collections, Wellesley College Library, Wellesley MA, USA.

names for his kind of garden design, *ferme ornée* being only one of them. The term was used in the mid-18th century in a rather light-hearted, even self-deprecating, manner, and it described really an attitude to appreciation as much as it described a thing. Shenstone as a young man, even an educated one, appears to have used the term without realizing it already had a history, in fact and in implication going back a generation, and even that was based on ancient wisdom and precept. If Shenstone knew that Charles Hamilton at Painshill and Philip Southcote at Wooburn had also made what he called a *ferme ornée*, he did not know that Switzer had also written about it, and designed several, if not many. That is quite extraordinary, especially as his remarks about "Ruinated Places" in *Unconnected Thoughts* are most Switzeresque. They will not be the first, and certainly not the last, young men of fashion to be ignorant of the obvious.

It may be true that by the late 1730s the predisposition to appreciate landscape, to *make a pretty landskip out of one's possessions,* as *The Spectator* had it, had become so accepted in these islands as to be almost universal. By the 1740s as is abundantly clear from John Rocque's 1746 *An Exact Survey of London* (Rocque 1746) that the suburbs of London contained many pocket landscapes. At usually much less than 20 acres they are too small to count with Switzer, but for their creators many of these approach the status of *ferme ornée*. Pope's house at Twickenham was very well known at the time, and remains famous with students of literature. From the evidence that Rocque shows (unlike the contemporary plan published by John Serle) not only was it a diminutive Cirencester, but its kitchen gardens were equally large. Curiously, unlike nearby Riskins, Pope formally kept his *utile* separate from, if contiguous to, the *dulci* parts, although, since they are two halves of the same thing, it is certain he frequented one as often as the other. Pope was the hero Horace Walpole wished to emulate when he acquired a small house and grounds nearby and renamed it Strawberry Hill. Famous for its early exploration of Gothic revival, his grounds were meant to be as up-to-date as he could make them, and as the chief critic and historian of what he called *Modern Gardening* who could be better? Walpole employed his 5 acres, ultimately expanded to 14, of flat rectangular ground facing onto the Thames in a perfect suburban *landskip*, very likely the first. The north-west edge contains his long, skinny but marvellous *Gothick* confection of a house, which generated more than enough visual associations for the gardens. Along the west and south sides he planted a wooded belt, which, if exceptionally thin, was still most effective. That left a large, if rectangular, lawn, and that Walpole managed to conjure into three zones of *park* by rough diagonal divisions. The east side contained the continuously moving scene of the Thames with its passing traffic against the wooded Surrey bank. But here all is *dulci*, with *utile* banished.

Shenstone had a neighbour who married an heiress to reinforce an already funded viscountcy at Enville, or at Hagley a courtier to whom the Prince of Wales made a gift of a monumental column complete with a statue, and whose father had an office whose income produced enough extra wealth to build the new house. Thus, sometimes commentators speak of his position almost with pity, but Shenstone, by any objective judgement, will be thought the luckiest of men. His life is pictured in the favourite day-dream poem of the century, *The Choice*, as a life of civilized indolence and lack of care. Walpole was the son of the first prime minister, and cannot have had an especially happy boyhood, and his father was not only powerful but a rich Norfolk landowner and well connected to others similarly placed. Young Walpole's life was more sociable than Shenstone's, and he was a remarkably generous correspondent. He was critically interested in the arts, loved gossip and seems to have been fascinated with people, especially fashionable and powerful ones and all their doings. There is little about the *taste* of the mid to later 18th century that Walpole does not have views about, and usually an interesting story to tell as well. With these two, and their similarly placed friends, the making of landscapes is widened from the landed and very powerful, Switzer's *Noblemen* and *Gentlemen*, that is, men of power and wealth and a secure landed position in society and government, to include their second sons and nephews, ministers of the Church of England, poets and some school-masters. As the *ferme ornée* had been a slight joke heretofore, a convenient bolt-hole or second seat near London for Bathurst, or a toe-hold for recently disgraced great men such as Lord Bolingbroke, or entry-level introduction to English country life for Lord Glenorchy (Jacques 1983), with Southcote at Wooburn and then Shenstone and others it becomes an end in itself, a delight to aspire to. From their time, and largely through their example and works, others even less well-off will soon begin to want a little place and a garden to make into a pretty *landskip*.

Of Hagley we know hardly anything of the grounds adjacent to the old house, an even earlier and slightly more modest relic of olden times than Enville. Whatever the nature of these the design focus at Hagley lay in the outlying fields, which like those of its neighbours were hilly, leading to upland grounds, varied and amenable more to pasturage than cultivation. This is where the Lyttletons, first Sir Thomas, and shortly and more famously his son George, begin to ornament their fields and start to call them *lawns*. Their improvements in the 1730s and 1740s were not only in advance of their closer neighbours, but at the same time even in advance of their more fortunate kinsman (brother-in-law and uncle) Lord Cobham. He is ornamenting the fields of his longed for successful acquisition of the other half of Stowe, and is doubtless an example to admire, if not actually to imitate. Sir Thomas Lyttleton had subscribed to the *Practical Husbandman* papers (and his gardener, Philip Rowley, had ordered four sets), which attests to his continuing interest in developing his grounds: he specifically laid claim to critical parts of Hagley including the Sham Castle and the Cascade in the late 1740s. However, his son George was also much involved in the period from 1735 when Frederick, Prince of Wales with exceptional generosity gifted the column in commemoration of himself. If these were not sufficiently knowledgeable contributors to engender the famous scheme there is also Pope (whose field, Pope's Lawn, was originally home to the Prince's gift) but also Shenstone, similarly honoured nearby, and James Thomson, whose *Seasons* was revised to include a section in praise of Hagley. No designed landscape (apart perhaps from Stowe) has had the benefit of quite so many distinguished potential true begetters (see Symes and Haynes 2010 101–111). Indeed, William Pitt, more famous for his parliamentary career, was also active in advising at these.

What is abundantly clear is that Hagley, whatever might still have existed near the old house, was not the kind of design that was drawn up beforehand, even in the seeming negligent manner Kent had employed. Someone doubtless made the string of ponds which is to become the *spine* of the design. That feature is necessary for the scheme but does not generate it. Rather, all parts take their qualities from the association of ideas they bring forth, and the placement of ornaments within the fields of this hilly and irregular part of the estate. It was close enough to the old house and its grounds for easy access, but owed nothing to them formally. It was not even on axis: indeed, when the new house was built, the Prince's Column was re-sited to form a strong axial relationship between it and the centre of the main front, rather suggesting a *return* to the old goose-foot scheme of radiating axes, in which the view to the Theseus temple balances the view to the bottom of the cascade-ponds sequence.

The Lyttletons may have followed Cobham's scheme for the Elysian Fields, as did perhaps the Burdetts of Formark in their *Alderie*, maybe Lord North at Wroxton too, but I think not. The precise date of the cascades and the associated pools is unknown, but thought to be early: indeed, their management and formation are critical to any serious improvement of this part of the estate, and might therefore be very early indeed. By the 1730s forming a stream in such a manner has become one of the elements any sensitive and up-to-date improver wished to employ. When skilfully managed with well-made walks it could make a very pleasing alternative to the terrace walk, or an axial walk in a parterre. Sensibly, it responded to the nature of Hagley's place. It also made it easy for the imagination of both owner and visitor to be engaged to reference to a scene in an *Eclogue*, or some description of Dryden's or Pope's, or even a scene redolent of a *landscape* picture. In 1749 *The Rotundo* was added at the top of Shenstone's field on the "axis" of the cascades. The first of many images of Hagley which were drawn, then engraved and printed for visitors and other admirers, was this very "scene". The garden-for-walking function has now been removed from the architectural setting of the house as centre and replaced by a more informal and rural one.

And this *new* element also allowed an easy means to visit and enjoy the further, heretofore more rural, parts of the *Extensive Garden*. At Hagley a short detour to the right led into a field division known as Milton's Bank leading to his Seat, while just beyond was Pope's Lawn. Further north was another field or lawn with commemorative reminders of Shenstone. This quite large series of plantations was connected on the southern side by woodland which appears to be a part of an *enfilade* plantation whose walks could always lead back to the house. There also was the site of the famous

Sham Castle, by neighbour and amateur architect Sanderson Miller. This was not only a landmark; it gave shelter and a place to rest, and it also gave colour and a sense of history to the place it graced, in Switzer's sense "in the form of some Antiquated Place". And all these Lawns – North, Castle, Elm Avenue or Thomson's – were also productive fields. At Hagley in the 1750s the *utile* and *dulci* very much obtained in the same place.

Enville is a perfect image of an 18th century layout whose design has come about by accretion. The style and size of the house, which had figured in Robert Plott's *Natural History of Staffordshire* of 1686, clearly would have had a garden of similar stature, not perhaps of the standard London and his partners provided, but still appropriate, and this garden remains at the core of the scheme recorded in the survey of about 1750. This had been augmented earlier in the century, probably in the 1720s, when the woodland with its axial walk, and large cabinet with apsidal extensions, was added. A further wilderness of semi-circular plan finishes the rectangular garden platform, which had a bastion at one corner, and may well have had others: the curious asymmetry of the main walk may or may not be the result of some quirk early in the garden's design life. Another large wilderness, with walks of the exaggerated serpentines sometimes called *Sharawaggi* and later by the French *anglo-chinois*, is on the south-east, and butts against a largish fish pond, like others at Enville curiously rectangular, even to this day. This large geometric and house-friendly ensemble has always sat comfortably within an estate of arable and woodland, with valleys, two with good sized streams, both dammed and providing ponds, all of which rise south of the house into upland pasturage suitable for sheep.

In the late 1730s the young Earl of Stamford moved his wife and growing family back to Enville, and they, like their near neighbours, began improving these grounds outside their garden. And like them they do not appear to have used professional advisers, except in the sense that in their large circle of friends there were many, not least Shenstone and Sanderson Miller, whose advice about landscape and design matters was sought and given with the authority of a professor. Lord Stamford was one of those who early recognized Brown's skills and recommended him for royal appointment (M Brown 2012), and the plan to "naturalize" the shape of the largest of Stamford's rectangular ponds certainly looks like a Brown design, but there is no archival evidence for it (Symes and Haynes 2010 plates 22 and 24). That design was not proceeded with, and the good reason for that is that the nature of the grounds at Enville did not really need Brown's intervention. Apart from the unfashionable shape of his ponds there was no real difficulty to overcome, and Brown was most welcomed and courted by those who did have real problems, such as large scale water management at Burghley, or engineering scale earth and stone reworking at Warwick Castle. The opportunities Enville offered were well within the management and direction of Stamford and his friends and neighbours.

Water

The management of water, generally, underwent great changes in the 1730s. The old fish ponds in Hyde Park had been there since the 15th century, and in 1730 Queen Caroline through Bridgeman began the work which caused these to be remade and joined together to form one lake, always known simply as The Serpentine. Of course its old straight banks remained, and the morphology of strings of ponds also remained, but the continuous turning through something less than a quarter of a circle of the new piece of water struck everyone as novel, and attractive. It was hardly the first made river, or indeed made lake, or properly pond, to be executed in England. There was the New River of the 17th century, of course, and more recently the new rivers at both Hampton Courts: in Herefordshire appropriately rural but irregular in the same manner as The Serpentine, whereas the one in Middlesex was rather more courtly and artful; both are still remarkable.

Lord Bathurst had one too, the rather famous one at Riskins, also of the second decade. But Switzer had never thought it essential, or even advisable, to show the water at Riskins as irregular when he prepared his illustration of it for his *Practical Kitchen Gardener* of 1727. According to Daines Barrington, Bathurst "was the first person who ventured to deviate from the straight line, in a brook which he had widened at Riskins . . . Lord Stafford, who had paid him a visit remarked how little it would have cost, to have made the course of the brook in a straight direction" (quoted in Martin 1984a 73). This was a small, if critical, part of Riskins, rather like the scribbled seeming afterthought still to be seen on an early design drawing for the Blenheim canals (see above Blenheim, figure 1.8). At Riskins the short serpentine arose from a spring grotto in the Menagerie and emptied into the canal head just south-west of where Switzer's *Epitomy* shows the house.

Although many still marvelled at the serpentine river's newness, by the 1730s serpentines were an established element. At Nostell Priory Switzer's "A Serpentine River coming out of Foulby Field" in the park looks pretty much like a real river although its almost parallel banks serpentine perhaps a trifle too much. Kent's contemporary treatment of the Alder within the Elysian Fields (designed to be seen up and down, that is, within the river, rather than from an elevated distant prospect) is similarly artful: rougher and more changeful in the Styx part, gentler in the Worthies and lower parts. It needs to be remembered that even to manage the edges of a stream requires much work and judgement, to dig a new one significantly more, and to alter the shape of a big body of water requires work of an engineering scale.

The design of Castle Kennedy, Dumfries-shire, is contemporary with Nostell Priory, and shares many of its characteristics. We know from Lord Cathcart's gossipy diary that Lord Stair was teased at court for employing his dragoons to carry out the digging works in his garden. He had plenty of soldiers to choose from, not only his veterans from Marlborough's time, but the best of the current army too. As he had fallen out with Walpole, so had Cobham and many more, and similarly both retired to make their gardens before their recall: in Stair's case to became Commander in Chief at Dettingen, and Cobham also answered his call to duty at Vigo. Stair's troops' efforts do not figure even on General Roy's very detailed survey of Scotland carried out for the Crown from 1746, but further details consistent with the layout appear in a survey for the works carried out there a century later by J C Loudon. From these we can follow the extraordinary land forms the dragoons made for Stair, well within the skills of men known for field fortification theory and practice, and following the designs perhaps of Switzer or William Boutcher.

Castle Kennedy is sited near the sea at Stranraer between two lochs, the Black and the White (see M Brown 2012 313 et seq). The "gardens" which occupy the isthmus are essentially woodland with major avenues and walks augmented by the marvellous treatments along the water's edge. As the far banks of the lochs are also planted, the water becomes not only the formal generator of the scheme but also its major part. It is as if the garden, playing the role of, for example, Stowe's Home Park, had been captured by the surrounding water. Like Exton or Formark the house sits in open space, originally a large rectangle; by Loudon's time this already large space continued southward to the water's edge, and by a parade also to the north banks. Blocks of forest trees furnished the ground, occasionally cut out into cabinets of various shapes, where it appears the dragoons took it in turn to play variations on themes of field fortification shapes as they might have done as musicians. This is even more celebrated at the water's edges, where the isthmus has been humoured into great curves or sections of straighter walks carrying the encircling double terrace walks separated by banks of sloped grass with ramps in glacis formation leading down to a beach walk. The variations natural to such a scheme give many differing views, but there are also variations in the land forms to make amphitheatres, sometimes distorted in the manner of modernist sculptures.

The easiest, and in many ways the wisest, way to form a new lake, after very careful observation and planning, is to build a dam, and wait for the flooded area to become a lake. This is what Switzer did at Exton. As Rutland is a flat county, to get a decent large piece of water means a long dam, and as the appearance of being made by nature is what is most desired, means have to be found to diminish the dam's prominence. At Exton the length is less critical because the dam is quite low, and had a rocky cascade with a prominent castle-like building always planned as its ornament. Lord North's dam at his new lake at Wroxton Abbey, Oxfordshire, is narrower than at Exton but much higher and therefore rather obtrusive: its bulk and rawness were not commented on as creating a problem at the time. It may well be the case that its early rendition in a print of the 1740s, among the last to be done in the surpassed fashion of one point perspective bird's-eye view, magnifies its artificiality. By the time amateur critics had acquired the skills and habit of free comment and might have condemned it, its equally high and prominent cascade and the associated serpentine run-off stream and grounds below the dam would have settled in, and the scene with its exotic and briefly very fashionable Chinese, and other, follies become familiar. Other pieces of water of these times are also, to later eyes, curiously *unnatural* at a time when the natural is so highly esteemed: yet, for example, no murmur of such discontent has ever been heard about the celebrated lake at West Wycombe, Buckinghamshire, thought to be directed by Robert Greening for Sir Francis Dashwood.

Blenheim, The Lake

To many critics, and historians as well, the lake at Blenheim is synonymous with the perfection of the man-made but natural seeming lake (Colvin 1993 174). I cannot concur with that, and simply note it. From the beginning of Switzer's career the *management* of these waters had been a central problem. And after the great duke's death his widow sought to resolve it. A design for it was published in the third volume of *Vitruvius Britannicus* in 1725, but this was not adopted, and could not have been realized as depicted. But we can observe from the survey made in 1763 that her efforts were largely successful, even if her previous actions to demolish Woodstock Manor had fatally undermined her attempt. In 1729 Switzer had called his reader's attention to it, "to see what a Pitch practical Hydrostacy is arriving to in *England*" (*Hydro* I 14), and may well have been responsible for it himself. In the intervening period, since works were stopped on it back in 1710, the canalized course of the Glyme had been perfected and flowed under the Bridge, connecting the old pond formed by the causeway linking the two sides of the park to the rest of the Glyme in its part canalized and artfully irregular course in the western half of the park. Switzer's Carriage remained in its place also. The lake Switzer referred to, and which John Spyers surveyed was, in fact, this north-eastern section on the Woodstock side of the Bridge, part of which is still called Queen Pool. The Duchess' Lake, like much else at Blenheim, has both a geometric and a picturesque seeming aspect. From the entry gate from Woodstock it will have appeared to be regular, if briefly so. The south bank of Queen Pool, directly opposite visitors on entry, was symmetrical. The old causeway to the left, which Switzer had 20 years before mimicked in his layout of the corresponding section of his water-carriage, becomes part of the "new" big composition whose bow shape is the site of the Old Manor with the Bridge and causeway dominant behind to either side. His old Carriage gives form to the new lake whose edge follows it precisely. The rest of the "lake" is formed of similar big and lazy curves, but in an asymmetrical composition. The "scene" has the clarity and sharp resolution of an early 18th century aesthetic sense, with not even a hint of the coming shaggy manner of the picturesque. There was then one cascade from Queen Pool into Colonel John Armstrong's central canal as the Glyme passed under the big arch of Vanbrugh's Bridge: its neighbouring narrower companion designed for the south now dispensed with, but Switzer's Carriage still running the Bridge and the Engine House there. Thus, maximum impact is achieved with the best style and minimal fuss . . . with no denigration of the Bridge; even the old ruins, had they survived, would have been happily presented.

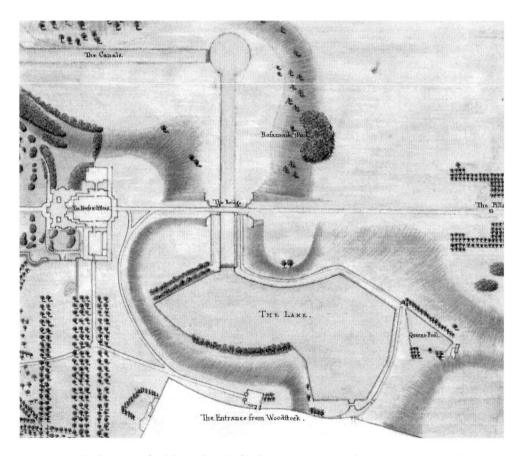

Figure 7.9 Blenheim, Oxfordshire: detail of John Spyers' estate plan, 1763 (north to bottom). Collection Centre Canadien d'Architecture/Canadian Centre for Architecture, Montréal.

In the later 1730s Brown made an early essay in the management of water, and on the Glyme as well. It will likely have been his first design, in 1739 at Kiddington, Oxfordshire. This occurred even before Brown had secured his appointment at Stowe, and appears to have been a chance engagement; although reported as early as 1813 (John Penn quoted in J Brown 2011 34), only recently has its significance been acknowledged. Kiddington lies a few miles north of Blenheim, and on the Glyme, 20 or so years before Brown was induced by the fourth duke, himself only born in that year, to vandalize the design then in place there. Even so this secured for Brown some of his greatest praise. The means he used at Kiddington were strikingly similar. Although the Glyme is a very small river it passes through topography that is quite changeful so that a small dam, and one out of sight, can have a spectacular effect, producing a convincingly natural looking lake. Because of the topography Kiddington's shoreline also shows curves which are a bit more rounded and robust than many contemporaries. To achieve that Brown had to resort to the same device we think Switzer used for the contemporary damming and flooding of the Nadder at Wilton, that is, digging an exaggeratedly curved channel into the far bank, thus leaving a largish island in view. That device, of course, not only makes the lake seem to be bigger with minimum extra digging, but also enhances the nature of the curve of its shoreline. The Kiddington lake is backed, closely, by an enclosing woodland belt, and is sloped from the grounds adjacent to the house by a seemingly natural but very large glacis-like lawn (very similar to the ones discussed above at Blenheim or at Nostell): to what extent Brown had to sculpt this into being we cannot presently say. However, it is clear that any requirement to do so was well within his abilities, and imaginative powers, despite his youth. The lake at Kiddington displays simply the best way to achieve a natural seeming lake in a designed landscape.

Late Parterres

The immediate setting of the house, and with it the ensemble of parterre and forecourt, remained strong, and both owners and designers appear to have been very reluctant to abandon these potent signs of grandeur and status. Even so the matters noticed by Walpole or the journalists of the *Gentlemen's Magazine*, or by the owners and designers themselves, are issues at hand, such as how will the parterre be formed and how defined? There were several steps in the transformation of the parterre. At places like Exton or Formark the parterre has become so large and axially disconnected from the house that it has become already something else, not quite yet a lawn, but very close: this is observable also in Kent's design of the Prince of Wales' gardens at Carlton House, St James', where there is a somewhat indeterminate parterre-like space adjacent to the house. A different treatment which achieves the same effect occurs adjacent to Badminton, Gloucestershire, where in 1750 Thomas Wright proposed an oval parterre-like space defined, similarly to the one at Carlton House, by loose shrubbery (see Laird 1999 127–128). The scale at Badminton is vastly larger, so large as to make its use as a parterre almost redundant. Like Bridgeman's very large and complex shaped axial pool at Kensington the Badminton "parterre" would have been recognized as such because of its still manifest balance about the central axis, whereas its actual shape would be lost. That, very likely, is just what Wright and other designers in this period wished. In fact, closer to the house, the "forecourt" to the great oval lawn/parterre is defined very ambiguously by pairs of groves of standard trees whose regularity is undermined by the ground being ornamented with two very differently serpentine streams. By the time Wright's middle feature in this design is reached, the blocks of woodland shaped as though they are shrubbery but on a much larger scale lie beyond long straight sections of "avenue" defining the broad axis. The composition is finished by an open park with clumps in a circular figure, as at Formark, but as there is also a very strong diagonal slant at the point it is reached, there is a real asymmetry as well.

At Lowther, Westmorland, in 1754 Francis Richardson proposed a modification to the scheme probably designed for the place by Switzer in the early 1730s. His proposal for the parterre and its extensions is a scheme which is both symmetrical and asymmetrical at once. Its symmetry remains, but by composing the lateral edges of the parterre as a series of whiplash curves almost in the manner of the flies in a stage set, the symmetry is undermined, and pleasingly and formally confused, so that its regularity, while recognized, is for all intents and purposes imperceptible. It is also very large, and empty, which also undermines its recognition as parterre. At the same time at Wimpole, Cambridgeshire, the parterre at Robert Harley's old house whose grounds had been laid out by Bridgeman in the 1720s was to be altered for Lord Hardwicke. Greening proposed two schemes to loosen the parterre. In the earlier the west side is to be defined by rather loosely planted singles and small groups of trees, to be "balanced" by similar clumps opposite, augmented by extra and larger closely planted clumps which "pull" the composition eastward; so from a standpoint in the middle of the house, or from the far end of the extended axial composition, symmetry remains, while from every other potential view point it is dispensed with in favour of a loose park-like area of which the old parterre is simply the most western part. His other scheme was less ambitious. It kept the thin gut of woodland against the walls of the west side, but made a bit thicker and arranged in a serpentine/bell shape, augmented with clumps in a Paisley-pattern. This was, very nearly, to be replicated on the opposite side, but with a Ha Ha taking the place of the woodland strip. The decision about which of these to adopt was the subject of some debate. This was doubtless true in most schemes for improvement, but documentation is available here to attest the obvious. Not only was Shenstone's opinion sought, but also that of the gardeners on site (Laird 1999 115). Contemporary with these designs is Brown's for Kirtlington Park, where he employed a recollection of the axial arrangement for the principal front. Although his bell shaped edges of the "parterre" are splayed out to seem like one of his more typical great sweeps, when the whole is seen axially, its other nature becomes clear. This we have also noticed at Stourhead and also at Wallington (above).

The Grecian Valley

Similar concerns impinged on the designs for the last part of Stowe. This was carried on by Lord Cobham in the later 1740s working with Brown, by then seemingly alone in directing Cobham's various projects for the large north-eastern part of the scheme. The parcel to be added was decided simply by extension of the east side of Hawkwell Field northwards until it crossed the line of the old Roman Road, always the north edge of the garden part of the Stowe design. These edges were defined by belts of woodland, exceptionally open at the north-east end, but with Ha Ha terrace walks with bastions to the inside. Thus, a new field of some 60 acres was made. As was always the case with Cobham, buildings played a major role, here the Cobham Monument at the east side is balanced by the Temple of Concord and Victory (so named in

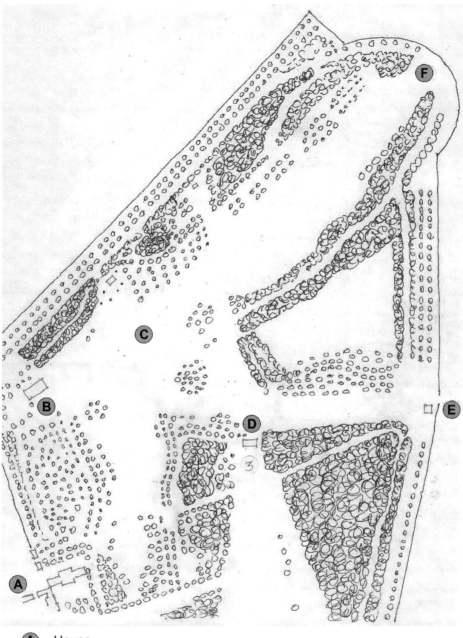

- A House
- B Temple of Concord and Victory
- C Brown's Dig
- D Ladies' Temple
- E Cobham's Monument
- F North-east Bastion, 1st site for Triumphal Arch?

Figure 7.10 Stowe House, Buckinghamshire: plan of the eastern additions, part of Hawkwell Field and Grecian Valley (north to top). Image by the author.

1763) near the house. The back of the Ladies' Temple and various relatively minor architectural ornaments were also to be accommodated. But the exact nature of the quarter is not clear, or, more precisely, various notions about what it could and ought to be seem to have been Cobham's and Brown's preoccupation. The design seems to have been even more than usually at Stowe a matter of experiment.

The winter season of 1746–1747 was when Brown thoroughly surveyed the "farmland and rough paddocks" of the quarter, and began digging and moving some 24,000 loads of earth, to form a great "sweep" planted with laurels, along the top of which Cobham then planned to set a number of statues (Brown 2011 55–56). This sweep was to be formed as part of an oval (a form Brown returned to at Buckingham House as elsewhere but never fully realized). It is not absolutely clear where that feature was to be, and it is sometimes referred to as an amphitheatre (Steenbergen and Reh 2003, 287), but the far east end of the new quarter is likely, and there a large part of it may be discerned from plans of this part of the gardens from 1753. Brown proceeded no further, "thinking that a summer's talk and tryel's about it may make it very fine thing" (Clarke n.d. [1971] 21). But Lady Grey (daughter of Glenorchy of Sugnall; see above) thought it very far from a "fine thing" when she saw it in 1748; her comments also allude to the intention then to have a piece of water between what she called the high banks to either side.

There is an alternative design which we might consider. Brown's reference to the sweep in his note to Lord Cobham was clear to its recipient, but may mislead us over 250 years later. The plan published in 1769 shows something that could be what Lady Grey reported was to became a pond, and also the work to which Brown referred as part of his sweep. Banks are indicated just to the east of the Temple of Concord and Victory which describe an oval space, not of the heroic size we associate with the mature Brown, but not inappropriate to the new temple. It would allow the pond to act as a kind of "centre", or epicentre, and being oval contracts towards a circle in the long view (from the south). Lady Grey also complained about the proposed vast buildings "larger and mightier than all the others" (G Clarke n.d. [1971]). If this were the design Cobham had in mind in 1747, Brown was prudent to hang back, and perhaps Lady Grey a perceptive critic.

The siting of the new temple was decided, and, as another visitor noted in 1747, the foundations of that "prodigious building based on the Maison Caree in Nimes" were in place. The siting of the Temple of Concord and Victory can be ascribed to Brown, although its designer has yet to be identified. It remained unfinished at Cobham's death, and was apparently modified during construction. But it is its siting and its neo-classical nature that are important when we consider Brown's part in the design that is to be followed. It is dominant, and not just because of its size, as it commands space in the same way the Ladies' Temple always has, and that is a good portion of the whole of Hawkwell Field. Another major feature was the Cobham Monument, not only designed but also built in 1747. That lies at a distance, and at an angle, on the edge of the gardens, and also at the edge of Hawkwell Field and this new quarter. It is big, tall, important and better seen at a distance. Assuming that Concord and Victory was meant to command the long view, then the angle of the axis between it and the monument is that of the right part of a goose-foot, roughly 30 degrees. The original siting of the Grenville Monument, also a column on base, but rather smaller and more decorative, occupied an angle similarly disposed, but to the left, at a position also on the long axis of the notional oval pond. That is most likely what Brown had in mind for this end of the valley, perhaps as a means of accommodating his client's express desire. Such a supposition makes the siting of the oval pond more sensible. The other ornaments in this part of the grounds were smaller ones, and convention might lead one to suppose that the other large building, as feared by Lady Grey, was meant to occupy the east end of the long glade on the very ample semi-circular bastion (or sweep). Such a building may never have been designed, but a prospect due east from Concord and Victory, with slant views occupied by family monuments, would place a prospect of nature (that is, nothing but the rising sun) in an appropriate and sublime position. It would be good to think that is what Brown would have preferred, and that design is the one which answers most of the evidence.

However, the Triumphal Arch, which was built in the 1770s on the vastly extended original north-south axis of Stowe on the highest ground between Stowe and Buckingham, was already being spoken of, and it has been suggested, very plausibly, that its first site was to have been the open bastion directly opposite the new Temple, with the family monuments, as it were, as flankers. Such a design would have vastly appealed to Cobham, and perhaps to Brown too.

But how were the plantations and open spaces in between to be managed? The plantings were a mixture of predominantly forest trees with shrubby under-planting, tending to exotics and to interestingly shaped and/or flowering species: these were arranged against the formal north edge and the eastern edge terrace in orderly rows, with much more closely planted belts of mixed trees and shrubs immediately in front, while clumps of trees or smaller groups of the mixed plantation – almost clumps but tending to a more Paisley-pattern – were loosely grouped adjacent to the edges of the open spaces. There is a progression, then, from the density of the edge through to the visually permeable interiors.

While there is fairly clear evidence about what was planted, it is rather less clear in the disposition of the open spaces whether Brown was dealing with avenues, with glades, with parterres or with something heretofore without a name. The quarter was sequestered; there is no obvious connection to the other parts of the gardens, and the visual hints, glimpses rather, that connect the Elysian Fields and Hawkwell Field are not present here. However, from the forecourt of Stowe there is an easy connection, but it is by way of the back of a greenhouse, or through seemingly secret close walks in the wooded belt. Similarly, the south terrace leads equally to it, and perhaps most easily. Still, that connection is not a direct one and is rather a surprising deflection by way of a little formal flower garden at the "junction" of the kitchen garden and the Elysian Fields' north end. From Hawkwell entry comes through a grove. However, first seen, it would have appeared as being in the middle of something not only new but mysterious too. This could be part of its programmatic intent. This quarter soon became known as the Grecian Valley from an early denomination of Concord and Victory, and it is certainly also enigmatic enough to stand in for a real Grecian Valley, Hadrian's Vale of Tempe laid out in his second century *Villa* grounds near Tivoli. There is no known narrative for the quarter, and it is more likely that Cobham and Brown had yet to resolve just how it was to become that "very fine thing" they both were working towards.

Formally, there are three important spaces: an "avenue" from the Temple to Cobham Monument; the "glade" from the south terrace and little flower garden, directed also at a family monument, Grenville Column; and the "parterre" fronted by the new Temple, and stretching eastwards to the garden's edge. The avenue is set up by the strong axis connecting the portico and the monumental column, and when examined more closely is either vestigial or virtual, for its edges are not those of an avenue. Rather, half is made up of two opposing slightly curved blocks of mixed tress and under-planted shrubs, which veers towards the back of the Ladies' Temple. Its other half is even less defined as it crosses the junction of the glade and the parterre with the help of a clump, but with the hindrance of Brown's oval pond. However, despite these ambiguities it acts like an avenue.

The glade part is easier to understand as a broader, somewhat diffuse, but still directional type of space already employed in various places in the 1730s. If entered from the terrace/flower garden it is by means of the open grove separating these two elements, then a directionally reinforced turn towards Grenville and the oval pond, with the grand new Temple's front looming surprisingly on the left side, but only after the visitor has well and truly entered the glade. It would be then that the whole composition could be seen as "that very fine thing" anchored at the new Temple, now with the avenue showing itself, and also, and most spectacularly, the new parterre. This is as much a parterre as the avenue would have been an avenue to George London. There is just the faint preview of the ambiguity Greening will very shortly propose at Wimpole, or perhaps Richardson's whiplash curves for Lowther. This formal looseness is very apparent in plan, much less so on the ground, and yet it is neither a mistake nor gratuitous. Brown seems to have attempted to meld the familiar forms and functions of gardens into a sort of abstracted image of itself. Whether Cobham was satisfied with their design is unknown, as he died in 1749 before it could be completed. For Brown it was an experiment, and these 60 acres can also stand as his first essay in designing

Figure 7.11 Stowe House, Buckinghamshire: J B C Chatelain's 1753 engraved view from the north of the Grecian Valley as designed by Lancelot Brown. Courtesy of Yale Center for British Art.

a whole place: if the new temple counts as the house or villa, and there were many who would have been proud and happy to make the exchange, then all the parts are present, even one captured field between avenue and parterre to show willing. It is still very much part of Stowe, but it also heralds something new.

The first opportunity for Brown to show what he could do independently was at Croome d'Abitot in south-east Worcestershire in the Severn valley, gently rolling country with the Malvern Hills forming a most pleasing distant close to the views westward. Brown knew this part of the world from his visit there in 1750. He naturally had met many people interested in garden design at Stowe, and doubtless shared with them his ideas about the works, and, of course, had their ideas and criticism in return. A better place to encounter potential partners in landscape making would be hard to imagine. Even in those times of *furor hortensis* when willing clients could meet the potential new professor on easy terms in the middle of great experiments there were still very few indeed who had both inclination and means to embark on such projects. The Denbighs, owners of Newnham Paddox, Warwickshire, began such works in the mid-1740s, and with the consent of Cobham used Brown, but these soon had to be put on hold. Brown had also begun improving Kirtlington, Oxfordshire (noted above), for Sir James Dashwood. He met other improvers as well as new employers while at Stowe, such as Sanderson Miller, who had improved his own Radway Grange, Warwickshire, from the late 1730s. They had met at Stowe in 1749, and on the trip to visit Miller to inspect his and other recent works in the district like Wroxton and Farnborough, Brown was also introduced through him to several important early projects, and far from the least of these was Croome Court.

Croome Court was an old estate with a squarish brick house in place surrounded by courts and gardens, and the kitchen garden was in good heart, but as this was not a main residence of the family, the place needed attention. However, Lord Coventry had begun some improvements, especially the beginnings of the long artificial river as part of an essential programme to drain the boggy grounds of Croome. So what greeted Brown was a somewhat tired looking place, still with boggy grounds near the house, but a prospect of exceptional beauty, and to the east good highish grounds from which to appreciate both. The new heir to Croome lived nearby, and had begun some works in the mid-1740s, although without much spirit of optimism as he associated the place with neglect and recent grief. Therefore, his meeting with Brown in 1750 must have acted as a spur, and he asked Brown not only to make proposals for the grounds but also, surprisingly, to advise on the house, a new church and other buildings. It appears that Brown's role, or reputation, or perhaps both, from Stowe was significantly more than as a garden designer, or a building designer, but as an architect of both, and all else. The commission was accepted with what was to become standard practice, the request that the client have a full survey of the place prepared for him.

Apart from the classic handsome prospect, the first quality that strikes one about Croome is emptiness. There are no great blocks of woodland and, given that it is a made landscape, few ornamental buildings. The church is, as it were, borrowed from the parish: otherwise, there is only the Greenhouse, the Rotunda and later a seat in the form of a monumental doorway. There is a named wood, Menagerie, a few big clumps of trees and an open grove with shrubbery under-planting. The rest, and there is lot of the rest, including further buildings, is made up of fields, with many single trees and small groups, large and very large, but still fields. They are separated from each other often by thin belts of woodland, and these belts seem somehow to enclose larger areas to make groups of fields into a larger element in the landscape. They produce silage, and provide pasturage for beasts, and may also occasionally be ploughed for other crops.

This whole array of seeming emptiness is divided along what appears to be its middle by a river: in one place it makes a small pond, it is sometimes broader but mostly rather narrow, and its serpentine route is a *natural* seeming one, not at all *Sharawaggi*. From higher ground along the east there is another division into two, noticeable as such only later. Also on the east side a line of woodland becomes a walled garden, then engages with a stable block, also of brick, and then becomes the stone house, regular and low but with higher corner towers. To the north, and then curving round towards the west, is another woodland, a belt as it turns out, which leads to the new parish church. Entry to the estate proper is eastward, skirting the woodland and walled garden to the front door, now clearly of a regular and handsome house in the latest fashion. This journey from relatively high ground, with the Malverns marking the western horizon, descends into the bowl of the Croome landscape. A turn to the north will show the wooded belt of the parish church curving round at a good distance, making its own horizon and enclosing the big field in front of the house, in which the church now appears as an ornament. There are the merest hints of a geometric resolution to this north space. Despite its proportions and scale being conventional Brown has more thoroughly abstracted this space, and extended it, than with the Grecian Valley. Although his scale is as heroic as Bridgeman's his forms betray no trace of underlying formality. That underlying formality is very much present, however well disguised, as John Phibbs' extensive research on "underlying geometry" has shown (see Phibbs 2006, 2007 and 2008).

These qualities are apparent to the south of the house. He makes his extension to the river curve eastward at the point one would expect a parterre to end, but here there is no parterre, and the open spaces to the south are on the order of six times larger than even the biggest parterres. The grove part of Croome Court, Brown's "Wray Wood", lies south-east of the garden door of the house, and on the highest ground within the gardens, and at its centre is a domed pavilion. This is not really visible from the house, although it reads effectively from other parts of the grounds, and it comes into view only when approached on foot. The loosely wooded and almost open grove is also a shrubbery or wilderness. It is meant for walking in, and for walking in without gum-boots, and the transition from the house is an easy one; a shortish stroll on well-drained turf (as if it were a terrace) leads past the stable and garden walls to a pair of *terms* at the beginning of the more wooded part, and also the beginning of the slope up the hill towards the domed pavilion, now in at least partial view. Exploration of the other parts of the grounds is equally easy, and the river is the most welcoming path to follow, especially towards the north-west, where the Orangery can be seen, and in due course a woodland with pool. But there is not even a hint at Croome of following a circuit: it is simply too large, and too diffuse. Its parts are composed with artistry without any overt pictorial narratives about any of them: that Croome is picturesque we may take as given, not only because of its manifest qualities, but also because Richard Wilson made his famous prospect of Croome from the south-west part of the park, strikingly similar to the view point the same artist had taken at Wilton. Nor has it ever been termed a *ferme ornée*, even though its fields are on the order of 80% of the composition and all grassed for pasturage. Brown had found his form at Croome, and it is best described as a Landscape Garden. He continues to make places in this way for another 20 years or so, usually, but sadly not always, with the same certainty that marks his masterpiece of Croome Court.

8 Legacy

In the foregoing chapters we have been able to give an account of Stephen Switzer's design ideas in both literature and practice. If there remain gaps owing to the present lack of knowledge we are fortunate that there is a good spread from apprentice works with George London and Henry Wise into the 1740s. This has allowed us to observe and discuss the development through time and in response to what started as untested and extraordinary and then in the 1730s begins to become the fashion. Even this corpus has its limits and comes with the appropriate warnings. It varies from the great details, including costings and the divisions of responsibilities of Caversham, through to the agreeably complete and dense large pivotal design for Nostell Priory, where much can be gleaned from simply the observation of the design itself. Even the abortive exchanges about the Ferriby House project give otherwise unknown insights into the desires of a sincere if aspirational commissioner, and would-be Man of Taste. It is anticipated that where we have had to propose, and to rely on, the attribution of works to Switzer, further research will confirm those as proven, or re-assign them to others. It is especially vexing that Marston should be so miserably bereft of illustration and commentary, since it covers such a long period of design development . . . coeval practically with Switzer's career as a consulting *professor*. Its commissioners were so distinguished and interesting, spanning from the *Battle of the Books* controversy to the first scholarly account of the works of Pliny the Younger.

Despite such regrets, we now have an alternative design history for the heretofore simplistic, or murky, period of 1700–1745, which will require that our inherited explanations be critically re-visited and queried. Building on Switzer's design career will bring greater clarity to the period more widely, and will also encourage examination of the works carried on then (whether fully realized or otherwise) and give a juster understanding of the qualities of those works in themselves. That will allow us to *see* them afresh, and not as harbingers of a coming taste, or pitiable examples of past fashion. Doubtless, therefore, many new projects will come to light and enrich further this important half century. Doubtless also there will need to be revisions in light of further information and analysis.

The conventional accounts, most convincingly Horace Walpole's, consist, briefly, of formal plots crowded with costly ornamentation and fussy plants (often clipped in imitation of sculpture) plus sculptures and water-works, within walled enclosures excluding park and countryside, but sometimes enlivened by (very costly) wrought iron gates or screens. All this prevailed at the turn of the 17th century. These were all to be replaced by the modern taste, ushered in by hints from Alexander Pope and Joseph Addison and by experiments by Pope himself, by Lord Burlington as the

"Apollo of arts" and by his "proper priest", the *father* (Walpole 1876 2 57) or *inventor* (Walpole 2 63) of the modern taste, William Kent, in the mid-1730s. It had then proceeded over the mid-century decades towards its perfection, and with Lancelot Brown and his *eleves* to mannerism.

However, informality, specifically the serpentine line of the *Chineses*, had been advocated and practiced by Sir William Temple in the late 1680s. As Walpole had castigated the layouts illustrated by Johannes Kip and Leonard Knyff for the seeming formality of the design (Walpole 1876 2 71), Switzer had reacted similarly to London's designs for Castle Howard (unwisely, but he got away with it), which resulted in Wray Wood at the very beginning of the 18th century; had been praised for consulting the genius of the place at Kensington before 1705 (that really puzzled Walpole); had discovered the joy of fields closely adjacent to a great garden by 1707; had also discovered the problems and potentials of ancient remains; and, with John Vanbrugh and others, had worked on solutions, part of which was the first irregular water course, all before 1710. He had embraced the wider landscape in works, and begun improvements to that adjacent landscape itself, from 1711. And before 1712 a documented landscape design, the prototype *ferme ornée*, or, as he preferred to name it then, *rural or farm-like garden*, was under way; and by 1715 he had published his first book. Thus, he had shown himself to be the first and chief promoter of the modern taste.

Walpole was not alone in getting his narrative of recent events wrong. Although the *Gentlemen's Magazine* noted Switzer upon his death as the well-known author of many books on agriculture, already his early role at Kensington Palace was unknown to the garden staff there, as William Stukeley noted in his record of his friend's death. Switzer died in June 1745, comfortably well-off, leaving his business in the care of his wife, Elizabeth, and their son, Thomas, then a student at St Johns Cambridge. He was buried at St Margaret's Westminster. He had recently issued the second edition of *Ichnographia Rustica* and had continued to operate from Westminster Hall as a seedsman and consultant. Switzer's literary legacy was carried on in the two posthumous editions of *The Practical Fruit Gardener* of 1752 and 1763. As part of the then new interest in the earlier part of the century and the genesis of the modern style, there was a single mention of his work as a designer in Daines Barrington's observations on landscape design in 1783 in *Archeologia*. But until the 1820s he appears to have been quite forgotten. By then Humphry Repton's extensive practice and theoretical writing had returned landscape design from the *Jardin Anglo-Chinois* vogue years of Brown's *eleves* and its antidote, the *picturesque*, to something much closer to Switzer's ideas. Francis Johnson's bibliography of early writers on gardening re-introduced Switzer, suggesting that he (not Kent) be considered as the Father of English Gardening.

Given the drift of garden history, from its earliest days, Switzer's reputation, when noticed, has invited dichotomy: he has been seen in terms of *either* and *or*: formal or informal, progressive or *retarditare*, French or English, for example. Most of the dichotomies apparent in reactions to Switzer's works derive entirely, or at the least substantially, from the very constructions raised to examine them. Naturally enough, this provides much scope for misunderstanding. The additions by the antiquary the Rev James Dallaway to the re-issue of Walpole's *Anecdotes* in 1876 well illustrates this. He had realized that there were loose ends that he could tie up, and Switzer was one of these. In his notes about King William's period Dallaway subscribed to Switzer's characterization of the faults of those days, but then went on to sweep him up in the new narrative as a party in those lapses. Confusing Switzer with Jean Tijou,

Dallaway makes Switzer the *most famous artificer* of the costly iron gates of Hampton Court (Walpole 1876 2 97). Continuing in his condemnation of vaguely foreign wrought sin, he thoroughly misreads Switzer's account of London's Dyrham. As he writes, not unkindly but with certain condemnation, Switzer ". . . describes 'a beautiful *rural* garden' at Dyrham, in Gloucestershire, which, of all his examples, is the most artificial" (Walpole 2 104). Dallaway then passes on to Addison, Pope and Thomas Whately and to orthodoxy.

J C Loudon attempted a more historical assessment of what Barrington characterized with regard to Leeswood's similarity to the earlier parts of Stowe, as being *in Bridgeman's first manner*. Loudon had based his observations on old designs and surviving schemes to join his contemporaries in accounting for artistic development in terms of dominant and usually national styles, classing Switzer as *Ancient* and *English*. Subsequent mentions of Switzer occur in arguments contemporary with the commentators: for example his work is brought in for support by those who still held landscape design as the default mode, or in ridicule by those who argued for the more eclectic borrowings from history, or the positive adoption of older styles, such as Reginald Blomfield in his earnest espousals of the manner of Queen Anne's time in *The Formal Garden*. Of Switzer's aesthetic sense there can be little doubt. But it is less accessible than "First follow nature . . ." or "Kent leap't the fence and saw . . ." Of course Switzer believed and practised both those things. But as Switzer's accounts are very thorough, and appeared when the taste in laying out grounds was quite different, that may have presented a problem – especially if the alternatives when they became the fashion seemed so easy and straight-forward.

Between Switzer's new edition of *Ichnographia Rustica* and the first comparable theoretical work on the subject is more than a quarter of a century. That was the period of unprecedented development of designed landscapes. Why should this be so, unless we conclude that the ideas he had put forward then were in the process of being implemented more fully as part of what had already been identified as the *modern taste* (Loveday 1890, 299)? In other words, there was no need for one. It is true that William Chambers' *Designs of Chinese Buildings, Furniture, Dresses, Machine and Utensils*, published in 1757, contained his "Of the Art of Laying Out Gardens among the Chinese", but this simply re-enforced the current vogue for the Chinese manner and also recalled Temple's *Essay* of 70 years past: it added nothing else. Much of this is effectively repeated in Chambers' later *Dissertation*. In that Chambers also showed his motive for writing about gardens a trifle too clearly: he was seeking commissions. So his condemnation of Brown's works as *insipid essays in the bare and bald*, like his earlier condemnation of the modern version of Wilton as having too much formality, was recognized as special pleading. George Mason rounded on him for that, as did Walpole and others.

William Shenstone's *Unconnected Thoughts on Gardening* appeared in the early 1760s as part of his collected works, and that gave further support for the idea of the *ferme ornée*, which incidentally is the closest to giving a name to the *modern taste*. Credit for that is given to Phillip Southcote, or Shenstone himself, but the name which crops up most often in that period is Kent's, as by common consent the true begetter of the modern taste. Soon the *modern taste* began to be systematized. Sir John Dalrymple as a very young man was early in the attempt in the 1750s (Tait 1979 44 et al, Cooper 2000 154 et seq). He had been brought up at Newhailles, near Musselburgh, one of the most interesting of early landscapes for with which Switzer may have been involved in the design (and perfectly preserved in its antiquity and still awaiting its restoration from the National Trust of Scotland). Dalrymple characterized situations by their topographical natures . . . flat, undulating, rugged and highland. Flat favours the formal and "people of little taste or feeling", undulating the informal beauty he associates with Kent, the rugged with rather the more romantic temperament, and the sublimity of highland topography men of long nobility, and great projects (Tait 1979 47). This work was known to Shenstone in manuscript from 1760, and was published anonymously as *Essays on Different Natural Situations for Gardens* in 1774.

But it is Thomas Whately's *Observations on Modern Gardening* of 1770 which becomes the successor to *Ichnographia Rustica*. This very much accepts the inclusion of fields and confirms the ancient Horation value of their mixture in his continuing espousal of the merits of the *ferme ornée*.

> Gardening, in the perfection to which it has been largely brought in England, is entitled to a place of considerable rank among the liberal arts . . . it is an exertion of fancy; a subject for taste; and being released now from the restraints of regularity, and enlarged beyond the purposes of domestic convenience the most beautiful, the most simple, the most noble scenes of nature are all within its province: for it is no longer confined to the spots from which it borrows its name, but regulates also the disposition and embellishments of a park, a farm, or a riding; and the business of a gardener is to select and to apply whatever is great, elegant or characteristic in any of them; to discover and to shew all the advantages of the place upon which he is employed; to supply its defects, to correct its faults, and to improve its beauties
> (Whately 1770, 1)

Although between 1745 and 1765 formality (of any sort) disappeared, and remained impossible for a generation, it was only so in these islands. The underlying belief in an imperceptible order in the universe also disappears from designed landscapes, that is, ceases to be expressed. This is far from the case elsewhere, notably, of course, in France. Versailles during the *Regence* had lost some of its lustre, certainly the lustre that comes with being synonymous with the leading political and cultural power. Although it had not so much declined it had not progressed either, and it had become a place to be criticized: it was and remained great, but it did not appeal to all as beautiful, and many of its characteristics were thought boring. The Abbe Laugier, writing in 1753 in the earliest neo-classical text on design, his *Essai sur l'architeture*, made just these judgements and chose rather to praise a different class of works by Andre Le Notre, such as Chantilly or Choisy. Those preferences of Laugier's seem to echo the praises Switzer had made on behalf of Forest and Extensive Gardens, as large, woody, varied and irregular. He also had a nearer target, the current very fashionable *rococo* taste in French gardens for the small and fussy. These mid-century French gardens had touches of cross channel modernity such as curving walks. As an antidote Laugier had commended the Chinese taste, but according to a contemporary critic should rather have cited "the beautiful simplicity of English gardens" (Hermann 1962 145). The French did regain the dignity of the *Grand Siecle*, and with Laugier's assistance, but only after their fondness for the *Jardin Anglo-Chinois* had had its time of fashion.

If Versailles, the major national building, could be criticized, what of the other national landmark, the Louvre? For essentially the same reasons these had been deemed the first truly modern buildings since antiquity (Levine 1999, 162). They had both been conceived as great works . . . unprecedentedly large, but also architecturally coherent and executed with the best materials and in a consistently grand manner (if not entirely admirable in every part), expressing a new programme, and the pride of the nation. If Versailles then lacked lustre the Louvre had remained internally incomplete. Whether two such exercises had been truly warranted remained an unresolved issue, and essentially then was irrelevant. In the early 18th century the Louvre had been colonized by various courtiers for their own uses and fitted out as grand apartments (even including roof gardens). But its very purpose was still doubtful. The Louvre was the largest building in the city, and its size and grandeur demanded a better and more fitting national purpose, and it became the principal project of the time. It became the kernel and generator of new quarters of Paris, using Le Notre's Tuileries Gardens as beginning. He had remodelled the gardens to good effect in the 1670s, transforming the large but unstructured mass of small gardens into one of the first coherent landscape scale projects. He had simplified the ten square beds, the stages nearest the palace, into three very large squares, whose major axes he turned diagonally, with huge basins of water centring the two nearest new squares, with the third seemingly elided in the middle, marking the beginning of the east-west axis with another big circular basin. This axis was made possible by his diminishing the wooded hill on the west side of the site, and then defining it by rows of trees. The simple effects of this master-stroke meant that all could be taken in at once, while at the same time disconcerting the eye to look in new directions, and defining a new kind of flower bed . . . one of very complex and non-orthogonal geometry. Thus, structure along with surprise and variety is achieved at first view, and a grossly oversized initial gesture appears comprehensible, even friendly.

The Seine defines the south side, and the old wooded bulwark immediately west of the Tuileries marks a sort of boundary with the axis defined only by double rows of trees to carry the line further west. Urbanization shortly begins to the north-east, where the Place des Victoires shows how a forest *rond point* can become an urban centre by replacing the wooded edge with arcaded shops with several floors of house above, and the first of many equestrian statues of Louis XIV, and this is followed by the Place Louis Le Grand (now Vendome) as the Parisian version of the squares beginning to be formed in London. Le Notre finishes his work at the Tuileries with another, even larger basin on axis, where its backing onto higher ground is formed into a satisfying introduction to the main axis, since 1712 the Champs Elysee. This is pressed into service from the 1750s as the Place Louis XV, and the Boldest Stroke of them all is begun.

The Cartesian coordinates pay homage to Rene Descartes and allow the universe to be planned, at least in principle. Just who should be credited with the invention of squared drawing paper, often called *graph paper*, is unclear. London paper dealers supplied it from the late 18th century, and Thomas Jefferson had discovered it in Paris in the 1780s. He used it for all his designs subsequently and thought it a wonderful regulator, both flexible and liberating while ensuring correspondence with an ordered Nature. He used it in laying out his *ferme ornée* in Virginia, Monticello, and he caused it to become the basis of the most extensive designing of landscape so far attempted. The National Land Ordinance of 1785 was established to aid the surveying of the Western Reserve, lands annexed to the new United States centred on Ohio. With the more extensive Louisiana Purchase its use covered and designed the heart of North America. Like Cartesian coordinates graph paper is always "there", but it is only when a farm, or town, is platted that convenience makes it the design guide as well. Revolutionary France had toyed with such an idea in 1789 when the National Assembly instructed that the whole of France be reconfigured as a great grid of departments, excepting only rivers and mountains as allowed deviation (Schaer et al 2000, 198). Surveyors in British America had used cardinal lines to lay out colonial towns, and the plans of these that were drawn by C J Sauthier, an Alsatian surveyor employed by Governor Tryon in North Carolina and in New York, show how flexible they could be. Sauthier's plans, such as the one of Edenton in the Albemarle region of North Carolina of 1769, show how the grid coincides happily with seeming haphazard development, and genuinely haphazard topography (Johnston and Waterman 1941, 48).

As Switzer very well knew, and taught in *Ichnographia Rustica*, geometric coordination is the basis of land surveying and thus always "there", whether the fields are irregular, formal or something in between. He had asserted that it is as easy to lay out an informal, that is, "natural", field as a rectangular one. Whether he convinced his complaining would-be surveyors is unknown. Certainly Scottish improvers clearly preferred the rectangular. This will likely figure in the cleavage between *utile* and *dulci* which soon begins. When Lancelot Brown, a consummate surveyor, began to provide his gardens throughout England, in an even more abstracted version than Switzer's and with no remaining evidence of art, and significantly had begun an artful manipulation of the landscape, he used orthogony but never celebrated it. This was new.

Henry Home (1696–1782), Lord Kames, makes these questions of taste philosophical. He was a lawyer and a judge, and his ideas are put with less strength and clarity than those of his neighbour, David Hume (1711–1776), but they are accessible and were widely read. In his influential *Elements of Criticism* Kames first writes of *designing* landscape. It is there that he attempted to bring order and clarity to the judgement of value in all the works of art: in three volumes he treats of the range including, for example, Dignity, Wit, Beauty of Language, Figures, and Gardening and Architecture. He, and others also, recognized his difficulties. The ability to discriminate with regard to the value of paintings was becoming part of the necessary equipment of civilized discourse. Kames was relatively magisterial, and wrote both as a philosopher and a *Man of Taste*. Kames recognized that gardening had potential beauties far beyond those of architecture, beyond beauty into the other side of the Enlightenment, the *romantic*. As he put it, "Gardening, beside the emotions of beauty by means of regularity, order, proportion, colour and utility, can raise emotions of grandeur, of sweetness, of gaiety, melancholy, wildness, and even of surprise or wonder" (Kames 1792, 3 296–297). So while Kames restated Switzer's injunction about regularity near the house and its quick introduction to more varied forms, he was more interested in the outlying parts. He credited to "Kent's method" the superior mid-century English style of embellished fields in which the raising of associations of ideas could be practised (Kames 1792, 3 304 et seq). And, of course, he was also one of the Scots Improvers himself, and had written about his efforts at Blair Drummond in Stirlingshire. His fields there were as regular as any of those of his neighbours, and he was doubtless proud of the fact. Although we are fairly certain that he had ideals in mind, such is not necessary: whether the parts he wishes to judge are regular or irregular is not important. Kames based his argument on Switzer's invitation to build in "imitation of some antiquated place" for the association of ideas which arise from such places. So it is their power to induce such responses . . . whether, and what kinds of, associations of ideas are conjured by the part of the garden under view. "A garden may be so contrived, as in various scenes to raise successively all it's different emotions. But to operate this delicious effect, the garden must be extensive, so as to admit a slow succession: for a small garden, comprehended at one view, ought to be confined to one expression: it may be gay, it may be sweet, it may be gloomy . . ." (Kames 1792, 3 297).

Parts of Cirencester might be amenable to a Kamesian critic; Rousham or the Elysian Fields at Stowe, or Rhual doubtless, would have done, as would the contemporary works at Stourhead, or parts of Nostell Priory in Switzer's design. One design was made in the later 1730s which not only answers perfectly to Kames but could well have been in his mind when he wrote the garden and architecture section of his *Elements of Criticism*. It was made by another Scots improver and a colleague, Sir John Clerk of Penicuik (see Spink in Willis 1974 31–40). It still exists and could very easily be restored to its 18th century perfection. Clerk described what he did, and what he had in mind in conceiving the plans of the place, in a letter to an old friend in the Netherlands, Dr Wilhelm Boerharve. Clerk wanted to extend a walk to a distant part of the grounds at Penicuik House beyond his kitchen garden. He wished it to be both an attractive and an entertaining, even memorable, walk. Just south of the kitchen gardens (their fruits safely beyond the ravages of his guests) his company are invited to cross the River Esk, where it is swiftly flowing and slightly scary, by way of a decidedly precarious and lightly constructed footbridge. At its far end they are presented with the wooded rough slopes of the high bank and the entrance to a dark cave. The terrors this might induce in visitors are heightened half way through by lines engraved into the walls about the old Sibyl at Cumae, doubtless embellished by their host. But soon light appears in the distance, where they all come out into a wooded and rose-bush bedecked sunny glade. Emotional resolution is achieved, and refreshment and fishing in Hurley Pond are offered in compensation. The final leg of this *enfilade* is by a pastoral and easy descent, which finishes the tour.

Kames' *Elements of Criticism* marked the beginnings of a critical and new distinction: the values to recognize in discriminating the merits of embellished fields were to Kames the business of art, in other words, of unalloyed *dulci*. By 1762 he had firmly excluded anything useful from contributing to the garden as a work of art, assigning to kitchen gardens and productive fields only relative beauty, and to gardens as ornamented nature the superior intrinsic beauty. His philosophy cannot allow these to be mixed. Kames also illustrates how timeless aspects of beauty and mutable ones may vary as polar "opposites" and colour our senses of them: so as we may recognize the cast of mind, *comme il faut*, or spirit of the age really as other terms for fashion, he could not. His was but the first of the *neo-classical*, as also of the *enlightened* discourse, about the principles of garden design. Soon his abolition of the mixing of *utile et dulci* on which Switzer had based all his work, and which brought Switzer's scheme to public notice and contributed so much to 18th century landscape design, will become generally accepted, and in the minds of those like Richard Payne Knight and Sir Uvedale Price will lead to the extreme version of the landscape garden, *The Picturesque*. In that mode connoisseurship is essential and even refined, and open only to those who may demonstrate the ability to appreciate it. Even after a restoration of more moderate taste, and a return to some formality and comfort, led by Repton, the productive parts of estates and their bucolic character are kept separate in designed landscapes. During the 19th century these virtues remained divided philosophically and in practice. When in the 1930s B Sprague Allen wrote her *Tides in English Taste* it was the *utile* aspect of Switzer's ideas that made them those of the *mere* gardener,

266 *Legacy*

clearly unable to fully appreciate poetic matters. And when Ian Hamilton Finlay began his improvements at Little Sparta, Renfrewshire, mixing garden making for pleasure and profit, it was the *utile* aspects which caused the local authorities to assess his place as a farm, and therefore liable to taxation: these he resisted in the noisy 1960s fashion of protest as *happening*, turning Charlotte Square into another *dulci* aspect of his efforts.

It is obvious of course, but still too often passed over, that as works like Stowe matured and grew older, the crisply defined empty (or seemingly empty) spaces in early 18th century designs, as well as the defined planted areas, became by that mature growth and age shaggy, and the most geometric pools through time are formally degraded: in old gardens nature takes art's edge away. So the informal but still decidedly crisp manner of the early 18th century would hardly be recognized after mid-century, and certainly would not be approved of in that style. On the other hand, as the Thomas Smith painting of Chatsworth circa 1740 amply illustrates, great formal schemes age exceptionally agreeably (to later eyes), becoming lofty or venerable. Caversham, like Chatsworth, was esteemed in the later 18th century, and Whately chose it as one of his descriptions in *Observations on Modern Gardening* (Whately 1770, 140 et seq). But Kames and his colleagues give a further role to this change of perception. The notion of *character* (which Switzer acknowledged) is one of the many definitions of value and means to judgement. But with later commentators it

Figure 8.1 Belton House, Lincolnshire: the new Waterwork from the south. Engraved view by Thomas Smith and François Vivares based on Smith's painting at the house. © National Trust.

is modified, so that a rough and grotesque water-work will come to be favoured . . . not in the crisp and contrasting emptiness of the designer's vision, but rather with all parts of this *scene* having, or at least favouring, the character of the whole. In other words, all must be gloomy and shaggy to give rise to the same kinds of associations of ideas. The most perfect examples of this could be seen in late 18th century works, and can now be sensed only through the writings extolling *The Picturesque* of Knight or Price, or in caricature in the former's contrasting illustrations of a place *dressed* and *undressed* (Hunt and Willis 1975 343).

In the centuries since Switzer's death the Landscape Garden, in one or another of its various expressions, has remained the default manner. Occasionally in restored sites there is a hint of the character of the early 18th century, at Painshill for example or at Stowe, but even there one has to rely on imagination to recall the designed state. A restored *ferme ornée* has yet to be attempted (Pierre DuPont's Longwood or his brother's Winterthur in Delaware come closest), and it retains an almost utopian allure. My farming friends and relations stubbornly refuse to take the idea of integrating farm and garden in one seamless design as a serious proposition. At the other extreme, the reclamation of derelict industrial areas has been accomplished using the theories of designed landscape: take as found, "strike from chance", combine profit and pleasure, and ameliorate in accordance with nature; and very large scale infrastructural works, such as motorways, have for nearly a century effectively become the focus for designing landscapes. At the core of all these, *Ichnographia Rustica* remains the best and most inclusive pattern we have.

The major motive in the art of the designed landscape was of course agriculture: the wealth of nations was its ability to feed itself, provide energy and resources and bring profit. Improvements in agriculture brought increased wealth. Already in Switzer's career were signs of revolutionary change; the iron fences of Chandos' Cannons, or Sir George Wynne's White Gates at Leeswood, were startlingly expensive luxuries which very soon became a means to stimulate extraordinary wealth when allied to increasingly ample supplies of coal, largely from the northern *improvers*. The expertise which created Switzer's cascades and water-works was soon put to providing an infrastructure to move manufactured goods and fuels cheaply about the country. By the end of the 19th century agriculture, land and landed estates had been supplanted as the source of wealth and power, overtaken by manufacturing and trade in cities. Keeping great estates in order became a luxury rather than the manifestation of prudent improvement. A desire to *make a pretty landskip of one's possessions* had not disappeared, but it had been concentrated in a much smaller area, and the number of potential improvers had grown from a group of the fortunate to many thousands. Loudon had shown how the impetus to improve could be carried out in a suburban context much smaller than Pope's or Walpole's. By the end of the century an aesthetic of improvement underpinned by John Ruskin, William Morris and others was in place in which the cottage and its modest garden patch were the prime source of what was to be admired, growing in size to include modestly larger places for the more fortunate, but rarely bigger than several acres, and always informed by the tenets of *Arts and Crafts*. Thus, gardens returned to room sized rectangular units whose compositions resemble the modest house they were so closely related to. All had become small, so plants as individuals were esteemed and horticultural improvement was encouraged: garden design rather than designed landscape led. Reference to the modest designs from the past was sought out for study and emulation, and for esteem. In these islands it was the later 17th century which held the most attraction, and the manner that grew up then had various names, but here is often called the Queen Anne Style. It was that kind of garden that Sir Reginald Blomfield (and others) lauded as the best national type.

Nearly 100 years ago there were signs that the early 18th century had begun to appeal again, not least because designing landscapes had by then become rare, and when attempted (as part of big infrastructural schemes like railways) was considered rather threatening. Surviving designed landscapes were so very rare in themselves that they began to become objects of esteem, as a neglected and powerful source of ideas. Curiously, they were also seen as of relevance along with 20th century notions of modernity, and to a large extent as an alternative to American or Continental modernism. There was also a growing academic interest in literature in English especially in the United States, where Pope and Dryden and a whole host of more minor characters, like Walpole, were treated seriously in universities. In London two young landscape designers, Christopher Tunnard and Frank Clark, still brought up under Arts and Crafts influence, saw the 18th century landscape garden as the most attractive and important of their Georgian inheritances. And they were modernists who saw clarity and abstraction in early 18th century designs as an appropriate context for a revived garden design in the 20th century, and they also wished to see the surviving landscapes now in suburban areas protected and conserved. Those in Surrey, like Chargate-Claremont, became major concerns.

Chargate-Claremont had gone through all the developments of the changing styles of landscape since Vanbrugh's and Switzer's time . . . augmented, as Claremont was by Bridgeman and Kent, then transformed by Brown for the Nabob Clive in the high phase of the Landscape Garden. It had later been a minor royal house, and retained that form into the 1930s. Surrey, and the other Home Counties, was then most attractive to house builders. Richings Park, as Riskins had become, was "saved" at the beginning of the 20th century by being made into a golf course, with its northern fringes transformed into a suburban settlement complete with a railway station. The house builders catered for those who wished to do what Walpole had done at Strawberry Hill: they wished to have their own small house with its own garden, but as they could not afford 14 acres they had to be content with very much less. Before planning had become nationally established such places as Claremont were seen as ideal sites for such development. It was to be parcelled out to make as many small house plots as could be fitted into its still ample acres. In their early practice as landscape designers Tunnard and Clark had the idea of conserving the grounds as a mature landscape garden, keeping the house for community uses and providing the new houses in a series of high blocks to the north-east, near the existing station. Their scheme did not go ahead then, although the idea was taken up at the Roehampton estate, also in Surrey. That became one of the most esteemed schemes for housing in parkland (see Tunnard, Jacques and Woudstra) and exerted an international influence.

Rarely, but notably, some few could afford a modern version of Strawberry Hill. In 1928 Bernard Ashmole bought 12 acres of countryside near Amersham, Buckinghamshire, and then commissioned Amyas Connell to design his stark white and rather cubist modern house and equally modern landscape, and called it *High and Over*. Its largely flat site is broken by a curving slope from south-west to east, and the house is sited on this ridge, and from that ridge it takes the orientations of two short wings containing the major rooms; a third service wing splits the difference, yielding the strong Y shape of the plan, which some modernists criticized as too *formalist*. The grounds share these formalities, presenting, hardly surprisingly given their date, an almost jazzy irregularity. The design has a series of elements, geometric in themselves but disposed in response to need, the nature of the ground, or the house. So, its forms, like those of the house, follow the functions. For example the main rooms overlook the south facing slope, divided by a Bold Stroke *balanced* by a big, exaggerated serpentine walk, terraced near the house and extended into woodland further out. This strikes a visitor as slightly Italian in character and may have responded to suggestions from the clients, who had been living in Rome. High and Over, if not quite the *ferme ornée*, is close to it. There are extensive kitchen and fruit quarters (in the regular checkerboard style of other modernist designers) and also woodland and park-like open spaces. It stored its own water supply in an appropriately modernist tower at the corner of the estate.

Together with Serge Chermayeff, Tunnard and Clark were involved in the design of a most admirable modern version of house and landscape. Like High and Over it was at the extreme end of modest, and despite being in the Sussex countryside it was still essentially a suburban exercise. It makes a reprise or homage to the classic Palladian house in a landscape. This was immediately seen as the 20th century response to the great schemes of the 18th century. *Bentley Wood* near Hallam in Sussex was designed and built by Chermayeff for his own use between 1935 and 1937. This house, and the idea of modern buildings in a cool minimalist classic landscape, became a trope of the modern movement (it even had a reclining Henry Moore sculpture as a mediating foreground). The design started as a linear one, similar in many respects to other works by Chermayeff in his former partnership with Erich Mendslesohn. A long terrace is a feature of all the schemes for Bentley Wood, and in a sense the terrace had assumed much of the role of the old garden, or parterre: it was the site of both kitchen and flower quarters, arranged as a series of repeating square beds comfortably within its broad pavement. This, whether part of a terrace or, more usually, *floating* in park-like greensward, was one of Clark's specialties, and shows up often in his earlier and later work. Tunnard illustrated their work using that element in *Gardens in the Modern Landscape* . . . and also the work of Jean Canell-Claes in Brussels, of Gabriel Gurekian at Hyeres and of A E Powell at Bristol. This checkerboard motif derives from Jefferson's grid and was used in the 1930s in many designs associated with the Surrealists. It had appeared also in an *Arts and Crafts* reprinted image of Hampton Court, Herefordshire, where Switzer's gridded kitchen quarters first re-appear. Tunnard had a penchant for *architectural plants* (as Loudon had dubbed them), the strong, singular and irregularly spreading specimen, often used as an accent. At Bentley Wood a surviving singleton oak adorns the terrace (and was spot-lit).

In the built project for Bentley Wood half of the terrace is rotated to run perpendicular to the house, and at the same time it forms the east end of a new element, the lower service wing, presenting a plain frontage to the entrance drive, and making a contrast to the higher main block of the house. This composition becomes a favourite in mid-20th century design. Internally, that is, within the purlieus of the house, both halves of the terrace make the *garden*, beyond which lies the larger piece of *landscape* . . . rolling lawns to thinned wood and backing into close woodland. The contrast between this almost *borrowed* landscape and the fully glazed reception rooms below and the glazed bedrooms above (opening onto a broad continuous balcony) is carried by the terrace as *garden*. The classic view of this appears as the frontispiece to *Gardens in the Modern Landscape*. There the borrowed landscape is shown across the strong grid of pavement, the gridded planting beds, and in a master-stroke the vertical and gridded glass screen . . . mimicking a Claudian Glass but acting as a windbreak for Henry Moore's *Recumbent Figure*. All this lasted a sadly short time, but through the esteem of early visitors and the publicity coming just at the outbreak of the world war its image became embedded in a generation of designers' imaginations.

Tunnard was recruited to join Walter Gropius at the Harvard Graduate School of Design in the summer of 1939. Chermayeff became bankrupt, and also left for America: he and Tunnard ultimately became colleagues at Yale. Clark stayed on in London, working as an air raid warden by night and, with no further design work to occupy his days, at the British Museum researching the history of 18th century landscape design. He was much encouraged in that by Rudolf Wittkower of the Warburg Institute. Clark's work "18th Century Elysiums: The Role of 'Association' in the Landscape Movement" was published in 1943, tying his argument, among others, to Switzer's call for designers to study Homer to learn to admire the grotesque (*IR* III 7–8). His more popular *The English Landscape Garden* appeared in 1948. He had great influence through the *Architectural Review*, where the notion of *Sharawaggi*, which he had re-introduced, was taken up to give support to an English kind of modernity based on The Picturesque, used initially in planning theory. Through contributor and sometime editor Nikolaus Pevsner and owner Hugh De Cronin Hastings the *Review* made this its cause. The latter's article (writing as I de Wolf) "Townscape: A Plea for an English Visual Philosophy" of 1949 (Ockman 1993, 114–119) shows that stance. Wittkower's own *Architectural Principles in the Age of Humanism* of 1949 re-introduced Andrea Palladio to modern readers, as had "The Mathematics of the Ideal Villa" by a student of Wittkower's, Colin Rowe, published in the *Review* in 1947. Thus, the lessons of mid-18th century landscape design are united with the best of criticism, and the most thoughtful new attitudes from Continental art history in the professional press and university teaching on both sides of the Atlantic.

With such an array of enlightened attitudes one might have hoped for the overdue assessment of Switzer's achievements, perhaps along the lines of Margaret Jourdain's *William Kent* or Dorothy Stroud's *Capability Brown* (1950 [1975]) or David Green's *Gardener to Queen Anne* about Henry Wise. Green had such a project in mind, and gave talks on the BBC Third Programme about him. In the event it was a rather different kind of book, not a monograph dealing with the works of an artist but rather a problematic place and project, and it addressed the design thinking of the men involved. Relying on evidence but not only documents it also addressed the fragmentary remains of the designs for building and landscape in trying to assess the roles of those involved. Thus, Laurence Whistler's *Imagination of Vanbrugh and His Fellow Artists* of 1954 is the most admirable study in the history of design . . . and goes a long way in assessing Switzer's contributions.

However, lingering doubts about having the formal and informal inhabit the same work of art, the both-and nature of Switzer's *utile et dulci*, seem to have continued to bother mid-20th century thought. This is summed up in one guiding feature then. That was the notion of the *spirit of the age*, to which Pevsner, in his many radio talks, was particularly prone (Games 2014). So the thoughtful perceived tendency became less an observation, and more a prescription. He played for the Modern Movement the role that Lord Kames had played for Modern Gardening. It perhaps clouded his eye and judgement. He also subscribed to the notion of national characteristics to the extent that he could admire Le Corbusier's intentions in the *Plan Voissin* for Paris, and even acknowledge its debt to developments in landscape in Britain, but as straight lines were French, he considered them not appropriate in England (by which he meant to include the whole island of Britain). Conversely, the *Sharawaggi* led notions of British modernity were not really likely, in his view, to find favour in France. Even Clark found Switzer's straight lines uncomfortable and a bit off-putting, although he kept that response to himself for a long time.

No one in Britain then, and probably also elsewhere, could really appreciate Le Corbusier's sense of landscape, and how landscape and building could be fused. Seeing his Villa Savoy, near Paris, as an abstracted Palladian design in landscape, as Rowe could, struck most as quite revolutionary, and a little taxing. The forms of such abstracted houses became attractive, and remain so. However, their very abstraction was ignored. None could see Le Corbusier's sense of landscape that was demonstrated (then only through photographs and now sadly destroyed) in his surreal apartment-garden on the Champs Elysee. There his, and his client Beitsegui's, *Bold Stroke* returns to the Right Bank's major axis (begun by Le Notre and continued by the Marquis de Marigny), which leads to the block and the apartment. It is lost, then reached again by a modern lift and a vertical serpentine path (the open spiral stair link), where from the roof garden/salon, it re-appears in perspective at the star and Arc de Triomphe. Le Corbusier could have taken the idea straight from Switzer's Manor of Paston. According to Samuel Johnson his most perfect idea of happiness was being driven swiftly in a chaise over the smoothly undulating greensward of the park while talking with a beautiful companion. Now and with only a minor alteration in mode of transport all can achieve precisely the effect of driving along a motorway: the translation of Switzer's style of *enfilade* for 20th century life occurred in the 1930s, with the Blue Ridge Parkway in North Carolina, where the reclamation of spoiled wilderness produced a blissful holiday drive, and then the early garden *freeways* of southern California, where highways were purposefully and skilfully integrated into the topography to unite utility and pleasure in a quick commute.

These examples – one surreal, the other simply conservative – are just two surprising echoes of an early 18th century garden theorist and his responses to landscape. When critics, historians and designers can see the past perhaps with the savage innocence of Le Corbusier, or with other new eyes, then early 18th century designed landscapes will begin to make more sense, and similar experimental developments may again become possible.

Envoi

For Switzer beauty derived from two sources, nature and custom. The former is timeless, and manifested, for example, in geometry, and in proportional relationships. Customary beauty comes from the senses and is mutable, as reflected in hunger, passion or fashion. For him his appreciation of nature, the Creation, is largely perceived sensually, mostly in seeing, what he calls "opticks." From the rules of "opticks" comes his explanation of the appeal of symmetry . . . because in small things beauty, like the human figure, buildings or elements of gardens like parterres, is rendered through balanced regularity, which is normally what we call symmetry. In things larger than can be apprehended easily in one view, beauty is manifested in other ways . . . as can be gleaned by the contemplation of nature:

> . . . *of all the Works of the Creation, none calls for our Attention more than the Superficies of the Earth, the Work of the Third Day. The Beautifulness there is in*

the Prospect of it the excellent Uses and Variety therein are Studies and Speculations that excel all others.

And amidst all; that of a Country Seat distributed with Judgement, may well be accounted one of the greatest; in this every Person makes to himself a Kind of new Creation, and when a Seat or Villa, is decently and frugally distributed in what a Harmony does it create in a virtuous Mind, besides, the many grosser Uses of it to the Body . . .

All other Employs have some things that are Pleasant in them, but in this there is a happy Composition of every thing that can possibly make Man's Life and Labour agreeable, and give an Innocent Gratification to all his Senses: The general View of his well dispos'd Seat gratifies the Sight, the numberless feather'd Choiristers that perching amongst his Woods, warble out their natural and melodious the Hearing, the refreshing Breezes of Air the Feeling, and the Palate is gratify'd by an almost innumerable Number of pleasant and nectareal Juices, and Fruits, and the Smell of Flowers, cheers the Organs of the Head in a wonderful manner. How sweetly glides the Blood thro' its several Offices, how exhilarated the Mind, and with what Fragrance and Joy (as out great Poet expresses it) does the Heart and the whole Frame of Nature overflow. How sweet are these Amusements to the Innocent and Virtuous, and how insensibly are they carried to adore that divine Power that has made them thus susceptible of their own Happiness.

To come nearer to our present purpose the Business of Gardening, Planting, and Husbandry, affords both the Mind and Body all that is good or agreeable to our Natures, and gives us the Opportunity of being more beneficial to Posterity than any other Study or Employ whatsoever.

(*IR* III iii–v)

Switzer's publications

Stephen Switzer, *The Nobleman Gentleman and Gardener's Recreation: Or, An Introduction to Gardening, Planting, Agriculture, and the other Business and Pleasures of a Country Life*, 1 volume, London: Printed for B Barker and C King, both in Central-Hall, 1715.

Stephen Switzer, *Ichnographia Rustica: Or, The Nobleman, Gentleman, and Gardener's Recreation. Being Directions for the general Distribution of a Country Seat, into Rural and Extensive Gardens, Parks, Paddocks &c. And a General System of Agriculture, Illustrated with great Variety of Copper-Plates, done by the best Hands, from the Author's Drawings. By Stephen Switzer, Gardener, Several Years Servant to Mr. London and Mr. Wise*, 3 vols, London: Printed for D Browne without Temple-Bar, B Barker and C King in Westminster Hall, W Mears, without Temple-Bar, and R Gosling in Fleet-street, 1718.

Stephen Switzer, *The Practical Fruit-Gardener, Being the best and newest Method of raising, Planting, and Pruning all Sorts of Fruit-Trees, agreeably to the Experience and Practice of the most eminent Gardeners and Nursery-Men. Revised and recommended by the Revd. Mr. Laurence and Mr. Bradley. Adorn'd with proper Plans*, 1 volume, London: Printed for Tho. Woodward at the Half-Moon over against St. Dunstan's Church in Fleet-street, 1724. 2nd ed 1731, "To which are added, Three New Plans, and other large Additions". 2nd ed reissued 1752, and 1763 "Recommended by John Mills, Esq. Editor of Du Hamel's Husbandry, and Author of the System of Practical Husbandry".

Stephen Switzer, *The Practical Kitchen Gardener: Or, A New and Entire System of Directions For his Employment in the Melonry, Kitchen-Garden and Potagery. In the several seasons of the Year. Being chiefly The Observations of a Person train'd up in the Neat-Houses or Kitchen-Gardens about London. Illustrated with Plans and Descriptions proper for the Situation and Disposition of those Gardens. To which is added, by way of Supplement, The Method of Raising Cucumbers and Melons, Mushrooms, Borecole, Broccoli, Potatoes, and other curious and useful Plants, as practised in France, Italy, Holland and Ireland. And also, An Account of the Labours and Profits of a Kitchen-Garden, and what every Gentleman may reasonably expect there from in every Month of the Year. In a Method never yet attempted. The whole Methodiz'd and Improv'd by Stephen Switzer, Author of the practical Fruit Gardiner*, 1 volume, London: Printed for Tho. Woodward, at the Half-Moon over against St. Dunstan's Church in Fleetstreet, 1727.

Stephen Switzer, *A Compendious, but more Particular Method, than has ever yet been publish'd, for the Raising Italian Brocoli, Spanish Cardoon, Celeriac, Fenochi, and other foreign Kitchen Vegetables . . . as also a more authentic Account of the La Lucerne, St. Foyne, Clover and other Grass Seeds, for the Improvement of Land, than is at present to be found in any Books of Husbandry, or Gardening . . . To which is added, the new but very useful Method of Burning of Clay, for the Improvement of Land . . . As also, an Appendix, wherein is contain'd a further and full Account of the La Lucerne . . . By S.S. Author of the Practical Fruit and Kitchen Gardner, &c.*, 1 volume, London: n.p., 1728. 2nd issue of 1st ed, recorded in L W Hanson, *Contemporary Printed Sources For British and Irish Economic History 1701–1750*,

1963, p406, and (R Hagedorn) "The First Edition of Switzer's *Brocoli*", *The Library*, ser. 5, vol 7, p58. Further editions recorded in Hanson: 2nd (with Author's name) 1728; 3rd 1729; 4th 1729; another 4th, Dublin 1729; 5th, 1731; and 6th 1735. There is besides these a revised 3rd edition of 1729, *A Compendious Method For the Raising of the Italian Brocoli, Spanish Cardoon, Celeriac, Finochi, and Other Foreign Kitchen Vegetables. As also an Account of The La Lucerne, St. Foyne, Clover, And other Grass-Seeds. The Third Edition Revis'd; and (from this Summer's Experience) made very perfect and compleat; especially that Part which relates to the Burning of Clay: In Which Is A Full Account of the first Methods of Lighting, Maintaining, Renewing, and Keeping the Fire continually in, by Means of a New-Invented cheap Kiln, which does the Burning with great Ease and Certainty, and is the chief Art which belongs to this Useful and Reasonable Improvement. By Stephen Switzer, Author of the Practical Fruit and Kitchen Gardener*, 1 volume, London: Printed for Thomas Astley, at the *Rose* in *St. Paul's Churchyard*. 1729.

Stephen Switzer, *An Introduction To a general System of Hydrostaticks and Hydraulicks, Philosophical and Practical. Wherein The most reasonable and advantageous Methods of raising and conducting Water, for the watering Noblemens and Gentlemens Seats, Buildings, Gardens, &c are carefull (and in a Manner not yet publish'd in any Language) laid down. Containing In General A Physico-mechanical Enquiry into the Original and Rise of Springs, and of All the Hypotheses relating thereto; as also the Principles of Water-Works, and the Draughts and Descriptions of some of the best Engines for raising and distributing Water, for the Supply of Country Seats, Cities, Towns corporate, &c. Deduc'd from the Theory of Archimedes, Gallileo, Torricelli, Boyle, Wallis, Plot, Hook, Mariotte, Desaguliers, Derham, Hawksbee, and others. Redu'd to Practice by Vitruvius, Bockler, de Caus, and other Architects amongst the ancient Romans, Italians, French, Flemmings, and Dutch, and much improv'd by later Practice and Experience. Illustrated and Explain'd by Sixty Copper Cuts, done by the best Hands, of the Principles which tend to the Explanation of the whole, and of rural grotesque, and cheap Designs for Reservoirs, Cataracts and Cascades of Water, Canals, Basins, Fountains, &c Collected from the best of the Italian and French Designs (together with some new ones of the Author's own Invention) few of which have ever appear'd in Books of Hydrostaticks, &c. In Two Volumes. By Stephen Switzer*, 2 vols, London: Printed for T Astley, at the Rose, S Austen, at the Angel in St. Paul's Church-Yard; and L Gilliver, at Homer's Head against St Dunstan's Church, Fleetstreet, 1729.

Stephen Switzer, *A Dissertation On the True Cythisus Of the Ancients. Proving that the Medicago or Cythisus Maranthae (Not the Bastard Sena, as asserted by a late Author) Is the Plant that was held in so great Esteem among the Romans. Also that it may be successfully made Use of for the Improvement of the most dry, barren, hill Land, as Lucerne has been for that which is moister and nearer a Level; and in every respect answer the Excellent Character given of it by Columella, Pliny, Virgil &c. In a Letter to a Nobleman, who favour'd this Enquiry. To which is added, An Account of the Great Profits which arise (if carefully managed) from sowing the Lucerne and Burning of Clay, the bad Success of which in some few Places may be entirely attributed to the Unskilfulness of those appointed to Manage it. Also a Catalogue of the Best Seeds, the Season of sowing them, and the Time of their Perfection. By Stephen Switzer . . .*, 1 volume, London: Printed for Thomas Astley at the Rose in St Paul's Church-Yard, 1731. 2nd ed, 1735.

Stephen Switzer, *The Country Gentleman's Companion: or Ancient Husbandry Restored: and Modern Husbandry Improved* . . . London, 1732. Re-issue of *A Compendious Method* . . . (5th ed, 1731) and *A Dissertation* . . . under new title page.

Stephen Switzer, *The Practical Husbandman and Planter: Or, Observations on the Ancient and Modern Husbandry, Planting and Gardening, &c Being Directions (deduced chiefly from Practice, rather than Books) for the Workman's Conduct in the Field, Wood, Apiary, Orchard, Fruit and Kitchen Garden Parterre and Distillery Garden; And all other Branches of Husbandry and Planting, Intersperesed with Notes Etymological, Philosophical, and Historical;*

with the Charges which attend , and the Profits which arise from every considerable Part thereof. To be continued Monthly till a general System is finished) By a Private Society of Husbandmen and Planters . . ., London: Printed for and Sold by S Switzer, 1733–1734.

Stephen Switzer, *An Universal System of Water and Water-Works, Philosophical and Practical In Four Books. Faithfully Digested, from the Most-approv'd Writers on this Subject, By Stephen Switzer. Containing I. An Historical Account of the Chief Water Works that were and are remarkable in Ancient and Modern Times; more particularly the Roman Aqueducts, &c and the Honour they have contributed to the respective Places where they have been used, II. The Different Hypotheses which have been laid down concerning the Original and Rise of Springs; of the Good and Bad Properties of Water; and the Best Manner of Discovering and Searching for Springs; and the Taking of True Levels, in order for the Conducting Water to its several intended Uses. III. Hydrostatical Experiments (relating to the Notion of Water) selected from the Most-celebrated Foreign and English Authors more particularly Doyle, Hooke, Wallis, Lowthorpe, &c. Also the full Description and Uses of Mechanical Engines for the Forcing Water to great Heights, and applying the same to the Watering Gentlemens Seats and Gardens, in a better Manner than any hitherto extant. IV. Some Curious Disquisitions concerning the Vacuum of the Ancients; the gravitation of Fluids; the Elasticity, Dilation, and Compression of Air; the best Methods of Conveying Water, and for making Reservoirs, Basons, Cascades, Cataracts, Rural Grotesque Canals, Fountains, and all Kinds of Ornamental Water-Works, V. A Collection of Designs for the Purpose from the most eminent Masters, finely Engraven on Sixty Copper-Plates, In Two Volumes*, London: Printed for Thomas Cox, at the Lamb, under the Royal Exchange, 1734.

Stephen Switzer, *Ichnographia Rustica; Or, The Nobleman, Gentleman, and Gardener's Recreation. Containing Directions for the Surveying and Distributing of a Country-Seat into Rural and Extensive Gardens, by the Ornamenting and Decoration of distant Prospects, Farms Parks, Paddocks, &c. Originally calculated (instead of inclosed Plantations) for the Embellishment of Countries in general; as also for an Introduction to a General System of Agriculture and Planting., Illustrated With above Fifty Copper \Plates, done by the best Hands, which, though first published above twenty years ago, has given rise to every thing of the kind, which has been done since. The Second Edition, with large Additions. By Stephen Switzer, Seedsman and Gardener at the Seedshop in Westminster-Hall*, 3 vols, London: Printed for J and J Fox, in Westminster Hall; B and B Barker, in the Bowling Alley, Westminster. D Browne, without Temple-Bar; and F Gosling, in Fleetstreet, 1742.

Works consulted

A

Rob Aben and Saskia de Wit, *The Enclosed Garden: History and Development of the Hortus Conclusus*, Rotterdam, 1999.
Joseph Addison, *Remarks on Several Parts of Italy*, London, 1753.
David Adshead, *Wimpole: Architectural Drawings and Topographical Views*, London, 2007.
Malcolm Airs and Geoffrey Tyack (eds), *The Renaissance Villa in Britain 1500–1700*, Reading, 2007.
Malcolm Airs and William Whyte (eds), *Architectural History after Colvin*, Donnington, 2013.
B Sprague Allen, *Tides in English Taste (1619–1800): A Background for the Study of Literature*, New York, 1958.
Malcolm Andrews, *The Search for the Picturesque: Landscape, Aesthetics and Tourism in Britain 1760–1800*, Stanford, CA, 1989.
[Anon.] "The Early History of the Houses Built on the Site of Marlborough Castle", in *Report of the Natural History Society of Marlborough College*, Marlborough, 1959.
John Archer, *The Literature of British Domestic Architecture 1715–1842*, Cambridge, MA, 1985.
Dana Arnold and Stephen Bending (eds), *Tracing Architecture: The Aesthetics of Antiquarianism*, London, 2003.
Robert Atkyns, *Ancient and Present State of Gloucestershire*, n.p., 1712.
Robert Tracy Atkyns, "Iter Boreale or the Northern Expedition", Paul Grinke MSS, Devonshire Place, London, 1732.
Hans Aurenhammer, *J. B. Fischer von Erlach*, London, 1973.

B

J Badeslade and J Rocque, *Vitruvius Britannicus, Volume the Fourth*, 1739; reprinted as vol. 2, New York, 1967.
Daines Barrington, "On the Progress of Gardening", *Archeologia* 7 1785.
Mavis Batey, "An Early Naturalistic Garden", *Country Life*, 22 & 29 December 1977.
Mavis Batey, "The Magdalen Meadows and the Pleasures of Imagination", *Garden History* 9:2 1981.
Mavis Batey, "The Way to View Rousham by Kent's Gardener", *Garden History* 11:2 1983.
Mavis Batey, "Horace Walpole as Modern Garden Historian", *Garden History* 19:1 1991.
Mavis Batey and David Lambert, *The English Garden Tour: A View into the Past*, London, 1990.
Geoffrey Beard, "William Winde and Interior Design", *Architectural History* 27 1984.
James Beeverell, *Les Delices de la Grand' Bretagne*, Leiden, 1707.
Ann Bermingham, *Landscape and Ideology: The English Rural Tradition 1740–1860*, London, 1987.

Marcus Binney, "Worksop Manor, Nottinghamshire", *Country Life*, 15 March 1973.
Wendy Bishop, "Whetham Wiltshire: A Switzer Garden?", *Garden History 40:1* 2010.
John Bold, *Wilton House and English Palladianism: Some Wiltshire Houses*, London, 1988.
Donald F Bond (ed), *The Spectator*, 5 vols, Oxford, 1965.
James Bond and Kate Tilly, *Blenheim: Landscape for a Palace*, Gloucester, 1987.
P Bouchenot-Dechin and Georges Farhat (eds), *Andre le Notre in Perspective*, Versailles, 2014.
John Boyle 5th Earl of Orrery, trans, C C Pliny jr, *The Letters of Pliny the Younger, with Observations on Each Letter*, Dublin, 1751.
Richard Bradley, *New Improvements of Planting and Gardening*, n.p., 1719–1720.
Richard Bradley, *The Weekly Miscellany for the Improvement of Husbandry, Trade, Arts and Sciences*, London, 1727.
Neville Braybrooke, *London Green: The Story of Kensington Gardens, Hyde Park, Green Park, & St James's Park*, London, 1959.
Paul Bremen and Denise Addison, *Guide to Vitruvius Britannicus*, New York, 1972.
Maurice W Brockwell, *Catalogue of the Pictures and Other Works of Art in the Collection of Lord St Oswald . . . at Nostell Priory*, London, 1915.
W A Brogden, "Stephen Switzer and Garden Design in Britain in the Early 18th Century", PhD thesis, 2 vols, University of Edinburgh, 1973, online www.era.ed.ac/bitstream/1842/6979/1/488466
W A Brogden, "Stephen Switzer: La Grande Manier", in Peter Willis (ed), *Furor Hortensis*, Edinburgh: Elysium, 1974.
Alison Brown, *Bartolomeo Scala 1430–1497 Chancellor of Florence*, Princeton, NJ, 1979.
Jane Brown, *My Darling Heriott: Henrietta Luxborough Poetic Gardener and Irrepressible Exile*, n.p., 2006.
Jane Brown, *Lancelot "Capability" Brown: The Omnipotent Magician 1716–1783*, Pimlico, 2011.
Marylin Brown, *Scotland's Lost Gardens: From the Garden of Eden to the Stewart Palaces*, Edinburgh, 2012.
Morris Brownell, *Alexander Pope and the Arts of Georgian England*, Oxford, 1978.
R O Bucholz, "Thomas Herbert, 8th Earl of Pembroke", in *DNB*, London, 2013.
Howard Burns et al, *Andrea Palladio 1508–1580: The Portico and the Farmyard*, London, 1975.

C

Colen Campbell, *Vitruvius Britannicus, or the British Architect*, New York, [1715, 1718, 1725] 1967.
R Campbell, *The London Tradesman*, London, 1747.
Robert Castell, *The Villas of the Ancients Illustrated*, London, 1728.
[Earl Cathcart.] "Jethro Tull: His Life, Times and Teaching", *Journal of the Royal Agricultural Society of England*, 3rd series, 2 1891.
John Cattell and Susie Barson, *St Giles House, Wimborne St Giles Dorset: Historic Buildings and Areas Research Department Reports and Papers B/023/2003*, English Heritage, 2003.
Douglas Chambers, "Painting with Living Pencils: Lord Petre", *Garden History 19:1* 1991.
D D C Chambers, *The Planters of the English Landscape Garden: Botany, Trees and the Georgics*, New Haven, CT, 1993.
Douglas Chambers, "The View from Woburn Farm: Looking Out/Looking", *Studies in the History of Gardens 19* 1999.
Douglas D C Chambers, "Petre, Robert James, Eighth Baron Petre (1713–1742)", in *Oxford Dictionary of National Biography*, 2004, online, May 2008, www.oxforddnb.com/view/article/53220 [accessed 13 Sept 2014].
William Chambers, *Designs of Chinese Buildings, Furniture, Dresses, Machine and Utensils*, New York, [1757] 1968.

Sir William Chambers, *Dissertation on Oriental Gardening*, Farnborough, [1772] 1971.

H F Clark, "Eighteenth Century Elysiums: The Role of "Association" in the Landscape Movement", *Journal of the Warburg and Courtauld Institutes* 6 1943.

H F Clark, "Lord Burlington's Bijou, or Sharawaggi at Chiswick", *Architectural Review* 95 May 1944.

H F Clark, *The English Landscape Garden*, London, 1948.

Ernest Clarke and G E Mingay, "Jethro Tull", in *DNB*, London, 2014.

G B Clarke, *The Seventeenth Century House and Gardens at Stowe*, reprinted from *The Stoic*, Buckingham, March 1968.

G B Clarke, "William Kent Heresy in Stowe's Elysium" in Peter Willis (ed), *Furor Hortensis: Essays in Honour of H F Clark*, Edinburgh, pp 49–56, 1974.

G B Clarke, "The History of Stowe – VII, The Vanbrugh-Bridgeman Gardens", offprint from *The Stoic*, Buckingham, n.d.

G B Clarke, "The History of Stowe–XIV, Lancelot Brown's Work at Stowe", offprint from *The Stoic*, Buckingham (n.d. but 1971).

G B Clarke (ed), *Descriptions of Lord Cobham's Gardens at Stowe (1700–1750)*, Buckinghamshire Record Society, Buckingham, 1990.

George Clutton and Colin Mackay, "Old Thorndon Hall, Essex: A History and Reconstruction of Its Park and Garden", *Garden History Society Occasional Paper No. 2*, 1970.

William Cobbett (ed), *The Horse-Hoeing Husbandry, or, A Treatise on the Principles if Tillage and Vegetation*: *Wherein Is Taught a Method of Introducing a Sort of Vineyard Culture into the Corn Fields, in Order to Increase Their Product and Diminish the Common Expense* . . . by Jethro Tull, London, 1829.

John Cockburn, *Letters of John Cockburn of Ormistoun to His Gardener 1727–1744* (Scottish History Society), Edinburgh, 1904.

D R Coffin, *The Villa in the Life of Renaissance Rome*, Princeton, NJ, 1979.

D R Coffin, "The Elysian Fields of Rousham", *Proceedings of the American Philosophical Society 130*, 1986.

D R Coffin, *Gardens and Gardening in Papal Rome*, Princeton, NJ, 1991.

D R Coffin, *The English Garden: Meditation and Memorial*, Princeton, NJ, 1994.

C H Collins Baker and Muriel I Baker, *The Life and Circumstances of James Bridges, First Duke of Chandos*, Oxford, 1949.

L Junius Moderatus Columella of Husbandry in Twelve Books: and His Book Concerning Trees, London, 1745.

H M Colvin, "A Scottish Source for English Palladianism?", *Architectural History 17* 1974.

H M Colvin et al, *The History of the King's Works: Volume V 1660–1782*, Edinburgh, 1976.

H M Colvin, *Biographical Dictionary of British Architects 1600–1840*, Murray, 1978.

H M Colvin, *Essays in English Architectural History*, New Haven, 1999.

H M Colvin, J M Crook and Terry Friedman, *Architectural Drawings from Lowther Castle Westmorland*, Leeds, 1980.

H M Colvin and John Newman (eds), *Of Building: Roger North's Writings on Architecture*, Oxford, 1981.

H M Colvin and Alistair Rowan, "The Grand Bridge in Blenheim Park", in John Bold and Edward Chaney (eds), *English Architecture Public and Private: Essays for Kerry Downes*, Hambledon, 1993.

Jean-Louis Cohen, *Le Corbusier: An Atlas of Modern Landscapes*, New York, 2013.

Michael Conan (ed), *Perspectives on Garden Histories: Dumbarton Oaks Landscape Colloquium XXI*, Washington, DC, 1999.

T P Connor, "Henry Herbert, Ninth Earl of Pembroke", in *DNB*, Oxford, 2004–14, online www.oxforddnb.com

David Coombs, "The Garden at Carlton House of Frederick Prince of Wales and Augusta Princess Dowager of Wales: Bills in their Household Accounts 1728 to 1772", *Garden History 25:2* 1997.

Scott Cooper, "A History of Ornamental Structures and Buildings within Scotland's Gardens and Designed Landscapes: From the 11th Century to 1840", PhD thesis, Edinburgh College of Art, 2000.
Countess of Cork and Orrery (ed), *The Orrery Papers*, 2 vols, London, 1903.
J W Croker (ed), *Letters to and from Henrietta, Countess of Suffolk, and Her Second Husband, the Hon George Berkeley 1712 to 1767*, 2 vols, London, 1824.
Michael Cousins, "Hagley Park, Worcestershire", *Garden History* 35:1 2007.
Michael Cousins, "Ditchley Park: A Follower of Fashion", *Garden History* 39:2 2011.
W L Creese, *The Crowning of the American Landscape; Eight Great Spaces and Their Buildings*, Princeton, NJ, 1985.
Eveline Cruikshanks and Richard Harrison, "Nicholas Lechmere 1675–1727", in R Sedgwick (ed), *History of Parliament*, Martlesham, 2002, online www.historyofparliamentonline.org/volume/1690–1715/member/lechmere-nicholas-1675–1727

D

Caroline Dalton, "'He That . . . Doth Not Master the Human Figure': Sir John Vanbrugh and the Vitruvian Landscape", *Garden History* 37:1 2009.
Caroline Dalton, *Sir John Vanbrugh and the Vitruvian Landscape*, Abington, 2012.
Stephen Daniels, *Humphry Repton: Landscape Gardening and the Geography of Georgian England*, New Haven, 1999.
Stephen Daniels and Charles Watkins (eds), *The Picturesque Landscape: Visions of Georgian Herefordshire*, Nottingham, 1994.
Margaretta Jean Darnall, "Pietro Crescenzi and the Italian Renaissance Garden" (abstract), *Journal of the Society of Architectural Historians* 31:3 October 1972.
Jean-Claude Daufresne, *Louvre & Tuileries: Architectures de Papier*, Liege, 1986.
Keir Davidson, *Woburn Abbey, The Park & Gardens*, London, 2016.
Daniel Defoe, *A Tour thro' the Whole Island of Great Britain*, London, 1738.
Benjamin Disraeli, *Coningsby*, London [1911] 1933.
Bonamy Dobrée and Geoffrey Webb (eds), *The Complete Works of Sir John Vanbrugh*, 4 vols, London, 1927.
Dublin Municipal Gallery of Modern Art *Irish Architectural Drawings: An Exhibition to Commemorate the 25th Anniversary of the Irish Architectural Records Association* (catalogue), Dublin, 1965.
John Dunbar and David Walker, "Brechin Castle", *Country Life*, 12 August 1971.

E

Andrew Eburne, "Charles Bridgeman and the Gardens of the Robinocracy", *Garden History* 31:2 2003.
"Charles Evelyn", *The Lady's Recreation*, Dublin, 1717.
John Evelyn, *Memoirs of John Evelyn Esq FRS* (William Bray, ed), 5 vols, London, 1827.
Nigel Everett, *The Tory View of Landscape*, New Haven, CT, 1994.
Patrick Eyres (ed), *Wentworth Castle and Georgian Political Gardening: Jacobites, Tories, and Dissident Whigs*, Stainborough, 2012.

F

William Falconer, "Taste of Gardening among the Ancients", in *Twenty Essays on Literary and Philosophical Subjects*, Dublin, 1791.
J-F Felibien des Avaux, *Les Plans et les Descriptions de Deux des Plans Belles Maisons de Compangne de Pline le Consul*, Paris, 1699.

280 *Works consulted*

Samuel Felton, *On the Portraits of English Authors on Gardening*, 2nd ed, London, 1830.
Celia Fiennes, *Through England on a Side Saddle in the Time of William and Mary: Being the Diary of Celia Fiennes*, London, 1888.
J B Fischer von Erlach, *Entwurf einer historischen Architektur*, Vienna, 1721.
J G Fitch (ed), *Palladius: Opus Agriculturae*, London, 2013.
Ophelia Field, *The Kit-Cat Club: Friends Who Imagined a Nation*, New York, 2008.
The Garden & Landscape of St Giles' House, Wimborne St Giles, Dorset, (English Heritage Report), 2007.
John Fletcher, *Gardens of Earthly Delight: The History of Deer Parks*, Oxford, 2011.
Richard Fortey, *The Hidden Landscape*, London, 1993.
Katie Fretwell, "Lodge Park, Gloucestershire: A Rare Surviving Deer Course and Bridgeman Layout", *Garden History* 23:2 1995.
J E Furse and D L Jacques, *Report of the Historical Interest of the Garden and Grounds at Leeswood Hall, Clwyd* (Garden History Society), London, 1981.

G

Christopher Gallagher, "The Leasowes: A History of the Landscape", *Garden History* 24 1996.
Stephen Games (ed), *Pevsner: The Complete Broadcast Talks; Architecture and Art on Radio and Television, 1945–1977*, Abingdon, 2014.
Ernest de Ganay, *Andre Le Nostre*, Paris, 1962.
John Geddie, *The Fringes of Edinburgh*, London, 1926.
Thomas Gent, *The Antient and Modern History of the Loyal Town of Rippon*, York, 1733.
The Gentleman's Magazine 1–15 1731–1745.
Sigfried Giedion, *Architecture and the Phenomena of Transition*, Cambridge, MA, 1971.
John Gifford, *William Adam 1689–1748: A Life and Times of Scotland's Universal Architect*, Edinburgh, 1989.
William Gilpin, *Three Essays: On Picturesque Beauty; On Picturesque Travel; and on Sketching Landscape: To Which Is Added a Poem, on Landscape Painting* (2nd ed, 1794), Farnborough, 1972.
Mark Girouard, "The Smythson Collection of the Royal Institute of British Architects", *Architectural History* 5 1962.
Mark Girouard, "Ambrose Phillipps of Garendon", *Architectural History* 8 1965.
Mark Goldie, "James Tyrrell (1642–1718) Political Theorist and Historian", in *DNB*, Oxford, 2004–14, online www.oxforddnb.com.
Andor Gomme, *Smith of Warwick: Francis Smith Architect and Master Builder*, Donington, 2000.
M L Gothein, *History of Garden Art* (W P Wright, ed, Mrs. Archer-Hind, trans), 2 vols, London, 1928.
John M Gray (ed), *Memoirs of the Life of Sir John Clerk of Penicuik, Baronet*, Edinburgh, 1892.
David Green, *Blenheim Palace*, London, 1951.
David Green, "Father of English Gardening", *The Listener*, 3 September 1953.
David Green, *Gardener to Queen Anne*, London, 1956.
The Guardian, 4th ed, 1729.

H

Earl of Haddington, *A Treatise on the Manner of Raising Forest Trees, &c. In a Letter from the Right Honourable the Earl of _____ (Haddington) to His Grandson*, Edinburgh, 1761.
R Hagedorn, "The First Edition of Switzer's Broccoli", *The Library* 7:5.
L W Hanson, *Contemporary Printed Sources for British and Irish Economic History 1701–1750*, Cambridge, 1963.

Eileen Harris, "Architecture of Thomas Wright", *Country Life*, 26 August, 2 September and 9 September 1971.
Eileen Harris, *British Architectural Books and Writers 1556–1842*, Cambridge, 1990.
John Harris, *Gardens of Delight: The Rococo English Landscape of Thomas Robins the Elder*, 2 vols, London, 1978.
John Harris, *The Artist and the Country House*, New York, 1979.
John Harris, "The Anti-natural Style", in Charles Hind (ed), *The Rococo in England: A Symposium*, London, 1986.
John Harris, "A Pioneer in Gardening", *Apollo* October 1993.
John Harris, *The Palladian Revival: Lord Burlington, His Villa and Garden at Chiswick*, New Haven, CT, 1994–1995.
John Harris, *The Artist and the Country House from the Fifteenth Century to the Present Day*, London, 1995.
John Harris, "Is Chiswick a 'Palladian' Garden?", *Garden History 32:1* 2004.
Henry Harrison, *Surnames of the United Kingdom*, 2 vols, London, 1918.
J E Harrison, "The Development and Content of Stourhead Gardens: Recent Findings, Insights from an Eighteenth Century Poem and the Visit of Carlo Gastone Della Torre Di Rezzonico in 1787", *Garden History 43:1* 2015.
Vaughan Hart, *Sir John Vanbrugh; Storyteller in Stone*, New Haven, CT, 2008.
John H Harvey, "The Family of Telford, Nurserymen of York", *Yorkshire Archaeological Journal* 42 1969.
A G L Hellyer, "A Great Northern Garden", *Country Life*, 20 May 1971.
Michael Herrman, *Hypercontextuality: The Architecture of Displacement and Placelessness*, Rome, 2011.
Wolfgang Herrmann, *Laugier and Eighteenth Century French Theory*, London, 1962.
Wolfgang Herrmann, *The Theory of Claude Perrault*, London, 1973.
W A S Hewins and R Mitchison, "Robert Maxwell (1695–1765), Agricultural Improver and Writer", in *DNB*, Oxford, 2004–14, online www.oxforddnb.com.
Michael Hill, *East Dorset Country Houses*, Reading, 2014.
Thomas Hinde, *Capability Brown: The Story of a Master Gardener*, London, 1986.
Historical Manuscripts Commission, *Manuscripts of the Earl of Carlisle*, 15th Report, Appendix VI, 1887.
Historical Manuscripts Commission, *Manuscripts of the Earl Cowper*, 12th Report, Appendixes II and II, 1888–1889.
Historical Manuscripts Commission, *Report on the MSS of the Duke of Portland*, 13th Report, Appendix VI, 1901.
Edward Hughes, *North Country Life in the Eighteenth Century: The North-East, 1700–1750*, London, 1952.
J D Hunt, *Garden and Grove: The Italian Renaissance Garden in the English Imagination 1600–1750*, London, 1986.
J D Hunt, *William Kent; Landscape Garden Designer: An Assessment and Catalogue of His Designs*, London, 1987.
J D Hunt, *The Figure in the Landscape: Poetry, Painting and Gardening during the 18th Century*, Baltimore, 1989.
J D Hunt, *Gardens and the Picturesque: Studies in the History of Landscape Architecture*, Cambridge, MA, 1992.
J D Hunt, *The Picturesque Garden in Europe*, New York, 2002.
J D Hunt and Peter Willis (eds), *The Genius of the Place: The English Landscape Garden 1620–1820*, London, 1975.
Christopher Hussey, *The Picturesque Studies in a Point of View*, New York, 1927.
Christopher Hussey, *English Country Houses: Early Georgian 1715–1760*, London, 1956.
Christopher Hussey, *English Gardens and Landscapes 1700–1750*, London, 1967.
Christopher Hussey, "Culverthorpe", *Country Life 54* 1923.

Christopher Hussey, "Rhual, Flintshire", *Country Life* 93.
Christopher Hussey, "Leeswood, Flintshire", *Country Life* 99.
Christopher Hussey, "Gardens of Wilton House Wiltshire", *Country Life*, 134, 25 July 1963.

J

David Jacques, "Gardening on the Sugnal Demesne", *Garden History* 12:1 1981.
David Jacques, *Georgian Gardens: The Reign of Nature*, Batsford, 1983.
David Jacques, "The Grand Manner: Changing Style in Garden Design, 1660–1735", PhD thesis, 2 vols, University of London, 1999.
David Jacques and A J van der Horst, *The Gardens of William and Mary*, London, 1988.
David Jacques and Jan Woudstra, *Landscape Modernism Renounced: The Career of Christopher Tunnard (1910–1979)*, London, 2009.
Gervase Jackson-Stops, "The Cliveden Album I", *Architectural History* 19 1976.
Gervase Jackson-Stops, "The Cliveden Album II", *Architectural History* 20 1977.
Gervase Jackson-Stops, *An English Arcadia 1600–1990*, London, 1991.
John James (trans), *The Theory and Practice of Gardening*, Farnborough, [1712] 1969. (Translation of A J D'Argenville's *La Theorie et La Practique du Jardinage*, Paris, 1709.)
Susan Jenkins, *Portrait of a Patron: The Patronage and Collecting of James Brydges, 1st Duke of Chandos (1674–1744)*, Aldershot, 2007.
G W Johnson, *History of English Gardening*, London, 1829.
G W Johnson (ed), *The Cottage Gardener* 6 1851.
F B Johnston and T T Waterman, *The Early Architecture of North Carolina: A Pictorial Suvey*, Chapel Hill, 1941.

K

Henry Home, Lord Kames, *Elements of Criticism*, 3 vols, Edinburgh, 1762.
R W King, "The Ferme Ornee: Philip Southcote and Woburn Farm", *Garden History* 2:3 1974.
Norman Kitz and Beryl Kitz, *Pain's Hill Park: Hamilton and His Picturesque Landscape*, Cobham, 1984.
Richard Payne Knight, *The Landscape, a Didactic Poem* (2nd ed 1795), Farnborough, 1972a.
Richard Payne Knight, *An Analytical Inquiry into the Principles of Taste*, Farnborough, [1808] 1972b.
Wybe Kuitert, "Japanese Robes, Sharawaggi, and the Landscape Discourse of Sir William Temple and Constantijn Huygens", *Garden History* 42:2 2013.

L

Mark Laird, *The Flowering of the English Landscape Garden: English Pleasure Grounds 1720–1800*, Philadelphia, 1999.
Denis Lambin, "Foxley: The Prices' Estate in Herefordshire", *Journal of Garden History* 7 1987.
Batty Langley, *New Principles of Gardening*, Farnborough, [1728] 1971.
Helen Lawrence, "New Light on Thomas Archer as Garden-Maker", *Garden History* 38:1 2010.
Claudia Lazzaro, *The Italian Renaissance Garden*, New Haven, CT, 1990.
David Leatherbarrow, "Character, Geometry and Perspective: The Third Earl of Shaftesbury's Principles of Garden Design", *Journal of Garden History* 4 1984.
David Leatherbarrow, "Architecture and Situation: A Study of the Architectural Writings of Robert Morris", *Journal of the Society of Architectural Historians* 44 1985.

David Leatherbarrow, "Character, Geometry and Perspective, or How Topography Conceals Itself", in *Topographical Stories: Studies in Landscape and Architecture*, Philadelphia, 2004.
James Lees-Milne, *English Country Houses; Baroque 1685–1715*, London, 1970.
David Lemming, "Sir William Thomson [of Ebberston] 1678–1739", *DNB*, Oxford, 2013, online www.oxforddnb.com.
Ben Lennon, "Burlington, Brown and Bill: The Landscaping of Tottenham Park and Savernake Forest in the Eighteenth Century", *Garden History* 39:1 2011.
J M Levine, *Between the Ancients and the Moderns; Baroque Culture in Restoration England*, New Haven, CT, 1999.
W S Lewis and W H Smith, *Yale Editions of Horace Walpole's Correspondence*, New Haven, CT, 1937–1983.
Robert Liddiard (ed), *The Medieval Park: New Perspectives*, Oxford, 2007.
George London and Henry Wise, *The Complete Gard'ner: Or Directions for Cultivating and Right Ordering of Fruit Gardens and Kitchen Gardens by Monsieur De La Quintinye*, London, 1704.
J C Loudon, *An Encyclopaedia of Gardening*, London, 1824.
J C Loudon, *The Landscape Gardening and Landscape Architecture of the Late Humphry Repton, Esq., Being His Entire Works on These Subjects*, Farnborough, [1840] 1969.
J C Loudon, *A Treatise on Forming, Improving, and Managing Country Residences*, 2 vols, Farnborough, [1806] 1971.
J Loveday (ed), *Diary of a Tour in 1732*, Edinburgh, 1890.
Arthur C Lovejoy, "Nature as Aesthetic Norm", *Modern Language Notes* 47 1927.
M A Lower, *Patronymica Britannica Dictionary of Family Names of the United Kingdom*, London, 1860.
Jacques Lucan, *Composition, Non-Composition, Architecture and Theory in the Nineteenth and Twentieth Centuries*, Lausanne, 2012.

M

James Macaulay, *The Classical Country House in Scotland 1660–1800*, London, 1987.
E MacDougall and W F Jashemski (eds), *Ancient Roman Villa Gardens: The Tenth Dumbarton Oaks Colloquium on the History of Landscape Architecture*, Washington, DC, 1987.
John Macky, *A Journey through Scotland*, London, 1723.
Edward Malins, *English Landscaping and Literature, 1660–1840*, London, 1966.
Edward Malins and The Knight of Glin, *Lost Demesnes: Irish Landscape Gardening 1660–1845*, London, 1976.
Elizabeth Wheeler Manwaring, *Italian Landscape in Eighteen Century England*, London, 1965.
Alfred Marie, *Jardins Francais Crees a la Renaissance*, Paris, 1955.
Joanna Marschner, *Queen Caroline: Cultural Politics at the Early Eighteenth Century Court*, New Haven, CT, 2014.
Sarah Markham, *John Loveday of Caversham 1711–1789: The Life and Tours of an Eighteenth Century Onlooker*, Salisbury, 1984.
Peter Martin, *Pursuing Innocent Pleasures; the Gardening World of Alexander Pope*, Hamden, CT, 1984a.
Peter Martin (ed), *British and American Gardens in the 18th Century*, Williamsburg, 1984b.
S W Martins, *The English Model Farm: Building the Agricultural Ideal, 1700–1914*, Oxford, 2010.
William Mason, *The English Garden: A Poem in Four Books*, with notes and commentary by W Burgh, Farnborough, [1783] 1971.
Robert Maxwell of Arcland, *Select Transactions of the Honourable The Society of Improvers in the Knowledge of Agriculture in Scotland*, Edinburgh, 1743.

T J McCormick, *Charles-Louis Clerisseau and the Genesis of Neoclassicism*, Cambridge, MA, 1990.

Michael McGarvie, "Marston House: A Study of Its History and Architecture", *Somerset Archaeology and Natural History* 118 1974.

Michael McGarvie and John Harvey, "The Revrd George Harbin and His Memoirs of Gardening 1716–1723", *Garden History* 11:1 1983.

Jenny Milledge, "Sacombe Park Hertfordshire: A Bridgeman Landscape", *Garden History* 37:1 2009.

Anthony Mitchell, "The Park and Garden at Dyrham", *The National Trust Year Book 1977–78*, London, 1978.

Christopher Morris (ed), *The Journeys of Celia Fiennes*, London, 1947.

Robert Morris, *Lectures on Architecture* (1–8, 2nd ed 1754; 9–14, 1736), bound with *An Essay Upon Harmony As It Relates Chiefly to Situation and Building*, Farnborough, [1739] 1971.

Timothy Mowl, *Historic Gardens of Gloucestershire*, Stroud, 2002.

Timothy Mowl, *Historic Gardens of Dorset*, Stroud, 2003.

Timothy Mowl, *Historic Gardens of Wiltshire*, Stroud, 2004.

Timothy Mowl, *Historic Gardens of Worcestershire*, Stroud, 2006.

Timothy Mowl, *The Historic Gardens of England Oxfordshire*, Stroud, 2007.

Timothy Mowl and Dianne Barre, *The Historic Gardens of England Hertfordshire*, Bristol, 2009.

Timothy Mowl and Jane Bradney, *The Historic Gardens of England Series: Historic Gardens of Herefordshire*, Bristol, 2012.

Timothy Mowl and Brian Earnshaw, *An Insular Rococo: Architecture, Politics and Society in Ireland and England, 1710–1770*, London, 2000.

Timothy Mowl and Diane James, *The Historic Gardens of England Series: Historic Gardens of Warwickshire*, Bristol, 2011.

Timothy Mowl and Marion Mako, *The Historic Gardens of England: Cheshire*, Bristol, 2008.

Timothy Mowl and Marion Mako, *The Historic Gardens of England Series: The Historic Gardens of Somerset*, Bristol, 2010.

Andrew Murray, *The Book of the Royal Horticultural Society 1862–1863*, London, 1863.

J R Murray, *A Tour of the English Lakes with Thomas Gray & Joseph Farrington RA*, London, 2011.

Katherine Myers, "Shaftesbury, Pope, and Original Sacred Nature", *Garden History* 38:1 2010.

Katherine Myers, "Ways of Seeing: Joseph Addison, Enchantment and the Early Landscape Garden", *Garden History* 41:1 2013.

N

Erika Neubauer, "The Garden Architecture of Cecil Pinsent, 1884–1964", *Journal of Garden History* 3 1983.

A N Newman, "The Political Patronage of Frederick Lewis, Prince of Wales", *The Historical Journal* 1:1 1958.

Mark Newman, *The Wonder of the North: Fountains Abbey and Studley Royal*, Woodbridge, 2015.

O

Jean Ockman (ed), *Architecture Culture 1943–1968; A Documentary Anthology*, New York, 1993.

Laurie Olin, "William Kent: The Vigna Madama and Landscape Parks", in Alexander von Hoffman (ed), *Form, Modernism and History; Essays in Honor of Edward Sekler*, Cambridge, MA, 1996.

Laurie Olin, *Across the Open Field: Essays Drawn from English Landscapes*, Philadelphia, 2000.
George Omond, *The Arniston Memoirs*, Edinburgh, 1887.
Arthur Oswald, "Breamore, Hampshire", *Country Life*, 20 June 1957.

P

Andrea Palladio, *The Four Books of Andrea Palladio's Architecture*, New York, 1965.
Linda Parshall, "C C L Hirschfeld's Concept of the Garden in the German Enlightenment", *Journal of Garden History 13* 1993.
Claude Perrault, *Ordinance for the Five Kinds of Columns after the Method of the Ancients*, Santa Monica, 1993.
Nickolaus Pevsner (ed), *The Picturesque Garden and Its Influence outside the British Isles*, Washington, DC, 1974.
John Phibbs, "Projective Geometry", *Garden History 34:1* 2006
John Phibbs, "Point Blank", *Garden History 35:1* 2007.
John Phibbs, "The View Point", *Garden History 36:2* 2008.
John Phibbs, "A List of Landscapes That Have Been Attributed to Lancelot 'Capability' Brown", *Garden History 41:2* 2013.
John Pinto, "The Landscape of Allusion: Literary Themes in the Gardens of Classical Rome and Augustan England", *Smith College Studies in History 48* 1980.
John Pomfret, *The Choice*, London, 1700.
Alexander Pope, *The Poetical Works of Alexander Pope, Esq.*, Philadelphia, 1830.
Alan Powers, *Serge Chermayeff: Designer Architect, Teacher*, London, 2001.
Alan Powers, "Modernism and Romantic Regeneration in the English Landscape, 1920–1940", in Therese O'Malley and Joachim Wolschke-Bulman (eds), *Modernism and Landscape Architecture, 1890–1940*, New Haven, CT, 2014.
Pierre de la Ruffiniere du Prey, "The Bombe Fronted Country House from Talman to Soane", *Studies in the History of Art 25* 1989.
Pierre de la Ruffiniere du Prey, *The Villas of Pliny: From Antiquity to Posterity*, Chicago, 1994.
Uvedale Price, *Essays on the Picturesque, as Compared with the Sublime and the Beautiful; and, on the Use of Studying Pictures, for the Purpose of Improving Real Landscape*, 3 vols, Farnborough, 1971.

R

S E Rasmussen, *Experiencing Architecture*, London, 1959.
S E Rasmussen, *Towns and Buildings*, Cambridge, 1999.
C C Reed, "The Deleval Estates in Northumberland", diploma thesis, King's College, Durham, 1962.
John Reid, *The Scots Gardener*, Edinburgh, 1766.
Humphry Repton, *An Enquiry into the Changes of Taste in Landscape Gardening*, Farnborough, [1806] 1969.
Christopher Ridgway and Robert Williams, *Sir John Vanburgh and Landscape Archiecture in Baroque England 1690–1730*, Stoud, 2000.
John Riely, "Shenstone's Walks: The Genesis of the Leasowes", *Apollo 110* 1979.
S K Robinson, *Inquiry into the Picturesque*, Chicago, 1991.
William Robson, "The Building of Deleval Hall", diploma thesis, King's College, Durham, 1956.
John Rocque, *An Exact Survey of the City's of London Westminster, Ye Borough of Southwark and the Country Near 10 Miles Round London*, Kent, [1746] 1971.
John Rocque, *A Topographical Map of Middlesex*, 4 sheets, London, 1754.
John Rocque, *A Topographical Map of the County of Surrey*, 8 sheets, London, 1768.
Kimerly Rorscharch, *The Early Georgian Landscape Garden*, New Haven, 1983.

Betsey Rosasco, "The Sculptural Decoration of the Gardens at Marly: 1679–1699", *Journal of Garden History* 4 1984.

Maren-Sofie Rostvig, *The Happy Man: Studies in the Metamorphoses of a Classical Ideal*, 2nd ed, Oslo, 1971 [vol I (1600–1700) 1954, vol II (1700–1760) 1958].

Royal Commission on Ancient and Historical Monuments (Scotland), *Stirlingshire*, 3 vols, Edinburgh, 1963.

Samuel Rudder, *A New History of Gloucestershire*, Cirencester, 1779.

S

Sabin Galleries, *A Country House Portrayed: Hampton Court Herefordshire 1699–1840* (catalogue of an exhibition), with an introduction by John Harris, London, 1973.

Frank Salmon, "Thomas Coke and Holkham from 1718 to 1734: The Early History", *The Georgian Group Journal* 33 2015.

Charles Saumarez Smith, *The Building of Castle Howard*, London, 1990.

R Schaer, G Claeys and L T Sargent (eds), *Utopia: The Search for the Ideal Society in the Western World*, New York, 2000.

K F Schinkel, *Berlin und Potsdam*, Stuttgart, 1991.

Leo Schmidt, Christian Keller and Polly Feversham, *Holkham*, Munich, 2005.

M F Schultz, "The Circuit Walk of the Eighteenth Century Landscape Garden and the Pilgrim's Circuitous Progress", *18th Century Studies* 15:1 1981.

Romney Sedgwick, *History of Parliament: The House of Commons 1715–1754* [Tyrrell of Shotover], Suffolk, 1970.

Dennis Sharp and Sally Rendel, *Connell, Ward and Lucas: Modern Movement Architects in England 1929–1939*, London, 2008.

Will Shenstone, *The Poetical Works of Will Shenstone*, London, 1793.

Steffie Shields, "'Mr Brown Engineer': Lancelot Brown's Early Work at Grimsthorpe Castle and Stowe", *Garden History* 34:2 2006.

Sir Robert Sibbald, *History Ancient and Modern of the Sheriffdom of Linlithgow*, Edinburgh, 1710.

M L Simo, *Loudon and the Landscape: From Country Seat to Metropolis*, New Haven, CT, 1988.

R A Skelton, *The Military Survey of Scotland 1745–1755*, Edinburgh, (reprinted from *Scottish Geographical Magazine* 83:1 April 1967).

John Slezer, *Theatrum Scotiae*, London, 1718.

L B Smith, "Charles Boyle, 4th Earl of Orrery, 1674–1731", PhD thesis, University of Edinburgh, 1994.

Michael Snodin, *Karl Friedrich Schinkel: A Universal Man*, New Haven, CT, 1991.

Michael Snodin, *Sir William Chambers*, London, 1996.

Anne Somerset, *Queen Anne: The Politics of Passion*, New York, 2012.

E Millicent Sowerby, comp, *Catalogue of the Library of Thomas Jefferson*, Washington, DC, 1952.

Joseph Spence, *Anecdotes, Observations, and Characters of Books and Men, Collected from the Conversation of Mr. Pope, and Other Eminent Persons of His Time* (Samuel Weller Singer, ed), London, 1820.

W W Spink, "The Planning of an Environment with Reference to the Penicuik Estate", M.Sc. thesis, Edinburgh University, 1969.

W W Spink, "Sir John Clerk of Penicuik Landowner as Designer" in Willis (ed), *Furor Hortensis Essays in Honour of H F Clark*, Edinburgh, 1974.

Clemens Steenbergen and Wouter Reh, *Architecture and Landscape: The Design Experiment of the Great European Gardens and Landscapes*, Basel, 2003.

Margaret Stewart, *The Architectural, Landscape and Constitutional Plans of the Earl of Mar, 1700–32*, Dublin, 2016.

Roy Strong, *The Artist & the Garden*, New Haven, 2000.

Dorothy Stroud, *Capability Brown*, London, [1950] 1975.

William Stukeley, *The Family Memoirs of the Rev. William Stukeley, M.D.*, 3 vols (Surtees Society vols LXXIII, LXXVI and LXXX), Durham, 1882, 1883 and 1887.
Howard E Stutchbury, *The Architecture of Colen Campbell*, Manchester, 1967.
M G Sullivan, "Gravelot, Hubert-François (1699–1773)", in *DNB*, Oxford, 2009 www.oxforddnb.com/view/article/11307 [accessed 13 Sept 2014].
Michael Symes, *William Gilpin at Painshill: The Gardens in 1772*, Painshill, 1994.
Michael Symes, *Mr Hamilton's Elysium: The Gardens of Painshill*, Hampstead, 2010.
Michael Symes, *The Picturesque and the Later Georgian Garden*, Bristol, 2012.
Michael Symes and Sandy Haynes, *Enville, Hagley, The Leasowes: Three Great Eighteenth Century Gardens*, Bristol, 2010.

T

A A Tait, "William Adam at Chatelherault", *Burlington Magazine* June 1968.
A A Tait, "William Adam and Sir John Clerk; Arniston and the Country Seat", *Burlington Magazine* March 1969.
A A Tait, *The Landscape Garden in Scotland 1735–1835*, Edinburgh, 1979.
Robert Tavernor, *Palladio and Palladianism*, London, 1991.
Sir William Temple, *Works*, 4 vols, Edinburgh, 1754.
Gladys Scott Thomson, *Life in a Noble Household, 1641–1700*, London, 1937.
Jethro Tull, *The Horse-Hoeing Husbandry* (William Cobbett, ed), London, 1829.
Christopher Tunnard, *Gardens in the Modern Landscape*, rev ed, London, [1938] 1948.
Roger Turner, *Capability Brown and the Eighteenth Century English Landscape*, Chichester, 1999.

V

Caroline Van Eck (ed) and David Britt (trans), *Germain Boffrand: Book of Architecture*, Aldershot, 2002.
Robert Voitle, *The Third Earl of Shaftesbury 1671–1713*, Baton Rouge, 1984.

W

Alison Wall, "Baynton Family (*per.* 1508–1716)", in *DNB*, *Oxford*, 2010 www.oxforddnb.com/view/article/71877 [accessed 17 January 2014].
Horace Walpole, "History of the Modern Taste in Gardening", in *Anecdotes of Painting in England*, Twickenham, 1780.
Horace Walpole, *Anecdotes of Painting in England* (James Dallaway, George Vertue and Ralph N Wornum, eds), 3 vols, London, 1876.
Horace Walpole, *Horace Walpole's Correspondence with George Montagu* (W S Lewis and R S Brown, eds), 2 vols, New Haven, CT, 1941.
Walpole Society, "Horace Walpole's Journals of Visits to Country Seats", Vol 16, Oxford, 1928.
Walpole Society, *Vertue Notebooks*, 6 vols, Oxford, 1930–1947.
W H Ward and K S Block, *A History of the Manor and Parish of Ivor*, London, 1933.
Charles Watkins and Ben Cowell, *Uvedale Price (1747–1829): Decoding the Picturesque*, Woodbridge, 2012.
David Watkin and Tilman Mellinghof, *German Architecture and the Classical Ideal 1740–1840*, London, 1987.
N F Weber, *Le Corbusier: A Life*, New York, 2008.
Susan Weber (ed), *William Kent Designing Georgian Britain*, New Haven, 2014.
Thomas Whately, *Observations on Modern Gardening, Illustrated by Descriptions*, 2nd ed, London, 1770.
Laurence Whistler, *The Imagination of Vanbrugh and His Fellow Artists*, Batsford, 1954.

E W White, *Rise of English Opera*, London, 1951.

Philip White, *A Gentleman of Fine Taste: The Watercolours of Coplestone Warre Bampfydde (1720–1791)*, Taunton, 1995.

Elizabeth Whittle, *The Historic Gardens of Wales*, Cardiff, 1992.

Tom Wilkinson, *Polite Landscapes: Gardens and Society in Eighteenth Century England*, Stroud, 1995.

Tom Wilkinson, *The Transformation of Rural England: Farming and the Landscape 1700–1870*, Exeter, 2002.

Basil Willey, *The English Moralists*, London, 1965.

Peter Willis, "Charles Bridgeman: Royal Gardener", PhD thesis, University of Cambridge, 1961.

Peter Willis, "The Work of Charles Bridgeman", *Amateur Historian* 6:3 1964.

Peter Willis, "Jacques Riguard's Drawings of Stowe in the Metropolitan Museum of Art", *Eighteenth Century Studies* 6:1 1972.

Peter Willis (ed), *Furor Hortensis: Essays in Honour of H F Clark*, Edinburgh, 1974.

Peter Willis, *Charles Bridgeman and the English Landscape Garden*, Newcastle, 2002.

Margaret Wills, *Gibside and the Bowes Family*, Chichester, 1995.

Heinrich Wolfflin, *Renaissance and Baroque*, London, 1964.

Kenneth Woodbridge, "Henry Hoare's Paradise", *The Art Bulletin*, 47:1 March 1965.

Kenneth Woodbridge, *Landscape and Antiquity: Aspects of English Culture at Stourhead, 1718–1838*, Oxford, 1970.

Kenneth Woodbridge, "William Kent as a Landscape Gardener: A Reappraisal", *Apollo 100* 1974.

Kenneth Woodbridge, "Irregular, Rococo or Picturesque?", *Apollo 108* 1978.

Kenneth Woodbridge, "The Picturesque Image of Richelieu's Gardens at Rueil", *Garden History 9:1* 1981.

Kenneth Woodbridge, *The Stourhead Landscape: Wiltshire*, London, 1982.

Giles Worsley, "Rokeby Park, Yorkshire", *Country Life* (part I, 19 March, part II 26 March, part III, 2 April 1987).

Sir Henry Wotton, *The Elements of Architecture* (Frederick Hard, ed), Charlottesville, [1624] 1968.

Wren Society, *Wren Society*, 20 vols, Oxford, 1924–1943.

Z

Bruno Zevi, *Towards an Organic Architecture*, London, 1950.

Acknowledgements

Writing this book has been a long term project. The research for it was done in Edinburgh and London, or perhaps one should say from Edinburgh and London, since there were many forays into the country. The major facts about Stephen Switzer's life were uncovered then, and the various contributions to his context, which have subsequently been much refined, were also established. The facts are illuminating, and much enriched by Switzer's own voice through his many books, and it has been a pleasure, and an honour, to toil alongside so many and varied distinguished *dix-huitiemistes*. The gaps in what we all know, and can agree on, are even more interesting, and the means to negotiate those with confidence has prolonged this work.

During that time the University of Edinburgh has made my thesis freely available. Many who helped me with that are acknowledged there, and many of those happily continue their support, ideas and snippets of information. My thesis has been consulted and photocopied regularly, and, when put on-line, consulted many times more. The facts there remain. These have been distilled also for Switzer's life in the new, that is, 21st century, version of the *Dictionary of National Biography*, now published by Oxford. Robert Gordon University in Aberdeen has provided me with ample means and time to reflect on Switzer's career and to rehearse it annually in my lectures to undergraduate architecture students, and also with honours, diploma and postgraduate students as they pursued their own research projects. At Aberdeen University students of art history and English literature have stimulated me time and again. And at various universities and colleges I have had the benefit of many students' attention and reactions, and so have colleagues in 18th century studies and the societies of architectural historians here and in America. My very distinguished and erudite colleagues in my two terms on the Gardens Committee of the National Trust for Scotland were patient and kind and great fun too. And of course the Garden History Society, which marks its 50th anniversary this year, has been quite indispensable.

What was thought of as a project to bring Switzer into book form took new life with the stimulus of Timothy Mowl's discovery of a survey of the Whetham estate in Wiltshire, and the further research on it by Sandy Haynes, which culminated in Wendy Bishop's article in *Garden History*. That work, alongside another piece of evidence discovered long ago at Hopetoun House near Edinburgh, was epiphany-like: all of a sudden there was a means to validate what had been impossible to verify before. The hospitality of Wendy and David Bishop, and Sandy Haynes, since then, and the lively discussions in Wiltshire, is most gratefully acknowledged. Through them Whetham could be imagined in its 18th century forms. I am obliged to John Money-Kyrle for his help and kindness, and to Dr Julian Money-Kyrle and family. At Spye Park the

Einthovens and their energetic staff were most excellent hosts, and revealed an unexpected resonance of earlier states. At Garendon, the Squire and Mrs de Lisle, and Peter de Lisle, provided a veritable symposium of garden history, which Lorren Boniface followed.

Wendy Bishop, John Harris, Sandy Haynes, Michael Symes and Judith Tankard have read parts of my text, and I am grateful for their observations and needful corrections. Michael Fraser has read the whole, and acted also as copy editor, and for that I am happy to acknowledge a debt that cannot be repaid. At Ashgate Val Rose has guided and encouraged as no one else could do. At Routledge my thanks go to Megan Hiatt and Sheri Sipka, and the art composition and editorial team at Apex CoVantage. I have sought advice to the point of importunity of a number of friends and scholars, owners and custodians: they have all responded cheerfully. These include David Adshead, Nancy Anderson, Chloe Bennett, Amanda Booth, Fiona Cowell, Christopher Dingwall, Scott Doig, Olivia Douglas, Patrick Eyres, Gordon French, James Halloway, Sue Hewer, Olivia Horsfall Turner, Lewis Hutchison, David Jacques, Julia King, Neil Lamb, Andrew Martindale, James Mullan, Katherine Myers, Jane Owen, Janet Patch, Judy Riley, Jonathan Scott, Eilidh Smith, Vanessa Stephen, Adam Swan, Lyall Thow, Lynne and Mike Watson, Robin Webster, Tom Williamson, Peter Willis, and Margaret Wills.

I wish to thank those who answered my questions, showed me their grounds and houses and often provided hospitality, and sometimes at very short notice, such as the staff at Beaumanor. Similarly, my thanks to those at Blenheim, the Duke of Marlborough, John Forster and Kate Bellinger; at Cirencester, Lord Bathurst and Grant White; at Cliveden, Peter Bunyan, Andrew Mudge and Phil Rollinson; at Taplow Court (now the Soka Gakkai International Grand Cultural Centre UK), Mike Yeardon, Robert Harrap and Robert Samuels; at Croome Court, Jill Tovey; at The Drum, Alan and Patrea More-Nisbett; at Dyrham, the National Trust staff; at Ebberston Lodge, the deWend-Fentons for fond memories of visits long ago and Justin Hobson, picture manager at *Country Life*; at Formark, Richard Merriman and Julian Hawtree; at Gisbourne, Kirsty McHugh; at Grimsthorpe, Adrian Wilkinson, the Lincolnshire Archive and the Grimsthorpe and Drummond Castle Trust; at Hopetoun House, Peter Burman, Simon Baillie and Richard Gillanders; at Lacock Abbey, Roger Watson; at Leeswood, the late Violet Fairbairn-Wynne-Eyton, David Jacques and Jane Furse; at Lumley Castle, Lord Scarbrough; at Newhailles, Robert Grant, Duncan Donald, Allen Patterson and Melissa Simpson; at Nostell Priory, Lord St Oswald; and at St Giles House, Lord Shaftesbury and Philip Hughes.

Arranging the details of producing suitable images (often carrying much essential evidence and therefore becoming as much documents as illustrations) from public sources has become rather fraught recently. I have followed the advice of my publishers, and also of the Society of Authors, where Kate Pool guided me through the finer points of copyright. I am happy to record that I have almost universally met with great kindness and inclinations to be obliging. To the institutions which hold great sources of visual documentation I owe thanks for many illustrations reproduced here. H M the Queen has graciously permitted the use of the Ricci studio painting of Upper Lodge, Bushy Park, from the Royal Collection. The most disinterested and charitable of institutions is the Yale Center for British Art in New Haven, whose extensive collection of images is made available without fee or fuss. Maria Singer was especially helpful. The Victoria and Albert Museum in London also make their extensive collections freely available for publications such as this one. The National Trust, Dr David Adshead and specially Miss Jenny Liddle deserve my fullest thanks for their advice and for the images of Nostell Priory, Cliveden and Taplow Court, and the Belton water-work. My thanks also go to Professor Ruth Rogers of Wellesley College, near Boston, for kindly providing scans of William Shenstone's sketch book of his works at The Leasowes, and granting full permission to publish it. To the principal archivist of Wiltshire Council and Gill Neal in Swindon my thanks are due for a scan of the survey of Lacock Abbey, and permission to use it here.

At the Bodleian Library in Oxford, I wish to thank Tricia Buckingham and Helen Gilio for exceptional efforts. The British Library in London (notably the King's Collection of maps and topographical drawings begun by King George III) and the National Library of Scotland, Edinburgh, George IV Bridge, and also the Map Room on Causewayside, provided excellent service. The Science and Society Picture Library representing the national Science Museums, London, provided the only photograph used, Henry Fox Talbot's *Beeches at Lacock* of 1844, and I am grateful to Sophia Brothers for her help. Caroline Dagbert at the Canadian Centre for Architecture in Montreal provided Spyer's survey of Blenheim. Durham University holds the Willis Collection and very kindly provided the photograph of the anonymous design for Lumley Castle, and I thank Mike Harkness, and of course my old friend Peter Willis. The archivists in Leicestershire, Staffordshire and Wiltshire provided information and permission to use the plan of Beaumanor, and a part of the survey of Aqualate; I am most obliged to Tim Groom for his notes on the public acquisition of that plan. At Derbyshire Records Office, Matlock, I thank Mark Smith and Becky Sheldon for photographs of the anonymous design for Formark, and to Keith Goodway, and Philip Heath, then heritage officer for the South Derbyshire District Council, for seeking my advice about this very interesting plan, and for providing the photocopies of it.

Index

Page numbers in italics indicate figures and tables.

Abb's Court (Bushy Park) 183, 184
Acres, Thomas 123, 124
Addison's Walk 34, 36, 37, 39
agriculture, landscape design and 267–8
amphitheater: Caversham 123; Chiswick
　House 167, 169; Kensington Palace 8, 22,
　35; Lumley Castle 135; Marston 94, 95;
　Nostell Priory 206
Ancaster, Dukes of 4, 158, 185; see also
　Grimsthorpe; Bertie family
Anchor Church, Formark 236, 237
ancient remains 30, 260
Aqualate 187–8
Architectural Principles in the Age of
　Humanism (Wittkower) 270
Arts and Crafts influence 267, 268, 269
axial walk: kitchen garden and 104;
　Lacock Abbey 152; Leeswood 102, 103;
　Whetham 74

Baldwyn, Charles (Aqualate) 179, 187
Bathurst, Allen 51; see also Riskins;
　Cirencester
basin: Carlton House 173; Chargate design
　project 39; Heythrop 32; locations for 65;
　Riskins 53; Upper Lodge 32
Beaumanor 219–23; see also William Herrick
Belton House (Lord Tyrconnel) 185, 186,
　266
Belvoir Castle (Duke of Rutland) 135–7, 186
Bentley Wood (Serge Chermayeff) 269
Bertie family 44, 61
Blenheim: central problem at 29–30; early
　Bridge-Canals 28; estate plan 29, 250;
　introduction to 3; lake at 249; lessons
　learnt from 30–1
Bold Strokes: Beaumanor 221, 222; Chiswick
　House 167; Cliveden/Taplow Court 110,
　112; Horton 183; Leeswood 102; Lodge
　Park, Cirencester 197; Manor of Paston
　64; Strawberry Hill 269

Bollo Brook, Chiswick House 168, 169
bowling green: Cliveden/Taplow Court
　and 111, 112; early landscapes and 94;
　Leeswood and 103; Rokeby Park and 176;
　Spye Park and 145, 147
Bowes, George (Gibside) 179, 181
Bowood 67, 71, 72
Boyle family 4, 82, 91, 106, 173; see
　Chiswick House (Lord Burlington); Lords
　Orrery, Marston and Britwell
Bretby 18–19
Bridgeman, Charles 196, 197, 198, 237
Bridge of Communication, Wilton 227, 228,
　230
broad walks 84, 89, 102, 152, 193
Broadley, Thomas see Ferriby House
Brompton Park Nurseries 15, 16, 19–20, 22
Brown, Lancelot 182, 231, 251–2, 254–8
Bushy Park: Abb's Court and 183; Upper
　Lodge at 32, 33, 35, 128, 145; see also
　Montagu

Cadogan, Lord see Caversham
canals see lakes and canals
Cannons 27, 79, 161, 267
Carlton House 163, 172–4
cascade-house 68, 69, 76, 77
cascades: Blenheim 30; Ebberston Lodge
　129; Exton Park 212, 214; Formark 235;
　Nostell Priory 201, 203, 204; Spye Park
　144, 145, 146–7; Whetham 68, 69, 73,
　75–7
Cassiobury 16–17
Castle House Marlborough 56, 140–2
Castle Howard: Lord Carlisle, Cirencester
　and 196; design of 20–3; grounds at 21,
　24; introduction to 3; prospect from the
　south 26; Stowe and 198; Switzer's role
　at 23, 27–30, 66, 260; topography of 23;
　working plan 24
Castle Kennedy 248–9

Caversham (Lord Cadogan) 119–24, 126, 156
Chandos project 27, 267
Chargate-Claremont project 37–43, 268
Chatsworth 67, 185, 211
Chermayeff, Serge 269, 270; *see also* Bentley Wood
Chiswick House (Lord Burlington) 164–72, 175
Cirencester (Lord Bathurst) 81–90, 192–8, 265
Claremont *see* Chargate-Claremont project
Clark, Frank 268, 270
Cliveden/Taplow Court (Frederick Prince of Wales, Lord and Lady Inchiquin [aka Orkney]) 105–13
Cobham, Lord 189, 238, 240–1, 252, 254–7
Common Court *200, 202,* 203, 209
Coningsby *see* Hampton Court
coppice gardens 74, 75
Corby Castle 177
country life 4, 6, 10, 30–2
courtyards 36, 39, 61, 111
Croome Court 231, 257–8; *see also* Brown, Lancelot

Dallaway, Rev James 260–1
De Caus design (Wilton) 7, 137, 139–40, 226, 227, 228, 229
Deer Course, Sherborne Lodge Park 196, 198
"Dutch Taste" 20, 58, 60, 69, 70
Dyrham 69–70

early landscapes: Cirencester 81–90; Cliveden/Taplow Court 105–13; Hampton Court 96–100; introduction to 79–81; Leeswood 100–4; Marston 91–6; Stourhead 114–18
earth-architecture 101, 147
earthworks 30, 94, 110, 147, 148
Ebberston Lodge 127–9
Eleven Acre Bottom, Stowe 237, 238
Ellison, Ralph *see* Park House, Gateshead
Elysian Fields, Stowe 241, 246, 248, *253,* 255
enfilade 32, 54, 185, 247, 271
Enville 241, 245, 247
Ernle, John-Kyrle *see* Whetham
estates: Aqualate 187–8; Beaumanor 219–23; Bowood 67, 71, 72; Cannons 27, 79, *161,* 267; Caversham 119–24; Chiswick House 164–72; Cirencester 81–90, 192–8, 265; Cliveden/Taplow Court 105–13; Croome Court 231, 257–8; Grimsthorpe 44–51; Hagley 245–6; Hampton Court 96–100; Heythrop 31–2; introduction to 2–3; The Leasowes 241–5; Leeswood 100–4; Marston 91–6; Nostell Priory 199–208; Oxfordshire 31–2; Riskins 51–8, 89–90; small size 186; Stourhead 114–18; Sugnal 186–7; Whetham 66–78; Woodstock (Blenheim) 27–8
Exton Park (Lord Gainsborough) 208–16, 249
extravagante bergerie (Lady Hertford) 51, 56

farm and farmer: character and pattern of 10; Chargate and 40, 41; disposition of 10; ideal 10; The Leasowes estate 242, 243; success in 159; Whetham estate and 73, 74; *see also* rural gardens
ferme ornée 186, 187, 242–5, 260–3, 267
Ferriby House (Thomas Broadley) 155–7, 259
field fortification 47, 49, 120, 248, 249
fields: Croome Court 257; early landscapes and 84, 87, 89; gardens and 265; Garendon Park 218, 220; Heythrop 31, 32; introduction to 6, 7; landscape design and 241; Leeswood 102, 103, 104; Cirencester Lodge Park 198; Marston 93, 94; Riskins 53, 54, 55; Wilton House 229
Fir Walk 113, 116, 117
fish ponds 51, 148, 214, 247
flanking walks 94, 122, 224
Forest Garden 14, 39, 41, 63, 181
forest trees: at Castle Howard 22; introduction to 14; at Cirencester Lodge Park 198; planting of 27; at Shotover House 129, 131
Formark (Burdett family) 233–7
fruit gardens and trees 12, *40,* 94, 135, 156–7

garden design: Beaumanor 220; Brompton Park Nurseries and 19–20; Cassiobury 16–17; Caversham *121,* 122, 123; Chargate 37–43; Bretby 18–19; Chiswick House 169; Cliveden/Taplow Court 105–13; Grimsthorpe 44–51; Holme Lacy 125; introduction to 6, 7; Leeswood 100–4; lessons learnt about 30–1; Longleat 17–18; Lumley Castle 134; Nostell Priory 204–5; Riskins 51–8, 89–90; Spye Park 144–6; Stephen Switzer and 19; Stourhead 114; as a whole place 63
Garden History Society 186, 232
gardening: history of 9–10; natural elements and 141; *see also* rural gardens
gardens: Carlton House *172;* Chiswick House 165, *166,* 167; Cirencester *81, 83, 194–5;* Cliveden/Taplow Court 108, 111; country life and 30–2; Croome Court 258; earliest description of 9–10; Ebberston

Lodge 128, 129; edges as a concern 6; Exton Park 209; Ferriby House 155; fields and 265; furnishings of 122–3; Grimsthorpe 44–51; introduction to 2–3; keeping them tidy 59; Kent's contributions to 172; Lacock Abbey *150*, 152, 154; meadows as part of 161–2; Shotover House 129; Spye Park 148; Stowe *238*; Studley Royal 133; terrace walks and 61; Wray Wood plantation as 25; *see also* Stephen Switzer

garden representations: Aqualate *187*; Beaumanor *220–1*; Belvoir Castle *136*; Blenheim 29, *250*; Bretby *18*; Cannons *161*; Carlton House *172*; Cassiobury *17*; Castle House Marlborough *140*; Caversham *121*; Chargate-Claremont *37, 40, 42*; Chiswick House *164*; Cirencester *192*; Cliveden/Taplow Court *105*; Dyrham *70*; Ebberston Lodge *127*; Exton Park *209, 210, 212–13*; Garendon Park *216, 218*; Gisbourne design *233*; Grimsthorpe *45, 47*; Hampton Court *97*; Heythrop, Oxfordshire *31*; Holme Lacy *126*; Houghton Hall *57*; Kensington Palace *8*; Lacock Abbey *150, 153*; The Leasowes *242, 244*; Leeswood *100*; Lumley Castle *133*; Manor of Paston *60*; Rhual *188*; Richmond Palace *162*; Riskins *52*; Rokeby Park *174–8*; Shotover House *130*; Spye Park *144, 146, 147*; Stourhead *116*; Upper Lodge Bushy Park *33, 35*; Whetham *66*; Wilton House *15, 138, 223, 225, 228, 230*

Garendon Park (Ambrose Phillipps) 216–19
Gisbourne design 232, *233*
Gothic 131, 194, 241, 245
gravel-pit amphitheater 8, 22, 35
Great Bridge, Wilton 224, 227, 228, 229
Great Oar Pasture 114, 115, 117
Grecian Valley 253, 255, *256*, 258
Grenville Monument 240, 254
Greta Garden 176, 178
Grimsthorpe (William Stukeley Berties) 44–51, 66, 126, 185
grotto work: Castle House Marlborough 141, 142; Chiswick House 170; Spye Park *144*, 147; Whetham 76; Wilton 139
grounds: Beaumanor *220–1*; Belton House 185; Belvoir Castle 137; Carlton House 173; Castle Howard 21, 24; Caversham 120–1; Cirencester 82, *83*, 85; Corby Castle *177*; Exton Park 208, 209, *210*, 215; Formark *234*, 235–6; Gisbourne design and *233*; Grimsthorpe 44, 50; Houghton Hall *57*; Lacock Abbey 150–1; The Leasowes 242; Leeswood *100*; Lumley Castle 134; Mereworth Castle *206*; Nostell Priory 203; Oxfordshire estate 31; Rhual

estate *188*; Richmond Palace *162*; Rokeby Park 174–8; Shotover House 129; Spye Park *142, 143*, 149; Stourhead *215*; Wilton 224, *225*, 226

Hagley (Lyttletons) 245–7
Ha Ha: Chiswick House and 165, 167, 168; rural gardens and 55, 62, 64, 74; Stourhead and 117; Stowe House 237; terrace walks 152, 210, 237–8, 241, 252 half-terrace walk 62, 117
Hampton Court (Lord Coningsby, Herefordshire) 28, 32, 33, 96–100
Hawkwell Field 252, 254, 255
hayfields 55, 71, 75
Herbert, Henry (Lord Pembroke) 223
Herrick, William 219, 220
Heythrop (Duke of Shrewsbury) 31–2
High and Over (Strawberry Hill) 268–9; and Bernard Ashmole and Amyas Connell 268
Hoare family, Switzer's bankers 176; *see also* Stourhead
Holme Lacy (Scudamores) 124–7
Home Park, Stowe 87–8, *90*, 192, 193, 237–8
Hopetoun House 68, 69
Horton 183, 184
Houghton Hall (Sir Robert Walpole) 57

Ichnographia Rustica 1715, 1718 and 1742; and Bertie family 44; and Duke of Ancaster 3; and Lord Coningsby 96; and Lord Pembroke 137
Inchiquin, Lord 99, 106, 108, 110–13
Introduction to a General System of Hydrostaticks and Hydraulicks, An (Switzer) 5, 56, 91, 183; and Hamilton and Lord Inchiquin, Cliveden/Taplow Court 106–8; and Lord and Lady Hertford, Castle House Marlborough and Riskins 56
Ivy Lodge Park 192, 193, 194, 196

Kensington Gardens 20, 22, 35, 53, 238
Kensington Palace 8, 20, 163, 170, 173
Kent, William 163, 168, 169, *171*
"Kent's notion" 170, 264
Kiddington 251
kitchen gardens: axial walk and 104; Beaumanor 221, 222; Holme Lacy *126*; Leeswood 102, 104; Marston 94; Rhual *188*; rural gardens and 59; Spye Park 148; Stourhead 115; Switzer's ideas about 12, 189; Wallington 182
kitchen quarters 55, 64, 86, 98, 148

Lacock Abbey (John Ivory Talbot) 149–55
Ladies' Temple, Stowe 252, *253*, 254, 255
lakes and canals: at Blenheim 249; at Castle Howard 23, 24; at Exton Park 211; at

Kiddington 251; at Leeswood 101–4; at Nostell Priory estate *200, 202*, 203, *204*; at Oakley Lodge (Cirencester Park House) 87; at Stourhead 115, 116, 117; way to form 249
landscape: Addison's interest in 34; appreciation of 244; Castle Howard 23; Cirencester 86–7; High and Over 268–9; introduction to 1; realization of 24; Shotover House *130*, 131
landscape design/designer: agriculture and 267–8; Aqualate 187–8; Castle Howard 25; Chiswick House 165, 169, 171; Cirencester 193–8; Ebberston Lodge 128; Exton Park 211; Ferriby House 156–7; fields and 241; Formark 233–4, 236; Garendon Park 217, 218; Grimsthorpe 46, 49; Lacock Abbey 151, 154; Nostell Priory *204*; qualities expected of 63; Rhual 188–91; Riskins gardens 55; Rokeby Park 175; Rousham and 239; Studley Royal 132; Upper Lodge Bushy Park 36; Wilton 139, 224, 227
lawns: as a design element 6–7; Hagley 246–7; Lacock Abbey 152; Leeswood 101, 102; Nostell Priory 200, 204; *see also* fields
The Leasowes 241–5
Le Corbusier's sense of landscape 270, 271
Leeswood (Wynne family) 100–4, 190, 261
Lime Walk 240
Lodge Park *192*, 193, 194, 196, 197–8
London, George 16, 18–20, 22–3, 25–7, 179
Longleat 17–18, 91, 112
The Louvre 27, 262, 263
Lowther (Lord Londsdale) 184, 252
Lumley Castle 106, 133–5

Manor of Paston 60, 61, 64, *65*, 116
Mansion House Woodstock 29, 30
Marston 91–6
meadows: early landscapes and 101, 103, 111, 112, 114, 115; gardens and estates and 161–2; Lacock Abbey 150, 155; Rhual 190; Wilton e 226, 227, 229
Merewoth Castle 206–8
Modern Movement 269, 270
Montagu, Charles 32, 183; *see also* Upper Lodge Bushy Park; Abb's Court
Montagu, George 174, 183, 189; *see also* Upper Lodge Bushy Park; Horton; Abb's Court
Mortham Tower 176, 177, 178
Moyser, James 200, 201, 202, 205

National Land Ordinance of 1785 263
natural elements: Belvoir Castle 135–7; Castle House Marlborough 140–2; Caversham estate 119–24, 126; Ebberston Lodge 127–9; Ferriby House 155–7; Holme Lacy 124–7; introduction to 120; Lacock Abbey 149–55; Lumley Castle 133–5; Shotover House 129–32; Spye Park 142–9; Studley Royal 132–3; Wilton 137–40
Nobleman Gentleman and Gardener's Recreation (1715) 4, 57, 60, 74, 86, 126; *see also Ichnographia Rustica*
Nostell Priory 199–208, 219, 248, 265

Oakley Great Park *192*, 193, 194
Oakley Lodge 84, 86, 87
open spaces concept 36, 39, 232, 255, 269
Ordnance Surveys 51, 91, 94, 179, 184
Orrery, Earls of (Boyle family), Marston and Britwell 3–5, 7, 91, 93, 95–6, 105–6, 158; and *Practical Fruit Gardener* 91, 105

paddocks 19, 74, 254
Palladian design: Chiswick House 167; Merewoth, Stourhead 3, 102, *206*, 207–8; Nostell Priory 201, 202, 203, 205, 207; Rokeby Park 175; Villa Capra 170; Wilton 224
Park House, Gateshead 179, 180
parkland: Caversham 120, 125; Chiswick House 168, 169; Dyrham 71; Formark House 235; Garendon Park 218; Grimsthorpe 48; Hampton Court 98; Lumley Castle 134, 135; Merewoth Castle 208; Spye Park 145, 148
parterres: at Beaumanor 222; at Bretby 18; at Cassiobury 17; at Castle Howard 25; at Caversham 122, 123; at Chargate 39; at Chiswick House 167, 168; at Cliveden 110; at Grimsthorpe 44, 47, *48*; introduction to 5, 6; at Kiddington 251; at Lowther 252; at Nostell Priory 200, *202*, 203; at Spye Park 145; Switzer's view of 62
pavilion: Blenheim 110; Chiswick House 166, 167, 168; Grimsthorpe 50, 51; Nostell Priory 201, 202; Riskins gardens 56; Shotover House 131, 132; Spye Park House *144*
Pembroke, Lord and Lady, Wilton 4, 137, 139, 223–4, 227–9; *see also* Henry Herbert
Petre, Lord Robert James 231–2
Phillipps, Ambrose 216, 217; *see also* Garendon Park
plantations: at Cirencester 84; at Ebberston Lodge 129; at Grimsthorpe 50; introduction to 9; management of 255; at Spye Park 149; Wray Wood 20, 23, 24
pleached walks 54, 55
ponds: at Formark estate 235; at Grimsthorpe 44, 47; introduction to 22, 23, 24; at Marston estate 91, 94, 95, 96;

at Shotover House 129; at Studley Royal 133; at Whetham 73, 74, 75; *see also* gardens
Pope, Alexander 51, 82, 162, 193, 238
Practical Fruit Gardener, The (Switzer) 5, 91, 105, 110, 135; and Orrerys, Marston 110
Practical Husbandman and Planter, The (Switzer) 151, 159, 181, 183, 184; and Lord Halifax, Horton and Abb's Court, 183–4; and Lord Londsdale, Lowther 184
Practical Kitchen Gardener, The (Switzer) 5, 189, 248; and Lord Bathurst, Riskins and Cirencester 248
Private Society of Husbandmen and Planters 160, 163

Queen Anne 20, 22, 27, 67, 82
Queen Pool, Blenheim 250

regulated Epitomy 53, *54*, 82, 86
reservoirs: Bessborough (municipal) 184; Castle Howard 25; Hampton Court 98; Nostell Priory 200; Spye Park 145, 147, 148; Whetham 73
Rhual (Griffith family) 188–91
Richmond Palace 162
Riskins (Bathurst, Hertfords [Percy Lodge]) 51–8, 66, 87, 89–90, 248
River Glyme 28–30, 249–51
River Nadder 7, 226
River Styx (or Alder), Stowe 240
rock-work 145, 169, 214
Rocque's plans 53, *54*, *162*
Rokeby Park 174–8
Rose, John 15, 16
Rousham design 172, 176, 239–40
Royal Gardeners 16, 20, 22, 81
Royal Gardens 15, 19, 123
Royal Society 3, 16, 139
rural gardens: Cannons and 162; Grimsthorpe and 44–51; how to make 58–66; introduction to 44; Rhual and 190, 191; Riskins and 51–8; smaller estates and 186; Switzer's image of *80*; Whetham and 66–78

Select Transactions 159, 160
serpentine paths 15, 135, 227, 271
serpentine river 197, *200*, *204*, 207, 248
Seven Rides 87, 89, *90*, *192*, 193–5
Sham Castle 246, 247
Sharawaggi (Temple) 270, 271
Shenstone, William 241–7, 261–2
Shotover House 129–32
Sidney's Walk 226, 227
Slade Meadow 116, 117
Society of Improvers 159–60, 183
Spye Park (Ann Bayntun Rolt, Lady Somerville) 142–9

St Giles House Wimborne (Lord Shaftesbury) 215–16
Stourhead (Hoare family) 114–18
Stowe 189–90, 198, 237–41, 252–3, 255–6
Strawberry Hill (Horace Walpole) 64, 245, 268–9
Stukeley, William 5, 7, 36, *37*, 46, *47*, *48*, *49*, *138*, 140, *141*, 144, 185, 211, 214, 224, 226
Studley Royal 4, 32, 53, 132–3
Sugnal 186–7
sunk fence *see* Ha Ha
Survey of London (Rocque) 244
Switzer, Stephen: Abraham Cowley and 15; as an apprentice 16, 19; Aqualate estate and 187–8; Beaumanor estate and 219–23; Bunny Park estate and 186; Bushy Park project and 32, *33*; Castle House and 140–2; Castle Howard house and 23, 27–30, 66, 260; Caversham estate and 119–24; changes in practice of 158–65; Chargate project and 37–8; Cirencester estate and 81–90, 193–8; Cliveden/Taplow court and 105–13; design ideas of 61–6; Ebberston Lodge and 127–9; Exton Park and 208–16; Ferriby House and 155–7; gardening history's view of 9–10; Garendon Park and 216–19; Grimsthorpe gardens and 44–51; Hampton Court estate and 96–100; Holme Lacy house and 124–7; improvers of 178–88; introduction to 1–5; John Evelyn and 14; Joseph Addison and 34–6; Lacock Abbey and 149–55; Leeswood estate and 100–4; legacy of 259–72; Lucius Columella and 11–12; Lumley Castle and 133–5; manner of business 180; manner of writing 56–8; Marcus Cato and 10–11; Marston estate and 91–6; Midland Tour 184–5; Nostell Priory estate and 199–208; notion of style 19; Park House and 180; regulated Epitomy and *54*; reputation of 260–1; Rokeby Park and 176; seeds trade by 5, 158; Shotover House and 129–32; Spye Park House and 142–9; Stourhead estate and 114–18; Stowe House and 238–9; Studley Royal and 132–3; Sugnal estate and 186–7; treatment of great men and 12–13; villas and 11; Whetham estate and 66–78; William Kent and 163; William Russell and 16; William Temple and 14–15; Wilton House and 137–40, 223–30

Temple, Sir William 14, 52, 260
Temple of Ancient Virtue 240, 241
Temple of Concord 252, 254
Temple of Venus 9, 216, 218, 237
terrace walks: Beaumanor 222; Caversham 122; Exton Park 210; gardens and 61; Ha

Ha 152; Leeswood 104; Lumley Castle 134–5; Rokeby Park 176; Whetham 71; Wilton 139–40
Thames valley 40, 122
Theory and Practice of Gardening (D'Argenville) 4, 13, 154; translation by James 6, 57, 79, 163
Thorndon design 231, 232
topography: of Castle Howard 23; of Dyrham estate 70; of Exton Park 208, 211; of Grimsthorpe 49
Tottenham Park 165, 190, 196
tree-lined walks 37, 122
triumphal arch 208, *216*, 217, 218, 219
Tunnard, Christopher 268, 270
Tything Plan Whetham 71, 72, 74, 76, 77

Unconnected Thoughts on Gardening (Shenstone) 261
Upon the Gardens of Epicurus (Temple) 14
Upper Lodge 32–3, *35*, 84, 128, 183

Versailles 262–3
Villa d'Este Tivoli 13, 14
villas: at Chiswick House 168, 170; Columella and 12; description of 11; Palladian 176
Villas of the Ancients Illustrated (Castell) 6, 161
vineyards 12, 75, 77

walks: axial 74, 102, 103, 104, 247; broad 84, 89, 102, 152, 193; at Chargate 40; at Cliveden 111; flanking 94, 122, 224; gravel 222; introduction to 5, 6; at Lacock Abbey 152, 154; as objects of design 59; pleached 54, 55; quadrant 55, 122; rural gardens and 64–5; straight 25, 87, 151; tree-lined 37, 122; woodland 40, 74, *88*, 93, 190
Walpole, Horace 63–4, 174, 196, 231, 244–5
Walpole, Sir Robert 51, 58, 101, 105, 131, 198, 228, 240, 241; *see also* Houghton
water carriage 77, 98, 250
water gardens: management of 247–8; Spye Park 145; Upper Lodge Bushy Park 32; Whetham 75; *see also* fish ponds
water-works: Belton House 266; Ebberston Lodge 128; Exton Park *213*, 214; introduction to 5, 7; Marston 96
Whetham (John-Kyrle Ernle) 66–78
Wilton House (Sir Philip Sydney Pembroke) 137–40, 223–30
Windsor Castle 53, 55, 111, 112, 113
Winn family 200–2, 205; *see also* Nostell Priory
Wynne family *see* Leeswood
Wise, Henry 2, 3, 16, 79, 123
woodland gardens 74, 93–4, 96, 152, 154
woodlands: Chargate-Claremont project 38; Cirencester 88; Exton Park 208; introduction to 14; Nostell Priory 206, 207; Rhual *188*; Studley Royal 133
woods: landscape design and 63; Rhual 190; rural gardens and 59
Woodstock estate 27–8
Wray Wood plantation 20, 23, 24, 25, 26
Wright, Thomas 251, 252
Wye valley 97, 98, 124, 125